Beside the Bard

TRANSITS:
LITERATURE, THOUGHT & CULTURE, 1650–1850

Series Editors
Kathryn Parker, University of Wisconsin—La Crosse
Miriam Wallace, New College of Florida

Transits is a series of scholarly monographs and edited volumes publishing beautiful and surprising work. Without ideological bias the series seeks transformative readings of the literary, artistic, cultural, and historical interconnections between Britain, Europe, the Far East, Oceania, and the Americas between the years 1650 and 1850 and as their implications extend down to the present time. In addition to literature, art, and history, such "global" perspectives might entail considerations of time, space, nature, economics, politics, environment, gender, sex, race, bodies, and material culture and might necessitate the development of new modes of critical imagination. At the same time, the series welcomes considerations of the local and the national, for original new work on particular writers and readers in particular places in time continues to be foundational to the discipline.

Recent titles in the Transits series:

Beside the Bard: Scottish Lowland Poetry in the Age of Burns
George S. Christian

The Novel Stage: Narrative Form from the Restoration to Jane Austen
Marcie Frank

The Imprisoned Traveler: Joseph Forsyth and Napoleon's Italy
Keith Crook

Fire on the Water: Sailors, Slaves, and Insurrection in Early American Literature, 1789–1886
Lenora Warren

Community and Solitude: New Essays on Johnson's Circle
Anthony W. Lee, ed.

The Global Wordsworth: Romanticism Out of Place
Katherine Bergren

Cultivating Peace: The Virgilian Georgic in English, 1650–1750
Melissa Schoenberger

Jane Austen and Comedy
Erin M. Goss, ed.

For a full list of Transits titles go to https://www1.bucknell.edu/script/upress/series.asp?id=33

Beside the Bard

SCOTTISH LOWLAND POETRY IN THE AGE OF BURNS

GEORGE S. CHRISTIAN

LEWISBURG, PENNSYLVANIA

Library of Congress Cataloging-in-Publication Data

Names: Christian, George S., author.
Title: Beside the Bard : Scottish lowland poetry in the age
of Burns / George S. Christian.
Description: Lewisburg, Pennsylvania : Bucknell University Press,
2020. | Series: Transits: literature, thought & culture | Includes
bibliographical references and index.
Identifiers: LCCN 2019025628 | ISBN 9781684481811 (paperback) |
ISBN 9781684481828 (hardback) | ISBN 9781684481835 (epub) |
ISBN 9781684481842 (mobi) | ISBN 9781684481859 (pdf)
Subjects: LCSH: English poetry—Scottish authors—History
and criticism. | Scottish poetry—18th century—History and
criticism. | Scotland—In literature.
Classification: LCC PR8567 .C48 2020 | DDC 821/.09413—dc23
LC record available at https://lccn.loc.gov/2019025628

A British Cataloging-in-Publication record for this book is available
from the British Library.

Copyright © 2020 by George S. Christian

All rights reserved

No part of this book may be reproduced or utilized in any form or by
any means, electronic or mechanical, or by any information storage
and retrieval system, without written permission from the publisher.
Please contact Bucknell University Press, Hildreth-Mirza Hall,
Bucknell University, Lewisburg, PA 17837-2005. The only exception
to this prohibition is "fair use" as defined by U.S. copyright law.

⊖ The paper used in this publication meets the requirements of the
American National Standard for Information Sciences—Permanence
of Paper for Printed Library Materials, ANSI Z39.48-1992.

www.bucknell.edu/UniversityPress

Distributed worldwide by Rutgers University Press

Manufactured in the United States of America

Strange whim of the people! They demand their history from the hand of the poet and not the hand of the historian. They demand not a faithful report of bare facts, but those facts dissolved back into the original poetry from whence they came.

—Heinrich Heine

CONTENTS

	Introduction	1
1	Burns's Ayrshire "Bardies": John Lapraik and David Sillar	19
2	Burns and the Women "Peasant" Poets: Janet Little and Isobel Pagan	43
3	Alexander Wilson and the Price of Radicalism	71
4	Lady Nairne: Burns's Jacobite Other	97
5	"In the Shadow of Burns": Robert Tannahill	127
6	Burns and the Jacobins: James Kennedy and Alexander Geddes	153
	Conclusion	183
	Acknowledgments	187
	Notes	189
	Bibliography	225
	Index	243

Beside the Bard

INTRODUCTION

EVER SINCE ROBERT CRAWFORD ISSUED a call to "heighten awareness of the current position of Scottish Literature which remains too often either ignored or lumped in with 'English,' its cultural inflections and position airbrushed away in syllabuses across five continents," numerous scholars, predominantly from within the Scottish academy, have done substantial work in establishing Scottish literary history and criticism as a distinct academic discipline.[1] Unquestionably, the poetry of Robert Burns has occupied a central position in this project. Indeed, as Gerard Carruthers's volume for the Edinburgh Companions series and recent monographs by Nigel Leask, Carol McGuirk, Corey Andrews, and Alex Broadhead amply demonstrate, Burns scholarship continues to grow apace, enriching our understanding of the poet, his language, and his cultural context.[2]

A fortunate by-product of this scholarship has been an increase in critical attention given to contemporaries of Burns who attempted to follow him into the late eighteenth-century literary marketplace. Still, much remains to be done. As critics situate Burns within larger eighteenth-century local, national, and transnational contexts, such as, for example, enlightenment and improvement (Leask), cultural production and reception (Andrews), and sociolinguistics (Broadhead), they not only suggest fruitful new approaches to understanding the "genius" Robert Burns but also raise new questions regarding the specific social, political, and economic conditions that contributed to the extraordinary rise of one Ayrshire farmer to international celebrity but not of others who followed in his train. Noting that "few critics have taken much notice" of the works of laboring-class poets writing "in the shadow of Burns," Corey Andrews asks, "Why Burns alone and not other labouring class poets? Is 'genius' a sufficient explanation, even now? If not, how can we account for the continuing neglect of an ample and important body of work, written by men and women originating from the same social, cultural, and national milieu as Burns? We may have more to learn about the experiences of the Scottish labouring class from such poets than from Burns himself."[3] As Andrews points out, Burns's immense reputation continues to inform and, in

[1]

some ways, determine the contours of analysis and criticism of the poetry of his contemporaries. Indeed, in Crawford's magisterial general history of Scottish literature, *Scotland's Books*, he names this period the "Age of Burns," affirming a now well-established eighteenth-century Scottish poetic canon composed of the vernacular voices of Allan Ramsay, Robert Fergusson, and Burns[4] (themselves connected to a venerable early modern tradition of Scottish bards and makars), together with the Anglo-Scot poet James Thomson, the primitivists James Macpherson and James Beattie, and the romanticist Sir Walter Scott.[5] Andrews's question—why Burns alone?—invites consideration of the poetry of Burns's contemporaries and reconsideration of the canon and its constitutional principles in an effort better to understand both Burns's poetry and "the experiences of the Scottish labouring class."

At the same time, however, evaluating this "ample and important body of work" has to account for widely varying degrees of reception, both in its own historical moment and in the two centuries that followed. As Andrews and others have shown, for example, Burns's fellow Ayrshire poets John Lapraik and David Sillar struggled financially after taking substantial losses on their own publishing projects. Janet Little, a third Ayrshire poet who enjoyed the patronage of Burns's friend and patron Frances Dunlop, did somewhat better, eventually selling eight hundred copies of her *The Poetical Works of Janet Little, the Scotch Milkmaid* (Ayr, 1792) to more than 650 subscribers (including Burns and James Boswell). But even she, like Lapraik and Sillar, never published a second volume of poetry.[6] Having achieved fame as a "Scotch bard," Burns did not go out of his way to welcome new aspirants, notoriously complaining to Mrs. Dunlop, "my success has encouraged such a shoal of ill-spawned monsters to crawl into public notice under the title of Scots Poets, that the very term, Scots Poetry, borders on the burlesque."[7] But as Andrews also observes, while Burns's reaction to competition in the literary market may not cast the best light on his sense of loyalty to old friends or similarly situated laboring-class poets, the crucial question involves whether and the extent to which Burns's very success as a literary phenomenon, expressly validated by the tastemakers in the Edinburgh literati, militated against a broader acceptance of his contemporaries and their work.[8] If it is indeed the case that Burns's entry into the literary marketplace changed the conditions of access for other poets, as Andrews suggests, evaluating the cultural and historical influence of their body of work becomes complicated by virtue not just of the inevitable comparisons of their work to that of Burns but also of the spotty reception history of such poetry in general. In the relative absence of more verifiable measures of reception applicable to the Burns case—his publication history, his recognition by the cultural elites, his development of a number of powerful patrons, his extensive network of correspondents and admirers, and his posthumous fame—we must seek additional

INTRODUCTION

ways to evaluate the meaning and influence of these poets' presence in the cultural space that Burns dominated, a space so aptly termed the "Age of Burns."

The present study proposes that we read the work of Burns's contemporaries in terms of the *density* of linguistic production in the Scottish Lowlands during the Age of Burns. Drawing on the work of Michel Foucault, I understand density in two senses. First, it means a thickening of discourse, a kind of clustering and stratifying effect of signifieds around each signifier, whose original denomination has become obscured, if not lost, in the very history its presence enunciates. According to Foucault, we speak (and write) in languages replete with figures that bear traces of the resemblances they once identified, traces that form "the ring surrounding the domain of that which can be analysed, reduced to order, and known. Discourse dissipates the murmur, but without it it could not speak." For Foucault,

> The idea that, when we destroy words, what is left is neither mere noise nor arbitrary, pure elements, but other words—this idea is at once the negative of all modern science of languages and the myth in which we now transcribe the most obscure and the most real powers of language. It is probably because it is arbitrary, and because one can define the condition upon which it attains its power of signification, that language can become the object of a science. But it is because it has never ceased to speak within itself, because it is penetrated as far as we can reach within it by inexhaustible values, that we can speak within it in that endless murmur in which literature is born.[9]

One might say that late eighteenth-century Scotland engendered a "literature" in this Foucauldian sense, one that Burns did much to fashion out of the discursive polyphony, fragments, and traditions of a linguistically sensitive and cosmopolitan culture stretching back into the medieval period. Burns's poetry, as Alex Broadhead has shown in illuminating detail, not only "reflect[s]the wider linguistic heterogeneity of eighteenth-century Scotland" (including its French, Latin, Italian, and Gaelic usages, as well as its local Scots dialects) but "reinvents the boundaries and possibilities of different linguistic varieties." Burns thus "liberates" readers from "deterministic understandings of language, identity, ideology, and the relationship between the three."[10] To put it another way, Burns's complex and polyvalent oeuvre penetrates the deep strata of signification, both revealing and creating meaning from ancient and elusive signs, so that we can hear the "endless murmur" of a literary language "speaking within itself." Scottish Lowland poets writing in the "shadow" of Burns likewise participated in this dense field of linguistic "archaeology," the common project of recovering the "inexhaustible values" of language and what those values reveal about lived experience in an era of profound

[3]

BESIDE THE BARD

change. Under the intense pressure of historical, cultural, and socioeconomic transformation, these poets too cracked open the hard casing of received linguistic forms, releasing their old histories of communal life, religious and class conflict, economic hardship, and national trauma into a world riven by revolution, war, and political crisis. Speaking to one another and about one another (and to their critics), reading and responding to each other's work, whether through traditional publishing or through myriad social or professional networks, print media, correspondence, pamphleteering, the broadsheet or the chapbook, religious congregations, songwriting, or even word of mouth, Lowland poets participated in the "birth" of the body of Scottish literature that came into being during the Age of Burns.

The second sense in which I use the term "density" is to describe the expansion and thickening of these discursive networks available especially to Lowland poets in the Age of Burns. During the last third of the eighteenth century, rapid urbanization converged with Enlightenment ideas of improvement to stimulate Lowland literary production. As Bob Harris has described, this new urban culture, "eminently practical [and] concerned with information, efficiency and progress, and 'improvement,' but defined in ways appropriate to environments shaped by commerce and, often, evangelical religious currents, . . . achieved its sharpest definition in the most dynamic commercial and manufacturing towns, such as Paisley, Greenock, or Dundee, but which was also evident in such places as Arbroath, Kilmarnock, Irvine, Dunfermline, Forfar, and Perth." Further, "commerce and religion were the twin poles of cultural life in many Scottish towns, affecting a broad cross-section of the urban population, which is easily underestimated in preference to concentration on the genteel."[11] Urban culture began to look increasingly "British" by providing access to institutions and practices that were familiar south of the Tweed but until now unavailable in a culture ruled by orthodox Calvinist Presbyterianism: assemblies and musical concerts, theater, schools, instruction in music and dancing, public lectures, exhibitions, subscription and circulating libraries, clubs and coffee houses, booksellers, and Masonic lodges.[12] Burns's early biography provides ample evidence of this change in the wind. Though a child of rural Ayrshire and never too far from the plow, by the age of twenty-five Burns had attended school in Dalrymple; studied English grammar and French with John Murdoch in Ayr; attended dancing school in Tarbolton (angering his conservative Presbyterian father); studied mathematics in Kirkoswald; founded what may have been the first debating society in rural Scotland, the Tarbolton Bachelors' Club; joined the Freemasons; and learned how to dress flax in Irvine.[13] Burns's experience lends credence to Harris's analysis and demonstrates the densifying network of connections that crisscrossed "Burns Country." Burns and his contemporaries, some drawn from this "broad cross-

[4]

INTRODUCTION

section of the urban population" and others from its rural environs, inserted themselves into the quickening environment, both in an attempt to take advantage of the commercial opportunities offered by a burgeoning readership and to stake a claim in an emergent national literature reflecting and establishing Scotland's place in an enlightened Britain and the wider world.

The commercialization of literary and cultural production that Harris and other historians of the period describe opened new pathways between poets and potential readers. From 1770 booksellers became a standard feature in urban Scotland, and by 1800 most Scottish towns and cities across the urban belt had subscription libraries, which were supported by ever-larger inventories of printed books.[14] Printers constituted the hub of an expanding network of information and textual exchange, becoming prominent figures in their communities as a result. Outstanding examples include Peter and John Wilson of Ayr and Kilmarnock (printers for Burns, Lapraik, Sillar, and Little), John Mennons of Irvine, George Miller of Haddington, David Buchanan of Montrose, Robert Tullis of Cupar and Fife, and William Scott of Greenock. The explosion of print also included more ephemeral products, such as "periodical miscellanies, collections of local verse, chapbooks of various kinds and a steady rise in the number of Scottish newspapers."[15] Vivienne Dunstan estimates that, in addition to booksellers and printers, as many as one thousand chapmen roamed Scotland in the late eighteenth century, selling items such as cloth, buttons, needles, handkerchiefs, and other everyday items but also inexpensive reading materials, Bibles, and psalms.[16] Murray Pittock has traced this history back to the early modern period, with hundreds of thousands of chapbooks in circulation, only a fraction of which have survived.[17] As we will see, the poet Alexander Wilson for a time made his living as a chapman whose wares included copies of ballad sheets or verse, ephemera now lost to the historian's eye.

It is difficult to say with any certainty how deeply this emerging print culture permeated the social hierarchy. Historians such as Harris and Dunstan note that archival materials, such as after-death inventories, subscription and circulating library catalogues, and stock lists of printers and booksellers, indicate "the propulsive power of print, finding its way into mainly (but not exclusively) the upper echelons of provincial lowland urban society, into the ranks of the growing number of professionals, prosperous merchants and tradesmen, and their families." This expansion remained uneven, however, and "the rate, extent and nature of absorption was heavily influenced by social rank, gender, occupation and by character and existing traditions of towns, especially (but not exclusively) religious ones."[18] Further down the social hierarchy, literate artisans, weavers, small tradesmen, and laboring-class Scots who could not afford either to buy books or to subscribe to

[5]

BESIDE THE BARD

more socially exclusive libraries and reading rooms still had access to "the culture of the tavern, the tap room and the weaving shop and cottage," as well as, in the wake of the advent of popular radicalism in the early 1790s, "a wave of book clubs . . . in radical hotspots in the west and central lowlands; for example, Kirkintilloch and Renton in Dunbartonshire, Fenwick in Ayrshire, Alva in Stirlingshire, as well as Paisley with its burgeoning population of weavers."[19] In these clubs, working men clubbed together to buy reading material and share subscription costs to radical newspapers such as the Foxite *Morning Chronicle* (regularly read by Burns and to which he frequently contributed poetry), the *Scots Chronicle*, and the *Edinburgh Gazetteer*.[20] As Harris notes, however, popular enlightenment was "of an informal, unorganised nature, which remains largely invisible to the historian. Popular enlightenment, in so far as it occurred, did so in towns where elites viewed the bulk of the population and any hint of radical enlightenment with deep suspicion. By the early nineteenth century, cultural and social boundaries were being drawn ever more rigidly and carefully in many towns as part of a drive towards greater efficiency, order and amenity."[21] Thus the weight of conformity bore down on poets such as Burns as well, further restricting access to the bourgeois literary market, especially for laboring-class poets.

Carol McGuirk's compelling illustration of the emergence in 1786 of Robert Burns, the author of *Poems, Chiefly in the Scottish Dialect*, from Robt. Burness, the financially and emotionally distressed writer of *The First Commonplace Book* (1783–1785) and *The Kilmarnock Manuscript* (1785–1786), amply illustrates this problem. McGuirk argues that Burns's biographers subdivide Burns's experiences during this period when they should view them as "a sustained emotional storm on many fronts: the vindictive wrath of Jean Armour's parents; the humiliation of being packed out of the country [his family in near bankruptcy and forced to give up the lease to Mossgiel farm, Burns considered emigrating to Jamaica to take a job as an overseer on a slave plantation]; the resentment over public penance for fornication; and yet also the faint if fading hope that publishing his *Poems* would change the game."[22] In McGuirk's reading we see an aspiring laboring-class poet under intense pressure to conform to economic and social expectations and despairing of the future of his art, while at the same time hoping that his art will rescue him from these same oppressive forces. We will encounter this phenomenon in poets such as John Lapraik, David Sillar, Alexander Wilson, Robert Tannahill, and Janet Little as well, all of whom, like Burns, felt that the pull of their often precarious and marginal class positions (subject to sudden downward mobility in the hard economic times of the 1780s and 1790s) undercut the push of their poetic ambitions in a literary market that was increasingly regulated by changing critical standards dictated from above.

[6]

INTRODUCTION

What emerges from this brief survey of a dynamic late eighteenth-century market for literary production, broadly speaking, is a bifurcated system in which social and economic elites—predominantly the landed and professional classes (which generally included tenant farmers such as Burns)—enjoyed broad access to an enlightened and polite literature of improvement, history, moral philosophy, and belles lettres, whereas the "lower" artisanal, small trade, and laboring-class orders accessed less formal and less expensive networks of literary circulation. At the same time, as a struggling tenant farmer who performed manual farm labor alongside his workers, Burns (as did his fellow Ayrshire poets John Lapraik and David Sillar and weaver poets such as Alexander Wilson and Robert Tannahill) straddled an ambiguous and permeable class boundary, self-identifying with both the "enlightened" and laboring classes, and experienced the vicissitudes of sudden and precipitous change in his social and economic position. The evidence certainly suggests that well-educated tradesman and workers, though they often lived far more economically precarious lives in material terms than did their genteel counterparts, were as hungry for the products of print culture as their social "betters" were and aspired to elevate their class status through its consumption. At the same time, we should not underestimate the continuing influence of religious orthodoxy on reading habits at all levels of Scottish society. While "improvement" and progressivism may have been in the air, religious texts continued to loom large in the collections of wealthier private citizens, in the peddler packs of roving chapmen, and in parish and parochial libraries affiliated with the Kirk.[23] The Auld Licht remained alive and well during this period (especially in Burns territory around Glasgow and the Southwest), and the kind of rural piety seen in "The Cottar's Saturday Night" can be read in an experiential as well as sentimental mode.

As previously noted, Burns's spectacular success in negotiating and shaping this vibrant literary culture complicates the task of assessing the work of Burns's contemporaries and their contribution to the development of "Scottish" literature during this period. Moreover, the precise nature of Burns's "genius" remains under critical construction, inviting fresh approaches to Burns's contemporaries as part of the larger project of expanding the disciplinary boundaries of both "Scottish" and "British" literature. In entries on Janet Little, Carolina Oliphant (Lady Nairne), and Isobel Pagan for *The Biographical Dictionary of Scottish Women*, for example, Valentina Bold challenges critics to "rescue" Little's literary reputation (which Bold herself has taken a large role in doing), pay "renewed attention" to the "range and ambition" of Lady Nairne's poetry, and give "more detailed critical consideration" to Pagan's poetry, which has, "hitherto, largely been considered as an appendix to Burns's."[24] More generally, Gerard Carruthers has drawn attention to the importance of using the same diverse modes of critical discourse to read Scottish literature

[7]

BESIDE THE BARD

as have commonly been employed to interpret other "national" literatures. "The future health of Scottish literary studies demands this," Carruthers argues, "if it is to be in line with other areas of literary study and so as to be prevented from becoming merely a minor adjunct to the discipline of history."[25]

This study aims to perform some of the work that Andrews, Bold, and Carruthers advocate, taking as its subject poetry composed by Scots who lived and worked in near proximity to Burns and in the urban milieu of Lowland Scotland, where the thickening of social, economic, political, and cultural networks was most pronounced in Burns's time. Limiting the examination to Lowland poets, in my judgment, is justified by the density of this milieu, considered with regard to its linguistic complexity and variety, its broad access to a variety of modes of literary production, even for poets writing from the margins of class and gender, and the availability of both formal and informal means of disseminating poetry to a public eager for reading material. Even so, there are more poets that meet these criteria than I have space to discuss, so my selection of specific poets has been determined in the first instance by Burns's demonstrable influence on them, their direct responses to Burns's influence, and their uses of the form, language, and subject matter of Burns's poetry. In the second instance, I have selected poets who participate in the Burnsian project of establishing a "national" literature that asserts Scottish distinctiveness within an enlightened British state. This common project bound these poets together and makes it possible to consider alternative poetic approaches to the vexed problem of Scottish identity that may or may not align with Burns's "bardic" version. Finally, I have sought poets who represent a wide range of subject positions in late eighteenth-century Scottish society. The rural "ploughman" typology that came to characterize Burns and his poetry, not only for much of his life but also posthumously (and that critics have significantly problematized in the past twenty-five years), has to some extent obscured the urgency with which the literary production of late eighteenth-century Scottish society more generally engaged with the promise and uncertainty of "modernization." By drawing on the poetry of Burns's contemporaries who occupied divergent class, gender, occupational, social, and political positions, I hope to show the ways in which poetry framed the "problem" of Scotland and self-identification as a "Scot" in a world of loyalties in conflict.

THE "PROBLEM" OF SCOTLAND

The historian Christopher Harvie has theorized that "the uniqueness of Scotland lies in the power of a civil society divorced from parliamentary nationalism, and

[8]

in an intelligentsia, which, lacking a political centre, was divided between two loyalties. . . . The red Scots were cosmopolitan, self-avowedly enlightened and, given a chance, authoritarian, expanding into and exploiting bigger and more bountiful fields than their own country could provide. Back home lurked their black brothers, demotic, parochial, sensitive about community to the point of reaction, but keeping the ladder of social promotion open, resisting the encroachment of the English governing class." According to Harvie, the "red" and "black" Scots formed an "uneasy alliance" in order to regulate "the rate of their own assimilation to the greater world, the balance which underlay integration in 'Britain.'"[26] Harvie's Stendhalian characterization, suggestive of the push and pull between militaristic, colonial adventure and insular, suspicious, yet pragmatic parochialism, transcends any simple or reductionist interpretation of Scottish "nationalism." Indeed, Harvie argues that in order to understand Scottish aspirations, one must turn to Thomas Carlyle, who argued that the Scots were "filled to the heart with an infinite religious idea. . . . Thought, conscience, the sense that man is denizen of a Universe, creature of an Eternity, has penetrated to the remotest cottage, to the simplest heart."[27]

Harvie's notion of "two Scotlands" yoked together in a tense yet mutually constitutive relationship, however, leaves women and many laboring-class men in a rather more marginal position. This sense of exclusion found expression in the poetry of late eighteenth-century Scots of all ranks of life, from the tavern songs of the mendicant Isobel "Tibbie" Pagan to the satires of the weaver and packman Alexander Wilson to the Jacobite lyrics of the aristocratic Lady Nairne. The sheer linguistic and topical variety of this poetry—its shifting degrees of "redness" and "blackness," its negotiation of complex social, political, economic, and religious affiliations, its self-consciousness and wonderment at an "enlightened" yet in many ways traditional world, its recognition of the benefits and costs of assimilation into a transnational state and global economy, its insistence on moral commitment and loyalty to one's own—fulfills the Foucauldian project of generating a national literature out of the "inexhaustible values" of language, of language that refuses to sit still and goes on making new meaning in each specific usage and context. To put it another way, Carla Sassi and Silke Stroh contend that "poetry's malleable and contingent nature points towards a complex and fluid idea of national identity—an idea that continually shifts between and across the historical and the domestic, the cultural and affective aspects of identity." Rather than "reconstructing an organic and consistent development of the Scottish nation through an overview of its poetic production across several centuries," Sassi and Stroh "chart . . . the different textual communities that, at different times and from different, even conflicting stances (ideological, linguistic, and geopolitical), have created and promoted ideas of nation and home within the boundaries of present-day Scotland."[28]

As conceptions of late eighteenth-century "Scottishness" and "Britishness" continue to evolve in academic discussion and popular debate, the time is ripe for renewing the analysis of one such "textual community," Burns's Lowland contemporaries, in both historical and literary terms. This analysis should also contribute to the ongoing examination of Scottish poetry's relation to the larger British, Anglophone, and transnational poetic traditions. As Robert Crawford urges in an afterword to the second edition of his seminal work *Devolving English Literature*, Scotland must "engage in debate with the rest of the world, reasserting not only its own awareness of itself as a nation, but also its sense of being part of an international community. Poets, novelists, and critics can all play their part in this, and it seems best . . . to suggest ways in which Scottish literature both projects and can be seen from international perspectives."[29] Crawford implies that Scotland exists as a diverse reading community—a critical consciousness—far beyond its juridical borders or the limits of political sovereignty, however those limits may expand or contract. As eighteenth-century Scots looked for ways to conceptualize Scotland's place within a powerful military-fiscal state and global empire, poets participated in the creation a "grammar" for this project, a complex of historical, cultural, and linguistic associations, ideas, imaginative self-projections, discursive modes, and material practices that situated "Scotland" within national and transnational space.[30]

Before turning to the poets, however, I must first establish what "Scottishness" and "Scotland" mean for purposes of this analysis. Mary Jane Scott argues that eighteenth-century Anglo-Scots poets such as James Thomson deserve to be considered as *Scottish* poets, rather than as exclusively English or British ones, and she recognizes this very problem of categorization: "For Scottishness is a stubborn thing. It is not simply a matter of language or locale. It takes more than a Scottish birth-certificate, or a vocabulary sprinkled with Scotticisms, to make a Scottish poet. It is all those intangible influences—religious, historical, educational, aesthetic, geographical, linguistic, literary, and broadly cultural—which work together to determine national and individual character."[31] For Scott, "Scottishness" evokes multiple bases of Scottish identity, speaking at once to the political and communal "nation" and to the ubiquitous Scottish presence in world culture. From this perspective, Scottishness constructs a kind of universal category available to anyone linked to Scotland by virtue of "broadly cultural" interpenetration. What makes Scottishness so "stubborn," perhaps, is its refusal of signification within any standard geopolitical terminology. No one knows exactly what constitutes Scotland or Scottishness, certainly not in the way we understand the constitution of

[10]

INTRODUCTION

England or the United States. When Robert Crawford, for example, retails the story of Mario Vargas Llosa's journey to Kirkcaldy and Abbotsford in search of Adam Smith and Walter Scott (citizens of the world if there ever were any), he does it to show the profound influence of Scottish literature on the wider world, as well as the immense culture industry that nineteenth-century Scotland has produced for world consumption.[32] In addition to its other presences, both concrete and evanescent, Scotland might be said to exist as a kind of corporate entity engaged in global commerce, an entity that, lacking political sovereignty, has nevertheless established a "nation" sustained by an aggressively marketed national culture. Lord Dacre may have considered this type of nationhood—tartan, pipes, and Burns night haggis feasts—as "invented" out of a collective sense of historical inferiority and loss (if not outright hucksterism), but he underestimated the capacity of Scots to "invent" a nation that allows one to "be Scottish" because one "feels" real emotional attachment to, if not affection for, his or her Scottishness.[33]

The notion that the construction of Scottishness involves a process of imaginative and emotional self-projection, rather than establishing a stable identity, also draws on recent work of Carol McGuirk and others on Robert Burns. Pointing to the efforts by Andrew Noble, Patrick Scott Hogg, and Liam McIlvanney to situate Burns as a politically and intellectually sophisticated "radical," McGuirk argues that Burns simply cannot be characterized in specific categorical terms.[34] Instead, in the context of the revolutionary period of the late 1780s and 1790s, Burns refashions a Scottish past fraught with historical crisis for the purpose of creating a "potentially utopian space that Burns defines as 'Scotland' . . . a place of free motion and strongly conveyed emotion. He critiques tyranny through a richly equivocal double vision of a glorious if embattled Scottish past and free-moving, free-speaking Scottish—and world—future."[35] McGuirk's reading of Burns's Scotland as a place of "free motion and strongly conveyed emotion" questions the possibility that Scotland can exist in anything other than a permanent state of incipience. It seems paradoxical to imagine an "essence" as always becoming and never fully present, but McGuirk suggests the paradox nonetheless. To extend McGuirk's theorization a bit further, my approach to Scottishness borrows from the Bergsonian insight that feelings or emotions cannot be fully experienced or named until they have already passed into memory, meaning that "being" must necessarily describe the shadow or impression of a past identity as well as the flux and reflux of present experience.[36] In this sense, the experiencing subject knows no present that it can think; the self can only hope to achieve consciousness of its own pastness as it recedes, gazing backward, into an indeterminate future that can only be imagined in an already archaized form. "Feeling" Scottish, then, connotes

[11]

BESIDE THE BARD

experience that passes into consciousness through a complex process of memorializing Scotland.[37]

But what does it mean to memorialize "Scotland"? Historians have long struggled to determine Scotland's precise status and influence in English, British, Atlantic, and world history, indicating that post-1707 Scotland eludes definitive signification.[38] In a superb demonstration of the nexus between social and literary history, for example, Christopher Smout argues that eighteenth-century "North Britain" refers to a geographic location and political affiliation assigned by an extremely narrow "enlightened" class (Harvie's "red" Scots) with an enormous investment in that particular form of authority (which included the authority of English over vernacular languages). At the same time, he recognizes that people on the ground lived and worked through "a sense of Scottishness" that in part supplanted and negated such authority. Colin Kidd prefers to use the term "North Britishness" to describe a hybrid identity in which post-Union Scots essentially replaced allegiance to the ancient Scottish nation with a strong patriotic identification with "English institutions, liberties and economic developments." Kidd emphasizes the Anglicizing and assimilationist impulses of the eighteenth-century Scottish political and economic elites, though he recognizes that Scottish religious, linguistic, and cultural distinctiveness tended to thwart development of a "comprehensive vision of British nationhood that drew on the history of both Scots and English."[39] Tom Devine steers a middle course, noting that three centuries of Union have fostered both national pride in a Scotland rich in its own distinctive history, culture, and tradition and a generally stable Scottish Unionism.[40]

Moreover, perceptions of the extent to which an indigenous Scottishness might meaningfully contribute to a form of cosmopolitan Britishness could shift substantially in a short period of time, contingent on domestic and foreign news, the waxing or waning political fortunes of specific figures, or the activities (or perceived activities) of people quite removed from the professional, university, and Kirk environments in which the debate played out. For example, as the relatively positive response to the early stages of the French Revolution gave way to widespread paranoia associated with the terror in France and the sedition trials at home (only to be followed by general war weariness and dissatisfaction with the Pittite regime), one can track destabilizing intensities that registered in the politer regions of literary canon-making.[41] The controversy over Burns's posthumous status as a vernacular, English, or British poet (which has never quite been settled) and the political values connected to the "appropriate" classification of Burns offers a case in point.[42] What passed for a robust vernacular contribution to "British" poetry in the mid-1780s, when Burns reached the apogee of his cosmopolitan fame, quickly became a dangerous and potentially subversive egalitarian "otherness" during the

[12]

INTRODUCTION

radical phase of the revolution, with its concurrent social and political unrest in Scotland.[43] Burns's "construction" as a national poet reflects the shifting political and cultural priorities bound up with the question of Scotland.[44] Follow the politics and there the language will be—or is it the other way around?

Historians and literary critics have frequently identified poets such as James Macpherson and Walter Scott as primary agents for packaging Scottishness for English consumption in the second half of the eighteenth century, largely through the collection and reproduction of the traditional oral culture of both the Highlands and Lowlands.[45] It might be said that "Britishness" as a national or cultural identity consists in large part of Scotland made digestible to the English, largely by the exertion of socially and politically aspirant "red" Scots. Lord Dacre notoriously takes the most extreme view, as we have seen, but more mainstream discussions of the nature of "Britishness" continue to emphasize the asymmetrical involvement of Scots in imagining Britain.[46] In a finely nuanced discussion of Burns's and Scott's roles in antiquarian quests to recover a unique and usable Scottish linguistic and literary past, the late Susan Manning observes that, although antiquarianism was a European-wide phenomenon, in "Scotland's case . . . the passing of tradition and custom was typically described as a process initiated or accelerated by the Union. . . . It is perhaps more productive to regard the condition of Britishness as offering Scottish writers a range of rhetorical resources with which to explore the implications of 'being modern' in the post-Union period."[47] Manning implies that "Britishness" is a discursive strategy for describing the necessarily fragmented and composite identities out of which the modern nation-state is constructed, as opposed to an individual or national identity in itself. This implication in turn suggests that Scotland's eighteenth-century experience of incorporation into an imperial England made it possible for poets such as Burns, steeped in neoclassical English literature, and Scott, with his enlightened professional education, to establish an entirely new "imperial grammar."[48]

But the cases of Burns and Scott do not entirely dispose of the question. As Janet Sorenson suggests, just as imperial grammars are constructed from disparate linguistic materials, they can be similarly refashioned to produce "progressive transnational links."[49] I take her to mean that linguistic reformation can contribute to, in Virginia Woolf's terms, "freedom from unreal loyalties."[50] In the context of late eighteenth-century Scottish Lowland society, the question of real and unreal loyalties riveted the participants in that society with particular intensity and urgency. For example, Leith Davis asserts that eighteenth-century collections of Scottish music and songs were "produced within the context of a British market which valued difference only to contain it within a wider hegemonic system." These "publications, particularly toward the end of the century, also served to

[13]

unsettle any sense of British cultural homogeneity not only by positing a different national culture within Britain but by challenging the primacy of literacy and of print, assumptions through which British culture asserted itself."[51] Davis thus suggests that "feeling Scottish" might bring us closer to understanding the national, ethnic, class, and gender differences that divide us and to liberating us from their repressive grasp.

Moreover, as Manning emphasizes, people perform their identities (whether national or otherwise), and these performances depend on the availability of broadly accessible, usable rhetorical and aesthetic resources. As we will see, eighteenth-century Scottish poets found little in English history to assist them in fashioning a "North British" identity. Standard Whig paeans to the glories of the English constitution or Tory patriotic hymns in praise of crown and church struck many Scots like a hammer on the head. As John Pocock has observed, England's interest in the 1707 Treaty of Union emphasized Scotland's incorporation and effective elimination as a free and unpredictable agent in European affairs. The English "acquired empire, in this case at least, not in the lapidary 'fit of absence of mind,' but out of unwillingness to consider their relations with others in any conceptual form, with the result that these could take no other form than that of an extension of the system to which they were accustomed. They had reasons, however— it may be further said—for this extreme and now and then appalling self-centredness."[52] Eighteenth-century Scots, who attempted to construct a meaningful form of British identity through which their felt Scottishness could be located, could count on no reciprocity south of the Tweed, forcing them back on their own historical and rhetorical resources.[53] Indeed, Scottishness and Britishness make two sides of the same coin, and any conception of post-Union Scottishness cannot exist independently from a correlative and often hegemonic British identity.[54]

This study reveals a striking lack of consensus and considerable skepticism about the truth value of elite claims regarding the nature and composition of the nation and the direction of history, despite the broad underlying Whiggishness of post-Union Scottish society.[55] As fractious as that society had been in prior centuries under conditions of frequent dearth, military occupation, and political instability, Scotland in the Age of Burns might not appear particularly exceptional, given the precarious state of the economy, periodic popular disturbances, and the increasing repression of even moderate reformist politics (not to mention the more radical elements, such as they were).[56] And, indeed, as we have seen, general enthusiasm for enlightenment and improvement, the watchwords of an emerging provincial urban commercial, professional, and industrial economy, watered down the heady brew of French republicanism and historical materialism. A number of possible

[14]

INTRODUCTION

futures thus existed at this historical moment.[57] They were not necessarily mutually exclusive, but the conflict between "red" and "black" visions of Scotland's future was fought out in part in the poetry of Burns and his contemporaries. Colin Kidd pertinently speculates that "British literature might lurk in the interstices between disciplines [of history and literary criticism], a kind of no-man's land that lies between the high literary matter which interests literary scholars and the broader political and social themes which attract historians."[58] The purpose of this study is to explore those interstitial spaces.

CHAPTER OVERVIEW

Chapter 1 examines the work of two of Burns's best-known Ayrshire contemporaries, John Lapraik and David Sillar. Lapraik and Sillar shared Burns's educational and social background, published volumes of poetry inspired by Burns's Kilmarnock edition, and engaged many of the same subjects and genres as Burns, though to disastrous financial effect. These poets, onetime friends of Burns, shared an ambiguous and self-conscious relationship with their counterpart, particularly as his literary fame grew in the late 1780s. At the same time, their verse engages the effects of "improvement" and social and economic change in Ayrshire in ways that diverge significantly from the Burns model. As we will see, Lapraik and Sillar exemplify the "black" and "red" Scot paradigm. The world-weary, pessimistic "black" Lapraik registers the dark side of enlightened "improvement" and assimilation to the imperial, global economy, whereas the opportunistic "red" Sillar sees change as offering Scots the chance to make a distinctive national contribution to the British composite state.

In chapter 2, we turn to two women "peasant" poets from Ayrshire, Janet Little, the "Scotch Milkmaid," and Isobel "Tibbie" Pagan. Little, who unsuccessfully sought Burns's patronage, adapted Latinate classical modes—lyric, panegyric, elegiac, and pastoral—to explore the decline of the feudal order and its implications, particularly for the "peasantry" and women. Her poetic meditations on standards of literary acceptance draw attention to the disadvantages that laboring-class women poets faced in competing for critical attention in Burns's wake. Pagan was known to Burns through at least one of her songs, and she occupied the extreme margins of gender and class. Pagan's poetry deploys her lack of social and economic agency to establish a liberatory space from which she evaluates and renders judgment on the moral failings of Muirkirk society at a historical moment when the old moral economy is giving way to the globalizing forces of industrialization.

[15]

Chapter 3 takes up the Scottish poetry of the Paisley weaver Alexander Wilson, who actively emulated Burns and achieved a large measure of poetic success in Lowland Scotland before his political radicalism (and penchant for poetic libel) caught up with him, forcing his emigration to America. Wilson's poetry, even at its most intensely local, voices a powerful sense of national crisis and its implications for domestic and personal well-being. Wilson, the radical whom Burns himself did not quite become, was among the first poets to register the large-scale effects of industrialization, articulated in deeply moving tragic or bitterly satirical strains the stresses of a society under siege by external forces of change and dissolution. Sympathetic to Burn's New Licht moderatism, republicanism, and progressivism, Wilson's poetry describes the emergence of an identifiably modern working class under conditions of subjection to capital.

Chapter 4 explores the poetry of the aristocratic Carolina Oliphant, Baroness Nairne (hereinafter referred to as Lady Nairne). Her songs and poetry take a complex and ambivalent view of Scottish history, interrogating the purpose of "national" poetry and the effects on women of the transition from feudalism to "modern" civil society. Lady Nairne avidly followed Burns in the antiquarian project of song collecting and composing, producing some of the most popular Jacobite songs in the Scottish tradition. Frequently characterized as apolitical, sentimental, and elegiac laments for the lost cause, Nairne's songs construct a female Jacobite "other" that problematizes the political and social coding of Jacobite verse as practiced by Burns.

Chapter 5 examines the work of the Paisley weaver Robert Tannahill, whose posthumous popularity as a songwriter during the Victorian period rivaled that of Burns and Nairne. Like Wilson, whom he revered, Tannahill self-consciously wrote "in Burns's shadow," producing a remarkable range of vernacular and English poems exploring the domestic effects of war and social disruption during the early Napoleonic era. But unlike Wilson, Tannahill veiled his radical political commitments in verse that emphasizes the destructive masculine economy of "improvement" and the disastrous effects of imperial war and conquest on Scottish society.

Contrasting Tannahill's carefully coded politics, chapter 6 turns to the overtly Jacobin poetry of the Edinburgh weaver and "seditionist" James Kennedy and the Catholic intellectual Alexander Geddes, whose unorthodox religious views and republican politics deprived him of both his ecclesiastical appointments and social position among the enlightened elite in Scotland. Kennedy's decision to compose largely in English enables him to mimic loyalist discourse while subverting its appeal to British patriotism. His poetry deconstructs "Scotland" as an alternative site of national identity, holding it responsible for complicity with the repressive British state, and finds potential social cohesion in class identification. Geddes,

[16]

INTRODUCTION

by contrast, situates "Scotland" not in opposition to England or Britain but in relation to its Roman and European intellectual traditions. His Latin, Scottish vernacular, and English verse draw deeply on humanist universalism as a basis for pan-European political liberty and social equality. In contrast to Burns, neither poet could or would mask his political commitments sufficiently to survive the savage political repression of the 1790s.

1

BURNS'S AYRSHIRE "BARDIES"

John Lapraik and David Sillar

BURNS SCHOLARSHIP HAS LONG NOTED the existence of a community of Ayrshire poets with links to the bard, chief among them John Lapraik and David Sillar. This chapter examines the work of these two poets, with regard to both their direct relationship with Burns through exchanges of epistolary verse and the specific ways their poetry compares to Burns's linguistically and thematically. As two of the three poets most frequently identified as having unsuccessfully attempted to follow Burns through the narrow aperture between literary obscurity and fame (the other, Janet Little, will be considered in chapter 2), Lapraik and Sillar emulated the Burns model in some ways but not others, indicating that the Ayrshire soil bred distinct kinds of poets with their own approaches to the socioeconomic challenges of their environment and the potential for poetry to mediate social change and "improvement."[1] A closer study of their poetry may also contribute to answering Corey Andrews question, why Burns and not his "others"? In this sense, considering Lapraik and Sillar as literary "failures" may tell us much about the criteria for "success," both in Burns's historical moment and in literary criticism since then, but perhaps more importantly about the local conditions that produced the Burns phenomenon in the first place.

Recent work on Burns has begun to pay close attention to the extensive connections between Ayrshire, Enlightenment, and modernization. In a magisterial study of Burns and pastoral, Nigel Leask reminds us that later eighteenth-century Ayrshire was not "an obscure provincial backwater" but rather was "linked by the discourse and practice of improvement to the birth of the modern capitalist age."[2] During the lifetimes of Burns, Lapraik, and Sillar, "improvement" announced itself to Ayrshire not only in the rationalization and commercialization of agriculture but in

[19]

BESIDE THE BARD

> the rise of manufactures, country banking, and the booms and busts of the new credit economy, war, and empire, accompanied by religious and cultural enlightenment. Ayrshire was also highly "globalized," to the extent that its landed elite benefited disproportionately from colonial expansion in the Caribbean and India, while rich and poor alike suffered palpably from the loss of the American colonies. . . . If at times Burns's poetry mounted a "zigzag" criticism of improvement, elsewhere (especially in the Kirk poems, with their bitter satires on religious prejudice) it fully endorsed the rational spirit of enlightenment. After all, his formidable literacy was itself a product of Ayrshire's provincial enlightenment, distinguished by new civic institutions, turnpike roads, and postal service, facilitating the circulation of newspapers and letters. The fact that Burns never attended college doesn't mean that he was "Heaven-taught."[3]

This view of Ayrshire sits side by side with the image of tenant farmers and their laborers toiling to wrest a bare subsistence from the soil or, to quote Andrew Noble, of "the domestic squalor and poverty in which [Burns] mainly lived."[4] Rather, the hard times that beset farmers like Burns and his brother, Lapraik, and Sillar's father (the young Sillar left the farm to open a grocery business) could be felt at all levels of society, if not in equal proportion.[5] Viewing Ayrshire as part of a "globalized" community of interest, tied together by thickening networks of exchange, technology, and communications, situates Burns and his contemporaries as literal producers, not only in the new economy but in the emerging literary discourse of an enlightened, "rational" society.[6] As we will see, Lapraik and Sillar conduct a similar "zigzag" critique of improvement, showing ambivalence about its moral and economic effects (though in Lapraik less "satirical" in its treatment of religious orthodoxy), while generally endorsing the "formidable literacy" that the institutions and innovations of the new economy afforded.

Moreover, the rational, literate, and globalizing Ayrshire pictured by Leask and the literature of "improvement" illustrates the extent to which traditional landed society of lairds, tenants, crofters, and laborers had already given way to a more urbanized provincial society consisting of lawyers, teachers, bankers, clerks, tradespeople, shopkeepers, artisans, and workers of all sorts, or as John Barrell has put it, "the rural professional class" that created "the landscape of parliamentary enclosure."[7] As Leask points out, the tenant farmer Burns "occupied the middle rung on the social hierarchy of the rural Lowlands, the most precarious lower edge of that rung, it is true, but still not too far below" Barrell's rural professionals.[8] While Leask notes that Burns worked in the fields alongside his hired hands, he nevertheless employed them for wages.[9] According to Leask, this made Burns a "labouring" but not a "labouring *class* poet."[10] Indeed, the same goes for Lapraik, who inherited land and leased it for farming, and Sillar, who left the farm for town

[20]

life as a grocer and then a teacher. This distinction associates the poetry of "improvement" composed by Burns and his contemporaries with the middle ranks (albeit lower middle ranks) of Scottish society, producing forms of social, political, and economic identity that differ in significant respects from those produced by laboring- or servant-class poets, such as, for example, Janet Little and Isobel Pagan. Read together, Burns, Lapraik, Sillar, and other similarly situated provincial poets thus form a kind of choric voice that articulates both the aspirations and anxieties of an emergent "middle" position between traditional and "modern" forms of wealth and the division of labor, aristocratic patronage and the mass literary market, local identity and "Scottishness" or "Britishness."

At the same time, however, the fine distinction between a "laboring" or "laboring class" poet becomes complicated by Burn's self-identification (and extended experience) with manual labor and the chronic financial difficulties that he and his family could never seem to escape. As noted in the introduction, his transformation from the struggling tenant farmer Robert Burnes and aspiring poet Rob Burness to Robert Burns, author of *Poems, Chiefly in the Scottish Dialect* signifies Burns's acute awareness of the ambiguous relationship between "objective" categories of socioeconomic status (which class?) and self-representation (laborer/enlightened farmer/poet/Scotch bard). Burns's case is complicated also by the critical reception of his poetry, which to some degree objectified (and commoditized) Burns as a laboring-class poet but also empowered Burns to fashion a public persona as a national bardic figure. To confuse matters further, the Edinburgh critics who cast Burns as a native plebeian genius urged him to grind the rougher edges off some of the vernacular poems that made his reputation to begin with. As Carol McGuirk points out, the "capital's literati (many of them clergymen who may have disliked the flippant tone of the religious satires), recognized Burns's extraordinary gifts but rejected his evident resolve to infiltrate the poetic canon, abolishing the standard-English monopoly of literary diction. . . . The resistance to Burns broke out most strongly following his premature death in 1796, but even in 1787 Hugh Blair, who advised Burns on the second edition of *Poems*, evidently insisted on genteel counterbalance: all those asterisked disclaimers at the head and foot of Burns's pages."[11] Burns's class position thus remains difficult to pinpoint, perhaps illustrating the interaction between an increasing fluidity of social categories and the enhanced possibilities for self-fashioning in a late eighteenth-century world of loosening class boundaries.

The question of whether and how Burns's Ayrshire contemporaries may have influenced him remains an open one. Gerard Carruthers wonders whether there was "a ready-made poetic community in the geographical area around him within which Burns is locating himself" or whether "it is his fictional projection, to some

[21]

BESIDE THE BARD

extent, that creates a later reality." In any event, Carruthers doubts that "Burns was readily slotting himself into a vibrant Ayrshire Scots poetry writing community" but rather believes that "the idea of the 'Bards on the Bonie Doon' was largely a creative fantasy (not unhelpful, however, even in its one-sidedness) when Burns conceived it in 1784, and remained so until his own published success largely spawned a shoal of imitators who did not do much for the reputation of poetry in Scots."[12] Still, Carruthers acknowledges that Lapraik and Sillar composed poetry contemporaneously with Burns, even if they later "tidied" their previous output or produced new material for publication once they realized the extent of Burns's success.[13]

Leask takes a somewhat more positive view of the "vibrancy" of the Ayrshire circle of poets. Noting the dual meaning of "bardie" as a diminutive of "'bard'—in the grandiose Ossianic sense"—but also as "bold, impudent of speech," Leask imagines the "Ayrshire bardies" as seeking "a vent for their frustrated aspirations in a swaggering poetical rejection of social emulation in a class-bound society, and (in quieter moments) a more introspective desire for sentimental 'self-improvement.' Inspired by Ramsay and Fergusson, as well by English poets such as Shenstone, Goldsmith, and Gray, they circulated their verse epistles in manuscript, taking advantage of Ayrshire's new roads and postal service (Lapraik was himself postmaster in Muirkirk)."[14] From this perspective, Burns appears rooted in a poetry-writing community that shared common occupations, values, and, at least for a time, companionship. Moreover, the fact that neither Lapraik nor Sillar followed Burns very far down the vernacular path seems curious if we hold them to have significantly modified their respective oeuvres in the tail of Burns's comet. The titles of their volumes do not particularly parrot Burns's, make no claim to the "Scottish dialect," and utilize the traditional *forms* of Scots poetry, such as Standard Habbie or "Cherry and Slae" stanzas, but without the Scots language. Perhaps they believed that they could not match Burns's talent in vernacular poetry and could not "tidy" their poetry nearly enough to pass muster under the literary standard established by Burns. But perhaps what they had to say about their world demanded different linguistic choices than Burns made. I will investigate the latter possibility.

Despite the high hopes of Lapraik and Sillar, they did not reach a readership that extended very far beyond the local or regional. Still, as Leask, Bob Harris, and others have pointed out, the rapid pace of provincial urbanization that changed the physical landscape of the Scottish Lowlands altered the literary landscape as well. Later eighteenth-century local or regional poets acquired access to printers, booksellers, and dealers in literary materials that did not exist in the days of Ramsay and Fergusson. The densifying communications and transport infra-

[22]

structure built to service an increasingly globalized economy could also be used to disseminate ideas, particularly on the "modern" subject of improvement and its dramatic effects on Scottish society. The "nascent petit bourgeoisie," to use Leask's term, experienced this quickened pace of life and used poetic discourse to speak to others in their class who experienced the same "booms and busts of the new capitalist economy, particularly the long repercussions of the Ayr Bank failure of 1772, as well as the terrible weather and worse harvests of the early 1780s."[15] By virtue of some timely patronage and success in negotiating the literary market-place, Burns achieved sales in the thousands in Scotland, England, and beyond. Poets such as Lapraik and Sillar could only count the number of their readers in the hundreds. But as Fiona Stafford, speaking of Scottish Gaelic poets, reminds us, "To judge poetry by the size of its audience . . . can be a rather dubious proce-dure, whether the assessment is based on contemporary responses or represents the verdict of generations. As literary canons have come to be seen as shifting and amorphous, critics have grown wary of making absolute pronouncements on the importance of earlier poets, while the assumption that a small, local audience is somehow less valuable than a mass readership seems decidedly unsafe."[16] There is no question but that Lapraik and Sillar enjoyed a "small, local audience," but because Robert Burns formed part of that audience (and they formed part of his), these poets have become integral to Burns's reception and to understanding the nature of his appeal. At the very least, taking Lapraik and Sillar on their own ground, so to speak, can tell us much about Burns's "bardies" and the community that grounded Burns's representations of rural Lowland society.

JOHN LAPRAIK: "IMPROVEMENT" AS ESTATES SATIRE

Son of a relatively affluent Ayrshire landowner, John Lapraik was born in 1727 near Muirkirk at Laigh Dalquhram. He attended parochial school, where he received a literary education. His father left him the family estate, which Lapraik augmented by leasing the lands and mills of Muirsmill. In 1754 Lapraik married Margaret Rankine, whose brother, John, a tenant farmer in Adamhill, Tarbolton, belonged to the same Ayrshire circle as Lapraik.[17] When Margaret died following the birth of their fifth child, Lapraik married again in 1766 to Janet Anderson, the daughter of a local farmer; the couple had nine children. Lapraik lost the family lands in the aftermath of the spectacular financial collapse of the Ayr Bank in August 1773, a fate he shared with many farmers who took advantage of the bank's liberal lend-ing practices.[18] His slow decline into bankruptcy played out over more than a decade, culminating in his commitment for a short time to an Ayr debtors' prison

[23]

BESIDE THE BARD

in 1785, where he composed many of the poems that later appeared in his *Poems, on Several Occasions* (1788).[19] Lapraik subsequently accepted a position as postmaster at Muirkirk and later opened a public house adjacent to the post office. He died on May 7, 1807.[20]

In the same year as Lapraik's imprisonment for debt, he made Burns's acquaintance. In "Epistle to J. Lapraik: An Old Scotch Bard," April 1, 1785, first printed in the Kilmarnock edition (1786), Burns recounts hearing a song attributed to Lapraik:[21]

> There was *ae sang*, amang the rest,
> Abbon them a' it pleas'd me best,
> That some kind husband had addrest
>   To some sweet wife:
> It thirl'd the heart-strings thro' the breast,
>   A' to the life.
>
> I've scarce heard ought describ'd sae weel,
> What gen'rous, manly bosoms feel;
> Thought I, 'Can this be *Pope* or *Steele*,
>   Or *Beattie's* wark?'
> They told me 'twas an odd kind chiel
>   About *Muirkirk*.[22]

As the Canongate editors observe, Burns's comparison of Lapraik to Pope, Steele, and Beattie (not to mention later in the poem to Allan Ramsay and Robert Fergusson) is "hyperbolic in the extreme."[23] Robert Crawford is more forgiving of Lapraik's skills, crediting him with helping Burns establish a local idiom in which his democratic politics could be "couched in warm, unthreatening language. . . . Companionable tone, rather than revolutionary politics, achieves a result whose implications, recognized alike by the young William Wordsworth and subsequent generations, are powerfully revolutionary."[24] Nigel Leask, on the other hand, considers Lapraik "a lesser poetic talent than Sillar."[25] In either case, critics agree that Burns's friendship with the two men was central to the formation of his own aesthetic, not only providing "a necessary literary environment" for the aspiring poet but helping him express his "spark o' Nature's fire."[26]

Lapraik's *Poems, on Several Occasions* was published in Kilmarnock in 1788. The volume contains more than forty poems and songs on various subjects and in various verse forms. A few of the poems feature the Scots vernacular, such as his "Epistle to R****T B****S" and the Burnsian dialogues "The Herd and Dog" and "The Devil's Answer to the Poet's Address," but most speak primarily in an Angli-

[24]

cized poetic voice. Lapraik's oeuvre likewise imitates favorite Augustan genres: pastoral (for example, the volume begins with a seasons cycle, "Spring," "Summer," "Harvest," "Winter"); didactic poetry ("In Praise of Charity," "A Query after Happiness," "Time, How Thoughtlessly We Let It Pass," "The Well-Meaning Jobber's Lamentation"); speculative verses ("Man's Creation and Fall"); ode ("On Melancholy," "On Solitude," "On Ridicule"); and elegy ("Elegy on G**** B***"). There are a few other epistolary poems, but they are not as numerous as in Burns's or Sillar's volumes. The following selections focus on Lapraik's verses relating directly to "improvement." They reveal deep ambivalence about the social and economic effects of improvement, classing Lapraik with English poets preoccupied with the loss of English rural values and the moral barrenness of "modern" commercial capitalist society.

Indeed, much of Lapraik's poetry comments on contemporary economic and social conditions in Ayrshire. These poems concern themselves with the history of the moment, the struggles of farmers and rural folk in the grip of larger economic forces over which they have no control. Generally speaking, the poems lack the elegiac tone associated with the rural poetry of English poets such as Gray, Cowper, and Crabbe. There is little sense in the poems of a golden age of rural life, now lost in the mania for agricultural improvement and commercial exploitation, although the plague of wealth-seeking inflicts Scotland just as pervasively as it does England. Scottish farming had always been a harsh and uncertain living in the best of times, but in Lapraik's world of financial collapse and bankruptcy, the business must have appeared unsustainable for the traditional small farmer. While historians tell us that the late eighteenth century witnessed a large-scale economic "take-off" in Scotland, partially based on more rational and productive agricultural practices, Lapraik's poetry narrates the cost of improvement in terms of the destruction, not of a rural idyll, but of the social order itself.[27]

For example, in "On the Distressed Condition of Honest Farmers,"[28] the poet begins,

> If man's possesst of *common sense*,
> He may well see, at the first glance,
> Mankind a *common system* is,
> > And should support
> Each other, in their stations here,
> > And them comfort.

> The Governor of all the earth
> Has made each being that draws breath,
> And ev'ry priv'lege that man hath

[25]

BESIDE THE BARD

> 'S receiv'd from GOD;
> Then why should stupid mortals boast
> In this abode?

Burns, for example, frequently uses Standard Habbie measure for satirical purposes but also as part of his "reinvention" of pastoral.[29] Lapraik employs it here in a heavily moralistic strain that recalls Sir David Lindsay's *Ane Satyre of the Thrie Estatis* (1552), an estates satire in the tradition of Chaucer, Gower, and other medieval British poets. Both poems emphasize how human corruption undermines the "common system" that God created. Lapraik's use of the term "common sense" suggests the Scottish school of philosophy of that name, but Lapraik's equation of "common sense" with "common system" reconceptualizes an empirically based approach to ethics as grounded specifically in Christian ethics.

Lapraik's moral economy, in which lairds, farmers, and laborers share a cooperative, paternalistic ethos rooted in the land, hardly constitutes an idealized or allegorized state, however.[30] Despite the traditional, even medieval ring of Lapraik's poem, it registers the influence of enlightened moral philosophy, urging the rich in "modern" fashion: "And if man would impartial be, / He may see't well, with half an eye, / The man who is of *high degree* / Is much ador'd; / Yet still the *pleb'an* is of use / Him to uphold." As Louisa Gairn has observed in her discussion of Burns's representations of "the precariousness of rural life, including the often unjust relationship between landowners and rural workers," Burns draws on Adam Smith's *Theory of Moral Sentiments* (1759), specifically Smith's influential concept of the "impartial spectator" who enters sympathetically into the feelings of others, to address inequities of class in the agrarian economy.[31] Lapraik's appeal to the man of "high degree" to put himself in the place of the "pleb'an" echoes Smithean Anglicized diction, in contrast to Burns's vernacular usage in "distress" poems such as "The Twa Dogs: A Tale."[32] Lapraik's former status as a landowner and lessor of farmland to tenant farmers (such as the Burns family) who has fallen beneath his hereditary social rank may account for his linguistic selection here, as he addresses members of his own class in the polite language of improvement, rather than the truly "ple'ban" tongue of Caesar and Luath.[33]

Indeed, Lapraik's inherited class position does not inhibit him from representing the actual *condition* of the laboring poor, though it may make him less comfortable expressing himself in the *vernacular* of the laboring poor.[34] For Lapraik, men work, drudge, and "what not" for meager wages and bare subsistence. A man of high degree depends on the "pleb'an" for his daily bread, but he also shares the common man's fate to a greater or lesser degree. Scotland is not England, at least not the England of much eighteenth-century rural poetry. While

[26]

vast inequities exist between rich and poor, as they do in England, the symbiosis between them produces a different effect than reflections on a ruined landscape and regrets for England's imagined pastoral past. Instead, the poet strikes a Smithean pose, again urging landlords imaginatively to change places with their hungry workers:

> But would the *Lairds* submissive be,
> And *Landlords* of whate'er degree,
> And think one moment, then they'll see
> > I'm not mistaken,
> 'Tis *Lands o'er dear* and *Factors keen*
> > Make such a *breaking*.

Oppressed by high rents and rapacious agents, those who work the land may one day "break," leaving the increasingly absentee lairds cash starved and capital poor. The repetition of terms and images connoting cataclysm further emphasizes the poem's political cast: the "breaking" point cannot be far away, and when it occurs, the "common system" will fail, landlords and laborers alike.

Lapraik's complaint against the landlord class continues in "Honest John's Opinion of Patronage."[35] This poem takes the form of a dialogue between friends, composed (with the exception of the first stanza, which ends in a triad) in octosyllabic rhymed couplets. Unlike the direct speech in the "Honest Farmer," the dialogic method distances the poet from the speaker in the poem. Here "Honest John," who may be an alter ego of the poet John, accuses the lairds of corrupting the Kirk by forcing the congregations to accept their sons and protégés, thus prostituting the church to the temporal power of the ruling elites:

> Good morrow neighbour; what's your news?
> Tell what you ken, pray, don't refuse.
> Says he, The folk's all in a rage,
> And blame the Church for *Patronage*.
> Sir, my opinion is the same
> With those men who the Church do blame;
> *Curst Patronage* usurps a pow'r,
> And makes our Church a *common who—e*.

Similar to "On the Distressed Condition of Honest Farmers," the poem recalls the anticlericalism of estates satire, in which the bishops (in the older Catholic format of anticlerical criticism) exploit the church for personal profit and fill its pulpits with the doltish second sons of aristocrats (or their own natural children). Figuring the Kirk as a "common who—e," moreover, draws on a virulent strain of

[27]

BESIDE THE BARD

anti-Catholicism that had not yet exhausted itself in the mid-1780s, when memories of the anti-Catholic riots in Edinburgh and Glasgow in 1779 and the 1785 Gordon Riots in London were fresh. Honest John's critique appears aimed in part at the "New Light" moderates who controlled Kirk government for much of the second half of the eighteenth century and with whom Burns has been closely associated.[36] Yet even so, Lapraik's speaker does not default to "Auld Licht" orthodoxy, with its frequently dour Calvinism, but maintains an enlightened philosophical position, lamenting the "dissensions throughout the land" that patronage causes. The poem then calls for healing: "The bond of all Society, / By *Patronage* is forc'd to fly; / If men, true friendship cannot stay, / Where men are void of charity." The awkward and ill-fitted rhymes in these couplets register the dissension that the speaker laments, as if the speaker yearns to rhyme "Society" and "charity" but cannot bridge the social divide that has split Scotland's most important national institution.

Here the "breaking" warned against in "Honest Farmers" is refigured as a breakdown of the "Society" of believers. Honest John voices sound Calvinist doctrine here, rejecting any biblical authority for lay patronage or church government. At the same time, no matter how well intentioned or "wise" the patron may be, the very act of usurpation implied in the presentation of a clergyman violates the social bond between the lords and the commons. The paternalism intrinsic to the estate critique found in "Honest Farmer" does not extend to the essentially democratic and egalitarian sphere of Presbyterian faith. The lairds penetrate that sphere not only at their own risk but at the risk of profound social disorder, a potent threat given Scotland's unhappy experience of seventeenth-century religious conflict. The poem continues with something of a history lesson tracing the purity of the early church, the Constantinian imposition of prelacy, and the subordination of the church to the secular, political ends of the state. But as in "Honest Farmers," the poem concludes by pulling back on the critique before it reaches a revolutionary pitch, asking Scots "why should we so much complain, / Of *Antichrist* and *Pope of Rome*, / Since arbitrary pow'r is us'd, / In settling Priests, though still refus'd?" Here the poet places the blame for social dissension not on fabricated external threats but squarely on a failure of civil society and ecclesiastical government to reconcile the interests of the lairds and the congregations.

Indeed, Honest John questions whether the Reformation achieved anything other than the substitution of one ruling elite (the lairds) for another (the pope).[37] The "arbitrary pow'r" long associated with popery (and the deposed Stuart monarchs) is simply in different hands. Britain's claim to Protestant liberty, embodied in the territorial constitution and the free institutions of Parliament and church, has become a cruel sham, not worthy of the blood of martyrs. Moreover, Honest

[28]

John's complaint implies no Jacobite nostalgia for lost Scottish independence or the courtly society of a ruling monarch in Holyrood. The poem's reference to Haman, who, according to the book of Esther, with his wife, Zeresh, plotted the massacre of the Jews in ancient Persia, deepens the poem's sense of political treachery and betrayal.[38] Moreover, figuring "relig'ously inclin'd" Scots Presbyterians as a persecuted "Chosen People" complicates the post-Union project of assimilating Scotland into the British imperial domain and reconciling Presbyterian orthodoxy with Enlightenment social ideals and philosophical skepticism. The poem reflects this uncertainty by concluding in an interrogatory mode, pleading with Scots to put aside doctrinal differences to knit "Society" back together again.

Paralleling the economic and social moderatism of "Honest Farmer," the speaker in "Honest John" tends to religious conservatism yet worries about the threat that orthodox Calvinism, pursued, for example, to the level of rebellion as in the seventeenth century, poses to "British" Scotland. To complete this trilogy of complaint poems, the poet takes aim at financial bubbles created by easy credit. As we have seen, the 1773 failure of the Ayr Bank (also called Douglas, Heron & Company after two of its original shareholders, Patrick Heron of Heron and Sir Archibald Douglas) ruined Lapraik and hundreds of others, including the 225 partners who lost more than £660,000.[39] According to one historian, the causes of Douglas and Heron's dissolution included "trading beyond their means; divided control by permitting branches to act independently; forcing the circulation of their notes; giving credit too easily; ignorance of the principles of business; and carelessness or iniquity of officers."[40] In "Observations on the D——S AND H—N B—K," the poet returns to Standard Habbie, but this time in a more detached satirical mode than in the personal complaint of "Honest Farmers."[41] But as in the first two complaint poems, the use of English marks the speaker's position in the middle ranks of society: the landowners and tenant farmers who lost the most in the failure of the bank. The first four stanzas of the poem perfectly describe a credit bubble, a periodic occurrence in eighteenth-century Britain, where financial regulation was virtually nonexistent. In the first stanza, the good times seem to roll, but "The Notes amongst men were too plenty: / They took their glass and were right canty; / They little thought, That plenty, when 'tis misimproven, / Brings men to nought." As the bubble expands, the poem's language emphasizes the slipperiness of signifiers of financial instruments: "There's credit here for every soul," and "credit went o'er all the country"; "If he's well-back'd, without control, / He shall have Money"; the all-too-plentiful "Notes." Each term seems interchangeable, seemingly solid and tangible but in reality without "backing" or "control" (or, as Marx and Engels famously put it sixty years later, "All that is solid melts into air"). Moreover, in the first stanza, the poet plays on the word "plenty," first

[29]

BESIDE THE BARD

using it to indicate the deceptive perception of wealth conferred by the free availability of credit and then ironically revealing the deception by deploying the word
in its traditional sense of real, tangible plenitude, sown and reaped by the sweat of
one's brow. By the third stanza, the bubble has burst on the hapless farmers, who
suffer every day from "hornings"—a Scottish legal term connoting a "process of
execution issued under the signet directing a messenger to charge a debtor to pay
or perform in terms of the letters, under pain of being 'put to the horn,' i.e. declared
rebel."[42] In this process, the king's messenger actually blew three blasts on a horn,
proclaiming the debtor an outlaw and "air landis and gudis eschete."[43]

After bemoaning the failure of the scheme and the descent of the creditors,
the poet concludes,

> Those consequences are so bad,
> That many wish they ne'er had had
> Such *credit*; for they're us'd, by G-d!
>   Not like to men;
> Yet seldom own that they themselves
>   Were much to blame.

> Man, *Agar's wish*, should not exceed,
> To pray for what's his daily bread:
> Industr'ous he should be indeed
>   To gain the same;
> But if his bread should scanty be
>   He none should blame.

As in "Honest John's Opinion of Patronage," Lapraik again interweaves biblical
and political allusions, at once evincing the world-weariness associated with the
people's eternal Job-like suffering, produced partly by their own vanity and pride
but also by their too-trusting good nature, taken advantage of by the creditors that
"us'd" the farmers "Not like to men." The resigned poet cites "Agar's wish," found
in Proverbs 30, verse 2: give me not wealth or poverty.[44] Though the poem sounds
a cautionary note about the dangers of an easy-money economy, it does not issue
a clarion call to the oppressed rural proletariat to rise up in a green revolution and
burn down the banks. In this collapse, the lairds, tenants, and workers suffer one
and all. The remedy to their condition lies in the moral and practical realms of
labor, not politics, which likewise aligns the poet's voice with the spirit of the old
moral economy. Though one's bread may be "scanty / He none should blame." The
poem, like "Honest Farmers" and "Honest John's Opinion," ultimately takes an
enlightened philosophical position, leavened with Old Testament wisdom: humble

[30]

thyself in the presence of God and the suffering of others. Sympathetic identification, in good Smithean fashion, can restore peace of mind, if not plenty.

Lapraik's Anglicization of the traditional Habbie stanza, as well as his selective use of biblical and Scots history to weave a fabric composed of elements of the old moral economy and a popular Presbyterianism softened by Enlightenment imaginative sympathy, strikes a distinctive pose when compared to Burns's vernacular complexity. Whereas, as Alex Broadhead has argued, Burns used vernacular Scots to expand the ability of language to represent experience, test the boundaries between low and high spheres, and explore the reach of different languages, Lapraik's English poetry, at least as represented in these three poems, seems to speak in the monologic tone of the middle ranks of Scottish Lowland society, steeped in the religious and historical traditions of their forbearers but attuned to the social and economic aspirations represented by improvement and linguistic assimilation.[45] Christopher Harvie's contention that the "vitality of the Enlightenment depended on semi-independence, conscious decisions by men working within the estates, who realised their strengths and weaknesses, and the need to control the drive to integration" maps closely onto Lapraik's poetic sensibility.[46] Even in economic decline, Lapraik held a respectable position in the estates as a former landowner and postmaster, much like Burns, who, likewise fallen on hard economic times, made the move from tenant farmer to excise officer. Lapraik and Burns are thus variations of Harvie's "black" Scot typology: "demotic, parochial, sensitive about community to the point of reaction, but keeping the ladder of social promotion open, resisting the encroachment of the English governing class."[47] They may differ from one another in their degree of "blackness"—Burns certainly seems more "demotic" but less parochial than Lapraik, we might say—but both advocate for communitarian values, even while looking for "social promotion" in the publication of their poetry.[48]

Broadhead reads Burns's epistle to Lapraik as a rejection of "the promise of social and personal improvement that was typically thought to accompany the learning of Latin and Greek in favor of an ideal of 'honest labour.' In this way, the metalanguage of the poem is bound up with the policing of social boundaries."[49] As we have seen, Lapraik, like Burns, sides with the "folk" against aristocratic values, also promoting the value of honest labor but doing it in a biblical "metalanguage" that softens the often sharper political edges of Burns's poetry about rural economic distress and divisions in the Kirk. Sadly, the Paisley weaver poet James Maxwell took great pleasure in the financial failure of Lapraik's volume and the disappointment of his subscribers, while also taking a swipe at his younger and more illustrious counterpart:[50]

[31]

BESIDE THE BARD

He sure hath lost it ere he came again.
His budget sure from off his back hath gone,
For grammar, rhime, or reason he hath none.
His brother B——does him by far excel,
And is a bolder advocate for hell.[51]

Maxwell's doggerel, as Nigel Leask has pointed out with respect to the poet's response to Burns's "Address to the Deil," itself suffers from "stilted English diction and metrical ineptitude," almost as though Maxwell composes in a language he neither speaks nor inhabits.[52] Whatever we think about the value of Maxwell's critique, Lapraik's poetry does not attempt to imitate the linguistic pyrotechnics of Augustan poets but speaks in the language of the poet's social class to a community of readers he knows and respects—and who know and respect him. Corey Andrews observes that Lapraik recognized that he and Burns had "different Muses" and that Lapraik's verses to Burns "speak to Lapraik's age and experience and suggest his sense of the chasm separating his literary efforts from Burns's."[53] I would add further that he wrote poetry in an effort to recuperate some sense of communitarian solidarity in an era of rapid provincial urbanization, which he figured in the distress of farmers and tradespeople ruined by the Ayr Bank failure and the fierce contentions between "Auld" and "New" Lichts in the Kirk.

Fittingly Muirkirk did not forget its "lesser" bard. On July 18, 1914, just days before the outbreak of the Great War, members of the Lapraik Burns Club gathered in a field near Lapraik's birthplace to dedicate a memorial cairn to the poet's memory. As reported by the *Muirkirk Advertiser*,

> Mr Thomas Weir, the father and poet laureate of the Club, expressed great pleasure in being there, where, 129 years ago, honest-hearted auld Lapraik had his home. Mr Weir repeated all the epistles betwixt Burns and Lapraik in his own surpassing style, and referred to the meeting of the poets, probably in 1785. Our poet was the oldest in the list of the contemporaries of Burns, and was much loved by the National Poet for his sterling qualities.
>
> He was indeed Burns's model in "A Man's a Man for a' That."[54]

Lapraik may never have succeeded in competition with Burns in the literary marketplace, but he is permanently linked to the greater poet and to the production of Lowland Scottish literature during this period. His unmannered and direct speech, perhaps, more closely resembles the Wordsworthian poetic diction of "men speaking to men" about their common humanity than that of either vernacular poets or imitators of Augustan English—a different Muse, indeed.

[32]

DAVID SILLAR AND SCOTTISH BOURGEOIS NATIONALISM

David Sillar was born in 1760 at Spittalside, near Tarbolton. Sillar left his father's tenant farm as a young man to open a school at Commonside. Finding little financial success in teaching, Sillar moved to Irvine and opened a grocery business. The first we hear of Sillar's association with Burns is during the Lochlea period of Burns's residence near Tarbolton.[55] The younger poet joined Burns's social circle and became a prominent member of Burns's Bachelors' Club, formed in 1781 in Tarbolton.[56] According to Sillar, a close friendship grew up between the two men:

> Mr. Robert Burns was some time in the parish of Tarbolton prior to my acquaintance with him. . . . Whether my acquaintance with Gilbert [Burns] was casual or premeditated, I am not now certain. By him I was introduced not only to his brother, but to the whole of that family, where in a short time I became a frequent, and I believe, not an unwelcome visitant. After the commencement of my acquaintance with the Bard, we frequently met upon Sundays at church, when, between sermons, instead of going with our friends or lasses to the inn, we often took a walk in the fields.[57]

Sillar's apparently small means during the hungry 1780s induced Burns to write his "Epistle to Davie, a Brother Poet," in which he encourages Sillar "ne'er to fash your head, / Tho' we hae little gear; / We're fit to win our daily bread / As lang's we're hale and fier."[58]

Indeed, the cost for Sillar to produce his own volume of poetry helped drive him and his grocery shop into bankruptcy. Like Lapraik, Sillar was committed to a debtors' prison, where he presumably begged the five pounds he needed to pay his debt. Sillar turned to teaching, this time opening a school for the instruction of sailors in navigation. This venture proved more financially rewarding, eventually yielding Sillar an annual income of a hundred pounds (about what Burns earned as an excise officer) and enabling him to marry (twice) and raise children. Unlike Lapraik, who never fully recovered from financial disaster and lost caste in the bargain, Sillar prospered, ultimately inheriting the farm at Spittalside from a younger brother and a healthy sum of money from two elder brothers who traded in Africa. Sillar now had sufficient independent wealth to give up the navigation school. He retired to Irvine, where he became a magistrate and died in 1830.[59]

As in Lapraik's case, Sillar's association with Burns has earned him increasing critical attention in recent years, though more extensive review of poems other than his epistle to Burns has yet to be done. Corey Andrews, for example, reads Sillar's epistle to Burns, in contrast to Lapraik's, as focused on reminding Burns of his origins and exhibiting "a self-confidence born from familiarity with the poet, who has been sufficiently demystified through years of friendship. Sillar's praise is enunciatory, declaimed with the authority of an equal, a 'brother' poet." He also notes that "to Sillar, Burns owes his fellow labouring-class poets an opportunity to also 'win a horn' and speak to 'ears unborn.'"[60] Andrews's characterization of Burns, Sillar, and other "brother" poets as "laboring class," as we have seen, is problematic, but most critics who have considered the question agree with Andrews that Burns benefited from his aesthetic relationship with "Davie."[61]

While Sillar's poems exhibit some of the same anxieties and insecurities of caste as those of the older Lapraik, they do not hark back to estates satire or socioreligious allegory. Instead, Sillar treats contemporary Scottish economic and social conditions as a function of the alienation of Scots from their "true" identity. At the same time, his affinity and shared poverty with Burns do not produce a similar political reaction. We see very little of Burns's republicanism or overt reference to Scotland's heroic age of independence. Instead, Sillar appears content to remain within the ambit of "common sense" virtue, much as Lapraik does. But Sillar's poems are more heavily inflected by Scots vernacular than Lapraik's, marking him as more of a "national" poet in this respect.[62] Whereas Lapraik sometimes uses Scots to emphasize caste distinction, Sillar seems more conscious of the language's demarcation of cultural boundaries between the Scottish and English national variants. From this perspective, I would argue that Lapraik is the more versatile poet with regard to genre (though Sillar certainly demonstrates familiarity with genre), while Sillar explores more deeply the use of Scots as poetic language.

Sillar's *Poems*, published in Kilmarnock in 1789, contains more than fifty poems and songs.[63] This selection features Sillar's handling of political, social, and economic subjects, as well as his "national" characteristics. One of the early poems in the volume, "To the Critics, an Epistle," claims for the poet a similar "lad o' pairts" status as that attributed to Burns. Invoking Allan Ramsay ("Few praises to our songs are due; / But pray, Sir, let's hae ane frae you"), the poet pleads for critics to take into account his humble rural origins:

> I gat my learnin's at the flail,
> An' some I catch'd at the plough tail.
> Amang the brutes I own I'm bred,
> Since herding was my native trade.

Though James Paterson takes Sillar at his word, the poet's "scanty learning" is every bit as good as Burns's and Lapraik's, though he may have spent his youth "catching at the plough tail" on his father's farm.[64] Indeed, like Lapraik's, Sillar's poems

[34]

BURNS'S AYRSHIRE "BARDIES"

not only reflect an intimate knowledge of the Bible (as we might expect from both men's parochial-school training) but also demonstrate familiarity with classical genres and contain allusions to Greek and Roman mythology and poetry, church and national history, and contemporary doctrinal controversies. Burns's meteoric ascent to cultural prominence in Edinburgh by assuming the modest role of an untutored genius is no doubt on Sillar's mind, but it is equally important to the poet to establish his poetic identity as an imitator of Ramsay, Fergusson, and Burns.[65] The poet reiterates this self-identification in the "Epistle to R. Burns," in which the poet by praising Burns inserts himself into the line of succession:[66]

> Brave RAMSAY now an' FERGUSSON,
> Wha hae sae lang time fill'd the Throne
> O'Poetry, may now ly down
>   Quiet i' their urns,
> Since fame, in justice, gies the crown
>   To Coila's BURNS.[67]

Compare Lapraik's "Epistle to R****T B***S,"[68] which, in contrast to Sillar's over-drawn panegyric, seeks not to embrace and emulate the bard's identity as a Scottish poet but to distance the poet from it:

> But on the tither han', should folk
>   Me for my nonsense blason,
> Nae doubt I'll curse th'unlucky day,
>   I listen'd to your fraisin.[69]

Here we see the trope of modesty once again, but despite the poem's intensive use of Scots, the poet gives no explicit praise for Burns's revival of an "authentic" Scottish idiolect. Indeed, the acknowledgment of Burns's fame appears as an afterthought (the poet's reflections on his life struggles and creative exhaustion, as we have previously seen, dominate the poem) and remains limited to hoping for the preservation of the younger man's "Name" and "honour," hardly Scottish national attributes. Even the form of the poem—four-line stanzas with octosyllabic couplets rhymed *abcb*—resists the "national" Standard Habbie revived by Fergusson and others.

Sillar's more overt nationalism might mark the generational gap between the older and younger Ayrshire poets and stake out different ideological ground. Lapraik's critique of the "old" and "new" Scotland makes no gesture toward an idealized Scottish past of political and cultural independence but appeals to communitarian values and the biblical virtues of honest labor and self-sufficiency. Sillar, on the other hand, recasts the question of communitarian identity in nativist terms;

[35]

BESIDE THE BARD

what is needed to compensate for the loss of the ancient Scottish polity is the reestablishment of Scottish identity on "indigenous" cultural aesthetic principles.

This aesthetic nativism is again made explicit in "Epistle to the Author, by J. H*******N."[70] The poem, likewise composed in Standard Habbie, presents itself as a letter to Sillar from a poet recently arrived in Irvine, where he finds "Sic plenty o' Ramsaic men" as to render Ayrshire a second "Parnassus":

> *Horace* an' *Virgil* baith did sing
> O' woods, rivers, an' ev'ry spring,
> O' mountains an' each harmless thing;
>   An' mayna we
> Mak woods an' hills aroun' us ring
>   In poetry?
>
> They sang Tiber, that flow'd thro' Rome,
> Meander, an' swift Hermodoon;
> An' mayna we in Irvine Town,
>   Wi' equal flame,
> Sing Irvine, Ayr, Garnock, an' Doon,
>   As weel as them?

Here the local Muse combines a judicious imitation of classical models with Scottish sociability. If Edinburgh resembles the "Athens of the North," in which every educated man is a philosopher, Ayrshire mirrors the Attic countryside, in which every farmer spouts poetry. At the same time, the displaced narrative of the poem (the newcomer appears carried away in a gush of emotion) may be read to ironize the writer's characterization of Ayrshire's aesthetic landscape. His rhyme is "ill spun," and the comparison of Irvine, Ayr, Garnock, and Doon to Greece and Rome stretches the limits of hyperbole. Yet the poet's sincerity and desire for friendship "without design" distinguish him from mere fame-seeking poetasters. He identifies with the communal values intrinsic to "real" Scots poetry, the poetry of the hearth and the fields, of work and play. In late eighteenth-century Scottish poetry, the rural landscape is still peopled and generative, as Thomas Crawford has put it, of an active aesthetic of "love, labour, and liberty."[71]

A third example from Sillar's volume makes a powerful claim for Scots as the language of "indigenous" British poetry. Introducing an extended didactic poem called "The Duel,"[72] the poet announces,

> Give ear a' people, while that I rehearse
> *Britannia's follies* in her native verse:
> Nor think our foibles, tho's they're clad in satin,

[36]

> Deserve their painting frae the Greek or Latin.
> A Scotchman's ears shou'd never tak offence,
> Because his failings are na wrote in French.
> A country's dialect still will do maist good,
> Within the bounds where 'tis best understood.

The poet, a self-identified "Scotchman," proclaims an intention to "rehearse / Britannia's follies in her native verse" (rhymed couplets of iambic pentameter) and sends "a Scot amang you" for that purpose. At this level the poem engages in the kind of "code-switching" that Alex Broadhead identifies with Burns's poetry. Code-switching involves "an alternation between linguistic varieties that . . . 'creates communicative and social meaning.'" Broadhead argues "that while a language, such as Scots, may for an audience, community, or society carry connotations of informality, intimacy, or vaguer qualities such as earthiness or vitality (that is, macro-level social values), it is up to the participants in a conversation to flag up those associations or, alternatively, to reject, ignore, or modify them. Correspondingly, when Burns switches (for instance) from poetic English to Broad Scots, it does not necessarily follow that his tone or attitude shifts from formality to informality or from distance to immediacy or his focus from the general to the particular."[73] Sillar likewise evinces sensitivity to linguistic communities of interest, unapologetically addressing Scots speakers in their own tongue, claiming that his Scots "dialect" best suits a discussion of serious subject matter like "Britannia's follies," and inviting his Scots auditors to identify "Britain" with "Scotland." The use of language separates true Scots from those to whom Scots is "unknown"; the poet trains his sights on enlightened natives who purge Scotticisms from their dialects and then treat native speakers as objects of Johnsonian scorn. The poem thus hyperbolically establishes binary categories of "Scots" and "English" that, as Colin Kidd reminds us, were not that clearly "nationalistic" in reality.[74] Nevertheless, in Andersonian terms, Scottish identity is determined imaginatively and linguistically.[75] Situating the Scottish, and indeed the "British," nation within language allows Sillar to reach across caste boundaries in a way that Lapraik, for example, does not attempt. Whereas Lapraik bases his critique of Scottish society primarily on socioeconomic grievances, Sillar suggests the reconciliation of historically determined caste tension through a common "British" language.[76] Moreover, this type of nativism can be highly aggressive when activated by resistance, particularly by resistance from within the nation itself. One cannot help but read this poem as a rebuke to the Edinburgh literati and their attempts simultaneously to claim and deracinate Burns. It also explodes the concept of the "Caledonian antisyzygy" by insisting on a unified Scottish identity that strips away the supposed contradictions of Scotland's history of political conflict and religious disputation.[77]

[37]

BESIDE THE BARD

The poem then veers off into a blistering critique of the Hogarthian rake, a locus classicus of eighteenth-century aristocratic "Englishness." While the poet conventionally chastises the idle, propertied classes for a variety of sins, he nevertheless marks these sins as characteristically and specifically English. Later in the poem, when describing the "gentlemen" antagonists' drunken argument over a woman, the poet "code-switches" into an allegorical mode, attributing their lust to "little *Cupid's fire*" and comparing their mounting anger of the erstwhile duelists to "*Pluto's or Mogul's* . . . furious rage." As we have seen in the poem's introduction, classical languages belong to the cultural elites bent on eliminating Scottish national distinctiveness through unionist assimilation. English gentlemen speak in foreign tongues, and their emulation of foreign manners and vices contaminates the purity of indigenous Scottish love and courtship. At the climax of the poem, the poet steps between the combatants:

> O Happy for you, that aid was sae near,
> Which sav'd your life! an' wha, withouten fear,
> His ain did venture, while he stood between
> Your horrid arms, which look'd saw stern an' keen.
> This ventrous hero merits your regard,
> An' tender friendship, as his just reward;
> For doing what he nobly dar'd to do,
> An' offer'd life a sacrifice for you.

The Scotchman's "heroic" intervention not only avoids bloodshed but reverses the current of linguistic practice and its correlative moral taint. The "tender friendship" of the plebeian, plain-speaking Scot trumps the supposed chivalric values of the English gentleman, claiming for Britannia a revised polarity based, at least initially, on national difference rather than assimilation. But can a Scotchman and an Englishman share the common ground of friendship in the face of such difference? The poet is not so sure, and the English may be irredeemably incorrigible. As the poet laments in the final couplet, "but turpid actions never can affront / The man wha's led by Satan, pride, or ———." We are left to imagine the final rhyme with "affront," but there is little suggestion of any real or lasting reformation of English attitudes. "The Duel" thus becomes a figure for national rivalry, but not simply an Anglo-Scottish rivalry. The poem also targets assimilationists who repudiate Scottish linguistic and cultural identity in hopes of currying favor with an alien invader. Scots, the poet tells us, would rather extend the hand of friendship than start a fight, but they are not afraid of a fight if one is foisted upon them.

Even so, Sillar has no clearly articulated political program, whether Jacobite or constitutionalist Whig. In his "Epistle to J. W****N, Student of Divinity,

[38]

Edinburgh,"[78] his relative indifference to doctrinal differences seems evident
as well:

> Will ye appear i' the *New Light*,
> Which pits sae mony in a fright;
> Or come an' *Orthodoxian Wight*,
> > Inspir'd an' proud,
> An roarin' H-ll wi' a your might
> > Tae please the crowd?
>
> Whate'er ye are, be sure an' fix't;
> Opinions ne'er haltin' atwixt;
> Whilk hath right mony fair perplext,
> > An' wi' ilk doubt,
> An' win' o' doctrine, hafflins mixt,
> > An' drove about.

As Liam McIlvanney has persuasively argued, Burns draws on his Scottish Presbyterian inheritance in two distinct ways: "the New Light, with its subjection of
all forms of authority to the tribunal of individual reason," and "the traditional
contractarian political theory long associated with Presbyterianism."[79] Can a similar claim be made for Sillar? The poet demands that the young student declare
his partisanship in the disputes currently (and seemingly endlessly) riving the Scottish Kirk. He asks whether the young divine will preach Old or New Light doctrine: "will ye be flytin' or be fleechin' / Wi' silly fock; / Or will ye free them frae,
or keep them, / 'Neath yon auld yoke?" This verse is particularly emphatic, given
its alliterative effect and use of the archaisms "flytin'" and "fleechin'." "Flyting," a
noun connoting the practice of trading abusive invectives with a poetic rival, is
associated with sixteenth-century Scottish poets such as William Dunbar ("The
Flyting of D. and Kennedie," 1508) and Alexander Montgomerie ("The Flyting
betwixt M. and Polwart," 1585).[80] In this sense of the term, the poem may be read as
a flyting—or at least as an invitation to a flyting—directed at the young scholar who
refused to acknowledge Sillar's missives. It can also mean reproaching or rebuking,
which here characterizes Old Light preaching.[81] "Fleeching" denotes coaxing or
wheedling, presumably typical, in the poet's view, of moderate, "enlightened" Presbyterianism. Neither option comes off as particularly appealing in the poem.

Still, the poet advises the student to pick a side and "fix't"; "haffling," or
shilly-shallying, it seems, is even worse than acting the "Orthodoxian wight,"
"roarin' H-ll wi' a' your might." At the same time, however, he asks what inspires
the Old Light ranters who "deal d-mn-tion": "Wha is't, think ye, dis them inspire /
Wi' sic awfu' kin' o' fire?" As for the poet, he does not want to get close enough to

[39]

BESIDE THE BARD

find out, "for fear o' yon." While not explicitly counseling the student to avoid the radical Calvinist "yoke," Sillar nevertheless distances himself (and, by implication, all reasonable people) from those "fock . . . sae fell" who demonize others based on religious difference. Indeed, "flytin'" over religious doctrine, as Lapraik likewise lamented in "Honest John's Opinion of Patronage," threatens the "nation" itself, undermining Scotland's imagined unity and enabling its absorption into the British state. Internal bickering over obscure theological niceties only serves English interests. The political resistance to Hanoverian rule, once and for all crushed in the aftermath of the Jacobite Rebellion of 1745, has turned inward, dividing the Scottish nation along sectarian lines. In the end, it makes no difference which side the student chooses. Either way "the trade which we ca' preachin'" no longer carries the banner of Scottish identity, which even the martyrs of the Covenanting tradition did, in spite of their excesses. For the poet, religion should be considered as both a native characteristic and a matter of private conscience. It should not establish a standard of public morals or conduct nor determine an individual's membership in a social body. If in "The Duel" Sillar throws down a linguistic gauntlet for the national community, this poem maps the nation's value system as more broadly Presbyterian, communal, and egalitarian. Similar to Lapraik, Sillar thus negotiates the Old Light / New Light controversy not by taking sides, as Burns does, but by advocating the redirection of internal energy away from divisive doctrinal controversies to a broader justification of Scotland's claims to a native identity.

In an instructive discussion of Burns's relation to the rise of the concept of "genius" in eighteenth-century philosophy and literary theory, Corey Andrews asserts, "Achieving repute as a poetic genius in the mold of [William] Duff and [Robert] Blair was a short-lived affair, and Burns's publicity proved to be ultimately confining to his efforts to be recognized as a major British poet. The more he worked to become a Scotch bard, the more he effaced himself as a 'poetic genius' writing solely by means of inspiration. As this process took place in the 1790s, Burns sought to redefine himself as the 'genius of the nation' rather than a mere 'poetic genius.'"[82]

As we have seen, Andrews goes on to argue that Burns's efforts to "nationalize" his genius produced a backlash against other poets who sought Burns's patronage to legitimize their own literary ambitions in a highly competitive market.[83] Indeed, the door to fame slammed shut on poets such as Lapraik and Sillar almost as quickly as it opened for Burns, not only, as Andrews observes, emphasizing "the considerable risks involved for labouring-class poets seeking to express themselves in print" but illustrating the extent to which Burns's "genius," which by definition was sui generis, excluded them from the national literary field altogether.[84]

If Lapraik and Sillar could not "surmount prejudicial judgments of literary value used to dismiss the efforts of labouring-class poets," part of the problem was

[40]

that provincial regions such Ayrshire, undergoing the processes of rapid urbanization and assimilation into a global imperial economy, did not reflect the same values as the professional literary culture in Edinburgh.[85] Burns's transition from a provincial "ploughman" poet to a one-off rustic "poetic genius" and finally to the "genius of the nation," all with the active intervention and assistance of the professional literary class, shifted the standard of taste further away from provincial poets who expressed communal concerns in plainer language that did not measure up to Burns's "extensive intertextuality . . . studded with allusions to contemporary literary figures and movements."[86] Still, Lapraik and Sillar are luckier than most, in that they live on as part of the Burns legacy.

2

BURNS AND THE WOMEN "PEASANT" POETS

Janet Little and Isobel Pagan

AS VALENTINA BOLD HAS POINTED OUT, Janet Little's poetry has been read as imitative of Burns's, though this trend has changed with increasing critical attention to the work of eighteenth-century women "peasant" poets in general.[1] Isobel Pagan's poetry, on the other hand, has received relatively little attention, possibly on account of its intensely local topicalism. The critical history of these poets connects to Burns in other ways as well. Though Burns extended an albeit limited patronage to Little and Pagan's "brother bardies" Lapraik and Sillar, he notoriously rejected his friend (and Little's patron) Frances Dunlop's request for him to review Little's poetry (though he did ultimately subscribe to a volume). He likewise had heard of Pagan and adapted the beautiful song for which she is best known, "Ca' the Yowes to the Knowes," though he did not acknowledge the link to the Muirkirk songstress.[2]

In contrast to Lapraik and Sillar, however, Little had a champion in Mrs. Dunlop, who was willing to assist her in the solicitation of subscribers, 650 of whom bought eight hundred copies of her single volume, *The Poetical Works of Janet Little, the Scotch Milkmaid* (1792).[3] Her subscription list includes numerous professionals (attorneys, clergymen, teachers, physicians) and merchants in Edinburgh, Glasgow, and across the Lowlands, members of the aristocracy, a significant number of women, and even a few readers in England and Ulster. Little's readership, speaking broadly, cuts a fairly wide swath through the middle ranks of Scottish society in growing provincial Lowland towns such as Paisley, Kilmarnock, and Dumfries, as well as in the suburbs of Dundee, Perth, Edinburgh, and Glasgow. This suggests a potentially wider circulation of Little's work than that Lapraik or Sillar enjoyed. Who is missing from Little's list, with the possible exception of James Boswell, are the literary opinion leaders that helped canonize Burns. The lack of this type of cultural patronage doubtless contributed to Little's failure

[43]

to achieve national status, once again demonstrating, in Corey Andrews's terms, that working "in Burns's shadow was a thankless enterprise, one which needs to be re-evaluated for the insights into literary success and failure provided by his 'brother' and 'sister' poets."[4] Andrews speculates that Burns, and later Hogg, succeeded partly because they cannily negotiated mainstream Scottish literary culture in ways the others did not or could not. Despite the formidable advantage of a substantial patron, which the laboring-class Little possessed over her male middle-class counterparts, the door slammed shut on her as well.

Isobel Pagan, on the other hand, never quite reached the threshold. Marginalized by her gender, indigence, and lack of formal education (Pagan could read but not write), Pagan relied primarily on oral performance to transmit her poetry and songs to the gentry and peasantry in the Muirkirk area who patronized her unlicensed tavern.[5] Her local fame was sufficient to induce her friend William Gemmell, a Muirkirk tailor, to transcribe the poems that were eventually published in Glasgow in 1803.[6] She had to have known Lapraik, who operated a licensed public house in Muirkirk (in addition to being the village postmaster, as we have seen). In Lapraik and Pagan's day, Muirkirk had a population of about twenty-five hundred souls, many of whom were employed by the Muirkirk Iron Company, which commenced smelting pig iron mined in the area in 1787. The mining and smelting industries brought Muirkirk into the global economy, connecting the town to the port of Glasgow and to Britain's larger industrial grid. An account written around 1820, thirteen years after Pagan's death, describes the village in less-than-flattering terms:

> The village, as a place of residence, can be tolerable only by the hardy and prosaic class who actually inhabit it; its dense envelopment in murky smoke—its deeply dingy or sepulchral tints from coal pits and furnaces—its unmusical and deafening clang of rude vulcan operations—and its environment with a landscape of treeless, heathy, moorland hill, render it to persons of taste and sensitiveness almost the beau ideal of what is disagreeable and dreary. Coals are obtained for private consumption at about 3s 6d or 3s 9d per ton. The village has three friendly societies, two large circulating libraries, two inns, and more than usual proportion of ale-houses, and annuals fares, ill-attended and of inconsiderable importance, in July, August and December.[7]

This view of Muirkirk combines a Dantean aesthetic with an enlightened interest in economic and social detail found in Sir John Sinclair's *Statistical Account of Scotland* (1791–1799). The industrial characteristics that make Muirkirk offensive to genteel sensibilities mark Muirkirk's relative prosperity and integration into British commerce. Muirkirk was among the "smaller towns" in the industrial belt that, according to Bob Harris, saw "the most impressive growth up to 1800."[8] The presence of "two large circulating libraries" seems remarkable given the town's population, indicating, as Harris has shown, "a powerful impulse or drive to 'improvement' predicated on a core set of cognitive values—pragmatic, rational, progressive—and confidence that, with the aid of reason and experiment, improvements were eminently realizable."[9] Moreover, the "more than usual proportion of ale-houses" likewise suggests a "popular provincial urban enlightenment" available to the literate laboring class in mining, manufacturing, or "single-occupation" towns that "provided more congenial environments for its development partially hidden from often fiercely conservative-minded elites."[10]

Though the indigent Pagan existed on the social and economic margins of this world, as we will see, she achieved a certain notoriety, if not celebrity, in the environs of Muirkirk that enabled her poetry to survive its obscure origins. It is not difficult to imagine that under slightly different historical circumstances— for example, if Pagan rather than Little had enjoyed the patronage of Frances Dunlop—her "untutored" verses would have struck a similar chord as those of Burns. Then again, her gender, like Little's, may still have inhibited wider acceptance of her poetry. Be that as it may, Pagan's work probably survives because it was produced in a rapidly industrializing and "progressive" society. Her poetry registers this change, contrasting with Little's meditations on the feudal hierarchy of a rural estate. Taken together, the poems of Little and Pagan offer insight into how laboring-class women responded to equally vexing questions of identity in an improving age as their male counterparts, but from even more marginalized gender and social positions. At the same time, their poetry conveys the experiences of women who, though forever coping with the deep structures of a patriarchal society, managed to record their voices and set them loose into a vibrant provincial culture undergoing transformative change. Little, Pagan, and other women "peasant" poets thus became actors in and shapers of the history they lived.

JANET LITTLE: THE "SCOTCH" MILKMAID?

Janet Little was born in 1759 at Nether Bogside, Ecclefechan, Dumfriesshire. According to James Paterson, her "parents were not in circumstances to afford her more than a common education; but she was early distinguished for her superior capacity and love of reading."[11] She served in the family of a clergyman in Glasgow,

BESIDE THE BARD

worked for Burns's patron Mrs. Dunlop, and rose to head dairymaid of an Ayrshire estate, then under lease to Mrs. Dunlop's sister. She married another servant of the estate, John Richmond, and raised his five children by a previous marriage. She also joined a Dissenting congregation at Galston, a sizable village of more than three thousand souls in East Ayrshire.[12]

Little produced a single volume of poetry, published in 1792 by the Ayr printers John and Peter Wilson and dedicated to her patron Flora, Countess of Loudoun.[13] Like her fellow Ayrshire poets Lapraik and Sillar, Little composed a broad variety of verse in formal Augustan and, in a few cases, vernacular modes, featuring significant generic, rhythmic, and metrical variety. The fifty-four selections in the volume include odes, a large number of pastoral love poems, elegies, satires, epistolary poems, and didactic verse. Paterson's judgment that Little's poems are "not destitute of merit, while all are unexceptionable in point of morality, and bear evidence of a cultivated, well-regulated mind" is remarkably complimentary (if patronizing), given that he attributed to Sillar an utter "lack of genius" and to Lapraik "little of the genius of poetry" (though Paterson credits him with "good sense").[14] Additionally, Little was more than willing to cloak herself in Burns's mantle and market to potential patrons as an untutored poetaster, the "Scotch Milkmaid."[15]

Though Little does not generally engage in *direct* political or social commentary in the poems, her critique of Anglo-Scottish culture and the dominant Augustan poetic conventions that she perceives as discriminating against women and the laboring poor have received increasing critical attention in recent years.[16] Little's identity as a woman *and* a plebeian poet, while limiting her access to more direct forms of political discourse, produces a certain ambivalence toward the cultural elite's valorization of Burns and his particular Scottish idiom. Still, her poetry, like that of Burns, Lapraik, and Sillar, resists local parochialism, while warning of the danger to women of overly masculinized constructions of a martial Scottish nation.[17]

Scholars have focused most of their attention on three of Little's poems that refer to Burns. Most recently, Corey Andrews discusses Little's relationship to him in terms of Burns's mediation of the literary marketplace. As Andrews notes, "For aspiring poets like Little, Burns's literary acclaim was a daunting precedent for their own emulation, frequently leading them to express considerable doubts about their own prospects for recognition."[18] Aligning with Moira Ferguson, Leith Davis, and Margery McCulloch, Andrews reads Little's poetic responses to Burns as particularly marked by "resentment . . . highlighting the unfair advantages he enjoyed due to his gender."[19] Yet at the same time, Andrews contends that Little "both valorizes and delimits the scope and measure of his body of work. Burns's poetry is

[46]

expressly valued for being Scottish poetry, perhaps even more upon account of its own exceptional merits. In this respect, her appeal to Burns differs greatly from the gender- and class-based approaches of her 'brother' poets Lapraik and Sillar."[20]

I am interested here in the specific ways in which Little, in Andrews's terms, "valorizes and delimits the scope and measure" of Burns's poetry. While emulating Burns in many respects, Little also stakes out her own distinctive poetics, influenced by, yet independent of, her luminous counterpart. In "An Epistle to Mr. Robert Burns, Dated July 12, 1789," Little begins with the conventional flattery, often shared between Ayrshire poets, aligning her with the Scottish vernacular tradition, equally inspired by classical authority as that of the English and now reanimated by Burns's authentic "genius."[21] Indeed, Burns's poetry is more "British" than that of the pantheon of English national poets. In exceeding Addison, Pope, Johnson, and even "Sure Milton," Burns has restored classical vitality to British poetry, his "bonnie homespun speech, / Wi' winsome glee the heart can teach / A better lesson, / Than servile bards who fan and fleech / Like beggar's messin."[22] Little thus lauds Burns for restoring Scots vernacular to its central position as a "national" poetic language but "delimits the scope and measure" of Burns's poetry by demoting his English poetry to lesser status.

This commentary on Augustan or Johnsonian norms continues in a distinctly gendered perspective in "On Reading Lady Mary Montague and Mrs. Rowe's Letters."[23] While this poem might be read as a straightforward acknowledgment of a woman poet's debt to her illustrious predecessors, reading it in the context of Little's critique of English poetry yields a more ambiguous interpretation. In the first two stanzas, the poet lauds Lady Montague for winning "mankind's" praise in her "gay" circle, thus emphasizing her class position, as well as her dependence on the critical judgment of the male framers of aesthetic standards. When Elizabeth Rowe eclipses Lady Montague as Britain's most popular poet, she likewise commands the admiration of critics such as Addison, Pope, and Johnson for her "virtue and wit," conforming to the very "model" of Augustan poetic success. Though Rowe's first volume of poetry, published in 1696 under the pseudonym Philomela, defends a woman's prerogative to write poetry, her most famous poem, "On the Death of Mr Thomas Rowe" (published in 1717 and again in 1720 as an appendix to Pope's *Eloisa to Abelard*) deploys impeccable Augustan rhymed couplets of iambic pentameter. As Little implies, such imitation is "ingen'ous" but somehow wanting. To follow in the footsteps of Montague and Rowe, the poet suggests, might earn the "silent" admiration of male critics, but it would hardly liberate aesthetics from the Johnsonian

[47]

BESIDE THE BARD

straitjacket that constrains, among others, working-class women seeking to join the ranks of the poets. Indeed, the form of the poem—four-line stanzas featuring couplets consisting of one line of iambic pentameter and an adjoining line of iambic tetrameter, rhymed *abcb*—varies and enlivens the stately Augustan didactic verse for which Rowe has been praised, implying that Little's versatility in the use of rhyme and meter differentiates her from those poets who dutifully compose the standard English line.[24]

English practitioners of Augustan aesthetics come in for yet another round of vernacular guff in "Given to a Lady Who Asked Me to Write a Poem."[25] The first two stanzas of poem, composed in rhymed couplets of iambic tetrameter, edgily emphasize the imitative, derivative, and superficial qualities of Augustan verse: "Swift, Thomson, Addison, an' Young / Make Pindus echo to their tongue, / In hopes to please a learned age; / But Doctor Johnson, in a rage, / Unto posterity did shew / Their blunders great, their beauties few." The poem's harsh dismissal of the most popular early eighteenth-century English poets, as well as the debilitating aesthetic standards that afflict Augustan verse more generally, go well beyond satire or the self-justificatory conventions of poetic modesty often found in plebeian poetry. As in the epistle to Burns, Little yokes English aesthetic standards to the social pretenses of aristocratic society and its pedantic confusion of real learning with the empty imitation of Greek and Roman genre poetry. Johnson's denunciation of artificial verse forms in favor of literature he believed faithfully mirrored nature, most famously Shakespeare, seems little improvement, primarily because it privileges linguistic purity (metropolitan London English) and moral uniformity over local, regional, and even national language variants and traditional poetic forms and subject matters.[26]

Yet at the same time the poem betrays a distinct awareness of the risks associated with Burns's fame and a too-near self-identification with the particular circumstances under which the Edinburgh literati have constructed Burns's popularity: "But what is more surprising still, / A milkmaid must tak up her quill; / An' she will write, shame fa' the rabble! / That think to please wi' ilka bawble." The awkward rhyme of "rabble" and "bawble" stands out here. Is it a "shame" for a milkmaid to presume to the poetic arts or seek a commercial market for her wares among the rabble? The issue, the poet tells us, is what type of challenge the vernacular poetics of Burns and his counterparts actually pose to dominant discourses of art and politics. While Little herself remained loyal and deferential to her patrons, her landlords, and her "betters," her poetics nevertheless pinpoint the challenge that laboring-class women poets can pose to metropolitan cultural standards.

Burns's flirtation with Jacobinism and Scottish nativism, for example, may seem far more politically subversive than the milkmaid's "bawble," but his

[48]

undoubted "skill" in wielding vernacular language meets metropolitan approval nonetheless, partly on account of his "untutored genius": "Yet Burns, I'm tauld, can write wi' ease, / An' a' denominations please; / . . . / An' Nature trace whare'er she goes; / Of politics can talk with skill, / Nor dare the critics blame his quill." This curiously secondhand recounting of Burns's broad popularity in Scotland inserts a critical distance between the speaker in the poem and the ploughman, marking the uneasy relationship that Burns's others shared with their rival.[27] One can even detect a note of resentment, as Andrews has observed, as the poet anticipates the savage criticism she is likely to receive in response to her poetic offering while the arbiters of Scottish taste grant Burns free passage: "May she wha writes, of wit get mair, / An' a' that read an ample share / Of candour ev'ry fault to screen, / That in her dogg'ral scrawls are seen." This stanza marks the poet's gender in the strongest possible terms. Not only is poetry a vocation unfit for rural boobs and dunces—Burns the exceptional ploughman-poet proves the rule—but, as Leith Davis has argued, a woman poet is especially suspect and subject to even more exacting critical scrutiny than her male counterparts are.[28] Indeed, Johnson's dictum about women poets constitutes sufficient commentary in a poem that rejects Johnsonian categories altogether. Yet the critic's choral voice in the poem is not even Johnsonian; it is Scottish and belongs to the Edinburgh literati who have canonized Burns while disdaining all other similarly situated poets.

Little voices this ambivalence toward Burns in "On a Visit to Mr. Burns."[29] When her efforts, promoted by Mrs. Dunlop, to establish a correspondence with Burns failed, Little attempted to visit him at Ellisland, only to find him debilitated by a fall from his horse. This lively poem, written in English in common meter or ballad form, begins with the giddy effusions of an overawed enthusiast, as the poet pinches herself as if to awake from a dream: "Is't true? or does some magic spell / My wond'ring eyes beguile? / Is this the place where deigns to dwell / The honour of our isle?" Noting Burns's failure to acknowledge Little's prior communications, the speaker's anticipatory elation at the long-sought meeting flees before an imagined encounter with the injured party:

> Hark! now he comes, a dire alarm
> > Re-echoes through his hall!
> Pegasus kneel'd, his rider's arm
> > Was broken by a fall.
>
> The doleful tidings to my ears
> > Were in harsh notes convey'd;
> His lovely wife stood drown'd in tears,
> > While thus I pond'ring said:

BESIDE THE BARD

> "No cheering draught, with ills unmix'd,
>   Can mortals taste below;
> All human fate by heav'n is fix'd,
>   Alternate joy and wo."

Mock tragedy has rarely been more exquisitely expressed.[30] The poem serves up a comic image of Scotland's national poet falling off a pretentiously named yet stumbling horse. While the poet's wife weeps uncontrollably, the milkmaid delivers a solemn moral platitude, but for whose benefit? Indeed, the poem may be read as self-consolation for Little's fantasy that the real Burns would live up to the idealized national muse, not for the suffering poet or his hapless wife. Even if meant for Burns, her deterministic "pond'ring" in a larger context suggests her subordinate position as a woman plebeian poet. Poetry cannot be extracted from the politics of class and gender that produces and classifies it; no independent Republic of Letters exists outside of established hierarchies.

The poem's final stanza dribbles away in ambiguity, as Little vaguely imagines addressing him: "With beating breast I view'd the bard; / All trembling did him greet: / With sighs bewail'd his fate so hard, / Whose notes were ever sweet." While Little quotes her self-reflexive dialogue, she omits what she said to Burns when she "did him greet." Instead, she recounts the physical manifestations of an intense anxiety, even suggesting that Burns's presence is already past. His "sweet notes" once existed for Little in her dream-like illusions, but all that remains is a fallen idol. This sense of Burns's absence reinforces the mock tragedy of Burns's fall and emphasizes the poem's real tragedy: the critical aesthetic judgments that exclude laboring-class women poets from a share of the poetic laurels.

A lesser-known poem, "On Seeing Mr.——Baking Cakes,"[31] mirrors "On a Visit to Mr. Burns," this time in a comic mode:

> As Rab, who ever frugal was,
>   Some oat-meal cakes was baking,
> In came a crazy scribbling lass,
>   Which set his heart a-quaking.
>
> "I fear," says he, "she'll verses write,
>   An' to her neebors show it:
> But troth I need na care a doit,
>   Though a' the country knew it.

The silent Burns of the previous poem finds his voice here, one inflected by insecurity and self-vindication. Not only is the "frugal" baker Rab nervous that a "crazy

[50]

scribbling lass" might compete with him in the literary marketplace, but she might also attract the attention, even the affection, of women readers. Moira Ferguson has pointed out that Little may have felt some sexual attraction to Burns, but even if this is the case, Little nevertheless critically examines this reaction as part of the Burns phenomenon as a whole.[32] For Little, Burns's supposed appeal to women goes hand in hand with the aesthetic standards that have set him up as an untutored, natural genius. His very masculinity enables this elevation; the same verse written by a milkmaid would suffer unendurable derision, if it were noticed at all.[33] The contradictory characterization of Rab's poetic economy as an "honest shifty," as opposed to that of the "crazy scribbling lass," further unravels the seeming objectivity of aesthetic norms. Literary criticism, at least that practiced by the guardians of culture in Edinburgh and elsewhere, masks an exercise in identity politics. Rab's "shiftiness" suggests that he is unreliable and manipulative, and his vindicatory self-confidence boasts of his ability to put one over on both the maids and the arbiters of polite culture. One may excuse a randy baker for practices that would condemn a maid. Moreover, the Rab in the poem consciously manufactures and markets his "cakes" for public consumption. Rab's overt commercialism indicates an aesthetic economy at odds with the idealized conception of the poet as a divinely inspired and naïve medium of Scottish identity. Instead, in the poem Rab's cake becomes a fetish, an object of fickle popular taste, a momentary fad, a commodity. The cult of celebrity surrounding the baker Rab is as fleeting as the cakes are "thin" and "crump"; the poet, it seems, reveals himself little more than a crier hawking his wares at market.

The poem concludes with a blunt assessment Rab's motives, which have little do with the production of culinary art: "Some ca' me wild an' roving youth; / But sure they are mistaken: / The maid wha gets me, of a truth, / Her bread will ay be baken." Rab's interest in sexual exploitation is thus intimately connected to his art. Underneath his fear of figurative emasculation by the "crazy scribbling lass" lies the fear of actual emasculation, a loss of sexual prowess. A woman poet, as Johnson says, must be put down like the animal she is, else the whole hierarchy must fall. In light of this poem, Burns's broken arm in the "Visit" takes on additional meaning; the instrument used to write poetry can be equated with the instrument used to bake a maid's bread. In both cases the presence of the female competitor threatens Rab's identity as a poet and a man. Little shrewdly demonstrates the inexorably gendered nature of aesthetic standards, created by elite men for their own self-preservation. God forbid that a woman should crash the party.

As the Burns poems show, Little can rely on the sympathy of neither her fellow poet nor the marketplace of critics and consumers. The poem "To My Aunty,"[34] which immediately follows "An Epistle to Mr. Robert Burns" in the volume,

BESIDE THE BARD

suggests that the only true judge of a working-class woman's poetry is another woman with experience of the poet's world. As she recounts to her aunt, her anxiety over critical standards manifests itself in a dream, in which "Voratious critics by the way, / Like eagles watching for their prey, / Soon caught the verse wi' aspect sour, / An' did ilk feeble thought devour; / Nor did its humble, helpless state, / One fraction of their rage abate." Here the dreamer imagines releasing her poetry into a Burnsian aesthetic economy that depends, as Corey Andrews points out, on two types of "credit": Burns's "power of consecration" over the work of "brother" and "sister" poets such as Little and the "credit . . . bestowed upon Burns by his critics, who had 'consecrated' him as an exceptional 'poetic genius.'"[35] The poet's anticipatory defensiveness is striking, as is her self-doubt at the wisdom of women attempting to publicize their poetry at all for fear of provoking the "rage" of "Voratious critics."

The following stanzas humorously describe a typology of men who control the publishing economy and, ultimately, its products and producers, which includes a Mackenzian pedant "of high pretence, / To taste an' learning, wit an'sense / Was at the board the foremost man, / Its imperfections a' to scan"; an editor who "in an unco rage / Revis'd the volume page by page"; a trimmer who "So much fear'd his brother's scorn, / The whole escap'd his claws untorn"; and a flatterer who "whisp'ring told each man apart, / That he the volume much esteem'd." Once again the capitalistic nature of aesthetic production rears its head, revealing a division of labor in the culture factory that criticism has become. The reduction of poetry to commodity has the concomitant effect of converting criticism into advertising. The dreamer awakes unedified and unable to extract meaning from this impenetrable, circular system, in which criticism is no more than part of the entertainment, a contrived response within a structure of dominant and subservient personalities vying for celebrity. Burns expresses a similar sentiment in "Epistle to J. Lapraik," scoffing, "Your Critic-folk may cock their nose, / And say, 'How can you e'er propose, / You wha ken hardly verse fra prose, / To mak a sang?'"[36] As both Little and Burns observe, the "business" of criticism effectively seals off poetry and the poet from the direct experience and knowledge of the public, performing a one-way mediation that arbitrarily accepts certain aesthetic materials but not others for packaging and sale.[37]

Little makes this exclusion explicit in the apparently innocuous poem "An Epistle to a Lady," addressed to her patron who is away from Loudon caring for her ill daughter.[38] Following the standard self-deprecating introduction begging pardon for the poet's presumption in composing the poem, the poet turns to news from the estate, painting a pleasant scene contrasting an old matron reading the Bible and a young pair still in the first blush of postnuptial mutual satisfaction.

[52]

The poem appears to harmonize the spinster's chaste piety and the couple's hymeneal virtue, though the juxtaposition of the "sacred page" and the "little Cupid's flutt'ring" produces a jarring pair of images. Furthermore, the matron's "ease" and "thoughts unperplex'd" contrast with the couple's "social hearts," though the matron's friendship, the poet insists, "ev'ry virtuous mind must prize," while the couple "each other proves their constant aim." The placidity of the description veils an underlying solipsism, a resistance to real community and, perhaps more importantly, to work. With only the slightest of ironic readings, the "prudent" spinster, comfortably ensconced in her "elbow chair," may be rendered self-righteous and officious, the couple, entirely absorbed in their desire, cloying and mawkish. Indeed, the almost complete absence of sentimentalism elsewhere in Little's oeuvre suggests that the poet's report indicates that while the mistress is away, the servants will play.

This irony becomes more explicit in the next stanza, in which one servant "Such anxious care on others she bestows, / She quite forgets what to herself she owes," while another whose "Eyes, which at will, can give pleasure or pain, / On stupid Humphry Clinker shine in vain." The awkward rhyme in the third couplet of this stanza ("scan"/"one") draws attention to the poem's increasingly satiric mode. Indeed, "little foibles" are the stuff of domestic satire, mocking the initially pietistic description of the virtuous spinster and newlyweds and revealing the poet's real intent: to subject her counterparts on the estate to "strict inspection" and moral evaluation. Whereas a Raphael or Dante would allegorize the beauty of Matilda's mind or Celia's eyes, the milkmaid's rural pen is content to expose the one's affectation and the other's frivolity. In any case, everyone is wasting an enormous amount of time nosing around in each other's business and reading "stupid" novels. As applied to *Humphry Clinker* (1771), however, the pejorative adjective may at once signify the maidservant's ridiculous vanity and desire to be seen reading a novel that she does not understand, as well as allude to Smollett's self-conscious attempt, as Alfred Lutz has argued, "to recuperate contemporary Scotland, misrepresented in the dominant representations circulating at the time, in the present within the context of Britain. . . . *Humphry Clinker* does not present Scotland as a subject culture; instead, the novel imagines it . . . as a part of Britain, a part whose presence benefits both Scotland *and* England."[39] In a poem that satirizes the effects of modernity on the traditional social and gender hierarchy of the Scottish rural gentry, Little's reference to Smollett's riposte to English pretensions of superiority elevates the poem into the realm of "national" self-representation.

The profligacy going on upstairs is mirrored downstairs as well, where we see the "lower class" engaged in similar avoidance, including the "crazy-pated dairy maid . . . scribbling o'er these senseless lines to you." What kind of work is writing poetry? Is poetry written by a "dairy maid" intrinsically more valuable than the

BESIDE THE BARD

cook's gossip or the chambermaid's complaints? The poem explicitly marks the "lower class," though everyone identified in the poem seems equally otiose. But here the poet names herself, not as the "crazy scribbling lass" of "On Seeing Mr.——Bake Cakes"), but as one of the servants. Should we consider this identification as self-abasing or, in the ironic mode we have noted in many of Little's poems, as self-constitutive—or perhaps both? In other words, does the poet's self-identification as a member of the "lower class," as well as her repeated apologies throughout the volume, assert the positive value of plebeian literature vis-à-vis works of a privileged caste, whether the paintings of Raphael or the satires of Smollett? If so, just what is its value? As the poet says with respect to the cook, servants should work and not speak, yet the Scotch milkmaid persistently presses her "senseless lines" on her patron and the public.

The poem that follows is likewise a servant's report to his master, this time in the idiom made famous by Cervantes, Pope, and Burns, the domestic animal that speaks its mind.[40] "From Snipe, a Favourite Dog, to His Master," however, presents a somewhat different version of the sociopolitical allegory that Burns constructs in "The Twa Dogs: A Tale" and similar poems that pit a rapacious and effete aristocracy against an abused and exploited laboring class.[41] This poem has the same upstairs-downstairs view of the manor house as "An Epistle to a Lady," and, though the tone varies strikingly, the same *otium* prevails in the absence of the master. Snipe, who is accustomed to being chased out when he invades the kitchen around meal times, finds the cook idle and the upper house deserted. He then proceeds downstairs to try his luck with the lower servants; there old James, whom in the previous poem we see driving turkeys o'er the green, feeds swill to the pigs ("the soss is a dealing"). The pigs' "voracious" appetites and bad manners mark not only their vulgarity and lack of "feeling" but perhaps an existential threat to the refined upstairs Snipe. There is a Burkean whiff of revolution in the air, as the sullen swine turns unchivalrously on the refined Snipe, showing him no deference or respect for rank. The poem continues with a plea for the patron's speedy return, for "My friend Jenny Little pretends to respect me, / And yet sir at mealtime she often neglects me: / Of late she her breakfast with me would have parted, / But now eats it all, so I'm quite broken hearted." Jenny Little appears in cameo once more, this time not as a crazy scribbler but as what she is: a hungry farmworker. When the master is present, the lower servants feel compelled to sacrifice part of their scanty fare to feed the master's domestic pet. When the master is away, they hoard the food for themselves.

It can be easily forgotten that late eighteenth-century Scotland could be a very hungry place, suffering periodic food shortages and the social unrest that came with them. As Snipe "ransacks" the house for something to eat, even willing to

[54]

BURNS AND THE WOMEN "PEASANT" POETS

eat pig scraps if necessary, we catch a glimpse of this scarcity and the anxiety it produces. Even the lady of the house, it seems, must eat potatoes, the staple food of the poor in a country still in the late eighteenth-century hard-pressed by recurring food insecurity and economic vulnerability. We thus sense in the poem the insufficiency of the traditional agrarian base supporting a social hierarchy in need of economic diversification. What appears as laziness in the servant class in "An Epistle to a Lady" is rendered here as dearth, but in either case class antagonism strains the conventions of deference. When only "soss is a dealing," Burkean paternalism wobbles on its feet.

Little's sense of permanent exclusion from overdetermined categories of identity such as class and gender dominates the final poem in Little's volume, "To a Lady Who Sent the Author Some Paper with a Reading of Sillar's Poems."[42] The poem commences in a valedictory mode, for "the Muses are fled far away, / They deem it disgrace with a milkmaid to stay. / Let them go if they will, I would scorn to pursue, / And can, without sighing, subscribe an adieu. / Their trifling mock visits to many so dear, / Is the only disaster on earth I now fear." Here the poet acknowledges the futility of a "milkmaid" pretending to write poetry. Not only have the Muses abandoned her, but their prior visitation "mocked" her, humiliating her so deeply that she fears the "disaster" attendant on further poetic composition. This anticipation of failure goes beyond the conventional humility trope evident in other poems in the volume. For a milkmaid and a woman to invoke the Muses is "disgraceful" in at least two senses: as representatives of a privileged, masculine poetic tradition, they do not "grace" women poets, even aristocratic ones like Lady Montague or Elizabeth Rowe; and as guardians of that tradition, they deploy "disgrace" and "mockery" to shore up cultural boundaries against incursions by alien elements, primarily women and the laboring poor.

The poet goes on to claim kinship with other contemporary plebeian poets who have presumed to impose themselves on the aesthetes: "Sure Sillar much better had banish'd them thence, / Than wrote in despite of good manners and sense. / With two or three more, whose pretensions to fame / Are slight as the bubble that bursts on the stream. / And lest with such dunces as these I be number'd, / The task I will drop, nor with verse be incumber'd; / Tho' pen, ink and paper, are by me in store, / O madam excuse, for I ne'er shall write more." As we have seen, Sillar, Lapraik, and Little gave up poetry after a single foray into the tantalizing yet closed Burnsian market. The poet leagues herself with Sillar and "two or three more," the "dunces" who thought they could compete with the gifted ploughman. But whereas Sillar seems to have the power to "banish" the Muses, the milkmaid has no choice. The double bind of the milkmaid's gender and class position closes off even the limited access granted to the select few male poets, or perhaps simply the one.

[55]

BESIDE THE BARD

THE UNACKNOWLEDGED MUSE: ISOBEL PAGAN
AND THE REFUSAL OF BARDIC IDENTITY

Isobel Pagan's point of contact with Robert Burns is the beautiful lyric song "Ca'
the Yowes to the Knowes":

> Ca' the yowes to the knowes,
> Ca' them where the heather grows,
> Ca' them where the burnie rows,
>   My bonnie dearie.
>
> As I gae'd down the water side
> There I met my shepherd lad;
> He row'd me sweetly in his plaid
>   An' he ca'd me his dearie.
>
> Will ye gang down the water side
> And see the waves sae sweetly glide,
> Beneath the hazels spreading wide?
>   The moon it shines fu' clearly?
>
> Ye shall get gowns and ribbons meet,
> Cauf-leather shoon to thy white feet;
> And in my arms yese lie and sleep,
>   An' ye shall be my dearie.
>
> If ye'll but stand to what ye've said,
> Ise gang wi' you my shepherd lad,
> And ye may row me in your plaid,
>   An' I shall be your dearie.
>
> While water wimples to the sea,
> While day blinks in the lift sae hie,
> Till clay-cauld death shall blin' my e'e,
>   Ye shall be my dearie.[43]

The song appeared in volume 3 (no. 264) of *The Scots Musical Museum* (1790) and
was subsequently republished in Elizabeth Amelia Sharp's 1887 anthology of
neglected English, Scottish, and Irish women poets.[44] Sharp anticipated by a
century the reawakening of interest in women poets such as Pagan, arguing that
their relative obscurity could be attributed to "defective education, lack of broad
experience of life, absence of freedom to make full use of natural abilities, and the

[56]

force of public and private opinion, both of which have always been prone to prejudice her work unfavourably, or at best apologetically."[45] As we will see shortly, while Sharp's accusation of "prejudice" can certainly be seen in James Paterson's at times condescending appraisal of Pagan and her verse, at the same time Paterson's extensive and serious treatment of Pagan's biography and songs not only made her poetry more widely accessible to Victorian readers but also associated Pagan firmly with the eighteenth-century song and ballad tradition and probably influenced the appearance of "Ca' the Yowes" under Pagan's name in Arthur Quiller-Couch's *The Oxford Book of English Verse, 1250–1900* (1919) (although neither the poet nor the poem are "English").[46]

Pagan's obscurity was perhaps unwittingly compounded by Burns, who composed two versions of the lyric but, according to Pagan's biographer, "did not acknowledge Pagan as the original source."[47] Paterson credits Burns with "pruning" Pagan's original, which was edited by its publisher, Allan Cunningham, to excise "one verse, in which the heroine is made to express her apprehensions of a moonlight walk by the river side, though she had been before on the banks of the same stream, and 'row'd sweetly' in her shepherd's plaid."[48] Paterson adds that the "verse omitted for its indelicacy, is still farther characteristic of the Poetess of Muirkirk; and the assertion of Burns, who wrote in 1797, that the air or words were never before in print, to some degree corroborates Pagan's claim to the authorship."[49] Margery Palmer McCulloch, on the other hand, argues that Pagan transmitted the song rather than composed it, "for this courtship folksong is much more sophisticated in idea and expression than any of the verses printed under Pagan's own name. To say this is not to denigrate Pagan or her contribution to the eighteenth-century song tradition. She is representative of good local folk poets and singers who worked in the tradition of transmitting and adapting existing songs and airs for their own local purposes."[50] Taking a middle course, Kirsteen McCue argues that the poem "exemplifies two important aspects of songs of the period. Firstly, they commonly hailed from an oral tradition and consequently appeared in numerous different versions. Secondly, there was often difficulty in distinguishing lyrics written by men and women."[51] Most recently, Nigel Leask observes that "Burns's manuscript notes describe it as a 'beautiful song . . . in the true old Scotch taste, yet I do not know that ever the air or words, were in print before.' Although the song is sometimes associated with the singing of Isobel Pagan, an Ayrshire tavern keeper, Burns makes no mention of the fact, claiming that he collected it (and Clarke took down the air) from a clergyman."[52]

In any event, the conditions under which Pagan composed her verses were hardly propitious for the transmission of her poetry beyond her local milieu, though Burns's awareness of her suggests that Pagan was well-known in Ayrshire for her "song-making." Pagan was born in New Cumnock, Ayrshire, in 1741 or 1742 and lived for the remainder of her life in the Muirkirk area. Her autobiographical poem "Account of the Author's Lifetime" describes her education at age seven as being taught to read by "a good old religious wife": "She took of me more pains / Than some does now of forty bairns / With my attention, and her skill, I read the Bible that no ill."[53] Abandoned by her parents, allegedly because of a birth defect that lamed her for life, Pagan was thrown upon the world with no resources save a considerable supply of wits. A local landowner, Admiral Keith Stewart, gave her an abandoned brick house, once part of Lord Dundonald's tar works (the same as those lauded by Lapraik), which she inhabited for thirty years, operating an unlicensed spirit house and entertaining her patrons with "her dramatic monologues and bawdy songs."[54] Pagan's haunt was popular with the local peasantry, workers, and gentry, particularly in August, when grouse hunting (a frequent subject of her poetry) attracted sportsmen from the surrounding counties.[55] Pagan died in 1821 and, accompanied to her grave by a large crowd, is buried in the Muirkirk churchyard.[56]

Pagan's class and gender no doubt damaged her posthumous reputation in the nineteenth century and beyond. Even her *Oxford Dictionary of National Biography* biographer feels compelled to concede that "Pagan reputedly had a beautiful singing voice, but she was habitually drunk and unashamedly sexually promiscuous."[57] Paterson believes that people in the neighborhood of Muirkirk feared her tongue and temper: "However much her character and mode of life might be reprobated, few were willing to offend her by expostulations or remarks; and she attained a sort of ascendancy, which the fear of her sarcasm and her crutch alike combined in enabling her to maintain."[58] Indeed, her penchant for vicious satire and violent temper earned her the nickname "Wicked Tibbie." In this context, Pagan's poetry can be read as a bid for "ascendancy" in a culture that suffered her to exist on the margins. Even the "peasant" poet Janet Little held a comparatively secure and socially respectable place in the rural hierarchy, which enabled her to aspire to a measure of literary success and publish her work. Unlike the other Ayrshire poets we have examined thus far, "Wicked Tibbie" had no other access to the literary marketplace than her own voice and performance, the "wickedness" of which earned her a considerable local celebrity that eventually resulted in the publication of her poetry without the benefit of patronage.

Valentina Bold includes Pagan in a group of autodidactic women poets who suffered rejection at the hands of their male counterparts, patrons, and critics alike. "Women autodidacts," Bold writes, "were rarely treated as the equals of men" and "faced even greater obstacles in their quest for recognition. While 'Celebrated Female Writers,' like the morally and socially upstanding Joanna Baillie, won polite

[58]

BURNS AND THE WOMEN "PEASANT" POETS

acclaim, autodidactic women were neglected. Paradoxically, some of the most exciting poetry of the nineteenth century was produced by autodidactic women, especially in comparison to the effete compositions of contemporaries like Lady Nairne and Caroline Oliphant the Younger."[59] Together with Jean Glover and Janet Little, Bold argues, Pagan established "an autonomous tradition" that contested "peasant poet stereotyping," going "beyond their male counterparts in expressing some form of gender and class solidarity."[60] These poets prepared the ground for and deeply influenced nineteenth-century Scottish women laboring-class poets such as Janet Hamilton, Mary Pyper, Maria Bell, Isabella Craig-Knox, Jeannie Johnstone, Ellen Johnston (the "Factory Girl"), Jessie Russell, and Marion Bernstein. Bold's argument on behalf of a "tradition" springing to life in the shadow of Burns suggests that Pagan, Little, and other women poets constructed an alternative literary marketplace, one not determined by the dominant masculine standards of elite critical approval, financial success, and posthumous fame. Instead, these poets inhabit a collective form of aesthetic, economic, and gender identity that depersonalizes the individual poet of "genius" to push back against the triple bind of domestic servitude, gender subordination, and exclusion from educational and economic opportunity.

Like the other Ayrshire poets, however, Pagan feels compelled to preface her entry into aesthetic competition by comparing herself negatively to Burns. Upon Burns's death, Pagan penned this short apologia, "On Burns and Ramsay":[61]

> Now Burns and Ramsay both are dead,
> Although I cannot them succeed;
> Yet here I'll try my natural skill,
> And hope you will not take it ill.
>
> You know their learning was not sma'
> And mine is next to nane at a';
> Theirs must be brighter far than mine,
> Because I'm much on the decline.
>
> I hope the public will excuse
> What I have done here by the Muse;
> As diff'rent men are of diff'rent minds,
> My metre is of diff'rent kinds.

Whereas the other Ayrshire poets likewise deploy the trope of modesty to address a metropolitan critical audience in a Burnsian idiolect, Pagan seems more interested in moving beyond the Scottish vernacular and Standard Habbie of Ramsay and Burns. In the first stanza the poet, having pronounced their demise, refuses

[59]

BESIDE THE BARD

succession, announcing that her "natural skill," rather than imitation of learned models, will inform her art. She thus claims authority not in the classical mode of Lapraik, Sillar, and Little, with their invocations of the Muses of poetry, but in the only way a literally "untutored" peasant woman possibly can: she calls on her own "Muse," who inspires her to compose "metre . . . of diff'rent kinds." The cryptic allusion to her "decline" in the fourth verse of the second quatrain seems to refer to a dulling of the "brighter" learning of Ramsay and Burns. But, having stated previously that she had "next to nane," it appears that the poet speaks of something else. I think rather that the poem adumbrates a poetics of "decline" in the obsolescent sense of the word, a wholly experiential idiom that falls away or turns aside from the dominant Scottish vernacular poetry championed by the dead poets (though her physical decline at the age of sixty may be implied as well).

Viewed from this perspective, Pagan's better-known pastoral poems, "Ca' the Yowes to the Knowes" and "The Crook and Plaid," may be read as revising traditional genre poetry.[62] Pagan deploys pastoral as a medium for bringing the experience of erotic pleasure out into the open as a form of poetic expression.[63] In both poems the shepherd's implements are explicitly sexualized, mirroring the shepherd lad's obvious intentions. In the former poem, the shepherd's sweetheart takes some wooing before allowing the lad to row her "in his plaid," while in the latter, she conceals herself under it: "And when that he is wearied, and lies upon the grass, / What if that in his plaidie he hide a bonnie lass?" But in both poems there seems to be little doubt that the love relationship will not long survive the inevitable cooling of sexual desire. The lad's promise, "While water wimples to the sea, / While day blinks in the lift sae hie, / Till clay-cauld death shall blin' my e'e, / Ye shall be my dearie," seems predictably callow, given that the maid has already fallen to his blandishments, whereas in the second poem, "The prospect o' the summer can weel mak' us glad" indicates the fleetingness of passion before the chill of the "storms o' winter." The shepherd's habit of reading "in books of history that learns him meikle skill" points to his liking for erotic poetry ("There's nae sic joyous leisure to be had in any trade"), while the seemingly odd reference to King David in the final stanza of "The Crook and Plaid" refers not only to the shepherd king's humble occupational origins but also, given the overt eroticism of the poem, to his spectacular polygamy as well. We may also detect the patriot king imagery of Jacobite poetry, both in the erotic appeal of the "Highland laddie" trope and in the Davidic associations of the youthful Stuart prince, imbued with the purity of rural life, renewing the corrupt and urbanized kingship of the usurping Hanoverians.[64]

Jacobite themes, however, do not constitute a primary staple of Pagan's poetry in general, though parody and satire do. For example, Pagan's ability to adapt conventional verse forms to her own "Muse" manifests itself in a wonderful

[60]

BURNS AND THE WOMEN "PEASANT" POETS

mock-epic poem, simply titled "A New Song."[65] Here "a bold hero of late from the west" appears in Muirkirk to hunt moor fowl, only to become distracted by a local damsel.[66] On the brink of his conquest, however, the hero is pulled up short: "Being of stout heart, he did boldly advance, / His powder was quick, and the shot he let flee, / Tho' he could kill nothing at the Lumagee." This allusion to the hero's sexual incontinence is redoubled later in the poem, when "the brave shooter . . . loses much powder, tho' not with his foes; / If he wants ammunition, if a pout he does see, / He will surely remember the old Lumagee." Paterson may have this poem in mind when he speaks of Pagan's volume as "doggerel," but one can hardly argue that this burlesque misses its target.[67] As she does with the shepherd lad in the lyrical poems, Pagan figures the "hero from the west" as primarily interested in sowing his oats rather than tending to his business. More specifically, she equates hunting and lovemaking; masculine desire manifests itself in multiple acts of violence. A "pout" may signify either a partridge or a maid, but to the desiring machine, they amount to the same thing.

The poem further alludes to the hunter's class superiority, as he engages the maid in titillating chivalrous foreplay by offering "her meal pock to bear." The hunter's objective, a dead bird or a deflowered maid, seems equally desirable; the hunt is the thing, and the male aggressor is fully justified by rank and tradition to bag his prey. The final stanza identifying the hunter, however, gives us a taste of Pagan's legendary bite, as she turns the only weapon available to a defenseless maid against him. But the problem for women who are hunted, as the poem's narrator implies, is that the "brave shooter's" supremacy is not only physically but culturally assured before he ever loads his gun. The maid who refuses him at the Lumagee, who "made him turn back," may have evaded "the shot he let flee," but such an escape only provokes the hunter to renew the hunt with greater vigor. Still, Pagan's willingness to call out the hunter by name reveals something "diff'rent" about her Muse. While perfectly capable of imitating the forms of poetry used by learned men, a moment comes when she reveals (quite literally as we see here) the man behind the curtain—or under the plaidie.

The sexual incontinence of the "hero" in the previous poem mirrors the gluttonous appetites of a local squire in "The Laird of Glenlee."[68] Composed in eight-verse stanzas with varying irregular lines of iambic pentameter, hendecasyllable, and hexameter, this poem directs its satiric fire at a named figure, whose vulgarity the poem mimics in the grossest terms. The laird, who says, "Religion's a whim, I know nothing about it," boasts, "My belly's so big, with the weight of my paunches, / The grease of my sides hangs over my haunches." The laird's obesity renders him "unable for the pleasures of Venus": "And nothing like that is a pleasure to me, / With eating and drinking I nourish my genius, / I feed like a

[61]

BESIDE THE BARD

swine at the mill at Glenlee." Framed in terms of estates satire, the laird both personifies gluttony (and lechery as well), as one would find in medieval allegory, and identifies a specific local figure, who no doubt recognizes himself as the target of the broadside. Pagan does not even grant the buffoonish laird the humanizing style and wit of a Falstaff, instead convicting him by his own confession of the grossest incontinence. The laird's monologue, which commences in boastful and defensive self-assertion, unwinds itself, ending in shameless and almost masochistic self-loathing, particularly in the laird's description of his immense obesity in the third octave and his impotency in the fourth. To add insult to injury, the laird's sexual incapacity links to his cuckolding in his self-comparison to a "well horn'd" bull, and the images of castration multiply in the figure of the "wethers" slaughtered for the laird's table. By the end of the poem the laird compares himself to the "swine at the mill of Glenlee," parroting and parodying the Burkean slander of the seditious rabble, as well as emphasizing the lack of deference paid to the laird's local hereditary rank and status.

While "The Laird of Glenlee" is certainly a more scurrilous ad hominem assault than Burns, Lapraik, or Sillar might have produced, it is no less serious-minded than the social critiques of her male counterparts. Indeed, Pagan's social satire demonstrates a range of poetic forms and voices. A good example is the epistolary poem "A Letter to a Gentleman on the Death of His Pointer."[69] This simple common meter features both rhymed verses of iambic tetrameter (first, third) and iambic trimeter (second, fourth) yet takes as its subject not the hymn of praise usually associated with this form but lightly ironic social comedy or mock elegy. In the servant's informing her master of the death of one of his hunting dogs, she uses a formal diction suitable to the dignity of the occasion, though she occasionally backslides into the vernacular ("snifters," "spain'd"). Whether the master actually knows the pointer remains in doubt, for the servant has apparently "nursed" the dog herself since his weaning from "old Gabbens." Here the poem suggests the genteel practice of putting out children for wet-nursing, creating strong affective bonds between the children of gentlemen and their working-class "foster mothers," while rendering filial relations cold and distant. Moreover, the nursemaid's description of the dog's illness as the "snifters" and its unnecessary and probably harmful medical treatment heightens the comic effect but clouds the reader's perception of her good faith. When the servant speaks of her affections for the pointer, she identifies herself in the first-person singular, but when alluding to the dog's treatment, she shifts to the first-person plural, thereby diffusing any personal responsibility for his death. This sliding between individual and collective voice seems discomfiting; the sum of the parts—the nurse's love, the trivial illness, the dubious medical practice, and the dead dog—do not appear to add up to the whole

[62]

story. A hint of the menace from below seeps out between the grammatical cracks and slippery self-representations that the servant's letter offers: "We did all that we could for him, / In every respect: / And to prevent his trouble first, / We bled him in the neck." Something is not right on the estate.

This disturbance takes explicit political form in "A New Song on the Times."[70] Echoing similar social and economic concerns voiced by Burns, Lapraik, and Sillar from a decade earlier, in this poem Pagan initially postures her critique as a hymn of thanksgiving for the Treaty of Amiens (1801), which temporarily froze hostilities between France and the five powers, Britain, Spain, Prussia, Austria, and Russia. But the poem quickly turns to a recent past of distress and poverty: "Ye know its two long years and more, / The poor's been sore oppress'd, / And dealers who had ought to sell, / They try'd who could get most." Famine had struck Scotland (and parts of England as well) in the mid- to late 1790s, triggering meal riots and reactionary suppression of "seditionists" and radical malcontents. Vagrancy and homelessness heightened upper-class fears of social dissolution and overwhelmed parishes responsible for outdoor relief. Much of the popular anger, as the poem indicates, was directed at grain dealers, jobbers, and engrossers, but food scarcity and high prices could to some extent be blamed on short leases offered by the improving landlord class.[71] Pagan's ballad, however, avoids the kind of pietistic vitriol observed in explicitly radical poetry of the period, adopting an almost gentle, admonishing voice. Britain's ills stem from the sin of pride—military and commercial hubris—rather than from the noxious effects of party factions, Dundas despotisms, or Pittite repressions, which would undoubtedly continue unabated had "Providence" not "been so kind, / As take pity on the poor." The poem continues in this vein, urging the privileged to recognize their moral duties to "In time of need unto the poor," their "charity enlarge":

> If widow, or the fatherless,
>   Goes hungry from your door,
> You scarce a blessing can expect,
>   If you neglect the poor.
>
> And what you give, take my advice,
>   Give cheerfully away,
> You'll get it sevenfold restor'd,
>   I hope, some other day.

One can hear the echo of Blake's "Holy Thursday" in *The Songs of Innocence* (1789):

> Beneath them sit the aged men wise guardians of the poor
> Then cherish pity, lest you drive an angel from your door.[72]

[63]

BESIDE THE BARD

Pagan's ironic tone (as does Blake's), however, betrays the sharp edges of her address to "Ye justices and gentlemen," who, she plainly implies, are more like the Laird of Glenlee than "the aged men wise guardians of the poor." Gluttons and hoarders at home, they take a high-minded Burkean view of the established social order as dictated by the same "Providence" that the speaker invokes. The poor will always be with us; the poor are morally prone to laziness and drunkenness; the poor are a dangerous threat to property.

Indeed, after reminding the privileged of the parable of the camel and the eye of the needle, Pagan's speaker acknowledges their cant, anticipating the objections they will make to enlarging their charity: "For my part I am hearty still, / And ne'er sought charity; / But I'll regard them while I live, / That has been kind to me." This is a curious and certainly un-Blakean appendage. As a class representative of the poor, the speaker of the first eight quatrains may be perceived as a kind of collective social conscience, rehearsing formulaic moralisms and Christian compassion for widows and orphans and gently chastising the rich for their parsimony. But in the final pair of quatrains the speaker enters the poem as Isobel Pagan, who threatens those who have not "been kind" to her with the weapon of poetry. Uninterested in "charity," which she sees as a threat to her independence, Pagan becomes a personal nemesis of a different order than, for example, Burns's more generalized denunciation of political and social privilege in the choral drinking song that ends "The Jolly Beggars, a Cantata": "A fig for those by law protected! / Liberty's a glorious feast! / Courts for cowards were erected, / Churches built to please the priest."[73] Here, rather, she appears as an avenging angel or, perhaps more accurately, a Dionysian force that will "cheerfully" wreak havoc on the Burkean social order in Ayrshire. The repetition of the term "enjoy" in the last quatrain, the paradisiac ideal of the "feast of contentment," and the emphasis on "health" over "wealth" all suggest the return of the Golden Age, but a return enforced by the menacing "regard" of the androgynous Dionysus, who comes to redress the imbalance of the world in the guise of a woman peasant poet. Only a poet in Pagan's specific subject position, in fact, possesses the necessary moral authority to appropriate the law of the Gospels to the moral reformation of an iniquitous society. No Blakean bard after all, the poet erupts as a natural force from below that, through her independent, Dionysian selfhood, can, at least imaginatively, remake the patriarchy in her own image.

The last poem in Pagan's volume, simply titled "A New Song,"[74] narrates the bottom side of the hoped-for "peace" promised by "A New Song on the Times." Here Pagan deploys a nearly regular iambic trimeter (also often used by Blake), rendering a powerfully direct address to the same powers who in the previous song deliver the dubious peace. Composed under the threat of French invasion, the

[64]

poem begins with a conventional prayer that the "noble heroes, / Will pull the usurpers, / Success to King George, / Long may he wear the crown." The first octave mimics the loyalist appeal for all Britons to unite in opposition to the invader. But here the appeal sounds perfunctory, a kind of political catechism that must needs be honored only in its repetition. In the second octave, the speaker retails a rumor that Napoleon has been defeated (probably in Egypt) and that "one general Moreau" has succeeded him.[75] Be that as it may, we may still wonder why the speaker makes a special point of this supposed Scottish turncoat. Perhaps it accentuates the contrast between the "noble heroes" and "usurpers" mentioned in the first octave, but it might also draw attention to "King George," coded as the Hanoverian usurper in Jacobite poetry, and the possible restoration of the true Scottish monarchy with the help of French arms.[76] Moreover, rather than denouncing the traitor, the speaker abstains from judgment, leaving the issue of whether "his heart has been true" to the reader. This would seem to allow space in the poem for both Jacobite and loyalist resonances, clouding the issue of what it means to be "loyal."

In this ambiguous posture the poem turns to the kind of Britain the wars with France has created, conventionally attributing the prolongation of the war to "disputes at Parliament, / And bribery at home." The poem alludes to the harsh social reality that approximately one in four Scottish men between the ages of eighteen and forty-five served in the British armed forces during the revolutionary and Napoleonic periods, with higher concentrations from many parts of the country, particularly the Highlands and northeastern counties.[77] The commonplace observation that "For men to be made soldiers / The trade is broken down, / And leaves families mourning / In many a town" speaks quietly to the catastrophic economic and social effects of so many absent men (a phenomenon that also plagued Ireland and numerous rural English counties). When the speaker pleads with "every individual" to act justly and honestly, she does not urge dutiful acceptance of a Burkean status quo but, as in the previous poem, a moral revolution that will "make deceit to cease." War is a condition created and perpetuated, the speaker asserts, by those who profit most from it: financiers, landowners, grain dealers, and politicians who control lucrative military contracts. Though she admonishes them to be "just in their dealing, / Act no over-rise," this expression of utopian desire for a morally just nation can never be fully realized. The speaker's "real opinion / There soon would be peace" remains proleptic, for the interests of the British imperial state will always oppose it. In this sense, the poem arguably suggests the idea of a revolutionary "Scotsman" at the head of a French army, a Wallace, a Bruce, or even a Stuart. Perhaps the "Auld Alliance" has another life to live, and the real enemy lives next door, rather than across the Channel.

[65]

BESIDE THE BARD

Pagan's talent for updating the old argument for the moral economy in relation to contemporary events presents itself again in a mock panegyric to a Highland regiment that was quartered in the Muirkirk area to suppress radical dissent during the height of the Pittite repression. Simply titled "Song" and set to the tune "Campbells is Coming," the poem begins:[78]

> The Duke of Gordon's fencibles,
>> They're handsome here in Cumnock town;
> And at Muirkirk a party lies,
>> For to haud the reformers down.
>
> They're decent, I can say no less,
>> For any thing that I do see;
> And well they set the Highland dress,
>> Although they're bare aboon the knee.

During the revolutionary wars of the 1790s, Scottish fencible regiments served primarily, as the British military historian J. W. Fortescue has noted, "for the purposes of domestic police."[79] The Duke of Gordon's fencibles, commanded by the 4th Duke Colonel Alexander Gordon, kept an eye on disaffected colliers in the neighborhood of Cumnock, a market and mining town (and later the home of Labour Party founder James Keir Hardie).[80] But the speaker does not appear as interested in political unrest as she is in the nudity to which the Highland dress calls attention. The speaker's fixation on the sexual occupation of Cumnock and its environs constructs the Highlanders in xenophobic terms not normally associated with them; their assimilation into the service of the British state betrays their historical attachment to Scottish independence and converts their chivalric restraint into overt sexual aggression.

The speaker then proceeds, with mock naïveté, to identify individual members of the troop by name, protesting their decency but accentuating their predatory motives, particularly the regiment's piper: "And their musicianer, T—m S—w, / I think he's decent, blithe and young; / I vow he plays his trou— / Although he has the Highland tongue." While the speaker adopts a "boys will be boys" approach to the Highlanders' philandering, the poem's real bawdiness erupts when it comes to the local "maids in town and country round," who "love to dance the soldier's jig, / And swear they love their soldier still." Indeed, the explicit language of sexual exchange in these "bawdy" verses suggests that the "maids" use the only power available to them to turn the tables on the oppressors. Two can play this game, it seems; the predators have become the prey.

[66]

But the game is serious, and the speaker observes that local resistance to the occupiers takes multiple forms. While the soldiers "like Cumnock best, / Their sweethearts there they're swear to want," in Muirkirk "they are more shy / Because the colliers are not scant," and local proprietors make them "pay boarding very dear" and "feed them with a beggar's meal." The images here become more ominous. Initially portrayed as the besiegers, the Highlanders find themselves besieged, holed up in fear of the same Muirkirk miners they came to "haud down" and at the mercy of the local innkeeper and merchants they are assigned to protect. The poem asserts both a defiant localism and anti-imperial animus, belying the breezy irony of the concluding quatrain: "But Providence the wars would cease, / That chearful hearts would dance and sing, / And every lad enjoy his lass, / And love his country and his king." The speaker returns to Blakean ironic mode, fiddling the tune of British state patriotism while East Ayrshire burns. Even more than the middle-class male poets' social critiques, Pagan directs her anger from below toward a utopic, if not millenarian, vision of the hypothetical social harmony of a feudal past (or a deferred future), in which the three estates enforced each against the other a moral economy based on Christian communitarianism. At the same time, Pagan's poetic subjects have little illusion that things will actually turn out that way: "But Providence the wars *would* cease, / That chearful hearts *would* dance and sing." The subjunctive mood places such a Golden Age beyond the real possibilities of politics and power. Recuperation, rather, inheres in the possibilities of poetry alone: "The road's not far, the night is good, / This I will sing, and gang my lane."

Pagan records the confrontation between property and liberty as pervasive in her social milieu. No relationship remains unaffected by the political and economic conditions of the day, except perhaps the poet's "independence" from the false consciousness created by contracts of adhesion, which for Pagan (as for Virginia Woolf more than a century later) can only be evaded by gifts of charity that are given freely and unconditionally. Moreover, Pagan's communitarian ethos implies that domestic, economic, political, or social relationships do not exist in separate spheres but are fundamentally public in nature. This is clearly seen in the philandering of the Highlanders, whose occupation of Cumnock tears the preexisting social web and weaves a new one in its stead.

Though Pagan calls on a deep tradition of estates satire to articulate contemporary social and economic tensions, she also demonstrates an acute awareness of the "modern" class antagonism that characterizes industrial capitalism. For example, another poem, also entitled "A New Song,"[81] celebrates the colliers' victory over management in a showdown over wages. An act of the Scottish Parliament

[67]

BESIDE THE BARD

in 1606 bound Scottish miners (and their children if the parents accepted earnest money for the bond) to the mines for life, a form of serfdom not finally abolished until 1799.[82] Historians now acknowledge that much of the impetus for the elimination of serfdom in the mining industry had little to do with humanitarian concern and much to do with reducing the cost of labor.[83] Pagan the poet, like the historian and Labour Party politician Thomas Johnston, takes the colliers' point of view, putting the issue in more direct, communitarian terms. In the poem we find many of the same grievances that nineteenth-century trade unionists, radical reformers, Chartists, and other labor interests would have to fight out all over industrialized Britain: the right to regular cash wage payments, freedom from the truck system, and a living wage. It is notable, however, that even the initial emancipation act, enacted in 1775, only phased out serfdom over time, and "any collier participating in an 'unlawful combination' for the raising of wages, before the day of his emancipation arrived," had two years added to his servitude (this included any efforts to establish or join a trade union).[84] When full emancipation finally came in 1799, Parliament assigned the task of fixing wages for colliers to local justices of the peace (hence the "plea" in the poem) and expressly extended prior acts of the Scottish Parliament against unlawful combinations to colliers.[85]

Pagan's song registers this tenuous balance between the "collective activity" of East Ayrshire colliers and the mine owners, whose agent "Should come so far from hame, / And leave his Lady and family, / And not the plea have won." Indeed, the bemused speaker observes the agent's attempts to propitiate the miners by treating the men with "a lib'ral part" and serving "A dinner for the children." While the miners "gratefully" accept the offered largesse, they apparently decline to modify their bargaining position. The speaker sheds crocodile tears when, despite the fact that "Providence hath favour'd him," the plea is resolved in favor of the colliers: "The company is made to yield, / And sore against their will." Pagan's poem sheds light on later historical analysis that "liberation was sought, not for the colliers, but for their masters."[86] Pagan's celebratory song, then, serves rather as a requiem *avant la lettre* for the rights of labor, which under the guise of "emancipation" have been shackled more than ever before. Although tied to the mines they worked, colliers exercised greater control over their labor, wages, and competition than they did under anticombination acts such as the one enacted at the masters' behest in 1799.

But beyond the historical moment that the poem captures—the last stand of labor before the full onslaught of capitalist laissez-faire economics—Pagan once again reveals the communitarian ethos that undergirds all of her "social" poetry. She also speaks for the "kiln-men" and their families, who often worked (and died) side by side for long hours under conditions of extreme hazard and discomfort.

[68]

BURNS AND THE WOMEN "PEASANT" POETS

For them, real independence lies far more in getting "their cash at twa weeks' end" than it does in Smithean political economy. Though the speaker pokes fun at the masters and their machinations, however, she makes no objection to a paternalistic economy that exchanges service for reasonable financial security. Indeed, only in such an economy can the entire community "profit." For this reason, the speaker wishes the masters well, for only in their prosperity can the community thrive. Moreover, there is "great honour" in the "fine appearance of the coal," a pride of place that does not attach to capitalistic enterprise.

This anticapitalist ethic also animates one of Pagan's most accusatory poems, marvelously titled "Muirkirk Light Weights."[87] The poem begins as a particularly juicy bit of gossip about a local "taylor" who "scrimpit weight for greed of siller," cheating the townspeople. The speaker paints with a broad brush: all merchants cheat their customers, and the "cult of commerce" masks the devil's religion. Moreover, the merchant class not only exploits the poor while admonishing them for their lack of piety but views such exploitation as merely part of doing "business." Only when the question comes to "Whether to hang themselves or no" do they feel any "doubt" of the propriety of their conduct. Once again we see the inflammability of local conditions, the insurrectionary potential of a community oppressed by military conscription and occupation, high food prices and dishonest business practices, and a prescriptive moral code that rewards hypocrisy and criminalizes pleasure. In response to "the oldest dealer's" fear of divine judgment ("What will be said at the last day?"), the tailor advises his brethren to make hay while the sun shines: "ne'er mind the last, / If we can but make money fast; / There will be large allowance gaun / For every dealer in the land." Justification by faith, it seems, has indeed supplanted the doctrine of good works, and the tailor reveals himself as a good nominalist: his assurance that "There will be a large allowance gaun / For every dealer in the land" reflects the moral salve that this form of Calvinism could provide to the troubled soul of Via Activa. The merchants do not take much convincing and return to their fraud: "Some broke off less, and some broke mair. / This practice did so long prevail, / Till poor workmen were like to fail." Again we see the poetic voice lamenting the failure of the communitarian ethic that could soften the sharper edges of the old moral economy. The speaker's alignment with the regulatory comprehensiveness of this economy questions both the Enlightenment emphasis on individual self-interest as the basis of moral action and social theories linking "improvement" with progress, civility, and peace. To put it another way, the speaker struggles with reconciling a particular form of "pro-business Protestantism" with its clearly deleterious effects on the well-being of the community. By pointing to the condition of the exploited "poor workmen" as the true measure of social progress, the speaker presents a Janus-faced perspective on

BESIDE THE BARD

the present. She deploys the communitarian ethos of the past to emphasize that a Protestant variant that sanctions and encourages acquisition perverts true religion, while gesturing toward a future in which the bitter antagonism between capital and labor will determine social relations.

Despite Pagan's lack of formal education, she proves herself as adept as her Ayrshire counterparts in the adaptation of common poetic traditions to the social and economic crisis in late eighteenth-century Scotland. Acutely aware of the traumatic disruptions in traditional social relationships attendant to massive shifts in the ethical basis of master-servant and seller-buyer relations, Pagan constructs in her poetry a consistent communal voice that privileges the virtue of horizontally organized reciprocity within a vertically stratified power structure. She does not seek to topple the power of the landowners, merchants, and moneymen but simply to subject their practices to the moral regulation of the people. Hers is a conservative voice, to be sure, but one that alludes to revolutionary radicalism coming around the circle from the other direction. At the same time, Pagan declines to recognize national or imperial claims or loyalties as paramount. Her allegory is thus not political but typological and, ultimately, eschatological.

3

ALEXANDER WILSON AND THE PRICE
OF RADICALISM

ON APRIL 28, 1788, ALEXANDER WILSON, A weaver and itinerant packman and sometime poet staying in Edinburgh, wrote the following to his friend David Brodie, a schoolmaster in Quarrleton, near Paisley:

> Know then, that last week I passed almost a whole night in company with three poets. One was James Kennedy, Ebenezer Picken—who is publishing his works, and the last and most glorious was the immortal author of that well-known ballad, "The Battle of Bannockburn," "From the Ocean, &c." Blessed meeting! Never did I spend such a night in all my life. O, I was all fire! O, I was all spirit! I had the honour of being highly complimented by Bannockburn for a poem which I wrote in praise of his sublime song. . . . I have now a more deep regard for the Muse than ever. I have the opportunity, and my views are more expanded than when I sung on the loom. . . . That you may long be happy in your noisy mansion to hammer wisdom through the dark walls of the blockheads' skulls; to teach the young ideas how to shoot; to pour instruction over the opening mind; to be a terror to evil-doers, and a praise to well-doers, is the sincere wish of
>
> Sir,
Your humble Servant,
Alexander Wilson

The unnamed author of "Bannockburn" may have been Gavin Turnbull, though no trace of the poems to which Wilson refers has been found.[1] But it is nevertheless clear that Wilson's experience of this heady brew of sociability and nationalist zeal made an epoch in what had been up to that point a hard-knock existence.[2] "Over the course of a life shaped by economic and political upheaval and curtailed by poverty and illness," writes Michael Ziser, "Alexander Wilson fashioned himself

[71]

BESIDE THE BARD

from a manual laborer into a popular poet and then into one of the pre-eminent men of science, art, and letters in the early American republic. . . . Considered in isolation, each of Wilson's two careers deserves (and has attracted) careful attention by specialists in Scottish Studies, literary history, labor history, and the history of science."[3] In the company of other eighteenth-century personalities studied by Kenneth Simpson, including Smollett, Macpherson, John Home, Boswell, Mackenzie, and Burns, Alexander Wilson deserves at least an honorable mention as a "Protean Scot."[4] In the essay "Robert Burns and the Scottish Renaissance," Richard Price calls him a "remarkable poet," and "if [Hugh] McDiarmid thought a post-Burns poet like Alexander Wilson of Paisley was something to be embarrassed about, he should have thought again. Burns's vigorous example might encourage the pawky but it also inspired, in Wilson's case at least, satire vigorous enough for a prison sentence and then effective exile in America."[5] Indeed, judging by the number of local memoirs and histories, biographies and encyclopedia entries, letters, scientific articles, and other materials relating to Wilson's Scottish and American careers as a Paisley weaver, poet, journalist, and ornithologist, Wilson merits a place on the list of the most enduring products of eighteenth-century Scottish literary culture.[6]

Born in Paisley in 1766 to a father who found legitimate work as a weaver (and perhaps more profitable enterprise in illegal smuggling and distilling), Wilson received an education at Paisley grammar school until shortly after his mother's death, when he was taken out of school and put to work on a farm. He was apprenticed as a weaver to his brother-in-law, William Duncan, in 1779 but did not care for the trade. He continued his education as an autodidact, writing poetry in the style of Milton, Pope, and Goldsmith. He read Burns's Kilmarnock poems, which inspired him to vernacular poetry, and spent several years as a packman, selling small textiles and books of poetry. As Andrew Noble has pointed out, "Like Burns, he combined his vernacular inheritance with early saturation in canonical and contemporary English poetry" and "was equally exposed to the stresses of the fluctuating, industrialising weaving trade."[7]

Wilson's ardent desire to "hammer wisdom through the dark walls of the blockheads' skulls" soon got him into trouble with local authorities back in Paisley. His libel against the factory owner William Sharp, "The Shark, or, Lang Mills Detected," was found out when Wilson, in an attempt to extort five guineas for preventing publication of the poem, foolishly wrote Sharp in May 1792. Sharp filed a criminal complaint, and Wilson was convicted. When Wilson did not pay the fine, the court committed him to Paisley Tolbooth for two weeks. His radical views resulted in a second arrest in January 1794. Rather than stand trial, Wilson sought the freer political climate of America, emigrating to Philadelphia with his nephew

[72]

that same year. His monumental *American Ornithology* (1808–1814), published by Samuel Bradford with engravings by the Scots émigré Alexander Lawson (including illustrations of 268 species, no less), counted among its patrons Thomas Jefferson and Robert Fulton, as well as other American literati, and had a significant influence on John James Audubon. Wilson was elected to the American Philosophical Society just before his death on August 23, 1813.[8]

Wilson's grammar-school education and subsequent autodidacticism resemble the experiences of Burns, Sillar, Lapraik, and Little, though his working-class origins and occupation as a weaver and packman both distinguish him from his male Ayrshire counterparts and sharpen his social and economic critique. Moreover, Wilson's vernacular poetry generally eschews feudal and nationalistic themes, whether couched in the heroic historiography of Scottish independence, the Jacobitic imagery of the Highland laddie, or the moralism of estates satire. Instead, Wilson's emphasis on social and economic justice, his republican political commitment, and his deism mark him as a radical and, in some respects, subversive poet (one of Tom Leonard's "radical Renfrew" voices), beyond even the most ardent expressions of plebeian egalitarianism in Burns.

Burns's influence on Wilson cannot be underestimated.[9] Though poor, Wilson was among the ninety subscribers in Paisley to the initial Edinburgh edition of *Poems, Chiefly in the Scottish Dialect*. Encouraged by his friends, most notably Thomas Crichton of Paisley, to emulate Burns, he attempted to raise subscriptions while traveling in the west of Scotland peddling his muslins and ribbons. This effort failed to generate much interest, leading Wilson to seek the patronage of William McDowall, a member of Parliament for Renfrew and investor in some of the new cotton mills springing up in the west-central Lowlands. McDowall, the proprietor of Castle Semple near Lochwinnoch, agreed to help Wilson obtain subscribers, while John Neilson, a leading Paisley printer, agreed to publish seven hundred copies of Wilson's volume in early 1790.[10] To generate interest in the book, Neilson printed several copies of Wilson's satirical poem "The Hollander, or Light Weight," which cast aspersions on a local silk manufacturer, William Henry.[11] Similar to Pagan's poetic takedown in "The Muirkirk Light Weights," the weaver poet calls out Henry "wi' vengeance big, / Resolv'd to ca'm his clashing; / Nor shall his cheeps, or pouther't wig, / Protect him frae a lashing / Right keen this day." But in contrast to Pagan's poem, here the systematic exploitation of the pieceworkers denotes a new economic system impervious to the moral suasion of the third estate.

In the poem the twenty-four-year-old poet combines a cultural awareness of the high Augustan style of Robert Blair and a vernacular Scots idiom that incorporates the linguistic variety of the Glaswegian working class of which Wilson

[73]

BESIDE THE BARD

was a part.[12] The poem, composed in the medieval Christ's Kirk stanza that Burns used to such great effect, draws on a conception of the moral economy familiar to us in plebeian poetry, particularly that of Lapraik and Pagan, but comes packaged with a potentially explosive political charge. The poem's speaker identifies himself with weavers doing piecework for manufacturers such as the unscrupulous "Willy." Like Wilson and many of his class, the weaver in the poem finds himself in chronic debt, both to the cloth buyers, who often advanced a discounted sum for work yet to be performed in order to take advantage of the "fellow's needin' clink, / To ca'm some threatenin's beagle," and to the pawnbroker, landlord, and merchant from whom he continuously borrows just to "satisfy his hungry soul, / A saxpence or a shilling / For fine some day." Class antagonism breaks out into the open when the "brave Hibernian boy," whose work Willy devalues for "Ilk wee bit trifling faut," refuses to bow to extortion. Imitating the boy's brogue draws on comic stereotypes of the Irish poor, who migrated in large numbers to Glasgow and the industrial heartland of Scotland in the later eighteenth and nineteenth centuries, but Wilson also taps into the property-owning class's deep-seated fear of the insurrectionary potential of the unruly Irish peasantry.[13] The boy's lack of deference to his social and racial superior registers an incendiary tension that burns through the poem's humorous tone.

The poem continues in this vein, retailing other stories of Willy's nefarious dealings and finally provoking the speaker to exclaim,

> O sirs! What conscience he contains,
> What curse maun he be dreein'!
> Whase ev'ry day is mark'd wi' stains
> O' cheating and o' leein!
> M'K****l, H*b, or throuther O*r,
> May swear an' seem to fash us,
> But Justice dignifies their door,
> An' gen'rously they clash us
> The clink each day.
> . . . .
> What town can thrive wi' sic a crew,
> Within its entrails crawlin'!
> Muck worms that maist provoke a spew,
> To see or hear them squalin'.
> Down on your knees, man, wife and wean,
> For ance implore the devil,
> To harle to himself his ain,
> An' free us frae sic evil,
> This vera day.

[74]

ALEXANDER WILSON AND THE PRICE OF RADICALISM

Masters who drive a hard bargain might be countenanced, but pious hypocrites like Willy and Jock, who exemplify nothing but the worst characteristics of the Protestant business ethic, are just as lethal to communal life as Lapraik's grasping estate agents or Pagan's unscrupulous merchants are. In the event, however, Wilson's libel cut a little too close once more. Like Sharp, Henry sued the poet, who denied that the Willy figure, identified in the poem's title as a "Hollander" and a "Light Weight," made any reference to the silk manufacturer, and even if it did, the poem did not accuse the manufacturer of any specific act of perjury or other moral turpitude. As might be imagined, Henry was neither persuaded nor amused. Speaking through his counsel in response to Wilson's defense, Henry fumed,

> In the Town of Paisley the rage for defaming peoples characters by writing poems & other papers of that kind have for some time past prevailed too much and if a check was not to be put to such practices it is hard to say to what length these scandalous publications might be carried; From the way in which the Defender treats the matter now under Consideration in his Answers your Lord'p will no doubt have some ideas of the liberties which they think themselves entitled to take & when you consider how easily the minds of the working people in a manufacturing town are inflamed & particularly those about the Town of Paisley of which we have already had too many instances, it is not doubted but your Lord'p will agree with the pursuer in thinking that a cheque can not be too soon put to such proceedings.[14]

Now we reach the heart of the matter: Wilson's poetry may inflame the "minds of the working people in a manufacturing town." Whereas Robert Blair's high-minded and abstract denunciation of liars and cheaters in his sermons pass as "polite literature," Wilson's poetic grievance against a specific liar and cheater threatens insurrection.[15] Indeed, Henry's fear that things could get out of hand if Wilson and others like him were not muzzled indicates a healthy circulation of this type of literature among the weavers and other artisans of Renfrewshire.[16] There is no further information about the outcome of the lawsuit, though the court apparently never entered a judgment or dismissed the case. Nevertheless, Henry's alarm over the inflammatory potential of poetry on the cadre of literate weavers and artisans in Scotland's industrial belt appears well founded, although the fact that the working people had as strong a preference for the sermons of the remarkable Paisley divine and church historian Robert Millar (1672–1752) as they did for poetic satires against leading industrialists indicates that they were not quite the "swinish multitude" that Henry thought they were.[17]

[75]

BESIDE THE BARD

Wilson's legal entanglements did not prevent him from becoming involved in the Paisley section of the Friends of the People or from continuing to publicize his poetry to potential subscribers. Raising money for the venture by weaving "40 ells (50 yards) of silk gauze at Lochwinnoch," Wilson entered a debate competition in Edinburgh on the question of "Whether have the exertions of Allan Ramsay or Robert Fergusson done more honour to Scotch Poetry."[18] Wilson took Fergusson's side and finished second by seventeen votes to Robert Cumming, who is said to have paid several dozen attendees (out of about five hundred well-heeled citizens) to vote for him. This poem, which was published in a new edition of Wilson's poems printed in Edinburgh in 1791, runs for 210 lines of iambic pentameter and is entitled "The Laurel Disputed; or, The Merits of Allan Ramsay and Robert Fergusson Contrasted."[19] In addition to bringing his work to the attention of a segment of Edinburgh polite society that was already familiar with Burns and stimulating subscriptions to his volume of poems, the poem stages a self-representation of the poet as part of the vernacular revival in eighteenth-century Scottish poetry.[20] It begins with the conventional trope of humility: "Before ye a' hade done, I'd humbly crave, / To speak twa words or three amang the lave; / No for mysel', but for an honest carl, / Wha's seen right mony changes I' the warl', / But is sae blate, down here he durstna come, / Lest, as he said, his fears might ding him dumb." In contrast to some of his contemporaries, who claim authorship while propitiating the polite audience for forbearance, Wilson casts himself as a mere performer of an anonymous poet's verses, establishing a self-reflexive mode in the poem that serves to ironize the staged "debate" and to focus attention not on the merits of dead poets but on the figure of a weaver who, defying local skepticism, finds himself among the metropolitan literati: "Trouth I was glad to hear ye war sae kind, / As keep our slee-tongu'd billies in your mind; / An' tho' our Elpsa ca'd me mony a gouk, / To think to speak amang sae mony fouk."

This theatrical prelude, with its mélange of mock humility and deliberate misrepresentation (the young poet on the make passing himself off as a "frank auld kintra man"), seeks both to meet the expectations of Wilson's polite auditors for a suitable "provincial" and to challenge those expectations by unveiling an aesthetically sophisticated working-class figure. Wilson cannot hope to match Edinburgh's adulation for Burns and his less politically threatening image as the "Scotch Bard," hence the double frame of the poem that distances the political radicalism associated with his artisanal occupation and local political affiliations.

The bulk of the poem is given over to a disquisition contrasting Ramsay and Fergusson. The speaker lauds Ramsay for restoring Scotland's pride of place in poetry over Dryden, Pope, and Augustan English poetry and making Edinburgh

[76]

a literary center once more: "Auld Reekie than, frae blackest, darkest wa's / To richest rooms resounded his applause." Ramsay's classical learning, satiric style, and talent for lyric enable him to speak both to "Learn'd fouk, that lang in colleges an' schools, / Hae sooket learning to the vera hools, / An' think that naething charms the heart sae weel's / Lang cracks o' gods, Greeks, Paradise, and deils," and to the "rustic that can, readin' See / Sweet Peggy skiffin' ow'r the dewy lee." But then "Up frae Auld Reekie Fergusson begoud, / In fell auld phrase that pleases aye the crowd, / To chear their hearts whiles wi' an antrin sang, / Whilk far an' near round a' the kintry rang." The speaker's panegyric identifies Fergusson's poetry with a folk culture of low characters, comic situations, ghost stories and superstitions, and social realism: "It's my opinion, John, that this young fallow, / Excels them a', an' beats auld Allan hallow; / An' shows at twenty-twa, as great a giftie / For painting just, as Allan did at fifty." One cannot but think that the young poet draws a self-comparison to the youthful Robert Fergusson, who "paints" from nature in the real language of the people. Such poets, the speaker proclaims, "Are true-blue bards, and worthy o' the name." This is a fine statement of aesthetic principle, decisively rejecting Augustan classicism in favor of the Scots vernacular tradition.[21] "The gleg, auld-farrant art" of the fifteenth-century bards and makars possesses real emotive power and embodies a people with a distinct language and culture. The poem is a tour de force of thematic and cultural allusion, a stage performance, and a masterpiece of self-invention.

A second "debate" poem, "Rab and Ringan," meditates further on the self-consciousness of a weaver poet performing in the metropolis.[22] The poet tells the story of two brothers, Rab, "a gleg, smart cock, with powder'd pash," and Ringan, "a slow, fear'd, bashfu', simple hash." Here we have an Aesop's fable. Rab goes off to college in Edinburgh, picks up a little classical learning, and falls in with a fast crowd: "Lost a' his siller wi' some gambling sparks, / And pawn'd, for punch, his Bible and his sarks; / Till, driven at last to own he had enough, / Gaed hame a' rags to haud his father's pleugh." Ringan, on the other hand, spends his time studying the ways of nature and becomes the parish minister: "Was deep, deep learn'd, but unco blate, / . . . / Sae meikle learning wi' sae little pride, / Soon gain'd the love o' a' the kintra side." The significance of the poem does not lie in the conventional argument over the virtues and temptations of the active and contemplative life, however. Note the specific types of knowledge the poet privileges:

He kend how mony mile 'twas to the moon,
How mony rake wad lave the ocean toom;
Where a' the swallows gaed in time of snaw,

BESIDE THE BARD

What gars the thunders roar, and tempests blaw;
Where lumps o' siller grow aneath the grun',
How a' this yirth rows around about the sun;
In short, on books sae meikle time he spent,
Ye cou'dna speak o' aught, but Ringan kent.

Ringan's virtue derives from his immersion in scientific study or, in eighteenth-century parlance, "natural philosophy." This aligns him with Scottish Enlightenment intellectual values, in contrast to the "English" classical education and gentlemanly pretensions that lure Rab to ruin. When read together with "The Laurel Disputed," "Rab and Ringan" may suggest the need for a revived national aesthetic based on *both* pre-Union vernacular (but learned) culture and the uniquely "Scottish" character of modern scientific and intellectual inquiry. Such an approach would be consistent with Wilson's attempts to attract a reading audience in religiously moderate and acculturated Edinburgh, as well as in the evangelical, plebeian public of modest means in Renfrewshire.

But Wilson's attempted self-assimilation into the Scottish Enlightenment cultural project of "completing the Union" could not be squared with his increasingly radical politics and working-class indignation against the masters. Like many adherents of the Friends of the People, Wilson initially represented himself as a constitutional reformist in the mold of the early French revolutionists.[23] But domestic events soon pushed Wilson in a more politically dangerous direction. As previously mentioned, in May 1792, Wilson penned an anonymous letter addressed to the Paisley manufacturer William Sharp threatening to publish a defamatory poem about working conditions at Sharp's mill if Sharp refused to pay five guineas. The poem, entitled "The Shark; or, Lang Mills Detected," once again utilizes the Christ's Kirk stanza to indict the exploitation of workers in an industrializing society.[24] It opens with a call to battle, summoning "Ye weaver blades! ye noble chiels, / Wha fill our land wi' plenty" to "Defend yoursels" from the Shark's "hellish greed." The speaker accuses the Shark of plotting with Satan "Ten thousan' fouk at ance to sink / To poverty and ruin!" The speaker refers to the "years on years" of labor "wi' head and heart" that has brought the skill of weaving "So nearly to perfection," contrasting the dignity of skilled artisanal labor with the moral corruption of capital. The following stanzas chronicle the depredations of "Lang Willy Shark," ranging from the standard social vices of gluttony, drunkenness, and lechery to the more serious offense of exploiting workers and their families.

All of this might pass for the same fit of pique that incurred the wrath of William Henry two years earlier, but in the incendiary climate of *The Rights of*

[78]

ALEXANDER WILSON AND THE PRICE OF RADICALISM

Man (1791) and heightened fears of working-class disaffection in the west country, the poem takes on a more ominous tone:

> Whiles, in my sleep, methinks I see
>   Thee marching through the city,
> And Hangman Jock, wi' girnan glee,
>   Proceeding to his duty.
> I see thy dismal phiz and back,
>   While Jock, his stroke to strengthen,
> Brings down his brows at every swack,
>   "I'll learn you frien' to lengthen,
>   Your mills the day."

The poem ends by imploring "thou unconscionable Shark" to repent his wrongs or "Thou'lt mind this reprehension / Some future day." Clark Hunter notes that some who knew Wilson thought the blackmail attempt so uncharacteristic that someone must have used him to get at Sharp.[25] Be that as it may, the sheriff (undoubtedly owing to Wilson's previous history) promptly arrested the poet, who did not help his case by initially denying that the poem was his and then confessing authorship but claiming that "Willy Shark" could not possibly be construed to refer to "William Sharp." Wilson found himself in and out of jail for contempt of court and made matters worse by allowing the poem to be published in violation of court order. He was forced to borrow money from friends, including the schoolmaster David Brodie, but he apparently never paid the fine owed to Sharp (though Wilson did burn two copies of his poem on the steps of the Tolbooth in Paisley).[26] Others came forward to stand security for his good behavior, which did not prevent Wilson from being arrested again in January 1794, for composing an advertisement for a meeting of the Paisley Friends of Reform.[27] The prosecution did not go forward, but Wilson had worn out his welcome in Paisley. Burns, whose flirtation with radical republicanism between late 1792 and early 1794 landed him in hot water with his employers at the Board of Excise (on whose employment the poet depended to support his young and growing family), could still draw on the friendship and patronage of figures such as the Board of Excise commissioner Robert Graham of Fintry. When the board investigated Burns's political activities in Dumfries during the winter of 1792–1793, he appealed to Graham, as Colin Kidd notes, in "two anxious letters . . . which set out the poet's adherence to the British constitution and the revolutionary principles of 1688."[28] Wilson's radicalism, culminating in serial imprisonment for a direct attack on the Paisley power structure, did not have to be inferred from a refusal to uncover his head when the

[79]

BESIDE THE BARD

orchestra played "God Save the King" in the Dumfries Theater or the Paineite echoes
in some of his late poetry.[29] As Gerard Carruthers puts it, "In this dangerous period
of the 1790s, Wilson had reached the limits of his Scots poetry expressiveness, and,
with the potential of future conflict with the authorities, he emigrated to America in
some despair but with not a little hope for a new life in a land that he, like so many
reform-minded individuals, saw as unencumbered by systematic political corruption."[30] Once the poet had earned enough money to pay for his passage, Wilson
and his nephew, William Duncan, embarked from Belfast on May 23, 1794.

Wilson's life as a Scottish radical may have ended when he put out to sea,
but not his career as a Scottish poet or Enlightenment scientist. Robert Smith, a
Paisley printer, published a volume of Wilson's "minor" poems in 1814, followed
in 1816 by another edition of Wilson's poetry, identifying the poet as the "Author
of American Ornithology." That same year, Neilson republished Wilson's poems,
together with biographical and bibliographical materials. Crossing the Irish Channel, John Henderson, a Belfast printer, published an edition of Wilson's poetry in
1844, which was edited by Thomas Smith Hutcheson (1822–1878) and subsequently
reprinted in 1853 and 1857. A new Paisley edition to support the Wilson Monument Fund came out in 1857 and another in 1876 edited by Rev. Andrew Grosart
(1827–1899) and printed by Alexander Gardner. One-off printings of Wilson's
most popular Scottish poems, such as "Watty and Meg," "Rab and Ringan," and
"The Laurel Disputed," as well as "The Foresters," a narrative poem describing
Wilson's expedition of Niagara Falls, continued well into the nineteenth century.
Wilson was also widely published in Scottish and American newspapers and literary magazines of the period, and his *American Ornithology* has been continuously
in print since its initial publication in Philadelphia in nine volumes between 1808
and 1814.[31]

WILSON AND THE CRITIQUE OF INDUSTRIAL CAPITALISM

Wilson's diatribes in "The Hollander" and "The Shark" have been read in relation
to Renfrewshire's industrial setting, and his biographer and editor Clark Hunter
calls Wilson "an innovator" of "this kind of protest, although the thought probably never occurred to him."[32] There can be little doubt in these poems that Wilson had the broader implications of the new capitalist business structure in mind.
When a single manufacturer can plot, as in "The Shark," "deeper schemes . . . /
Ten thousan' fouk at ance to sink / To poverty and ruin," we are in the presence
of an organized *system* of oppression far more insidious than anything the old moral
economy could generate.

[80]

We thus see in Wilson a consciousness that the British state and its economic base present two radically different faces to its own people: one of enlightened political economy and depersonalized standards of social progress, the other of murderous particularity in the classes of persons designated for use and ultimate disposal. Burns's turn to collecting and composing songs might evince a similar recognition and self-exilic response.[33] Indeed, Wilson and Burns had a vexed relationship. The two poets may have met in Edinburgh in 1791, though Wilson offended Burns in a review of "Tam o' Shanter," in which Wilson criticized a passage in the poem as having "too much of the brute in it." Burns responded, "If ever you write again to so irritable a creature as a poet, I beg you will use a gentler epithet than to say there is, 'too much of the brute' in anything he says or does."[34] Ever the promoter of laboring-class poets, Frances Dunlop even tried (apparently unsuccessfully) to encourage Burns to peruse Wilson's volume of poetry.[35] Wilson took Burns's neglect in stride and produced the long narrative poem "Watty and Meg; or, The Wife Reformed,"[36] which resembles "Tam" and became Wilson's most popular work, eventually selling more than one hundred thousand copies and circulating in chapbook and broadsheet form all over Britain, though Wilson himself only realized enough profit to pay off his debts to his printers.[37]

"Watty and Meg" poses as a domestic comedy in *The Taming of the Shrew* tradition, but beneath the comic performance lies a family structure deeply distressed by the harsh economic conditions of the working poor. When the poem was published anonymously, some people attributed it to Burns, though in contrast to the imaginative comic brilliance of "Tam," an undercurrent of despair and domestic abuse courses through its verses.[38] The poem begins in the tavern, where Watty's drinking companion remarks, "Something's wrang— I'm vex'd to see you— / Gudesake! But ye're desp'rate thin!" Watty responds by lamenting his marriage, which he implies only occurred as a consequence of sexual passion: "Lord! I wish I had been halter'd / When I marry'd Maggy Howe!" Maggy bursts onto the scene: her "well-kent tongue and hurry, / Darted thro' him like a knife; / Up the door flew—like a Fury / In came Watty's scawling wife." In the next three quatrains, Maggy pours forth a stream of invective, forcing Watty to leave off his "whiskey," and then follows him home, "Flytin' a' the road behin'." The tirade continues all the way through the front door, creating a public spectacle:

> Fowk frae every door came lamping;
> > Maggy curst them ane and a';
> Clappet wi' her hands, and stamping,
> > Lost her bauchles i' the sna'.

[81]

BESIDE THE BARD

> Hame, at length she turn'd the gavel,
>   Wi' a face as white's a clout;
> Raging like a very devil,
>   Kicking stools and chairs about.

As Maggy berates and threatens the cowed Watty with even greater vociferation, Watty announces his intention to go for a "soger." While the poem can be read in conventional terms as cautionary tale against overhasty marriage and the dangers of drink, it likewise depicts a deeply disturbed social milieu, in which husbands and wives heap one another with physical and psychological abuse, leaving a trail of broken homes and ruined prospects in their wake. As the historian Anna Clark has written, artisans in Scottish industrial towns and cities became increasingly associated with domestic violence as downward swings in business cycles pushed them to the margins.[39] Though the first half of the poem aligns its reader with the henpecked Watty, the second shifts the perspective to the terrified Maggy, now faced with the prospect of abandonment and homelessness with her children:

> Then poor Maggy's tears and clamour
>   Gush afresh, and louder grew;
> While the weans, wi' mounfu' yaumour,
>   Round their sabbing mother flew.

> "Thro' the yirth I'll waunner wi' you—
>   "Stay, O Watty! stay at hame;
> "Here upo' my knees I'll gi'e you
>   "Ony vow ye like to name;"

> "See your poor young lamies pleadin',
>   "Will ye gang and break our heart?
> "No a house to put our head in!
>   "No a friend to take our part!"

The poem locates the couple's salvation in a domestic contract, conditioned on Maggy's submission to her husband's authority and Watty's promise to provide house and home. Maggy and Watty consummate their pact accordingly:

> Down he threw his staff, victorious;
>   Aff gaed bonnet, claes, and shoon;
> Syne below the blankets, glorious,
>   Held another Hinnymoon!

[82]

Watty's payment of the marriage debt is a nice Burnsian touch, completing the comic restoration of the community and reestablishing the proper gender order. But the poem's internal violence suggests that comedy, while reassuring in an abstract sense, does not represent the true nature of filial or, more broadly, social relations. Milton, one of Wilson's favorite poets, has it right when he portrays the first marriage as drama, a titanic power struggle that leaves the parties emotionally traumatized and severely chastened. Bunyan, too, reunites Christian and Christiana, but only after harrowing their souls. While Watty and Meg are not called on to renounce anything more than the inconveniences of close proximity, their vows of mutual forbearance are all the more important for recognizing that quotidian relationships are at once the most difficult and most necessary to sustain.[40]

In this regard, the famous praise of "Tam o' Shanter" as true to "nature," given by A. F. Tytler (Lord Woodhouselee), should be reexamined.[41] Kate's abuse of Tam in the poem, colorful and entertaining as it is, has little of the affective quality that animates "Watty and Meg":

> *O Tam!* had'st thou but been sae wise,
> As taen thy ain wife *Kate's* advice!
> She tauld thee weel thou was a skellum,
> A blethering, blustering, drunken blellum;
> That frae November till October,
> Ae market-day thou was nae sober;
> That ilka melder, wi' the miller,
> Thou sat as lang as thou had siller;
> That ev'ry naig was ca'd a shoe on,
> The smith and thee gat roaring fou on;
> That at the Lord's house, even on Sunday,
> Thou drank wi' Kirkton Jean till Monday.
> She prophesied that late or soon,
> Thou would be found deep drown'd in Doon;
> Or catch'd wi' warlocks in the mirk,
> By *Alloway's* auld, haunted kirk.[42]

While Burns pens a wonderful and unmatched burlesque, Wilson's setting of a similar marital condition—a drunken husband and a neglected wife—refrains from emphasizing either Watty's rusticity or the Gothic aesthetic that at times identifies "Scotland" in the works of Burns, Walter Scott, and James Hogg. The Scotland of "Watty and Meg," rather, is pictured as a home under threat of dissolution, beset by alcoholism, rage, and depression. Here desperate families subsist on the razor's edge of utter destitution, pitiless employers grind and cheat their workers, "improving" landowners disperse whole communities to make way for sheep,

BESIDE THE BARD

and reactionary authorities harass anyone with stomach enough to protest. This Scotland is fast becoming deracinated, as voiced by the bereft matron in Wilson's lovely allegorical lament "The Disconsolate Wren":[43]

> "Nae mair I'll thro' the valley flee,
> "And gather worms wi' blissfu' glee,
> > "To feed my chirping young;
> "Nae mair wi' Tam himsel' I'll rove,
> "Nor shall e'er joy throughout the grove,
> > "Flow frae my wretched tongue;
> "But lanely, lanely, aye I'll hap,
> > "Mang auld stane-dykes an' braes;
> "Till some ane roar down on my tap,
> > "An end my joyless days."
> > So, lowly and slowly,
> > > Araise the hapless Wren;
> > While crying and sighing,
> > > Remurmur'd through the Glen.

The neologic term "Remurmur'd" preserves only a spectral presence in the empty landscape; the poem's beautiful final couplet leaves a ghostly epitaph for a ruined country. The mother wren's lament for her lost children makes an apt sequel to "Watty and Meg." For Scotland, national comedy may be suitably antiquarian and mythogenic in a post-Union, pan-British world, but the appropriate genre for lived Scottish historical experience can only be tragedy.

Even when Wilson dabbles in burlesque in the manner of "Tam o' Shanter," as he does in the "Elegy on an Unfortunate Tailor," the tragic effect of Scotland's "fall" is only barely concealed.[44] In this poem Rab the tailor meets a gruesome death when he stumbles into the river after a drunken orgy and a mill wheel crushes "his guts an' gear, / Like ony burrel." The poem makes it evident that, unlike the sexual play and voyeuristic pleasure-seeking of Tam's "alehouse ingle," Rab's milieu is characterized by addictive behavior, alcohol abuse, and hallucinatory episodes:

> Aft ha'e I heard him tell o' frights,
> Sad waefu' souns, and dreary sights,
> He's aften got frae warlock wights,
> > An' Spunkie's bleeze;
> Gaun hame thro' muirs and eerie heights
> > O' black fir-trees.
> . . . .
> Tho' aft by fiends and witches chas't,

[84]

An' mony a dead man's glowrin' ghaist;
Yet on his knees he ae time fac't
   The Deil himsel':
An' sent him aff in dreadfu' haste,
    Roarin' to hell.

While we are invited to be skeptical of the historicity of Tam's midnight-ride experiences, here Rab's elegist retails stories of the tailor's real or imagined encounters with natural and supernatural beings, not only as a moral fable but as part and parcel of the same sense of social dissolution registered in poems as diverse as "Watty and Meg" and "The Hollander."

MASTERS AND MEN: ENGLISH CAPITAL, SCOTTISH LABOR, AND THE CONDITION OF SCOTLAND

In "First Epistle to Mr. William Mitchell," a leader of a local radical faction in Paisley, Wilson returns to the idiom in which he excels even his quondam idol, Burns.[45] Here his description of the iconic figures of Scottish industrialization, colliers and lead miners, rivals John Robertson's representation of the conditions of the rural laboring poor:

Here mountains raise their heath'ry backs,
    Rang'd huge aboon the lift;
In whase dark bowels, for lead tracts,
    Swarm'd miners howk an' sift;
High owre my head the sheep in packs,
    I see them mice-like skift;
The herd maist like ane's finger, wauks
    Aboon yon fearfu' clift
        Scarce seen this day.

Wilson's use of the Christ's Kirk stanza is particularly effective in evoking the sublimity of the scene. The *a* rhyme—"backs," "tracks," "packs," "wauks"—pulses with the masculine energy of the workers, the immense physical effort involved in the enterprise, and the almost unnatural, if not diabolical, activity of mining coal and lead. On the other hand, the *b* rhyme—"lift," "sift," "skift," and "clift"— indicates the precarious nature of the mining environment, the threat of sudden death or crippling injury. Usually associated with Scottish nativity and independence and often with nostalgia for the innocent (or Jacobite) past, here the "mountains raise their heath'ry backs" not as a site of the shepherd's dalliance or hiding

[85]

BESIDE THE BARD

place for freedom fighters but as resources to be exploited and placed into the service of a globalizing industrial economy. The poem's speaker alludes to this change, noticing the sheep on the mountainside walking perilously close to the edge of the cut. This is a striking dual image as well, as the sheep walk could refer to the clearance of land as well as to the shrinking rural character of the Scottish Lowlands in the face of provincial urbanization. The description of the miners as a "swarm" ironically recalls the medieval figure of the perfectly ordered society of bees, comparing the miners to drones whose lives are perpetually on forfeit to the absolute authority of the queen/state. Until the turn of the nineteenth century, as we have seen, Scottish miners served their masters as serfs legally bound to the mine, and their dehumanization in the poem reflects their objective economic and social condition.

The next stanza further emphasizes the hellish quality of the miners' work:

> Here mills rin thrang, wi' whilk in speed
>   They melt to bars the ore in;
> Nine score o' fathoms shanks down lead,
>   To let the hammerin' core in;
> Whare hun'ers for a bit o' bread
>   Continually are borin';
> Glowre down a pit, you'd think, wi' dread,
>   That gangs o' deils war roarin'
>   Frae hell that way.

Wilson ranks among the earliest British poets to chronicle in verse an industrial process and its environmental effects. He draws on the Miltonic figure of Pandemonium, ironically contrasting the social order of the hive in the previous stanza with that of Satan's hell. In the hive drones serve the queen so that the colony can survive, a tyranny of sorts but a commonwealth nonetheless; in hell the fallen angels serve a tyrant so that God's creation may be destroyed, but even so they at least have a larger purpose. In this poem, the miners dig "for a bit o' bread," not to build a better world for themselves and their posterity. From their perspective, work is essentially objectless, undertaken solely to sustain their own lives before black lung or lead poisoning brings them to a painful yet merciful end. Moreover, the domestic idyll of "The Cottar's Saturday Night" appears much different in this poem. The ghost villages of late eighteenth-century English rural poetry may be deserted, but they do not house the toxic waste products of industrial capitalism. The speaker describes the miners' homes as detritus, clustered around the openings of "holes an' caverns" and perched on the heaps of slag where they "pick the pyles o' leaden ore." This is a dead community inhabited by

[86]

the dead, a zombie society in which death is not a negation of life but a constant state of being.

The poem incongruously frames the three stanzas describing the mine between lighthearted descriptions of the speaker's experience as a peddler wandering through the countryside. In the stanza preceding his coming upon the mine, the speaker waxes lyrically about the beauty of the countryside in conventional terms, praising the "spreadin' vale," "gltt'rin' burns," and "sleepin' lochs." But even the speaker's joy, which the view of the mine interrupts, betrays the complete absence of human life in the natural world. Nature may well be aesthetically pleasing and inspiring to the poet, but its emptiness destabilizes its meaning. In this sense Wilson's poem challenges Romanticist orthodoxy *avant la lettre*. I am thinking here of Wordsworth's "Tintern Abbey" (1798), in which the poet's remembered childhood experiences of nature "interfuse" with his present contemplation of a beautiful scene in which human activity (and suffering) is remote and negated in its distant acknowledgment:[46]

> Once again I see
> These hedge-rows, hardly hedge-rows, little lines
> Of sportive wood run wild: these pastoral farms,
> Green to the very door; and wreaths of smoke
> Sent up, in silence, from among the trees!
> With some uncertain notice, as might seem
> Of vagrant dwellers in the houseless woods,
> Or of some Hermit's cave, where by his fire
> The Hermit sits alone.

Wordsworth's viewer absorbs these signs of human habitation into his own construction of "poetry," in which humanity exists in a minor key that supports and clarifies the "truth" of Nature:

> To look on nature, not as in the hour
> Of thoughtless youth; but hearing oftentimes
> The still, sad music of humanity,
> Nor harsh nor grating, though of ample power
> To chasten and subdue.
> . . . .
> Therefore am I still
> A lover of the meadows and the woods,
> And mountains; and of all that we behold
> From this green earth; of all the mighty world
> Of eye, and ear,—both what they half create,
> And what perceive; well pleased to recognise

> In nature and the language of the sense,
> The anchor of my purest thoughts, the nurse,
> The guide, the guardian of my heart, and soul
> Of all my moral being.

Wilson's speaker can scarcely plumb these depths, but even a roving packman-poet realizes that a lead mine and its desolate surroundings are inassimilable to a high romantic rendition of the "still, sad music of humanity." Indeed, for Wilson the mine emblematizes in a tragic mode the fundamental antagonism between humanity and Nature. But this antagonism has a comic mode as well, as in the final stanzas of the poem the versifying packman is rudely butted into a stream by "A toop, who won'ert at [his] pack." The poem leaves the poet fishing his pack (and his living) out of the water: "Wi' waefu' heart, before it sank / . . . / And now they're bleaching on the bank / A melancholy washing / To me this day."

Whereas the Wordsworthian poet kneels before the shrine of Nature to receive both instruction and salvation, the Wilsonian one is violently ejected from it. Spying the peddler's pack of muslins—a product of industrial capitalism—the ram attacks, bringing down the full force of the natural world ("earthquakes, hail, an' thuner's blaze") on the head of the poet. The pack is flung into the stream, its bearer not far behind. The "melancholy washing" that the poet suffers at the behest of a hostile and avenging Nature belies the comic situation and recalls the tragic condition of the miners. One cannot have the world both ways; we are either for it or against it. Wilson's peddler-poet, who views the world from below, learns the hard way that the choice is clear and unequivocal. Wordsworth's creator-poet, whose panoptic gaze takes in the world from above, averts his eyes, still hearing "the still, sad music" but evading responsibility for it. Indeed, with the peddler's ruined worldly goods "bleaching on the bank," all he can do is reflect, not on Nature's benevolence and compensatory grace but on its bitter implacability.

If violated Nature no longer offers consolation for human suffering, it is not likely that any human construct, whether religious institutions or a sacralized conception of "Nature," can compensate for that loss. A stridently anticlerical poet, Wilson does not draw primarily on the tradition of estates satire that we have observed in Lapraik or Pagan but rather situates his critique of religious institutions and practitioners in the context of modern capitalist society. Indeed, Wilson's major contribution to a poetics of protest arguably lies in this direction. Similar to Blake's, his poetry discerns the structural relationship between large-scale industrial production and the institutional authority that enables and facilitates it.[47] Clerics, passing smoothly from their former servitude to aristocratic patronage, take their place in the division of labor on the side of capital, doing their masters' bidding as middle managers responsible for inculcating the moral values most

ALEXANDER WILSON AND THE PRICE OF RADICALISM

needed in an industrial society: sobriety, docility, and regularity. Wilson registers this move, for example, in a ballad entitled "Address to the Synod of Glasgow and Ayr."[48] Here the poet speaks plainly to "Ye very reverend haly dads, / Wha fill the black gown dously, / And deal divinity in blauds, / Amang the vulgar crously." His message, which "ne'er cam' through / Presbyt'ry or Session," rather "comes without digression / In lumps this day." The petitioner advises the "haly dads,"

> Ye wad do weel to feed your flocks,
>   And read your buiks mair tenty;
> Then ye wad better raise your stocks,
>   And fill your ha's wi' plenty.
> Morality and common sense,
>   And reason ye should doat on;
> For then ye're sure of recompense
>   Frae ladies and your patron
>   On sic a day.

This petition is not calculated to persuade the clerics to read it. The speaker's exhortation to "do weel to feed your flocks, / And read your buiks mair tenty" sarcastically alludes both to the clerics' relatively ample means (and given the poverty of so many Scottish congregations, these are very relative, indeed) and their failure to tend to their spiritual "flocks." The speaker then excoriates their hypocritical sermons on "Morality and common sense, / And reason" (one cannot help but think of the anodyne morality, for example, of Hugh Blair's sermons), which please the "ladies" and the clerics' "patron" but offer no tangible benefit to the poor. For the affluent classes, morality and common sense provide a comforting rationale for maintaining their privileges, while teaching the laboring poor to remain in their preordained economic and social positions. In this sense, Wilson, who, as we have seen, is sympathetic to Enlightenment demystification and intellectual improvement, nonetheless deplores the failure of Scottish moral philosophy to develop more humane doctrines that address the inequities intrinsic to "modern" class and economic structures.

The poem continues in this vein, building a more direct political critique of the patronage system and the moral and doctrinal abuses of the clerics. The speaker warns that "Sic things are but ill taen thir days, / When Liberty's sae raging; / And in her leel and noble cause / Ten thousands are engaging." The implication here is that, given the opportunity, congregations would elect much different pastors, converting the Kirk from a bastion of reactionary loyalism to an organ of social and political change. Coming from the deistic Wilson, this familiar rhetoric of Covenanting Puritanism transmutes into a call for the overthrow of

[89]

BESIDE THE BARD

Burkean authoritarianism, which places the preservation of property above all else. The popular energy once associated with puritanical Calvinism still dwells in the people, and the congregation has become the basic instrument of radical change. Dangerously invoking "Rights of Man" and "Tammy Paine," the speaker imagines the conflict pitting the king's court and Kirk against the people in terms of the "buiks" each propounds: the Synod's works of theology and moral philosophy on one side, Paine's *Rights of Man* on the other. Moreover, the speaker recognizes that the very Enlightenment that the moderate literati and their state sponsors embrace might also be used against them. This is a populism infused with the virtues of literacy, education, and, in Virginia Woolf's words, "freedom from unreal loyalties."[49] Wilson's brand of popular radicalism draws on the rhetoric of the Friends of the People movement of which he was part, appealing across national and imperial boundaries to a universal working man, English, French, and Scottish alike. In this respect, the speaker acknowledges that the enlightened military-fiscal state has proved merely another regulatory mechanism for co-optation and control, sapping any vestigial native identity that may threaten the metropolitan rule of property. What is needed, the speaker asserts, is an equally cosmopolitan and unified conception of labor. Ethnic, linguistic, and traditional identities have always been tools of the ancien régime, which skillfully manipulates them to divide and conquer, and will not provide the necessary materials for national reconstruction.

At the conclusion of the poem the speaker foresees the dawning of a new epoch free of the "power of clergy," "courtiers' craft," and "Auld Monarchy," in which "Democracy, trig and braw, / Is through a' Europe crawing / Fu' crouse this day." This peroration, stirring as it is, anticipates the counterrevolutionary response that will crush radical democratic movements and drive "true blue" democrats such as Wilson out of Britain altogether. Though it may be "through a' Europe crawing/ Fu' crouse this day," the speaker seems to recognize that the old regime remains dangerous and adaptable to modern conditions. The economic and social forces that produced the revolution in France might be present in Britain, but the "Fair Liberty" that the speaker seeks may be no match for the "dark and deep designs" of the churchmen and the government they serve. Indeed, the speaker's "Muse" *does* exaggerate, promising a new millennium but leaving the speaker resignedly to "pray good Lord to guide us." The revolutionary energy of the poem thus dissipates in the final stanza, implicitly acknowledging the overwhelming force that the interests of property actually wield. The Muse may escape this repression, but the speaker, with his democratic brethren, is left victim to "confusion."

The poet's counterrevolutionary premonition in "The Address to the Synod of Glasgow and Ayr" is fully realized in "The Tears of Britain," a 168-line narrative

[90]

ALEXANDER WILSON AND THE PRICE OF RADICALISM

poem that imitates the formal diction of eighteenth-century rural elegy (its head-note quotes Goldsmith's "The Deserted Village") to lament the destruction of the hopes for democratic reforms inspired by the French Revolution.[50] In this poem the allegorical figure of the "genius of Britain" displaces the proletarian anger of Wilson's vernacular poetry. The formal requirements of Augustan verse suppress insurrectionary impulses and redirect them into satirical and allegorical modes. But why would Wilson invest in this aesthetic distance, when the urgency of Britain's ills seems to demand his other Muse, the Muse of Protest? Like many of his counter-parts, Wilson adeptly utilizes Augustan aesthetic conventions and, in this respect, participates in the broad tradition of eighteenth-century British poets who deploy classical verse forms to express discontent with social, political, and moral condi-tions in British society. The division of the poem between the poet-reporter's dream vision and Britannia's lament has none of the self-reflexive irony or humor, for example, of Coila's visitation to Burns in "The Vision." Britannia, it seems, has no specific business with this poet, as Coila does with Burns. War's barbarity excludes irony, satire, or even epic, and the poet should not translate those "hor-rors" in a way that blunts their true nature. Wilson's "Britishness" in this poem thus befits the tragic consequences of war for all Britons. Literary nationalisms sim-ply do not seem appropriate to the occasion, especially when all are either dying or fleeing:

> 'Down yonder rough beach, where the vessels attend,
> I see the sad emigrants slowly descend;
> Compell'd by the weight of oppression and woe,
> Their kindred, and native, and friends to forego.
> In these drooping crowds that depart every day,
> I see the true strength of the State glide away;
> While countries, that hail the glad strangers to shore,
> Shall flourish when Britain's proud pomp is no more.

> 'Her towns are unpeopl'd, her commerce decay'd,
> And shut up are all her resources of trade:
> The starving mechanic, bereav'd of each hope,
> Steals pensively home from his desolate shop;
> Surveys with an anguish words ne'er can express,
> The pale sighing partner of all his distress;
> While round them, imploring, their little ones meet,
> And crave from their mama a morsel to eat.

Rural depopulation by enclosure, commercialization, and emigration is a common-place in British poetry from the mid-eighteenth century, even before the American

[91]

BESIDE THE BARD

and French wars added their toll in impressed seamen, dragooned foot soldiers, and militia conscripts. But Wilson's critique is more comprehensive in that it envisions the world as a zero-sum game, in which Britain's loss is the corresponding gain of "countries, that hail the glad strangers to shore." Nor is commercial or industrial capitalism per se to blame, not this time. In marked contrast to Wilson's vernacular poetry, state capitalism, when dedicated to the arts of peace, might also operate to the benefit of the "poor Manufacturer" and "his workmen," the "sad emigrants" and "starving mechanic." The question remains whether modern British capitalism itself, with its growing dependence on territorial empire (especially in the East), naval hegemony, and exclusive foreign markets, is at all compatible with peaceful enterprise. Britannia's anguished lament predicts that Britain's capitalistic dependence on extracting surplus labor from the workers will eventually result in a proletarian revolution:

> 'Shall then such a monster, a fiend so accurs'd,
> By Britons be welcom'd, embosom'd, and nurs'd?
> Shall they, on whose prudence and mercy we rest,
> Be deaf to the cries of a nation distrest?
> Yes!—scorn'd for a while my poor children may mourn,
> Contemn'd and neglected, depress'd and forlorn;
> Till bursting the bands of oppression they soar
> Aloft from the dust, to be trampled no more.

Who are the oppressors? The "gentlemanly capitalists" who started the war and profit by it?[51] The bankers and stock jobbers who speculate on war? The bondholders without whose investment in the national debt the British state could not wage war to begin with? Referring to this poem, Noble rightly points out that "the Scots were neither politically nor linguistically alien from their radical English compatriots, and cross-border fertilisation among radical writers was constant throughout the period."[52] I would add that Wilson's brand of radicalism is just as deeply informed by his Scottish Enlightenment milieu and self-education in canonical British poets as it is by his artisanal roots. While the appeal to the allegorized Ambition and Pride, which call forth War and banish "Hope, Commerce, and Wealth," appears conventional, the poem implies that they may actually be two sides of the same coin. That Hope is serially attached to the other figures does not make it synonymous with them but recognizes that Smithean political economy and moral philosophy cannot truly be reconciled. Capitalism, in other words, is incompatible with "sympathy." Rather, it thrives on precisely the economic and military competitiveness that Britannia deplores:

'When rights are insulted, and justice deni'd,
When his country is threaten'd, his courage defied;
When tyrants denounce, and each vassal prepares,
'Tis then that the soul of the Briton appears:
Appears in the stern resolution reveal'd,
To rescue his country or sink in the field;
Indignant he burns the proud foe to pursue,
And conquest or death are the objects in view.

Britannia views the war as another bloody episode in *European* history, in which for centuries dynastic states have fought one another for prestige and plunder but have joined forces to suppress "Liberty" whenever and wherever it threatened to usurp aristocratic and clerical privileges. There is very little sense here of attachment to local, historical, or cultural nationalisms. Indeed, Britannia here signifies Liberty, which is defined not in property but in *class* terms. As we have seen in Wilson's labor poetry, the world of industry and commerce collects feudal, ethnic, linguistic, and historical identities into two great aggregations: masters and hands. In this world Britannia sides unambiguously with the hands, as in English rural poetry it identifies with yeomen farmers and the "bold peasantry, their country's pride, / When once destroyed, can never be supplied." Even Burns in his most "radical" idiom does not quite approach this understanding of the real functional significance of the revolution. The *Rights of Man* provides a vocabulary for a poetics of equality (at least for the universal male), but it does not perceive the structural economic transformations that incarcerate the laboring classes in the workhouse of "free labor." The cruelest irony of this process, as Britannia acknowledges in the poem, is that the rhetoric of Liberty has been co-opted for use by the propertied classes as the fundamental characteristic of "Britishness," the idea that "free-born Britons" will not brook the "foreign" tyranny with which property interests are complicit. In stanza 16 Britannia asks, "Was Britain insulted, was justice refus'd, / Her honour, her quiet, or interest abus'd?" The response two stanzas later is not comforting:

'These shouts that I hear from yon wide western plains,
Where distant Hibernia lies panting in chains;
Those pale bleeding corpses, thick strew'd o'er the ground,
Those law-sanctioned heroes triumphing around;
These speak in the voice of the loud-roaring flood,
And write this stern lesson in letters of blood:
Oppression may prosecute, Force bend the knee,
But free is the nation that wills to be free.

BESIDE THE BARD

For Wilson (as for William Blake), as events proved, the United States is that nation, at least in its Jeffersonian imaginary. In this respect, Robert Tannahill's beautiful eulogy for the exiled Wilson expresses the departure from Scotland of its last "free" poetic voice:[53]

> Is there wha feel the meltin glow
> O sympathy for ithers woe?
> Come, let our tears thegither flow;
>   O join my mane!
> For Wilson, worthiest of us a,
>   For ay is gane.
>
> He bravely strave gainst Fortune's stream
> While Hope held forth ae distant gleam,
> Till dasht and dasht, time after time,
>   On Life's rough sea,
> He weep'd his thankless native clime,
>   And sail'd away.

Even accounting for the eulogistic hyperbole, Tannahill has it right that Wilson belongs in the company of Burns as one of the preeminent vernacular Scottish poets of the period. Burns died, perhaps, before he could do anything irrevocably foolish in politics, and cultural authorities anxious to claim his "genius" for nineteenth-century British uses largely, if not quite completely, sanitized his political reputation, while treating his moral failings as a species of local color to be expected of Scottish rustics. Wilson, however, remains inassimilable to this particular model of the poet of the people. To a greater extent than any of the Scottish poets we have discussed, Wilson was a poet specifically from and of the working class, though he in some respects sympathized with Burns's New Licht moderatism, republicanism, and progressivism.[54] Wilson must also be considered as an important contributor to the Scottish Enlightenment and its diffusion in the United States. It is one of the loveliest of historical coincidences that John Witherspoon baptized the infant Wilson at Paisley Kirk in 1766. There was something very powerful indeed in that water.

But leave it to Wilson to ironize his own self-representation and refuse to take himself too seriously. In this wonderful comic poem, "To the Famishing Bard. From a Brother Skeleton,"[55] Wilson emerges simply as a struggling young artist looking for his next meal:

> Aloft to high Parnassus' hill,
>   I heard thy pray'r ascending swift;

[94]

ALEXANDER WILSON AND THE PRICE OF RADICALISM

And are the Nine propitious still
    To grant thy wish, and send the gift?
Has kind Apollo made a shift,
    To roll down from his kitchen high
A sirloin huge—a smoking lift,—
    To feed thy keen devouring eye!
. . . .
If thou must eat, ferocious bard,
    Elsewhere importune for a dinner;
Long thou may pray here, nor be heard,
    And praying makes thee but the thinner.
Do like the lank, lean, ghostly sinner,
    That here presumes to give advice;
Ne'er court the Muse for meat—to win her,
    E'en starve, and glory in the price.

4

LADY NAIRNE

Burns's Jacobite Other

IN CHAPTERS 1–3 WE HAVE BEEN CONCERNED PRIMARILY with the work of "autodidactic" or "peasant poets" who were contemporaries of Burns: John Lapraik and David Sillar, Janet Little and Isobel Pagan, and Alexander Wilson. As Valentina Bold has argued, these poets "provided a vigorous alternative to the mainstream tradition of Scottish poetry." But as Bold points out, and as this study has amply illustrated, while the typology of the unlettered peasant poet as embodied by Burns (and later James Hogg) "allowed working class writers a limited critical acceptance and, increasingly, the inspiration of being part of a national tradition, . . . it actively discouraged poets of Nature's Making from experimenting with themes and styles which were seen as more appropriate for their self-styled superiors."[1] This double bind of poetic aspiration and critical condescension generally defeated their efforts to crack open the literary market as Burns had done so successfully.

If we think, as Bold suggests, in terms of an alternative national tradition of Scottish poetry in the autodidactic mode, how then should we read the poetry of the aristocratic Lady Nairne (Carolina Oliphant, 1766–1845)? Nairne avidly followed Burns's collection, revision, and production of Scottish songs and began both writing original verse and adapting existing verses to traditional music in the 1790s, though even to her friends she declined to disclose her authorship. Whereas peasant poets suffered from the stigma of their social inferiority, Nairne, for reasons of propriety associated with her social rank and gender, went to great lengths to conceal her identity from her publisher, Robert Purdie, who "for twenty years knew her only under the name 'Mrs. Bogan of Bogan.'"[2] Indeed, some of Nairne's most popular songs, such as "The Land o' the Leal," were attributed to Burns,[3] but subsequent nineteenth-century compendia of Scottish songs, such as Graham's *The Songs of Scotland* (1861), Tytler and Watson's *The Songstresses of Scotland* (1871),

[97]

Wilson's *The Poets and Poetry of Scotland* (1876–1877), and Henderson's *Lady Nairne and Her Songs* (1901), as well as the frequent republications of her songs beginning in the second half of the nineteenth century and continuing to the present, leave little doubt of her central importance to a tradition that Burns did so much to shape.[4] Still, as Carol McGuirk points out, "in Nairne's day, 'Unknown,' 'Anon' and 'Anonymous' were presumed . . . to be long deceased 'wonderful men' rather than living and breathing Edinburgh matrons. Nairne may have feared that her songs' high popularity would suffer if the word got out."[5] As McGuirk points out, the secret, which Nairne kept even from her husband, depended on the discretion of the all-women editorial committee of the *Scots Minstrel* (1821–1824), suggesting the striking power of bonds of friendship and solidarity between women in a society in which, as Nairne herself wrote, "still the balance is in favor of the 'Lords of Creation.' I cannot help . . . undervaluing beforehand what is said to be a feminine production."[6]

While it may not apply equally to men and women peasant poets, this "undervaluing beforehand" nevertheless links the poets of humble origins whom we have read thus far with the aristocratic woman who felt compelled to pass herself off as a purveyor of "anonymous" native literary productions rooted in the oral tradition. In this framework we can relate Nairne's work to that of Burns and other laboring-class poets and examine how we might determine, in William Donaldson's terms, "the exact extent of her work and its links with the rest of the tradition."[7] In this regard, Ian Duncan and Sheila Kidd have credited Nairne as "the most important songwriter after Burns and Hogg" and add that she "gives the tradition a decisively sentimental Jacobite tilt."[8] This "tilt" is only part of the story, however, for Nairne genders her Jacobite lyrics in ways that neutralize sentimentality and recover, to some extent, the political charge associated with nationalist verse of this kind. Here I rely on Leith Davis, who in her study of eighteenth- and early nineteenth-century Irish song takes a postcolonial approach that considers "music as a location of 'double inscription' . . . , a site that reflects the various ways in which colonizing and colonized identities were shaped, changed, and articulated through encounter."[9] As we will see in the selection of lyrics that follows, Nairne shows clear awareness of Scottish song's capacity for negotiating gender, class, and national identities in a society that, if not "colonized" in the Irish sense, suffered a significant loss of national purpose in the post-Union eighteenth century.

I argue that the beauty of Nairne's verse preserves and accentuates its political content, rather than displacing it. Read from this perspective, Nairne's poetry reveals a more ambivalent discourse about Scotland's past, present, and possible futures than most commentators, with the exception of Davis and McGuirk, have previously recognized. McGuirk invokes Homi Bhabha's notion of hybridity to argue that Nairne's (and Burns's) songs imagine "'Scotland' as a site of stubborn yet evocative dissonance, a place where fish vendors inspire art songs, royal princes weep as homeless outcasts, and every single speaker . . . has a problem with social consensus and/or historical outcome. . . . Burns's and Nairne's neo-Jacobite songs are hybrid in their emphasis on interaction between what were (historically) divided or antagonistic Scottish communities."[10] I concur with McGuirk's postcolonial reading and argue further that Nairne inflects this "dissonant" Scottish conscious-ness not only with an acute awareness of social, doctrinal, and national spaces of contestation but also with an awareness of gender.[11] The centrality of gender to the transmission of traditional Scottish oral culture in the medium of print has received a significant amount of critical attention in recent years. As Catherine Kerrigan points out, the ballad form (in which much women's poetry of the period appears) enables "a chorus of voices, different in class and education, but . . . offers a broad and complex picture of the psyche of women."[12] This examination of Nairne's poetry will reveal the specific aspects of this influence.

As previously discussed, unlike the dairymaid Janet Little and tavern keeper Isobel Pagan, Lady Nairne's status as a gentlewoman inhibited her from publish-ing under her own name. Little's gender and laboring-class position enabled her to appear in "public," though as we saw in her poetry, she negotiates her public position by ironizing it and projecting the persona of a bemused observer of the bottom side of rural genteel life. Pagan's social and economic marginalization, on the other hand, liberated her to render critical judgment on the morals of Muirkirk society, address corruption, and police the boundaries of the social order. These strategies were not available to Lady Nairne, who had literally to veil her author-ship and suppress publicity, even to the point of misleading her readers with respect to her gender. Only after Nairne's death in 1845 was she revealed as the author of numerous songs published initially in Robert Smith's six-volume collection *The Scottish Minstrel* (1821–1824).[13]

The double bind of her gender and high social rank goes hand in hand with her sincere Jacobite political sympathies, which by the latter half of the eighteenth century had settled into the broad consensus "grounded in a common Whiggery."[14] Born into the staunchly Jacobite family of Laurence Oliphant, laird of Gask, and Margaret Robertson Oliphant, a daughter of the chief of clan Donnachie (who were married while in exile in France, refugees of the '45), Nairne doubtless imbibed the "sentimental Jacobitism" that, according to Colin Kidd, "was indulged as a harmless diversion."[15] By the time she entered the literary market at the turn of the nineteenth century, however, Jacobitism was not quite a dead letter. Murray Pittock points out that in Burns's Jacobite lyrics, situated historically in a revolu-tionary era, "Burns foreshadowed both the nostalgic Jacobitism of sentiment, and the capacity of its living analysis of Scotland's plight to inhere in the language of subsequent struggles."[16] Pittock refers here to Burns's contribution to the development of nineteenth- and twentieth-century "Jacobitism of the Left." More recently, Pittock has shown the continuity between Jacobite material culture, language, and politics between 1688 and 1745, the radicalism of the 1790s, and insurgent nationalist movements in Ireland and Europe in the nineteenth century.[17] Positioned precisely at the historical juncture that Pittock here identifies, Nairne deploys the extraordinarily malleable Jacobite tropes to analyze what her poetry imagines as Scotland's domestic crisis, a crisis in which war and assimilation into a globalizing economy threaten to empty the nation of both its physical bodies and traditional modes of self-identification. As we will see, women bear a disproportionally heavy burden in the process of deracination.

But this is not how Victorian readers understood Nairne's songs (once they became aware of their actual provenance). Margery McCulloch observes that the reception history of her poetry has been deeply influenced by the eminent Scottish literary historian, biographer, and educator David Mather Masson (1822–1907), who wrote, "There is real moral worth in them all, and all have that genuine characteristic of a song which consists of an inner tune preceding and inspiring the words, and coiling the words, as it were, out of the heart along with it."[18] Masson's commentary, neatly complemented by George Henderson's assertion that Nairne contributed to "purifying the national song" from "coarse and worthless words," is of a piece with Victorian concerns with policing the propriety of Scottish lyrics to make them suitable for bourgeois "British" readers, particularly young women learning to negotiate the keyboard.[19] But it is also part of the effort of Masson and other Scottish literary figures (Alexander Geddes is an early example) to establish an "ethnogenesis" that recognized the Gothic origins of both Scots and English and "a common Saxon inheritance across the lowlands of medieval Britain." Indeed, Masson believed that Gothicism "underpinned the union" of Scotland and England and completed the historic destiny of the two kingdoms.[20]

Masson's political interest in assimilating Nairne's overt Jacobitism to a pan-British literary heritage elides interpretations of "national" poetry in terms of a specifically *Scottish* nationalist discourse and tends to emphasize the tune at the expense of the verse. McCulloch argues that even Burns "felt that the *tune*—often a traditional fiddle tune—was the locus of national identity. Where he felt that the words which had come with the tune were inferior to the quality of the tune itself, then he rewrote them to make them worthy."[21] McCulloch exemplifies this insight by comparing Burns's use of the traditional tune "Hey, tutti taitie" as the musical setting for "Scots Wha' Hae" with Nairne's adaptation of the same tune

[100]

for "The Land o' the Leal."[22] This adaptation produces, in McCulloch's reading, a "beautiful and moving song" that evokes "that eighteenth-century belief in our capacity to empathise with those less fortunate than ourselves."[23] By here alluding to the eighteenth-century genre of the sentimental novel, McCulloch implies, in terms similar to those of Masson, Henderson, and other Victorian critics, that Nairne's songs shy away from national questions, instead embracing "real moral worth."[24]

"The Land o' the Leal," for example, can also be read as addressing the concrete social and economic conditions that late eighteenth-century Scots, particularly those of the lower ranks of society, had to endure.[25] In the poem, which was first published by Robert Smith in 1821 under Nairne's pseudonym (and which after Nairne's death some of Burns's biographers claimed was composed by the dying poet), the speaker, a woman "wearin' awa'" from cold, hunger, deprivation, and grief, tells her husband that she desires death over a life of bodily and emotional suffering. Her dead child, "baith gude and fair," has only achieved "joy" by exiting life, though her parents "grug'd her sair." While the speaker now appears to accept her daughter's death as the will of heaven ("But sorrow's sel' wears past"), she hints at an underlying and unremitting anger at its injustice: "Sae dear that joy was bought, John, / Sae free the battle fought, John." This language of violent struggle (the internal rhyme "bought"/"fought"/"brought") contrasts sharply with the preceding verse, "The joy that's aye to last," and the speaker's appeal "to be free" echoes the defiance implicit in "Sae free the battle fought." Though the poem returns to quiescence in the final verse ("We'll meet, and we'll be fain"), such gladness as the poem offers seems little compensation for the burden of life that is always "wearin' thro'."

While the poem indicates a traditional expression of *contemptus mundi* that figures the universal Christian man as "sinfu'," the *sins* to which the woman refers—those that produce hunger and poverty—come at the hands of historically specific men. The "land o' the leal" may be heaven, but it is a Scottish heaven or, perhaps more accurately, a Scottish haven. The idea of the "leal Scot" who returns from exile to his native land politically codes this explicitly religious allegory in somewhat oppositional terms. Scottish subordination to English rule makes all "leal" Scots into exiles, whether they are forced to emigrate to clear sheep walks and hunting grounds in the interests of agrarian "improvement" (and to the benefit of the tiny class of Scottish landowners), to fight Britain's imperial and continental wars, or to leave the land for entombment as wage laborers in squalid industrial or commercial towns. The "land o' the leal" is thus an alternative Scotland, one free of the hegemonic structures of the military fiscal state and inhabited by native Scots with communitarian national values. Only in a Scottish community

[101]

BESIDE THE BARD

of the faithful might a child's death from cold and starvation—or a parent's from grief and overwork—ever stand redeemed.[26]

We find another variant of this communitarianism in "The Auld House."[27] Just as its English and Anglo-Irish counterparts by poets such as Cowper, Crabbe, and Goldsmith, the poem laments the decline of aristocratic paternalism and a "free" peasantry:

> Oh, the auld house, the auld house,
> What tho' the rooms were wee?
> Oh! kind hearts were dwelling there,
> And bairnies fu' o' glee;
> The wild rose and the Jessamine
> Still hang upon the wa',
> How mony cherish'd memories
> Do they, sweet flowers, reca'.
>
> Oh, the auld laird, the auld laird,
> Sae canty, kind and crouse,
> How mony did he welcome to
> His ain wee dear auld house;
> And the leddy too, sae genty,
> There shelter'd Scotland's heir,* [*Prince Charles Edward*—original note]
> And clipt a lock wi' her ain hand,
> Frae his lang yellow hair.

These stanzas emphasize the relative modesty of the Scottish gentry, in contrast to the rather grander proportions of the English squirearchy.[28] They also relocate social adhesion, family piety, and filial affection from the yeoman farmer's humbler social class, as in the English poems, to the gentry itself.[29] The laird's hospitality extends to one and all, while the leddy's grace and gentility imbue the community with domestic sanctity and racial purity, fetishized in the form of the young heir's / Bonnie Charlie's lock of blond hair. Just as in "The Land o' the Leal" and "Caller Herrin'," the poem envisages the community of faithful as Scottish and traditional, untainted by foreign or English interference, although the flora—"wild rose and the Jessamine"—connotes a broader literary association with English roses and white jasmine.[30] This floral locus classicus of British poetry is extended in the next two stanzas, which evoke sensual experiences traditionally associated with the Scottish Lowland countryside. The ubiquitous song thrush (mavis), blue bells, and pear tree deepen the poem's "Britishness," but at the same time they accentuate the emptiness of the landscape. Whereas the first two stanzas associate the flora with "cherish'd memories" of hearth and home, in the second they reveal the social

[102]

and economic changes that have undermined the old feudal hierarchy. Moreover, the poem's use of common meter mimics the English hymn form, but without the standard *abab* rhyme pattern. Instead, the rhyme varies somewhat, but generally follows an *abcb* scheme (though the fourth stanza, for example, contains one variant of *aaba* and one standard *cdcd*). These variations indicate a parallel disruption of literary and aesthetic traditions, as the very form of the poem distorts under the pressure of Scotland's cultural subordination in the British state. The auld house deserted and the children's voices forever silenced, the beauty of the "bonnie Earn's clear winding" is preserved only as an aesthetic production, a picture postcard featuring British rural scenery, mass produced for an increasing number of tourists and travelers from the South.[31] Unlike in the English empty-landscape poems, where the rural peasantry has been driven from the land by rapacious, capitalist landlords who enclose common land and tear down cottages, here the land has been lost altogether as Scotland's traditional economy assimilates into the English commercial system.[32]

The poem concludes with an elegiac pronouncement of the irreversibility of this assimilation:

> For they are a' wide scatter'd now,
> Some to the Indies gane,
> And ane alas! to her lang hame;
> Not here we'll meet again,
> The kirkyaird, the kirkyaird!
> Wi' flowers o' every hue,
> Shelter'd by the holly's shade
> An' the dark somber yew.

Their society destroyed, the sons of the gentry—Harvie's "red" Scots—have scattered to the four corners of the empire, seeking their fortunes as soldiers and sailors, merchants and planters, colonial administrators and East India Company clerks. Even the regulation of the seasons that governed the economic and social rhythm of the old agrarian society has lost its relevance in the new commercial, capitalist Scotland. Nothing here is cultivated except a romantic imagery of picturesque ruins; even the tropes and imagery of English landscape poetry have invaded and colonized the Scots vernacular. Even as the poem celebrates Scottish musical, poetic, and linguistic national traditions, it eulogizes their demise.

This colonization of Scottish culture, imagined as in transition in "The Auld House," appears more complete in "Her Home She Is Leaving."[33] This poem, composed in rhymed hexameter couplets, dispenses altogether with vernacular Scots

BESIDE THE BARD

(the only archaisms are the personal pronouns "thee" and "ye") in favor of elegant Augustan English:

> To the hills of her youth, cloth'd in all their wildness,
> Farewell she is bidding, in all her sweet mildness,
> And still, as the moment of parting is nearer,
> Each long-cherish'd object is fairer and dearer.
> Not a grove or fresh streamlet but wakens reflection
> Of hearts still and cold, that glow'd with affection;
> Not a breeze that blows over the flow'rs of the wild-wood,
> But tells as it passes, how blest was her childhood.

The Anglicized observer might be anywhere; unlike many of Nairne's "nature" poems, this poem strips away the insistent localism of particular river valleys, along with their national and linguistic associations. In this sense, the poem deracinates its origins, fully realizing the English colonization of Scottish poetic forms and vernacular still extant in "The Auld House." The predominant mood of the poem is elegiac detachment, a favorite Augustan mode that further identifies the poem with the dominant South British cultural tradition. Even the voice of the breeze, which the speaker rightly or wrongly assumes is narrating the blessedness of the old woman's youth, communicates to her in a language that does not seem to belong to her: it "tells as it passes, how blest was her childhood," but its primary effect is to conjure a dead past whose associations can only find expression in a dead language.

In the following stanzas, the poem's perspective shifts from the observer of the aged woman to the woman herself, who laments the necessity of her exile from "Ye high rocky summits," "ye ivy'd recesses," "thou wood-shaded river." Allowed to speak for herself for the first and only time in the poem, the woman seems curiously disassociated from the landscape. She does not refer back to the affective bonds that the speaker identifies in the first stanza as one source of the woman's "blessedness." It appears that she has no words for that kind of blessedness, and the speaker's imposition of an alien language on the woman effectively silences her. She queries the landscape of her native place, only to receive an echo of her own alienation from it: an exilic sigh and a whisper. We now see that the speaker has misconstrued the nature and meaning of the woman's reflections from the beginning: this final parting does not sanctify past associations but completes a process of erasure. When spring comes, the birds will sing once more, but the song no longer has meaning for the woman—it can never be "hers." As if to affirm this appropriation, the poem shifts back to the observer in the final stanza:

[104]

LADY NAIRNE

> The joys of the past, more faintly recalling,
> Sweet visions of peace on her spirit are falling,
> And the soft wing of time, as it speeds for the morrow,
> Wafts a gale, that is drying the dew drops of sorrow.
> Hope dawns—and the toils of life's journey beguiling.
> The path of the mourner is cheered with its smiling,
> And there her heart rests, and her wishes all centre,
> Where parting is never—nor sorrow can enter!

Here the observer naturalizes the old woman's imminent death in conventional terms of consolation. But note the dramatic contrast between this version of the *contemptus mundi* narrative and the one we see in "The Land o' the Leal." There the affective relations between the woman, her husband, and their lost child materialize in the Scots vernacular of the poem; they are felt through the woman's native language speaking *for itself.* In "Her Home She Is Leaving" none of this feeling survives. We get no sense of the woman's lived experience, suffering, and loss. The poem instead speaks over the woman, substituting pious sentiment for authentic mourning, cultural domination for self-representation.

Nairne's poetry continuously resists the forces of Anglicization. In sharp contrast to the deracination effected in "Her Home She Is Leaving," "The Banks of the Earn" projects a rousing Scottish patriotism in the martial vernacular of "Scots Wha Hae":[34]

> Fair shone the rising sky,
> The dew drops clad wi' mony a dye,
> Larks lifting pibrochs high,
> To welcome day's returning.
> The spreading hills, the shading trees,
> High waving in the morning breeze;
> The wee Scots' rose that sweetly blows,
> Earn's vale adorning.

This is Scotland resplendent; if the Augustan mode of the prior poem elides all traces of nativity, "The Banks of the Earn" renders Scotland as "Nature" itself. With the rising sun the larks' song transforms into the sound of pipes, the landscape flaps in the breeze like the Saltire. In the first stanza the poem deploys three of Scotland's "national" languages, Scots, Gaelic, and English, embracing a composite linguistic, historical, and cultural idea of the nation that unifies Lowlands and Highlands, Scots and Celts, country and city. The poet, who might be read as Dame Scotia, personifies the River Earn (*Uisge Eireann* in Scottish Gaelic)[35] in

[105]

BESIDE THE BARD

terms of the heroes of the Wars for Scottish Independence, "Where Wallace wight fought for the right, / And gallant Grahams are lying low":

> O Scotland! nurse o' mony a name
> Rever'd for worth, renown'd in fame;
> Let never foes tell to thy shame,
> Gane is thine ancient loyalty.
> But still the true-born warlike band
> That guards thy high unconquer'd land,
> As did their sires, join hand in hand,
> To fight for law and royalty.

It is instructive to compare Nairne's voice in the poem with that of Burns in "The Scotian Muse: An Elegy." This poem was first printed in the *Edinburgh Gazetteer* on October 1, 1793, in response to the sedition trials of Thomas Muir and the Rev. Thomas Fyshe Palmer:

> For him, who warm'd by *Freedom's* genial fire,
>   With soul unfetter'd, drags the *Despot's* chain,
> Perhaps thy hand attunes the living lyre
>   To soothe his woes by music's magic strain.
> . . . .
> Say (and, ye *Powers of Truth*, accordant join!)
>   'The time will come—that *Fate* has fix'd the doom—
> 'The *Friends of suffering virtue* shall combine,
>   'And hurl each blood-stained Despot to the tomb!'[36]

As Noble observes, "this is absolutely the only Scottish public radical poetry derived from the high Miltonic style."[37] But Nairne's lyric ode, while not "public radical poetry" in Noble's sense of the term, certainly participates in a similarly "high" style. I would argue that it too contains radical implications, but not of the same republican stamp as Burns's poem. The ostensible subject of the poem, the River Earn, embodies both Scotland's history of freedom from foreign domination and Burns's Scotian muse, whose song both recounts the "ancient loyalty" of the Scots and prophesies a new dawning of freedom through "suffering virtue." The kind of harmless nostalgia commonly associated with the safe domestication of Scottish heroes from the past, while present in the poem's memorialization of Wallace and the Grahams, only accentuates the shift to the *present* tense in the third stanza: "But still the true-born warlike band / That guards thy high unconquer'd land, / As did their sires, join hand in hand, / To fight for law and royalty." These yet-to-

[106]

be-sung heroes, like Burns's Scottish Friends of the People, fight tyranny in the here and now:

> Oh, ne'er for greed o' wardly gear,
> Let thy brave sons, like fugies, hide
> Where lawless stills pollute the rills
> That o'er thy hills and valleys glide.
> While in the field they scorn to yield,
> And while their native soil is dear,
> Oh, may their truth be as its rocks,
> And conscience, as its waters clear!

But what is the nature of this tyranny? Does the poem suggest a return to the royal prerogative and the Stuart monarchy, as fealty to "law and royalty" might suggest? For the poet, it seems, the immediate threat to Scotland's sovereignty is the "cult of commerce" that characterizes the modern composite British state.[38] Seduced by "greed o' wardly gear," Scotia's sons are faced with the choice of either preserving their nativity or engaging in British enterprise. Curiously, "British" enterprise appears limited in the poem to the business of the illegal distillation of whisky, which flourished (especially in the Highlands) during the post-Union regime of licenses and excise duties on spirits, both imported and locally produced. Here the poet's somewhat-priggish allegation that those brave Highlanders who once fought for Scotland's ancient freedoms are now too busy selling illicit moonshine to notice their loss masks a deeper estrangement caused by the Union.[39] Even the advance of a century does not seem to have erased the humiliation of economic subordination, which has emasculated Scotland's "brave sons" and "polluted" its former independence with the stain of economic dependency and illegal commerce.

Unlike Burns's rhetoric of republican "truth" and "virtue," Nairne's Scottish muse calls for a return to traditional "truth" and "conscience," a decidedly conservative, patrician position that, while it shares some of the rhetorical attributes of Jacobitism, accepts the political reality of the British state and recasts the argument in terms of a return to the moral economy. Thus the poem targets not the "blood-stained Despots" but the tyranny of the fiscal-bureaucratic state, which has burdened the Scottish nation with the debts of French and American wars while stifling its economic freedom through punitive excise taxes and English protectionism.[40] The insidious effect of commercial (and later industrial) capitalism, directed and enforced by the terms of the Treaty of Union, may have found expression in the Jacobite politics of 1715 and 1745, but by century's end Nairne's Dame

[107]

BESIDE THE BARD

Scotia engages in neither wishful republican thinking nor hazy feudal nostalgia. Her conservatism lies rather in a clear-eyed assessment of Scotland's actual condition as an economic colony of the British state and empire. Although the glittering promise of profits from trade and industry may have been realized by some Scottish participants in British enterprise (Harvie's red Scots again), the true measure of Scotland's predicament is found in the squalid Highland villages sustained by illegal distilling, the continuous low-grade warfare between smugglers and excise officers, and the diminishing social cohesion once fostered by feudal political and economic ties. In order for Scotland to clear its collective conscience and purge the pollution from the social body, it must either become an equal partner in a truly "British" state or liberate itself from English fiscal and economic policies. Nairne, at least in "The Banks of the Earn," sees no partnership whatever. Scotland is little more than an aesthetic accessory, an economic satellite, a labor pool, a sheep walk, a recruiting depot, and a graveyard where impotent and polluted "fugies" go to die.

We can see that the English overwriting of Scottish history implicit in the Union project produces a present dislocation from this heroic past that has severed Scots from any sense of localized self-identification. The beautiful elegy "Bonny Gascon Ha'" strongly registers this effect, as a familiar ruin associated with Wallace's martial feats is imagined in the present as a sign of the completed and inaccessible epic past:[41]

> Lane, on the winding Earn, there stands
>   An unco tow'r, sae stern an' auld,
> Biggit, by lang forgotten hands,—
>   Ance refuge o' the Wallace bauld.
>
> Time's restless finger sair hath waur'd,
>   And riv'd thy grey disjaskit wa';
> But rougher hands than Time's ha'e daur'd
>   To wrang thee, bonny Gascon Ha'.
>
> O! may a muse unkent to fame,
>   For this dim gruesome relic sue:
> 'Tis linkit wi' a Patriot's name,
>   The truest Scotland ever knew.

The poem begins in *Ozymandias* fashion with the striking image of the "unco tow'r, sae stern an' auld, / Biggit, by lang forgotten hands,— / Ance refuge o' the Wallace bauld." In this "epic zone," as Mikhail Bakhtin puts it, there is no need for

[108]

explanation of the hero's historicity, for "epic is indifferent to formal beginnings and can remain incomplete. . . . The absolute past is closed and completed in the whole as well as in any of its parts. It is, therefore, possible to take any part and offer it as the whole."[42] Wallace defeats the English at every turn, always against impossible odds and in the name of the Scottish nation that he eternally embodies. As Bakhtin says about *The Iliad*, "the plot-line of the tradition is already well known to everyone."[43] Thus, when we see in Burns, Nairne, and other poets references to Wallace and other Scottish "national" figures, the associations invoked in terms of the present condition of honorless subjection to the English do not merely register on a historical plane but as an absolute, irrevocable bereavement of national character. Indeed, as Steven McKenna has suggested, Burns's "youthful attraction" to the Wallace myth evinces "the desire to write a national epic, and this desire again shows his attachment not to history's victors but to the representatives of the struggle against those winners."[44] To put it in terms of an "English" national tale—the Arthurian cycles—the Norman aristocrats and courtiers who devised the Arthur legends to legitimize their conquest may have constructed a story that has many of the characteristics of epic, but it refuses the severance from the deep past, the closed circle, that for Bakhtin marks the national epic. Arthur's return remains open; the rise will inevitably follow the fall. In this respect, the Arthur legends are comic in nature and closer relatives to the modern novel. If we think in terms of this paradigm, as poets the Scots are indeed a tragedy-minded people. Their national tale is a true epic: Wallace will not come back; the circle is closed; those were indeed the "good times."

When in the second quatrain the poem turns from the Wallace plot that everyone already knows to the fate of its signifier, we see that "Time" (which is rigidly excluded from epic because it denotes movement, a lessening of distance, a collapse of the absolute) has the ability to decay the signifier (the tower) but not its signified (Wallace). This conventional allusion reaffirms the sanctity and immunity of the sealed epic past, but, unlike *Ozymandias*, the poem does not stop with convention. The poet ruefully adds, "But rougher hands than Time's ha'e daur'd / To wrang thee, bonny Gascon Ha'." Here the poet may refer to the immediate depredations of vandals or local builders looking for materials, but it would likewise appear that attempts are at work to repress the Scottish epic past in the service of promoting the modern British state. In the next quatrain the poet implores a "muse unkent to fame" to resist these attempts to overwrite Scottish national epic and, inspired by the tower, to sing the old songs once more. It is interesting that the poet should call on an *anonymous* voice for this purpose, as if calling out the poet's more notorious contemporaries for failing in this presumably national duty. The sought-after unknown muse likewise harks back to the "lang forgotten hands" that built the tower and, by implication, Scotland's heroic past. Indeed, the poet seems to suggest that poetry that is not so inspired, that is wedded to the open, assimilationist impulses of the present, cannot be considered as part of the national tradition. In this sense, the poet of "Bonny Gascon Ha'" strikes a pose similar to that of "The Banks of the Earn," calling on Scotland's "brave sons" to turn to the epic past for a means of self-identification and national expression.

At this point the poem also performs a semiotic transference in which the hall tower's signification of Wallace the "bauld" hero passes through the "unkent muse" back through the tower to a new signified, "a Patriot's name / The truest Scotland ever knew." This substitution for Wallace may seem too close an approximation for comment, but it functions not only to sharpen the opposition between the "true" muse/poet/patriot and the "rougher hands" of the second quatrain. Indeed, the "dim gruesome relic" is itself sanctified by the "Patriot's name" in a kind of ritual of transubstantiation. It is not that Wallace has transcended epic to become a sacrificial figure within a Christian soteriology (this might be a productive reading as well, though it would convert the Scottish national tale from tragedy to comedy, which does not seem quite appropriate to the poem), but that "true" Scottish literature, like Scottish patriotism, must meet the peremptory demands of its own *logos*, just as Christian allegory begins and ends with the Word incarnate:

> Just leave in peace ilk mossy stane,
> > Tellin' o' nation's rivalry;
> And for succeeding ages hain
> > Remains o' Scottish chivalry.
>
> What tho' no monument to thee
> > Is biggit by thy country's hands,—
> Engrav'd are thine immortal deeds
> > On ev'ry heart in this braid land.
>
> Rude Time may monuments ding doun,
> > An' tow'rs an' wa's maun a' decay;
> Enduring—deathless—noble Chief,
> > Thy name can never pass away.
>
> Gi'e pillar'd fame to common men,—
> > Nae need o' cairns for ane like thee;
> In ev'ry cave, wood, hill, and glen,
> > Wallace! remembered aye shall be.

One can well imagine what Nairne would have thought of the Victorian-era Gothic tower that now stands as the national monument to Wallace or of the authenticity

LADY NAIRNE

of the "national" feeling that raised the money to build it. This kind of forgetting in empty memorialization is precisely what the "rougher hands" of the poem seek to accomplish. The only true national response, the only way to "hain / Remains o' Scottish chivalry," is to leave the tower as it is. Moreover, the "mossy stane / Tellin' o' nation's rivalry" is the form of Scottish epic itself, the irreducible element that cannot be added to or detracted from. As Bakhtin puts it, "The epic world knows only a single and unified world view, obligatory and indubitably true for heroes as well as for authors and audiences."[45] Imitation, interpretation, and agrarian capitalism are violations.

It appears that the "unkent muse" has come forth: he is William Wallace. The poet turns in disgust from memorialization and directly addresses the chieftain by name, collapsing the chain of signification in the poem that batters at the "deathless" chieftain in a vain effort to overwrite Scotland's epic narrative. The elegy is not *for* Wallace or the heroic past he embodies but *by* Wallace for the country—and the nation—that its people have forgotten by talking "about it" too much. As in epic, there can be no distance between thought and action, no consciousness of time and history, no talking "about it" too much. To narrate a memory is to destroy it, to subject it to the solvent of time and "interest." "Bonny Gascon Ha'" describes nothing, remembers nothing, signifies nothing. It can only gesture in the direction of an epic wholeness entirely embodied in and identical with the nation itself.

We have reached an impasse. If poetry of the nation in its epic sense can only degrade it, then what, if anything, can be recuperated through the kind of literary nationalism in which Burns, Nairne, and others appear to be engaged? To ask this question another way, if one objective of poems such as "Bonny Gascon Ha'" is to preserve in pristine form the representation of national memory from assimilationist overcoding, what form should it take? As we have seen, each of the poets we have read thus far takes distinctive formal approaches to Scottish national subjects, including those we may think of as "British" or "English." This fact alone suggests the enormously productive nature of this impasse. Because the completeness of the national idea, which is only available in "ancient" forms, cannot be approached through art, the task of the poet is no longer to sing of the nation but to strip of meaning, with violence if necessary, any contemporary use of that term to signify the existence of a political or cultural entity that is the putative heir of its "traditions." Lady Nairne comes not to praise Scotland but to bury it.

[111]

BESIDE THE BARD

JACOBITISM AND THE AESTHETIC OF NATIONAL TRAUMA

If poetry must be silent in order to represent Scotland's true history, however, the experience of exile so prominent in the Jacobite song genre may still provide a basis for an art of national trauma.[46] "Songs of My Native Land" eschews the kind of objectless historical narrative we see in "Bonny Gascon Ha'" and suggests that the memory traces of Scotland's deep past can only be recuperated through transposition to an equally distant and inaccessible future.[47] The first two stanzas of the song rehearse the familiar nostalgia of old age for lost youth, the powerful yearning of an exile for the homeland, the consciousness of experience lamenting a former state of innocence, the memory of paradise. The song marks the nativity (in its national sense) of the singer by briefly dropping from the impeccable Augustan verse to the vernacular description of the "bonnie banks and braes / Where the winding burnie strays," but this is the only verse that betrays a particular national identification. Thus the "native land" of the first verse of the second stanza, while not geographically specific, may suggest local associations, but it may also suppress such associations in favor of an allegorical region, one that transcends and erases national difference. Moreover, it is curious that the "Strains of my native land," while they "thrill the soul," appear to regulate or confine the singer's imagination in some way. The singer apostrophizes these native "strains," lauding the "magic of / Your soft control." This "control," the singer tells us, has often "Soothed the pangs of misery, / Winging rapid thought away / To realms on high," implying that the native "minstrelsy" should distract and console with promises of eternal rest rather than reopening old historical wounds.

This distraction or consolation, though, is likewise another means of restraining the dogs of war pricked and provoked by poetic nationalism. By way of contrast, consider Burns's approach in his song "Frae the Friends and Land I Love" (1792):[48]

> Frae the friends and Land I love,
>   Driv'n by Fortune's felly spite,
> Frae my best Belov'd I rove,
>   Never mair to taste delight.—
> Never mair maun hope to find
>   East frae toil, relief frae care:
> When Remembrance wracks the mind,
>   Pleasures but unveil Despair.
>
> Brightest climes shall mirk appear,
>   Desart ilka blooming shore;

[112]

LADY NAIRNE

> Till the Fates, nae mair severe,
> > Friendship, Love, and Peace restore.—
> Till Revenge, wi' laurell'd head,
> > Bring our Banish'd hame again;
> And ilk loyal, bonie lad
> > Cross the seas, and win his ain.

This counterpart to Burns's better-known Jacobite song "Strathallan's Lament" (1788) seeks not to calm blood still hot from civil conflict but to arouse it.[49] Here the exile's return comes in a storm of steel and shot, his nativity inextricably linked to a specific national relationship with the Stuart cause rather than the sacralized prelapsarian Scotland of childhood. Moreover, Burns's singer equates the "Fates" with "Revenge," and "Friendship, Love, and Peace" with the restoration of the Stuart heir; the song gives no indication of a transcendental space in which the grievances of civil war may be reconciled either in the past or the future, which, as in Nairne, remain inaccessible to both poetry and politics. In this regard, it can be argued that Nairne and Burns approach the question of Scotland's past in much the same fashion (the past is epic and thus closed off to authentically national art), but they part ways with regard to the political uses of that past. To cite another example, the following song appeared without attribution in the *Edinburgh Morning Chronicle* in August 1795. Entitled "Exiles," the song laments the exile of Muir and Palmer following their conviction for sedition:[50]

> Scotland, once our boast, our wonder,
> > Fann'd by Freedom's purer gale,
> When thy Wallace, arm'd with thunder,
> > Bade the baffl'd TYRANT wail:
> O, our Country! Vultures rend thee,
> > Proudly riot on thy store;
> Who deluded, shall befriend thee?
> > Ah! do we thy lot deplore.

Patrick Scott Hogg, who found the song in 1996, has identified a number of markers that indicate Burns's authorship, both in its metrical and musical context and in its use of the Wallace iconography in the Bruce poems.[51] And as Noble and Hogg point out, "It is also wholly characteristic of Burns to take a Jacobite theme and recontextualise it in a Radical context."[52] As we have seen, Nairne does not make similar use of Wallace in "Bonny Gascon Ha'" and other patriotic songs but rather walls off this history and treats subsequent conflicts as essentially random events in an interminable civil-war narrative. At the same time, it might not quite be accurate to say that Burns in "Exiles" (if we accept Burns as the source of the

[113]

BESIDE THE BARD

song) adapts a Jacobite theme to the republican and anti-British context of the mid-1790s. Muir's and Palmer's radicalism, after all, was both cosmopolitan and pan-British, in that it sought to unite the Friends of the People movements in Scotland, Ireland, and England.[53] This ecumenicism seems a long way from Wallace's Scottishness and the assertion of Scottish national independence, and the promiscuous use of Wallace would seem to weaken the persuasiveness of the national epic. For Nairne, it is sincerer to submit to assimilation into British state culture than to brandish Scotland's "Holy of Holies" to even political scores.

Nairne's Jacobite songs, for which she is best known, thus evince a deep ambivalence toward the ethical propriety of using poetry to arouse nationalistic desire, whether for a return to feudal independence or for an advance to egalitarian republicanism.[54] What, then, is the precise function of reviving memories of the lost cause, particularly in the political climate of the late eighteenth century? Or to ask the question in another way, how do Nairne's Jacobite songs assess the permissible uses of the "Charlie trope" and help to establish a poetics of memory that refuses the violence at the heart of the national project itself?

Set to a traditional tune popular in Ireland and Scotland, Nairne's lyrics for "Wha'll Be King but Charlie?" begin by heralding the prince's landing in Scotland and summoning the clansmen to his standard: "Come thro' the heather, around him gather, / Ye're a' the welcomer early; / Around him cling wi' a' your kin; / For wha'll be king but Charlie?"[55] Already in this summons, however, lurks the threat of coercion. While the clansmen and "a' your kin" are invited to "round him gather," the intervening verse warns them that the warmth of their "welcome" will depend on the haste with which they muster to the royal presence. The song thus establishes from the outset a hierarchy that valorizes the true believers, while marginalizing the hesitant trimmers. Viewed through this lens, the herald's call to "crown your rightfu', lawfu' king" implies that putting a Stuart on the throne will merely substitute one system of patronage for another, and the question with which the first stanza concludes—"For wha'll be king but Charlie?"—seems too open-ended and ambiguous to elicit the fanaticism necessary to topple the British monarchy. Moreover, the herald's specific appeal to the MacDonalds anticipates the conflicting loyalties that that would divide Clan Donald between the Jacobites and Hanoverians during the 1745 rising.[56] The herald's nearly palpable anxiety that that the clan will *not* turn out "a' thegither," coupled with the herald's ambivalence toward the question of right, invests the song with a proleptic sense that the cause has already been lost. This prolepsis continues in the following two stanzas, as the herald hopefully proclaims the unification of Scotland behind the rightful monarch. But the poem distinguishes between the alleged commitment of the "Hieland clans" and the Lowland lords and lairds. The clansmen, with their

[114]

LADY NAIRNE

swords in hand, have "to a man declared to stand / Or fa' wi' Royal Charlie," whereas only "mony a lord and laird" have "Declar'd for Scotia's king an' law." This distinction makes explicit the questioning ambivalence of the herald in the first stanza. Does the cause consist in feudal loyalty to the person of the supposed anointed monarch ("Royal Charlie") or in a juridical understanding of succession ("king an' law")? The answer would seem to be both—or neither. When the herald returns again to the question "wha but Charlie?" she prefaces it not in the future tense as before ("wha'll be") but as a self-interrogatory ("speir ye"). Charlie's arrival in Scotland will force each Scot to examine his or her own historicity, the relation of each self to a complex of identities informed by authoritative discourses that appear to justify the destructive conflicts that divide them. For one to declare, to take a stand, requires an answer, not to the question of "wha'll be" but to that of "wha is." The herald's rhetorical query, rather than eliciting an affirmative response prepared in advance and conditioned on an uncertain contingency, functions instead to dissolve the factitious subjectivities that Jacobitism evokes in the minds of auditors to whom the herald appeals. In this sense the song *ostensibly* operates, in Althusserian terms, to interpellate subjects as Jacobites, to remind them that they are in fact the subjects they always have been and will be again.[57] But, at the same time, the belated recognition of this subjectivity—"I was a Jacobite and will declare myself a Jacobite once more"—defers its actuation, shifting the ground in which Jacobitism is rooted in both the distant past and the indefinite future. The present, the question of "wha is," exists rather in the moment in which variant discourses of Jacobite authority—Highland versus Lowland, personal loyalty to "Royal Charlie" versus. allegiance to Scotia's "king an' law"—are placed in direct contradiction. The one cancels out the other, and in the empty space of the present sits the historical fact of the Treaty of Union, the Hanoverian succession, and the British fiscal-military state. By forcing the subject to confront its immediate historical relations in this manner, Nairne's Jacobite song renders the historical impossibility of Jacobitism.

We may presume that the herald's alternative appeals to Highland feudal reminiscences (or, more accurately, warm feelings aroused by the prospect of feudal patronage) or Lowland legal proprieties have not entirely succeeded in stimulating interest in Charlie's cause. The final appeal goes directly to the heart of the matter: masculine aggression and domination of women. Charlie's cause must be "complete an' early," not in order to restore the monarchy, Scottish law, or feudal tradition but as a test of manhood. What rouses men to fight, in the poem's terms, is the threat to masculine dominion, not abstract political theory: "There's ne'er a lass in a' the lan', / But vows baith late an' early, / To man she'll ne'er gie heart nor han' / Wha wadna fecht for Charlie." Moreover, this dominion must be continuously

[115]

BESIDE THE BARD

asserted or forever lost, and it is asserted always and everywhere through warfare undertaken in the name and for the sake of women. Jacobitism, then, refers not only to a historical impasse but also to the misogyny intrinsic to the grammar of gender. To fight for a woman is not to protect her but to reinforce her absence from the competitive masculine order of things. Whether this affirmation flies the flag of Jacobitism or something else matters little, as long as there is another battle to fight.

If, as we have suggested, "Wha'll Be King but Charlie?" invokes the Charlie trope as an instrument for reinscribing patriarchal discourse, what can we make of a song such as "The Women Are A' Gane Wud"?[58] In this version of the Jacobite song, a male narrator bemoans Charlie's arrival in town as disrupting his domestic tranquility:

> The women are a' gane wud,
>   O that he had bidden awa!
> He's turn'd their heads the lad,
>   And ruin will bring on us a'.
>
> I ay was a peaceable man,
>   My wife she did doucely behave;
> But now, do a' that I can,
>   She's just as wild as the lave.
>
> My wife she wears the cockaude,
>   Tho' she kens 'tis the thing that I hate;
> There's ane, too, prined on her maid,
>   An' baith will tak their ain gate.

Here the prince figures as a sexual rival, the cockade as a mark of sexual posses-sion.[59] While Charlie has stolen the narrator's wife, the "Hieland lads" who fol-low in his train have literally eaten the narrator out of house and home; both have deprived him of the property that identifies him as a "man." It is interesting to note that the narrator uses the same term to describe the women and the High-landers ("wild"), perhaps implying that Charlie is as sexually attractive to the lads as he is to the lasses and that the nature of his power lies very much in a charis-matic personality that promotes itself as an object of desire or, to put it another way, as a pure expression of masculine desire that can only be explicitly recognized in the terms of compulsory heterosexuality. As in the previous song, which like-wise deploys Jacobite appeals to elicit an emotional response founded on threat-ened male sexuality, this song carries through on the threat, emasculating the "peaceable man" who refuses to declare himself one way or the other. Having lost the ability to brandish his property as a badge of masculinity, the woeful narrator,

[116]

who takes "nae part at a'," can no longer function within a political and economic system that demands that he take a side, if only to prove that he is a man.

The narrator concludes the poem by attempting to turn the tables on the persecutors who beset him from "baith sides." By associating the Jacobite cause with the return of papal authority, he rearticulates the anxiety of emasculation in terms of the threat of invasion by Catholic predators who seduce innocent Protestant women into acts of unspeakable Gothic horror and debauchery. This association also links back to the suggestion in the second stanza that Charlie's potentially homoerotic appeal is part and parcel of his false religious doctrine; indeed, as he passes by, Charlie leaves a lingering whiff of brimstone in the air. By positing Jacobitism as *itself* emasculating, "The Women Are A' Gane Wud" reverses the appeal to the auditor's manhood in "Wha'll Be King but Charlie?" and refigures authentic masculinity as a refusal of political commitment. But in both cases women lie at the heart of contending models of male self-assertion, in which the positive and negative uses of Jacobitism to define masculinity share common ground.

A wonderfully comic dialogue poem, "Ye'll Mount, Gudeman," reverses the polarity of "The Women Are A' Gane Wud" yet again by positioning its feminine protagonist as a rational actor faced with her husband's Jacobite "madness."[60] Here the "wud" woman, rather than responding conventionally to Jacobitic youth and beauty, assaults her husband in order to save him. As we have seen, the recurring question "But what ails the woman?" seems central to the enterprise of Jacobitism itself, which Nairne's songs and poems characterize as a complex interrelationship of gender, desire, and lack that produces a wide range of subjectivities. Indeed, Nairne's refusal to conflate Jacobitism and Scottish patriotism, or to overdetermine Jacobitism in terms of nostalgia or cultural nationalism, can be viewed as an influential counternarrative to the post-Union settlement, distinct from, for example, Burns's powerfully tragic "There'll Never Be Peace till Jamie Comes Hame" (1791):

> My seven braw sons for Jamie drew sword,
> But now I greet round their green beds in the yerd;
> It brak the sweet heart o' my faithfu' auld Dame,
> There'll never be peace till Jamie comes hame.—
> Now life is a burden and bows me down,
> Sin I tint my bairns, and he tint his crown;
> But till my last moments my words are the same,
> There'll never be peace till Jamie comes hame.—[61]

Hogg and Noble suggest that this poem does not merely gesture toward an "irretrievable" past but may have "a disturbing, resurrectionary potential as a prelude

[117]

BESIDE THE BARD

to political action."[62] If this is the case, how might we understand Nairne's comic response to the deeply traumatized experience of Jacobite rebellion related in Burns's song? Nairne's poem gives agency to the "faithfu' auld Dame" whose bereavement is known only through the masculine perspective of the song. Burns's speaker implies that the Dame gave her sons as a willing sacrifice to the cause, but even he seems to doubt the value of this gift; his "words are the same," but the "burden" that "bows him down" signifies a grief that the old slogans can no longer recuperate. In Nairne's version, however, the leddy interdicts the conventional yet inadequate narrative of loss and sacrifice, a self-assertion that, though expressed in terms of property, effectively neutralizes the "resurrectionary potential" of the laird's "true loyaltie." She asserts the only power available to her in a social order that grants men possessory rights to women as a means of preserving property: she instigates a rebellion of *property* in the defense of *propriety*, the property in herself that lies beyond her husband's proprietorship. Her remark "Had I kent the gudeman wad hae had siccan pain, / The kettle, for me, sud hae couped its lane" points in the direction of a domestic rebellion with perhaps more "resurrectionary potential" than a revolution that simply trades one feudal lord for another. When kettles begin jumping off stoves to attack menfolk bent on killing one another as part of a preening, atavistic display of homoerotic, chivalrous desire, then a space for political action may open that avoids the ritual slaughter of so many sacrificial lambs. It is not much to hope for, but perhaps in the long run the liberatory possibilities of revised gender relations might be the only means of redressing the extreme masculine violence that is the stuff of "history."

As we see in the lovely lament "The Lass of Livingstane," historical trauma is inscribed directly on the bodies of women, as well as in the collective memory of the nation as experienced by women:[63]

> Oh! wha will dry the dreeping tear,
>   She sheds her lane, she sheds her lane?
> Or wha the bonnie lass will cheer,
>   Of Livingstane, of Livingstane?
> The crown was half on Charlie's head,
>   Ae gladsome day, ae gladsome day;
> The lads that shouted joy to him
>   Are in the clay, are in the clay.
>
> Her waddin' gown was wyl'd and won,
>   It ne'er was on, it ne'er was on;
> Culloden field's his lowly bed,
>   She thought upon, she thought upon.
> The bloom has faded frae her cheek

[118]

In youthfu' prime, in youthfu' prime;
And sorrow's with'ring hand has done
The deed o' time, the deed o' time.

For the bereft women, however, such artifacts as martial honor neither console nor compensate. The marriage bed has become a grave, the bride's youth and beauty ravaged by grief and loneliness. With no remaining social function—all the lads "are in the clay"—the Lass of Livingstane becomes the thing she is named. Indeed, her death is predetermined by a kind of cultural suttee, an aesthetically beautiful self-immolation, to which the lovers and wives of dead soldiers are condemned, regardless of to whose side they belong. Burns's song "The Sodger's Return" articulates this expectation in disarmingly conventional terms:

The wars are o'er, and I'm come hame,
    And find thee still true-hearted;
Tho' poor in gear, we're rich in love,
    And mair,—we'se ne'er be parted!
Quo' she, my grandsire left me gowd,
    A mailen plenish'd fairly;
And come, my faithfu' sodger lad,
    Thou 'rt welcome to it dearly![64]

Patriotic discourses, whether deployed in the service of the imperial state or other national idea, depend on women remaining bound to property through the patrilineal line. If every time men went to war women declared their independence, there would not be much of a market for the parades, pageants, and ceremonials that glorify the nation. In the poetry of patriotism, men owe a duty of absolute loyalty to a national cause, while women owe that duty to men. Nairne asks whether women can properly be said to have a nation at all.

Women in Nairne's Jacobite poetry possess, at best, a derivative form of self-identification. But in "My Bonnie Hieland Laddie," Nairne extends her analysis of the gendered Scottish nation to question whether women's subjectivity is possible within a national narrative, particularly if that narrative is fundamentally chivalric.[65] The poem begins conventionally with the prince's landing in Scotland, but it quickly becomes evident that the female narrator can only parrot the masculinized rhetorical figures of Jacobitism:

Prince Charlie he's cum owre frae France,
    In Scotland to proclaim his daddie;
May Heaven still his cause advance,
    And shield him in his Hieland plaidie.

BESIDE THE BARD

> O my bonnie Hieland laddie,
> My handsome, charming Hieland laddie!
> May Heaven still his cause advance,
> And shield him in his Hieland plaidie

The images and signs of patriarchy overflow the poem's formal structure: prince, daddie, laddie, God. The prince's "cause" is figured simultaneously as a righteous and an erotic crusade, in which the apostolic character of the prince / Hieland laddie mixes with his charismatic sexual appeal (handsome, charming). In the second and third stanzas, the prince's overdetermined masculine beauty also reveals a homoerotic aspect, as his "gracefu' looks . . . / Made a' our true Scots hearts to warm." Indeed, the prince's power and authority seem entirely sourced in his body. Identified in the first stanza by legitimizing discourses of divine right, legal entitlement, and blood, here the patriarch's gaze transfixes the nation, eliciting from all "true Scots" a powerful emotional and physical response.[66] By contrast, the emasculated and sexually inadequate Geordie offers a union based on "commerce," recalling the opprobrium attached to the exchange of English gold for Scottish independence in 1707. Scottish nationalism thus inheres in a kind of collective unconscious, a deep structure of desire, which awakens when called forth by the God/king/father/lover, rather than in juridical, political, or feudal arrangements or "constitutions." One might even argue that this deep structure, as figured in the song, resembles a relationship in which "true Scots hearts" recognize in the father their own lack of a unified subjectivity, a recognition that the poem figures in highly eroticized terms of sexual union.

The romance closes with the language of marital fidelity ("And there's no ane amang them a' / That wad betray their Hieland laddie"). But this duty of loyalty runs in only one direction, as one would expect in romance. The "Hieland folks," whose desire for the God/king/father/lover figure unleashes the insurrectionary Id of Jacobitism and enables the marital union of the father and the Scots, are no more "free" in Charlie's embrace than they are in Geordie's. That "there's no ane amang them a', / That wad betray their Hieland laddie" goes without saying, as the father merges with the nation, subsuming it under the sign of divinely sanctioned "cause." As we have seen in "The Lass of Livingstane," where the consequences of masculine aggression always and everywhere fall on the broken women who remain to bear the physical and emotional traces of national trauma, the collectivized bride-nation in "My Bonnie Hieland Laddie" will suffer the same fate when Charlie, his cause in ruins, betrays it. Jacobitism cannot escape the mandate of its own romantic imaginary. It is about men competing violently with other men to "win" the body of a woman, figured as the girl—or the nation—left behind.

[120]

LADY NAIRNE

The beautiful lyrics of "The White Rose o' June" further reveal the gendered violence of representations of Jacobitism.[67] This song recasts the traditional "Ranting Roving Lad," published by David Herd, as well as Burns's own resetting of that traditional version, "The White Cockade" (1790):[68]

> My love was born in Aberdeen,
> The boniest lad that e'er was seen,
> But now he makes our hearts fu' sad,
> He takes the field wi' his White Cockade.[69]

> CHORUS
> O, he's a ranting, roving lad,
> He is a brisk an' a bonie lad;
> Betide what may, I will be wed,
> And follow the boy wi' the White Cockade.

> I'll sell my rock, my reel, my tow,
> My guid gray mare and hawkit cow;
> To buy myself a tartan plaid,
> To follow the boy wi' the White Cockade.
>   O he's a ranting, &c.

The traditional and Burns's renditions maintain the simple (and lovely) identification of the Jacobite cause with masculine youth and beauty, embodied in the song both by the speaker's lover and the bonnie prince himself. Indeed, here we see that Jacobitism relies on its sartorial attractiveness and its appeal to restless young men, discontented with the poverty and drudgery of life among the laboring poor. The lover's intention to sell her means of subsistence and follow the Pretender's army likewise indicates the decline of the traditional economy and the community it sustains, even if only by the barest margin. The "boy wi' the White Cockade" thus synecdochically figures a confluence of historical, social, economic, and political forces operating on the community, broadly conceived as "Scotland" under the rule of the British state. In Nairne's version, rather, the sign "white rose" defers such rough and ready identifications:

> Now the bricht sun, and the soft summer showers,
> Deck a' the woods and the gardens wi' flowers—
> But bonny and sweet though the hale o' them be,
> There's ane aboon a' that is dearest to me;
> An' oh, that's the white rose, the white rose o' June,
> An' may *he* that should wear it come back again sune!

[121]

BESIDE THE BARD

> It's no on my breast, nor yet in my hair,
> That the emblem dear I venture to wear;
> But it blooms in my heart, and its white leaves I weet,
> When alane in the gloamin' I wander to greet,
> O'er the white rose, the white rose, the white rose o' June,
> An' may *he* that should wear it come back again sune!

Nairne suppresses Burns's direct reference to the lover's sweetheart as a soldier in the Jacobite army, bringing it somewhat closer to the traditional song's initial emphasis on the lover's nonspecific restlessness. But Nairne substantially revises both songs by refiguring the "boniest lad" as the masculine third-person pronoun "he" and deferring its introduction until the end of the first stanza. While this usage emphasizes the conflation of the lover's and the Pretender's respective identities into the more general Jacobite trope of youth and beauty, it also concentrates attention on the feminine narrator rather than on the "ranting, roving lad" and eliminates any clear indication that the boy is the narrator's lover. Nairne further alters and varies the song's refrain so that it is slightly different in each stanza. The repetition of the phrase "the white rose, the white rose o' June" remains constant, but its modifiers change. In the first stanza, the narrator distinguishes the rose ("that's the white rose") from the other flora in the woods and gardens as "dearest" to her. Only then does she express her desire for the absent presence in the poem, the *he* that wears the rose. In the second stanza, the narrator describes the "emblem" of the Jacobites as "blooming" in her heart, rather than as the external sign of a political commitment. When she walks in the woods at dusk, she weeps "o'er" the white rose as she contemplates *his* return. Nairne thus reverses the spatial and emotional hierarchy of both traditional settings, which view the "roving laddie"—and Jacobitism itself—as an active force and his lover as pulled into his orbit. In Nairne's version, rather, the female narrator's desire acts on the indeterminate masculine absence, but only to defer, if not to repel, its return. The repetition of the final verse of each stanza, "An' may *he* that should wear it come back again sune," further distances the presumed object of her longing through the double usage of conditional modal auxiliaries "may" and "should." This grammatical deferral emphasizes the fact that the narrator's desire for the "white rose o' June" can only be fully satisfied in the melancholic and historical stasis of an eternal present, in which the hypothetical future return of the lover/prince/king is forever held in abeyance.

In the third and fourth stanzas, it becomes clear that the narrator can expect no such return. As the red rose forces itself into the narrator's field of vision, the lack at the center of her Jacobite desire fully reveals itself as Scotland. Moreover, as we have seen in many of the poems and songs we have discussed to this point,

[122]

LADY NAIRNE

the narrator concedes the historical substitution of the "fragrant and rich" red rose of England for the "scathed" and "blighted" white, while simultaneously denying it emotional allegiance ("there is nae spell to bind it to me"). The song's refrain becomes a dirge in the third stanza, where the fading white rose is apostrophized with the "O," the infinite circle with an absent center, the zero, the absolute and unimaginable state of nonbeing. The fourth stanza completes this process of exile, eulogy, and entombment. It is not even clear what type of agency exists in this world; the same "blast that tears the skies," while rooting England's "native oak" in James Thomson's "Ode: Rule, Britannia" (1740), has scattered Scotland's "true hearts" to the winds.[70] To "sing" the white rose, as the narrator implores, is to sing a silence. The only vestige of Scotland's auld crown, itself a ring that encloses an absence, is the *O* shape of the singer's lips as she utters her soundless lament.

THE DESERTED NATION: SCOTLAND AND THE FIGURE OF WOMAN

One of Nairne's most popular and beautiful poems, "The Lass o' Gowrie," announces itself as politically innocent in contrast to the overt political intensity of, for example, "The Banks of the Earn."[71] Yet the conventional pastoral casting of the poem masks a narrative of social displacement and emotional dislocation that attaches to Scotland's loss of territorial sovereignty and breaks down the moral coherence of traditional local and national identities. Composed in three octaves, each embedded quatrain consisting of three rhymed octosyllabic verses followed by an irregular refrain that returns to the poem's beginning ("Gowrie"), the poem places a young woman before a particularized landscape:

> 'Twas on a summer's afternoon,
> A wee afore the sun gaed doun,
> A lassie wi' a braw new goun
>   Came owre the hills to Gowrie.
> The rose-bud wash'd in summer's shower,
> Bloom'd fresh within the sunny bower;
> But Kitty was the fairest flower
>   That e'er was seen in Gowrie.

The first quatrain strongly differentiates the woman's appearance from the Edenic natural background. Her "braw new goun" marks her difference from nature, indicating on one hand her objective condition as social and sexual currency and on the other her objectified threat as a seductress. Her arrival in Gowrie, the site of

[123]

BESIDE THE BARD

Scotland's most fertile farmland (the "Eden," or Garden of Scotland) and the coronation seat of its ancient kings (the source of patriarchal authority), seems portentous and tracks the woman's dual identification.[72] In the first four lines the observer speaks heavily in the vernacular, emphasizing the historically specific social milieu in which the woman appears as the object of desire, even while suggesting that Gowrie simultaneously exists in the dimension of biblical or mythological prehistory.

The second quatrain ramifies this double allusion, emphasizing the woman's virginity amid the mounting sexual desire of the observer, who, in the poetic convention of romance, imagines "Kitty" as a rosebud. Accordingly, the observer's language shifts from the vernacular to a standardized English idiom. The observer's allusion to the "bower" heightens the prelapsarian tension of the scene, recalling the ambiguous introduction of Eve in book 4 of *Paradise Lost*, in which the innocent and unselfconscious sexual play is undercut by Eve's narcissistic fascination with her own image in the pool. The summer shower that has freshened the rose further suggests the woman's Miltonic self-regarding yet unrealized "vanity," the sin of pride always lurking in a woman's beauty, even as that beauty provokes in the observer the sin of lust while excusing it. Even the name "Kitty" suggests that the woman is trembling on the threshold of a change in her moral, as well as sexual, nature, as the innocent and playful kitten gives way to the devious and selfish cat. It is as if the fall has already happened, as indeed it has, and the poem's refrain— Eden/Gowrie—sounds like the tolling of a funeral bell.

The second octave takes up the prelapsarian setting of the first but with a creeping sensation of the observer's anxiety: "To see her cousin she cam' there; / An' oh! the scene was passing fair; / For what in Scotland can compare / Wi' the Carse o' Gowrie?" The observer feels obliged to disclose in passing that Kitty has come on family business, but his narrative abruptly shifts from this mundane and unpersuasive facticity to a panegyric more suitable to the pastoral frame. Once again, as in Milton, paradise appears never lovelier than in the moment immediately preceding its loss. For the second time in the poem, the observer alludes to the setting sun, as Kitty has arrived in the long twilight of a midsummer's eve. The image of the "blue hills melting into gray" possibly refers to the Sidlaw Hills from whence Kitty has come, the *Na Sidhbheanntan* of ancient times, with their cairns and supernatural associations with fairies. If Kitty recalls Eve in the first octave, here she might recall Titania, the unhappy goddess/wife in Shakespeare, whose love for a boy has disturbed the settled order of the fairy kingdom. As in the second quatrain in the first octave, the observer continues speaking in a stylized conventional voice, waxing rhapsodic on the beauty of the garden, as if trying to avoid the sense of disruption and estrangement wafted in with Eve/Kitty's appear-

[124]

LADY NAIRNE

ance. The observer asks uncertainly whether anything in Scotland can compare with the Carse o' Gowrie, as if seeking affirmation in the face of gnawing doubt.

The third octave reveals the observer's insincerity in previous ones, retrospectively clarifying his interest in the "braw new goun" that identifies Kitty as the desired object of his narrative snare. Pastoral and romance are here revealed as mechanisms by which the patriarchy has preordered the way of things in Paradise, whether the Father is figured as the God of Eden or Scotland's immemorial line of monarchs crowned at the ancient seat of royal power. The woman, with her maternal, natural, and demonic associations, has been created solely to fulfill the observer's desire. She has been fashioned from his body (Eve/imagination/fairy queen) for the sole purpose of gratifying his sexual and economic demands. The hard yet brittle casing of formal pastoral language shatters into the vernacular once more, as the observer's "wooing" takes on the cold instrumentality of social circulation and economic exchange. "Truth and constancy," the formal language of love, rapidly gives way to property concerns, as the wooer points to his "father's ha'" securely fortified against the blasts of nature. The Carse o' Gowrie, it seems, was never an Eden at all, just as Eden was not. Eve/Kitty appears in Eden/Gowrie when summoned, the lover's vows as illusory as Paradise itself. Only when Kitty sees the property does the lover's suit advance, her destiny always already fulfilled as property. The deal has already been struck, the preexisting contract solemnized, the transaction concluded. The poetic conventions of romance may now be dispensed with.

And so they are:

> Her faither was baith glad and wae;
> Her mither she wad naething say;
> The bairnies thocht they wad get play,
>   If Kitty gaed to Gowrie.
> She whiles did smile, she whiles did greet,
> The blush and tear were on her cheek—
> She naething said, an' hung her head;
>   But now she's Leddy Gowrie.

Here Kitty is bought and paid for in the crudest possible terms. Her father, delighted to get an unmarried daughter off his hands but reluctant to part with her dowry, her silent mother who knows her daughter's fate only too well, her younger siblings being fattened for the slaughter—all is as it is and always shall be. Kitty submits to the yoke, which has always been implicit in her existence, and disappears into *couverture*, just as all daughters of Eve. It is noteworthy that her title as "Leddy Gowrie" refers not to the local estate into which she has merged but to the chief

[125]

province and seat of authority of the ancient and independent Kingdom of Scotland itself. The poem's refrain, it seems, has always been she.

Though we have read the poem in feminist terms, the poem's politics of place seem no less urgent than those of "The Banks of the Earn." While the heir of Gowrie seems to have assured the continuation of the family property and the national hierarchy it supports, he nevertheless betrays a consciousness of the irremediable loss involved in the eternal transaction in which women are converted from one category or property into another. He knows enough to notice that Leddy Gowrie's "blush and tear" reveal the psychic cost of making the continued existence of nation dependent on the trade in women and their dualistic representation as generative and destructive, undercutting the notion of "Scotland" and its "brave sons" imagined in "The Banks of the Earn" and similar belated, national narratives. Indeed, the Scottish nation, like the feudal patriarchy that erected it, is as anachronistic as pastoral love poetry in the "polite and commercial" society of the eighteenth-century British state. "The Lass o' Gowrie" uncovers a deep-seated discontent, not only with old aesthetic, economic, and social forms and structures but with the late eighteenth-century North British conception of Scotland. As if Scotland's status in Britain as a junior partner at best and internal colony at worst were not galling enough to poets such as Burns and Nairne, Nairne goes beyond Burns to deconstruct the manly, martial representations of Scottish nationhood. Restoring Scotland's ancient independence may be desirable at some level, but it may not make any difference if the social and economic base that produces a figure such as Leddy Gowrie remains untransformed.

5

"IN THE SHADOW OF BURNS"

Robert Tannahill

ROBERT TANNAHILL, FOUNDER of the Paisley Burns Club and eulogist of the exiled Alexander Wilson, may have fancied himself as Burns's and Wilson's literary heir. Another of radical Renfrew's well-educated weaver poets, Tannahill was born in Paisley in 1774 and raised at the loom as an apprentice to his father, a silk gauze weaver, from the age of twelve. After two years working as a weaver in Lancashire, he returned to Paisley to tend his dying father in late 1801 or early 1802. There he lived with his mother until his death by suicide in 1810. Early biographers portray the sensitive and isolated Tannahill as living in desperate poverty, but other versions of his life, most notably that given by David Semple in 1876, depict a more comfortable and sociable Tannahill, who had money in a savings bank, served as the first secretary of the Paisley Burns Club, and was courted by admirers and fellow poets, including the Ettrick Shepherd.[1] But the predominant view is that Tannahill never achieved financial security. As Ian Duncan and Sheila Kidd have recently noted, although "Tannahill's songs enjoyed enormous nineteenth-century popularity," it came "too late . . . to lift him out of poverty and obscurity."[2]

Despite his poverty, in collaboration with the weaver and composer Robert Archibald Smith, as well as the musicians James Barr of Kilbarchan and John Ross of Aberdeen, Tannahill enjoyed notable success as a songwriter and compiler during his brief lifetime.[3] William Donaldson's biography emphasizes the usual eighteenth-century influences, Thomson, Shenstone, and especially Burns. Tannahill likewise "'mended' folk-songs," but his original songs, such as "Jessie, the Flower o' Dunblane," "Oh, Are Ye Sleeping, Maggie," "Thou Bonnie Wood o' Craiglea," and "Gloomy Winter's Now Awa'" further secured his posthumous reputation in the Victorian era. According to Donaldson, Tannahill's "stress on the

[127]

naivety of his work was misleading," and his real audience, like Lady Nairne's, consisted of "the burgeoning new early nineteenth-century drawing-room market, whose demand for popular art-songs, arranged for one or more voices with accompaniment for the piano and other instruments, was beginning to become commercially significant."[4] Indeed, as Penny Fielding notes, in the nineteenth century "Scottish song became a form of cultural capital in which certain distinctive qualities of Scottish language were drawn into a more generalised, polite version of labouring-class culture for middle-class consumption."[5] The weaver poet Tannahill's art thus fed the cultural appetite for "improvement" in bourgeois Britain.[6]

At the same time, Corey Andrews writes, "Throughout his brief career, Tannahill was acutely aware of writing in the shadow of Burns."[7] Certainly, Tannahill's shrewd appraisal of the commercial possibilities of antiquarian collecting and songwriting tapped by Burns, Walter Scott, and James Hogg promised a means of earning a living wage from his art that was not available to other weaver poets.[8] Tannahill apparently began submitting his songs and verse to periodical publications in London as early as 1800, when "Jessie, the Flower o' Dunblane" first appeared.[9] He published several songs in Glasgow in 1805, including some of his Burns poetry, and in the *Paisley Repository*, edited by the bookseller John Miller. Tannahill's dramatic poem in two acts, "The Soldier's Return," appeared first in this publication, together with "The Recruiting Drum" and "The Old Beggar." Donaldson and other biographers concur that Tannahill's songs quickly became popular because "his lyrics were easily committed to memory, particularly by the gentler sex," and in "every company where singing delighted the ear, in the cottage, in the hall, at concerts, and in theaters they were heard."[10] His first and only volume of poetry was published by subscription in 1807, selling out all nine hundred copies printed. When Tannahill proposed an expanded second edition to Archibald Constable, who turned it down, the poet responded by burning his manuscripts and descending into depression.[11] He continued to send both new and revised songs to various periodicals, including the *Scots Magazine*, until the year of his death. Subsequently, editions of Tannahill's poetry, some with memoirs penned by his friend and collaborator Robert Smith and selections of his correspondence, appeared throughout the nineteenth century in Scotland, England, Ireland, and the United States.[12] Tannahill's "The Soldier's Return" and "Jessie, the Flower o' Dunblane" were particularly popular in separate publication into the twentieth century, and "Jessie" continues in publication in digital media form on myriad British and American websites and even YouTube videos.

[128]

THE "PATRIOT" BARD?

Is there a "radical" Tannahill in the mold of Burns or Wilson to be found here, or simply an aspiring laboring-class producer of aesthetic goods for commercial sale? Christopher Harvie thinks that there may be a radical Tannahill, pointing out that Tannahill's Burns Anniversary Society in Paisley (1805) was subscribed by manufacturers, shopkeepers, and other employers who had been journeymen handloom weavers or employees in other trades, including James Scullock, James Tannahill, and William M'Laren, and who had in the early 1790s taken up French revolutionary ideals. Harvie also traces Burns's impact on the lower middling and working classes, artisans, tradespeople, small employers, and shopkeepers and concludes that Burns's "radicalism" may not have been an entirely posthumous production but was felt in the historical moment as well.[13] Steve Sweeney-Turner argues more forcefully for the radical politics of the self-described "unlettered Mechanic" who "co-founded the Paisley Literary *and Political* Club" and lived "in the midst of a growing Radical, Chartist and Republican hotbed of dissent in a 'disorganic' Paisley under the widespread influence of groups from the United Scotsmen through the Friends of the People."[14] Still, there is no record of Tannahill engaging in any specific political commitments or controversies of the kind that ended in Wilson's exile, nor do we find much in the way of imitation of Burns's republicanism. But Tannahill's active participation in the establishment of the Burns cult in the years immediately following the bard's death, rather than signifying a bourgeois appropriation of Burns, may suggest a more politically charged version of the weaver poet. Moreover, as Sweeney-Turner has argued, "it seems difficult to deny the political potential of his *reception* within his own class and profession."[15] Consider, for example, the following song, composed in 1807 in honor of Burns's birthday, to the accompaniment of the air "Britons, Who for Freedom Bled":[16]

> Haughty Gallia threats our coast,
> > We hear her vaunts with disregard,
> Secure in valour, still we boast
> > "The Patriot, and the Patriot-bard.
> > > But chiefly, BURNS, &etc.

> Yes, Caledonians! to our country true,
> Which Danes nor Romans could subdue,
> Firmly resolv'd our native rights to guard,
> Let's toast "The Patriot, and the Patriot-bard."

BESIDE THE BARD

Like Burns's "Does Haughty Gaul Invasion Threat?" (or "The Dumfries Volunteers," 1795), composed under a previous threat of French invasion, this is a fine drinking song, indeed, and its surficial ambiguity assures that no revelers will offend loyalist sensibilities.[17] But as an ostensible tribute to the "Patriot, and the Patriot-bard," the song complicates Burns's relation to those flattering epithets.[18] Composed as a proper Augustan ode, the song refuses the vernacular of its model, in effect "royalizing" the panegyric to the ploughman. While there may also be a Thomsonian gesture to a "Scottish" tradition, the song carries virtually no trace of nativity.[19] Burns appears as the "chief" of "ye glorious sons of song," but the singer omits the usual mention of Ramsay and Fergusson, leaving it unclear precisely who the other honored Scottish poets might be. Similarly, the panegyrist refers to the "Fathers of our country's weal, / Sternly virtuous, bold and free," presumably implying the roll call of Scottish heroes from the days of Bruce and Wallace. But rather than invoke the specific patriotic tradition of the Wars of Independence, the poet "others" the Danes and the Romans, hardly stirring stuff, it would seem, for "Caledonians . . . true." Does this archaism imply a tacit recognition that Caledonia really is a northern province of Anglo-Saxon Britain, whose enemies are the enemies of England, not the Anglo-Norman conquerors who strove to subject an independent Scotland to feudal vassalage?[20] Indeed, while the refrain insists that "Engrav'd in every Scotsman's breast, / Thy name, thy worth, shall ever be," one cannot help wonder how that inscription actually reads. Burns's patriotic appeal, whether in republican or Jacobite form, often comes off as unambiguously anti-*English* in a broad sense.[21] As we have seen, the composer suppresses this Anglophobia in the form, the content, and even the tune of the song. The question is whether we are to read this act of violence to Burns's poetic legacy (even in Burns's "loyalist" mode, he still says, "But while we sing God Save the KING, / We'll ne'er forget THE PEOPLE!") as an ironic revision dictated by political expediency or a deliberate misprision of Burns for some other purpose.[22]

Tannahill's popular comedy "The Soldier's Return" (1807) may help us answer this question.[23] Set to music by the distinguished Aberdonian musician John Ross, the following tribute to the Cameron Highlanders, veterans of several major engagements during the French war, divides the first and second scenes of the first act:

> Our bonnie Scots lads in their green tartan plaids,
>> Their blue belted bonnets, an feathers saw braw,
> Rankt up on the green, war fair tae be seen,
>> But my bonnie young laddie was fairest o' a';
> His cheeks were as red as the sweet heather bell,
>> Or the red western clud looking doun on the snaw,

[130]

His lang yellow hair owre his braid shoulders fell,
 An the een o' the lasses were fixed on him a'.

My heart sank wi' wae on the wearifu' day,
 When torn frae my bosom they march'd him awa',
He bade me fareweel, he cried "O be leel,"
 An' his red cheeks were wet wi' the tears that did fa',
Ah! Harry, my love, tho' thou ne'er shoudst return,
 Till life's latest hour I thy absence will mourn,
An' memory shall fade, like the leaf on the tree,
 E'er my heart spare ae thocht on anither but thee.

The song draws deeply on Jacobite typology, rehearsing the sexualized figure of the tartaned and feathered "bonnie young laddie" with "His lang yellow hair," as well as the "leel" sweetheart's vow of celibacy until his return, in this life or the next. But, in a manner similar to the Anglicization of Burns in the previous ode, it appears to redirect the insurrectionary energy of Scottish patriotism to endorse royalist political and imperial aims. These "bonnie Scots lads" are regular British military, and the enemy they march off to fight is Scotland's former partner in the "Auld Alliance." In the surrounding comedy, the heroine, Jeanie, betrothed to the local laird's servant who has followed his master to fight the French in Egypt (the somewhat incongruously named Hielan Harry), has been promised in marriage to an aging but wealthy bachelor, the buffoonish Muirlan Willie. Harry returns from battle, having saved the life of his laird, setting up a generational confrontation between the lovelorn Jeanie and her mother:

>   *Jean*. Mither, ae simple question let me speir,—
> Is Muirlan fat or fair wi' a' his geir?
> Auld croichlin wicht, tae hide the ails o' age,
> He capers like a monkey on a stage;
> An' cracks, an' sings, an giggles sae licht an kittle,
> Wi's auld beard slavered wi' tobacco spittle.—
>
>   *Mir*. Peace, wardless slut—O, whan will youth be wise!
> Ye'll slicht your *carefu'* mither's gude advice:
> I've brocht you up, an made ye what ye are;
> An' that's your *thanks* for a' my toil an' care:
> Muirlan comes doon this nicht, sae drap your stodgin,
> For ye must gie consent or change your lodgin'.

The comedy displaces the blocking paternal authority from Jeanie's father, Gaffer (the laird's tenant), who thinks his daughter's marriage with Muirlan a perversion

BESIDE THE BARD

of nature, to the scheming and covetous mother figure, Mirren. Muirlan, on the other hand, is feminized, portrayed as an addle-pated, gossipy old crone. In this respect, the Mirren-Muirlan pair stands for a traditional communal organization that consolidates wealth through the exchange of women. But this community has no positive valence in the comedy, which paradoxically aligns feudal hierarchy (laird/tenant/servant) with the proposition that, as Jeanie holds, "Love shoud be free." But what liberates "Love" is not the law of nature or an ideology of affective individualism and companionate marriage but Harry's devotion to the British state, symbolized in the play by his rescue of the laird:

> Then, as our rowers strove with lengthen'd sweep,
> Back from the stern I tumbl'd in the deep,
> And sure had perish'd, for each pressing wave
> Seem'd emulous to be a soldier's grave;
> Had not this gallant youth, at danger's shrine,
> Off'ring his life a sacrifice for mine,
> Leap'd from the boat and beat his billowy way,
> To where I belch'd and struggl'd in the sea;
> With god-like arm sustain'd life's sinking hope,
> Till the succeeding rowers pick'd us up.

"Hielan" Harry, who reveals that he is an orphan, turns down the grateful laird's offer to "raise his fortune," instead asking the laird to sponsor his marriage to Jeanie:

> Then, as in warmth I prais'd his good behaviour,
> He modestly besought me this one *favour*,
> That, if surviving when the war was o'er,
> And safe return'd to Scotia once more,
> I'd ask your will for him to wed your daughter;
> A manly, virtuous heart he home hath brought her.

The laird complies and soothes Mirren's ruffled feathers by giving her a gold ring, prompting her to exclaim, "It's goud, it's goud! O yes, sir—I agree. / Gaffer, it's goud! Yes, "Luve *shou'd aye be free!*"

This poem concocts a complex recipe for Anglo-Scottish or "North British" identity. The Jacobite figure of the "bonnie Hielan laddie" is first assimilated to an Anglicized Lowland social organization, where his native martial qualities can be used to protect the military fiscal state that his kinfolk once attempted to overthrow. Jeanie's erotic attraction to him, as in Jacobite romance, is closely identified with this martial habitus, as indicated in the marching song that frames the

[132]

comic treatment of Jeanie's love dilemma, but Harry nonetheless indicates his acculturation by speaking in perfect, high-minded Augustan heroic couplets (he apparently has forgotten Gaelic), a representative example of which runs, "Great is his soul! soft be his bed or rest, / Whose *only wish* is to make others blest." Mirren's and Muirland's greed and lack of interest in the supposed French threat to Britain's national survival, on the other hand, bolster the same English Scotophobia that the brave Highland regiments put to shame on foreign battlefields. But as T. M. Devine has written, "This 'Highlandism' was quite literally the invention of a tradition. What made it deeply ironic was not simply the actual historic Lowland contempt for ancient Gaelic culture that existed well into the eighteenth century but the fact that Highlandism took off precisely at the same time that commercial landlordism, market pressures and clearances were destroying the old social order in northern Scotland."[24] To make matters worse, as we see in the poem, the Lowland squires have co-opted the Scottish military tradition, which "had long been an important part of Scottish identity; now that was being decked out in Highland colours and the kilted battalions depicted as the direct descendants of the clans."[25] There is a great deal of theatricality in all of this that blurs the lines between Harry's "true" Scottish identity and the "invented" one he performs. Though he and his comrades look like "bonnie Hielan laddies," we cannot be sure that their "green tartan plaids," "blue belted bonnets," and "feathers saw braw" signify any particular "Hielan" heritage at all, much less indicate Scottish martial vigor. Indeed, the young lad must be torn from his lover's breast when "they march'd him awa'," his "red cheeks . . . wet wi' tears that did fa'." Jeanie's account suggests that Hielan Harry, whose martial persona has been created specifically to erase the Gaelic past by dressing it up in stage clothes and giving it a gun with which to kill Frenchmen, may not be a willing participant in this very British enterprise.

Moreover, in this regard, Hielan Harry performs the dual functions of defending the empire (he is sent to fight in Egypt, hardly the place to defend the homeland) and restoring Scotia's damaged reputation for manliness and virtue, which has been degraded by clowns such as Muirlan and conspiratorial women such as Mirren (whose loyalty must be bought with English gold in a kind of reenactment of the Act of Union). The laird legitimizes this new Scottish meritocracy, effectively adopting and gentrifying the orphaned soldier, who loses his "indigenous" Highland nativity and becomes fully incorporated into a deracinated British identity:

> *Harry.* While I was yet a boy, my parents died,
> And left me poor and friendless, wandr'ing wide,
> Your goodness found me, neath your fost'ring care

BESIDE THE BARD

I learn'd those precepts which I'll still revere,
And now, to Heav'n, for length of life I pray,
With filial love your goodness to repay.

The British state, in its "goodness," supposedly "found" the barbaric and benighted Scots, brought them the benefits of enlightened and polite culture and language, and gave them opportunities through war and imperial adventure to justify the subordinate status so generously and paternalistically conferred on them in 1707. As Gaffer opines at the end of the play, "Virtue ever is its own reward," as long as "virtue" is understood as respectful submission to a Scot's betters.

But the apparently anodyne acceptance of an assimilated Britishness featured in "The Soldier's Return" does not necessarily imply a strictly loyalist aesthetic. Virtue may be its own reward, but it must be remembered that in Tannahill's comedy virtue comes packaged with English cash and the promise of imperial opportunities that red Scots pragmatically accepted. This shadowed aspect of British loyalism reveals itself in Tannahill's song "Loudon's Bonnie Woods and Braes."[26] Semple describes the immediate context of the song, a great volunteer review held near Paisley in the fall of 1804:

> The whole of the Volunteers in the County of Renfrew, mustering nearly 5000 strong, were reviewed by the gallant Commander, General the Earl of Moira, on Thursday, the 4th day of October, 1804, in the large field on the north-west side of the Barnsford Bridge, near Walkinshaw, two miles from town. This review was among the earliest, if not the very first of Volunteer Reviews in Scotland, and occurred on a splendid day for the occasion. Business was suspended, and it became a joyous and grand holiday to all classes of the community. The brilliant appearance of so many thousands of Volunteers in their military uniforms,—the beauty and fashion of the surrounding country,—and the vast assemblage of citizens in holiday attire,—was a sight worth seeing. The review was a complete success; and from the cheerful smiles and merry laughs, it was evident that every confidence and reliance was placed in our Scots Volunteer lads that they would defend their households to the death. In the afternoon, an elegant entertainment was given in the Town Hall to his Excellency and suite, and a number of noblemen and gentlemen belonging to the County, officers of Corps, &c., &c. In the evening, his Lordship and suite returned to Glasgow.[27]

Though Tannahill's song was actually written as a tribute to Moira when the nobleman was called to active service in 1807, Semple's Victorian-era account of the solid loyalism of "all classes of the community" seems a far cry from Wilson's reading of Paisley as riven by class antagonism. While the threat of French invasion

[134]

"IN THE SHADOW OF BURNS"

and the rush to arms of the local volunteers (which included two of Tannahill's brothers) appear to have a leveling and unifying effect, Semple's interpretation nevertheless reflects the same historical amnesia that tends to reproduce narratives of Scottish stolidity during the period. The review that Semple describes undoubtedly has a bread-and-circuses flavor about it, but Tannahill's rendition of this species of loyalism takes on a much more ambivalent and darkened perspective in the song itself:

> Loudon's bonnie woods and braes,
>   I maun lea' them a', lassie;
> Wha can thole when Britain's faes,
>   Wou'd gi'e Britons law, lassie?
> Wha wou'd shun the fiel o' danger?
>   Wha frae Fame wou'd live a stranger?
> Now whan Freedom bids avenge her,
>   Wha wou'd shun her ca', lassie?
> Loudon's bonnie woods and braes
> Hae seen our happy bridal days,
> And gentle hope shall soothe thy waes,
>   Whan I am far awa', lassie.

One pauses over the lyricism of these lovely verses, which refuse excessive sentimentality while registering an authentic attachment to place and home. Indeed, this balancing of desire and reticence, of longing and stoic acceptance, in Tannahill's poetics of loss raises his songs to the level of those of Burns and Nairne. The Jacobite theme, however, emerges here in the service of British patriotism, as the speaker's "exile" to military service seems necessary to preserve "Britons law" and "Freedom." But when the speaker directs a series of queries to his wife— "Wha can thole when Britain's faes, / Wha wou'd shun the fiel o' danger, / Wha frae Fame wou'd live a stranger, / Wha wou'd shun her ca'"—they appear more calculated to convince the soldier *himself* to follow the flag than to assuage her grief at their parting. Indeed, appeals to honor, manliness, and "fame" have remained essentially unchanged since *The Iliad*; young men compelled to leave home to fight their masters' wars must be given some reason beyond the explicit or implied threat of coercion. But what reasons could ever be sufficient for his forsaken partner?

> Hark! the swellin' bugle sings,
>   Yieldin' joy tae thee, laddie;
> But the dolefu' bugle brings
>   Waefu' thochts tae me, laddie.

[135]

BESIDE THE BARD

> Lanely I may climb the mountain,
> Lanely stray beside the fountain,
> Still the weary moments countin',
> > Far frae love and thee, laddie.

Just as Lady Nairne refigures loss in the Jacobite song as largely a woman's trag-edy, Tannahill registers the contradiction inherent in a culture of masculine honor, which exalts women (and to a lesser extent children) as possessions in need of con-stant "protection" while requiring their protectors to desert them whenever the "swellin' bugle sings." The soldier's wife clearly recognizes this contradiction: to her, the "dolefu' bugle brings / Waefu' thochts." Again, her proleptic lament betrays no sentimentality, only a grim acknowledgment that his potential death on the battlefield announces her own. After all, is this not the inexorable logic of a soci-ety in which a married woman is covered by her husband's body and subsumed into his legal personality? In this aspect, Tannahill's poem gives voice to the wife's residual, aural presence. Her husband does not see her as much as he hears the echo of her dirge from within the totalizing discourses of duty and country that he has so deeply internalized: "Oh, resume thy wonted smile! / Oh, suppress thy fears, lassie! / Glorious honour crouns the toil, / That the soldier shares, lassie." His adoption of the imperative form of address cancels its consolatory intention and displaces it onto a different plane of existence. Prepared for self-immolation by a lifetime of acculturation to the patriotic cult of "Glorious honour," the sol-dier plays out his prescribed role as both a warrior and a preserver of the hearth. This self-suppression is an automatic response. His lover must be dutifully proud of his sacrifice and encourage him to fulfill it, and this is precisely how he imag-ines her with her "wonted smile." "Loudon's bonnie woods and braes," as it turns out, functions in the same way as Lady Nairne's "Land o' the Leal," an idyllic after-life in which the soldier and his lover will "spend our peacfu', happy days, / As blythe's yon lichtsome lamb that plays." When the soldier claims the protection of heaven, he does not mean that Providence will return him whole in this life, but only in the next. The beauty of Tannahill's poem is that these conventional pieties refuse the consolation they appear to promise. Just as his wife, who exists in the poem only as a production of the masculine economy of war and death, the soldier's presence is solely aural, as he repetitively chants the liturgy of violence that produces and reproduces him from one generation to the next, down through the ages. Tannahill's popularity with Victorian readers undoubtedly owes much to his ostensible loyalism and deference to social rank, while his compatriot Wilson's workingman radicalism makes him unsuitable for the polite drawing room, but I

[136]

would suggest that poems such as "Loudon's Bonnie Woods and Braes" deeply problematize these long-settled assumptions and reveal close affinities between these weaver poets.

The story of all wars is that the men who fight them do not come back, as seen in a sequel to "Loudon's Bonnie Woods and Braes," entitled "The Soldier's Funeral."[28] In this song, set to the air "Holden's Dead March," Tannahill abandons the vernacular common meter in favor of stately Augustan rhymed couplets of iambic pentameter: "Now let the procession move solemn and slow, / While the soft mournful music accords with our wo, / While Friendship's warm tears o'er his ashes are shed, / And soul-melting Memory weeps for the dead":

> Yet time-fretted mansions! ye mouldering piles!
> Loud echo his praise through your long vaulted aisles;
> If haply his shade nightly glide through your gloom,
> O tell him our hearts lie with him in the tomb.
> And say, though he's gone, long his worth shall remain,
> Remember'd, belov'd, by the whole of the men:—
> Whoe'er acts like him, with a warm feeling heart,
> Friendship's tears drop applause at the close of his part.

No proper patriotic sentiment appears out of place—manliness, heroism, Christian fellow-feeling define the true Briton willing to spend all in "the wars of his country." In the second octave, the soldier's humanity inheres in the sympathy he feels for the men he has just slain: "He fought like a lion, yet felt as a man; / For when British bravery had vanquish'd the foe, / He'd weep o'er the dead by his valour laid low." Here the acts of fighting and killing are curiously displaced from the soldier's "manhood," first onto the figure of the (British) lion that the soldier resembles in combat and then subsumed into the agency of "British bravery." The analogy could not be more complete—the lion fights to protect the pride and kills for food. British "men" require fighting and killing so that they may inhabit the human by weeping over the bodies of dead humans.

Unlike in the previous poem, however, there is no figure of the lover left behind, her grief softened by pride in the hero's brave sacrifice. But then again, why should it? As we saw in "Loudon's Bonnie Woods and Braes," the war narrative genders everything as masculine, right down to the warrior constructing a feminine alter ego that vindicates and redeems killing other warriors in a national cause. Tannahill here recognizes that a soldier does not live for his country but *always* dies for it. The beautiful verses enact the military march to which they are sung, playing out the ceaseless suicidal loop of masculine aggression and self-destruction.

BESIDE THE BARD

At the end of the song we see that the soldier's funeral is indeed the last act of a play, a tragedy, in which "Whoe'er acts like him, with a warm feeling heart, / Friendship's tears drop applause at the close of his part."

Read as a dramatic text, the patriotic discourse that the dirge publicly endorses falls to pieces under the pressure of its structural contradictions. In the second octave, the soldier's generous spirit animates the patriotism that "compell'd" him to join his country's war, but at the same time "He cheerful would say, all the world was his home." This cosmopolitan self-representation starkly opposes the insular patriotic nationalism that compels him to fight, placing the soldier in the paradoxical position of destroying his home in order to save it. At a logical impasse that he can neither reconcile nor evade, the soldier can only fight "like a lion" and feel "as a man." Personal moral responsibility for killing his brothers (the "world is his home," after all) is neatly cleaved from the physical act of murder, which is refigured as "valour," while the soldier's individual agency is collectivized in the trope of "British bravery." To "feel like a man," then, means the ability to mourn, and even to love, the fellow humans whom the soldier has been programmed to slaughter. To "act like a man," however, which the song ultimately urges the friends whose "tears drop applause at the close of his part" to do, means simply to butcher other men until one's part in the tragedy is played out.

When the poet initiates the lament in the first octave by personifying "Friendship" and "Memory" (in contrast to localizing grief and consolation as he does in "Loudon's Bonnie Woods and Braes"), he emphasizes the abstraction of moral agency from the murderous "acts of valor" for which the soldier is praised. Institutionalized practices of bereavement—funeral processions, lugubrious music, pious sentiment, hyperbolic eulogy—safely contain the horror and revulsion that would result if one's subjectivity somehow escaped the control of the state. All are equally kind, good, and virtuous in death, just as they are valorous in combat; moral states, it seems, are purely retrospective rather than aspirational or motivational. The song reveals that in the patriotic national state, a continuous identity is only possible in performance, in acting out a predetermined part in which one is both actor and spectator. Both are deeply structured, collectivized, and automatic; doing and not doing have the same result. Tannahill's song thus anticipates the Nietzschean demotic principle that collapses the cause-and-effect sequence. Dead bodies are just that.

As is the case with Tannahill's contemporaries, social rituals provide copious material for his poetry: courtship, marriage, fairs, war, celebrations, funerals. One of Tannahill's most popular songs, "The Kebbuckston Wedding," describes a rumbustious rustic wedding, with considerable local color, comic characterizations, and a touch of bemused condescension.[29] Philip Ramsay, Tannahill's 1838

[138]

"IN THE SHADOW OF BURNS"

editor, lamented that the "humour and spirit of this production are so appropriate, that it is to be regretted the author did not write more in the same vein."[30] Perhaps Tannahill thought he got it right the first time and did not feel the need for another go, but Ramsay's sentiments fully explain the nineteenth-century reception of Tannahill and his relative obscurity in the twentieth. Rather than give this ballad the extended reading it certainly deserves, however, I would like to concentrate on selected stanzas that, in my view, further demonstrate Tannahill's demythologizing aesthetic, as we have identified in the previous two poems.

"The Kebbuckston Wedding" begins in much the same way as Lady Nairne's "The Laird o' Cockpen":

> Auld Watty of Kebbuckston brae,
>   With lear and reading of books auld-farren,—
> What think ye? the body came owre the day,
>   And tauld us he's gaun to be married to Mirren;
>   We a' got bidding,
>   To gang to the wedding,
> Baith Johnny and Sandy, and Nelly and Nannie;
>   And Tam o' the Knowes,
>   He swears and he vows,
> At the dancing he'll face to the bride with his grannie.
>
> A' the lads had trystet their joes,
>   Slee Willy came up and ca'd on Nellie;
> Although she was hecht to Geordy Bowse,
>   She's gi'en him the gunk and she's gone wi' Willie.
>   Wee collier Johnny
>   Has yocket his pony,
> And's aff to the town for a lading of nappy
>   Wi' fouth of good meat
>   To serve us to eat;
> Sae wi' fuddling and feasting we'll a' be fu' happy.

The poem's emphasis on a wedding as a carnivalesque release, with plenty of fuddling, feasting, and trysting, follows a well-worn groove, but we must first pause on the pretext: Auld Watty's determination to wed Mirren appears based entirely on his "lear and reading of books auld-farren." This suggests that Watty's sudden desire has been engendered in part by a Quixotic obsession with tales of chivalry. The poet thus premises the nuptial rituals on an act of "bad" reading, a misprision of romance that promises nothing but trouble for the infatuated pedant. To paraphrase C. S. Lewis, chivalric romance deals in adultery, not marriage, but Watty appears to have missed the essential point.[31] His compulsive reading of

[139]

BESIDE THE BARD

romance, with its attendant titillation and exquisite restraint on the consummation of sexual desire, works him into an understandable passion, but rather than
dissipating it in dalliance, as do the "lads" that "trystet their joes" (who appear,
despite their lack of "lear," to have a much better understanding of "romance" than
Watty does), he confuses pleasure (sex) with business (marriage). That everyone
else in and around Kebbuckston recognizes Watty's error gives the poem its comic
piquancy, as they are far more interested in a temporary escape from the heavy
moral strictures imposed by the Kirk, which have ironically converted the sacrament of marriage into something resembling the pre-Reformation feast day that
the reformed Kirk sought to suppress.

This Cameronian hint is humorously taken up in a later stanza, which reads,

> Lowrie has cast Gibbie Cameron's gun,
>> That his old gutcher bore when he follow'd Prince Charlie:
> The barrel was rustet as black as the grun,
>> But he's ta'en't to the smiddy and's fettl'd it rarely.
>>> With wallets of pouther
>>> His musket he'll shouther,
> And ride at our head, to the bride's a' parading;
>>> At ilka farm town
>>> He'll fire them three roun',
> Till the haill kintra ring with the Kebbuckston wedding.

Scotland's confused history of religious and political violence erupts into the poem,
its Covenanter and Jacobite effusions of blood converging in the ancient musket
that will see service once more. Gibbie Cameron's gun materializes Auld Watty's
predilection for romance, representing a heroic past of ideological fervor and hope-
less causes. The motley "parade" that Lowrie leads with the gun indeed mimics
that of the Covenanting and Jacobite bands that preceded it, deftly overwriting
the wedding with ominous narratives of historical and cultural blind alleys. The
ritual practice of firing "three roun'" to rouse the countryside likewise suggests
the mustering of the militia to meet a perceived (or misperceived) emergency.
Scott's comic treatment of the false alarm in *The Antiquary* comes to mind, as
Lowrie's shots in the air could mean anything from the threatened French invasion to a rat killing, but here they signify nothing more than an invitation to a big
drunk staged at Watty's considerable expense. Seen from this perspective, the
interpretive ambiguity of Lowrie's alarming signal to gather at the Kebbuckston
wedding intensifies the comic sense of calamity in the entire enterprise, which
begins with Watty's misreading of romance and proceeds to empty out the political and religious ideologies of Scotland's turbulent past and present. Historical

[140]

eras and events—feudalism, Reformation, Revolution, Anglo-Scottish Union, and, finally, Anglo-French imperialism—come and go, but their artifacts, such as Watty's "auld-farren" books and Gibbie's gun, continue to command anachronistic social responses, whether they are wars or weddings. Watty's belated attempt to enact the chivalric narratives he loves is in this sense not very different from the Cameronians' effort to revive the Covenanting faith or Prince Charlie's to restore the Stuart monarchy. As Tannahill reveals, how and in whose interests these narratives are plotted ultimately determine their social and cultural effects. It does not take much twisting to make comic figures out of religious zealots or royal pretenders, rendering their pretensions ludicrous and absurd. Moreover, traditional history itself, with its earnest and solemn preoccupation with "great men and events," makes the same plot choices that the poet does in a ribald song such as this. For Tannahill, a rural wedding may be as bad an omen for social peace as the descent of Napoleon, or it might equally be an occasion for a riotous blowout. There is simply no absolute standard of value in any plotted narrative:

> Then gi'e me your hand, my trusty good frien',
>   And gi'e me your word, my worthy auld kimmer,
> Ye'll baith come owre on Friday bedeen,
>   And join us in ranting and tooming the timmer:
>   With fouth of good liquor,
>   Will haud at the bicker,
> And lang may the mailing of Kebbuckston flourish!
>   For Watty's so free,
>   Between you and me,
> I'se warrant he's bidden the half of the parish.

It is telling that the poem only mentions Watty in the first verse and the third to the last, and Mirren never appears in the poem at all. Weddings are not for the people who have them but for the "half of the parish" fortunate enough to be "bidden." What the uninvited half thinks goes unrecorded, but one of them would probably write a much different narrative than the bluff, companionable fellow who on Watty's behalf invites both his "trusty good frien'" and the "worthy auld kimmer" to the party. The Kebbuckston wedding marks a significant historical event in the life of the parish, but what significance and which parish? To one part it means the joy of carnival excess and comic freedom; to the other it offers the bitter cup of exclusion and a tragic missed opportunity for fleeting enjoyment in the midst of daily travails. The poet puts the story in the mouth of the former, but Watty's folly reverberates throughout the entire community. If Tannahill had written this side of the story, perhaps Ramsay and other nineteenth-century lovers of rustic quaintness would not have been so anxious to see "more in the same vein."

BESIDE THE BARD

SCOTLAND AND THE BODY OF A WOMAN

As we have seen in our examination of Lady Nairne's work, even in its most conventional and ostensibly "safe" forms, Tannahill's poetry sustains a deep and probing engagement with the political. This is certainly true of his best-known lyric, "Jessie, the Flow'r of Dunblane."[32] Philip Ramsay effused that "no Scottish song has enjoyed among all classes greater popularity. For this it is indebted at once to the beauty of the words and the appropriateness of the music composed for them by the poet's friend [Archibald Smith]."[33] This oft-imitated love lyric delighted its morally proper nineteenth-century performers, auditors, and readers, but despite its "appropriateness," a violent male fantasy perturbs the song's placid surface of melancholic chastity.

> The sun has gane doun o'er the lofty Benlomond,
>> And left the red clouds to preside o'er the scene,
> While lanely I stray in the calm simmer gloamin'
>> To muse on sweet Jessie, the flow'r o' Dunblane.
> How sweet is the brier wi' its saft faulding blossom,
>> And sweet is the birk, wi' its mantle o' green;
> Yet sweeter and fairer, and dear to this bosom,
>> Is lovely young Jessie, the flow'r o' Dunblane.

To begin with, the speaker's perspective places the setting sun between his field of vision and Ben Lomond, casting a lurid "red" hue to "preside o'er the scene." His peripatetic musing plays out in this light, which reflects both his intense sexual desire and his objectification of nature as a feminine vessel awaiting penetration by the male ("How sweet is the brier, wi' its saft faulding blossom"). As in Wordsworth, the wandering poet uses the tranquility of the "calm simmer gloamin'" to conjure up this passion, to recreate, partly through excited memory and partly by the action of the natural scene on the poet's faculties, the pleasurable emotional and physical desire he experiences when in close proximity to "the flow'r o' Dunblane." As the first stanza draws to a close, the poet has invested his lover with an exaggerated sensuousness; she is "sweeter and fairer" than nature and "dear to this bosom." At the same time, however, the poetic act of investing her with these supercharged feminine attributes *of* nature forcefully removes her *from* nature. The poet must appropriate Jessie to himself fully to enjoy her, just as men must conquer nature to achieve dominion over it. Jessie's body is a thing to be possessed and plundered, to be sure, but in a larger sense her enthrallment in the poet's mind as an exclusive subject of poetry subjugates her to his desire far more thoroughly than the mere satisfaction of physical lust. In poetry he can place her in a permanent

[142]

"IN THE SHADOW OF BURNS"

state of chaste readiness, as she opens up to receive his first approach in an infinitely repeatable moment of exquisite consummation. This, it seems, is what Victorian admirers of the song thought of as love.

The poet makes his possessory interest more explicit in the second stanza. Listing Jessie's generic qualities—modest, blithe, bonny—tells us nothing, nor does his insistence that "guileless simplicity marks her its ain." On the contrary, these commonplaces conceal Jessie behind a veil of conventional figures as effectively as if she were physically covered and secluded. The poet's motive for this defensiveness becomes clear in the next couplet, in which he condemns the "villain, divested of feeling, / Wha'd blight in its bloom the sweet flow'r o' Dunblane." Gesturing in the direction of the chivalric tradition, the poet's anxiety over the preservation of Jessie's maidenhood does not simply reflect a male desire for exclusive sexual prerogative. It also indicates that the production of desire through the representation of this prerogative carries with it a perverse, almost sadistic pleasure in imagining Jessie's "deflow'ring." In that ephemeral instant of gratification, the poet-lover dominates Jessie in two ways: sadistically, as a subjugated object, and masochistically, as an object subjugated by another, the "villain, divested of feeling." Indeed, it might be argued that the poet splits into ego and alter ego, the former the possessor of an "effeminate" poetic sensibility or "feeling," the latter the male animal that takes. As if startled and chagrined by this self-recognition, the poet shuts down his fantasy, apostrophizing the mavis to sanctify his aesthetic and sexual prurience in "thy hymn to the e'ening." The final couplet of this stanza repeats the first, safely veiling Jessie for his future enjoyment.

The third stanza, apparently added sometime after composition of the first two, is self-exculpatory. Guiltily retreating from the self-image of the voluptuary, the poet attempts to pass himself off as something of a prodigal who has come home to claim his birthright. He defines moral values in conventional terms of urban cosmopolitan rot and virtuous rusticity, but this somehow rings hollow. Though the poet says, "I ne'er saw a nymph I would ca' my dear lassie, / 'Till charm'd with sweet Jessie," he implies not only that eyeballing nymphs is all he has ever done but also that composing love poetry is little more than an onanistic exercise. Indeed, this impulse toward self-gratification is part and parcel of the same economy of sadistic and masochistic male pleasure that we see in the second stanza. In his determined quest for a nymph he would call his "dear lassie," he acknowledges that poetry provides a medium for coding the complex relationship between the imaginative and carnal selves inhabiting the same body, as well as for the cultural effects that such self-representation entails, particularly with respect to masculinizing gender identities and relations. It seems fitting that for years after this song was published, Tannahill's admirers sought fruitlessly for the "real" Jessie,

[143]

BESIDE THE BARD

the flower of Dunblane. That they did so speaks volumes for the double action Tannahill's song initiates: it projects male desire in the form of a female body but simultaneously reveals that the true object of desire is the poet himself. Searching for Jessie, it seems, is the self-reflexive act of "love" that characterizes the psychic economy that the poet—and the men of his culture—inhabit.

Tannahill further explores this self-reflexivity of the aesthetic act in "The Parnassiad, a Visionary View," a meditation on the depressing difficulty of achieving poetic fame.[34] As we have seen, the obscure labor of poets "in Burns's shadow" is entirely at the mercy of standards of taste over which they have no control. The signal success of Burns, however, only makes matters worse, as it establishes a transformative "new normal" that eclipses even the deftest skill at imitating and—it is to be hoped—reanimating classical genre poetry. Tannahill's use of the Parnassus trope both acknowledges this problem and recognizes his own supersession by the new poetics of "Nature" that Burns and others have forged:

> Come, Fancy, thou hast ever been,
> In life's low vale, my ready friend
> > To cheer the clouded hour;
> Tho unfledg'd with scholastic law,
> Some visionary picture draw
> > With all thy magic pow'r.
> Now to the intellectual eye
> > The glowing prospects rise.
> Parnassus' lofty summits high,
> > Far tow'ring mid the skies,
> > > Where vernally, eternally,
> > > > Rich leafy laurels grow,
> > > With bloomy bays, thro endless days,
> > > > To crown the Poet's brow.

This is one of Tannahill's most ambitious poems with regard to its metric construction. Composed in fourteen-line stanzas (sonnet form), each stanza begins with a pair of tercets, rhymed *aabccd*, the first two verses of which are iambic tetrameters and the third of which is iambic trimeter. These are followed by pair of quatrains composed in common meter, rhymed *efef* and *ghgh*. It is likely that Tannahill had Burns's vernacular version of the Spencerian or Shenstonian invocative mode in mind (as well as the direct influence of William Shenstone and other Augustan poets, as the poem itself indicates), though he does not attempt either Burns's Standard Habbie form or broad Scots diction (though, as we will see shortly, he does drop into the vernacular when describing his inadequacy as a poet). This complexity of form demonstrates the poet's ambivalence and self-doubt about his

[144]

"IN THE SHADOW OF BURNS"

craft and his motives for pursuing it. Which model should a poet follow? The "great" poets in the classical tradition—Homer, Virgil, Dante, Milton—were all successful imitators and, arguably, innovators. When Burns joined the company, he did it by leavening classical forms with his "genius," his fidelity to Nature. As we have noted in chapters 1 and 2, many of Burns's contemporaries for various reasons both lauded and resented this "genius," but Tannahill appears to locate his disappointment in a failure of the poet's "Fancy," which he invites to "cheer the clouded hour; / Tho unfledg'd with scholastic law, / Some visionary picture draw / With all thy magic pow'r." Tannahill's muse is thus an externalized version of himself, as opposed to the loftier visitants of the epic poets or even Burns's vision of Coila or Dame Scotia. Indeed, it might be argued that Tannahill crosses over into the romantic trope of the self-made poet, as exemplified, for instance, in Wordsworth's *The Prelude*.

But as the poet discovers, invoking the self as inspiration imports the very inadequacies that the poet seeks to remedy through the invocation itself. Fancy, it seems, is "unfled'g with scholastic law," a familiar self-deprecatory move in much of the poetry we have sampled, but here it comes tinged with the recognition that perhaps the poet cannot dispense with "scholastic law" and still hope to scale "Parnassus' lofty summits high." Imitation matters, and although poets may spurn older forms and subjects as outworn and anachronistic (Milton's rejection of classical and Renaissance epic subject matter and the constraints of artificial verse forms comes to mind), they must nevertheless master them in order to transcend them. Here the poet appears to feel this deficiency keenly; his Fancy comes uninstructed, bereft of one of the basic requirements of poetry's "magic pow'r." Having called for this problematic imagination, the poet's "intellectual eye" fantasizes about producing a "great poem," despite being already aware of the incompatibility of his desire and his talent. This incompatibility cannot be long repressed, and when it emerges into the poet's active consciousness, he proves unable to cope with the psychic strain:

> Sure, bold is he who dares to climb
> Yon awful jutting rock sublime,
>   Who dares Pegasus sit;
> For should brain ballast prove too light,
> He'll spurn him his airy height
>   Down to Oblivion's pit,
> There to disgrace for ever doom'd
>   To mourn his sick'ning woes,
> And weep, that ever he presum'd
>   Above the vale of Prose.
>   Then, O beware! with prudent care,

[145]

BESIDE THE BARD

> Nor 'tempt the steeps of fame,
> And leave behind thy peace of mind,
> To gain a sounding name.

This vision is obviously not the kind of inspiration the poet seeks when he summons his muse; indeed, the poem announces itself as a kind of antiepic, a demonstration of poetry composed without inspiration of any kind, whether supernatural or self-generated. Burns sought this inspiration in a national idea, a political commitment that helped him to reconcile his desire and talent in an integrated aesthetic production. Declining this muse, and the limitations it imports (Burns the plebeian radical, for example), Tannahill looks to the ancients and his more recent British avatars to establish a suitable national and aesthetic position from which this integration can occur. The poem implicitly asks the question, What kind of poetry might Burns have written had he lived into the Napoleonic years that Tannahill experienced? Could a poem like "The Vision," with its appeal to a specifically *national* muse, have been produced in reactionary, royalist Scotland increasingly being called on to defend the British state from external enemies?[35]

Perhaps Tannahill might have used this opportunity to recast Burns's "vision" as Britannia. But he firmly resists the allegorical mode that such a national appeal would entail; his Fancy cannot build such a framework. His choice rather appears to lie between some kind of fidelity to the self and a misappropriation of Burns's avatar (not to mention that of the British poets who went before him). At the same time, that fidelity leads to an "Oblivion" of obscurity and "disgrace." The "vale of Prose" of the second stanza coincides with "life's low vale" in the first, a place of seemingly dishonorable refuge for the ruined poet but also one in which "peace of mind" is still possible. To write poetry, in this sense, is "madness," mandating the poet's willing desertion of this same "peace of mind." Prose is the medium of sanity, sociability, and common sense. It is also the language of religion, philosophy, and enlightenment:

> Behold!—yon ready rhyming carl,
> With flatt'ry fir'd, attracts the warl'
> > By canker'd, pers'nal satire;
> He takes th' unthinking crowds acclaim
> For sterling proofs of lasting fame,
> > And deals his inky spatter.
> Now, see! he on Pegasus flies
> > With bluff, important straddle!
> He bears him midway up the skies,—
> > See! see! he's off the saddle!
> > > He headlong tumbles, growls and grumbles,

[146]

> Down the dark abyss;
> The noisy core, that prais'd before,
> Now join the gen'ral hiss.

As we have seen elsewhere, the fickle taste of the "noisy core, that prais'd before" can likewise condemn a poet too fixated on celebrity. This is a conventional enough lament, but how does it interact with the lack of "brain ballast" that hurls the poet down the "abyss" in the second stanza? It seems significant that this is the first instance in the poem in which the poet reverts to a vernacular strain to describe the "rhyming carl, / With flatt'ry fir'd, attracts the warl' / By canker'd, pers'nal satire." One thinks of Wilson or Pagan firing off poetic broadsides at real or perceived personal enemies, but Tannahill is also referring to Swiftean satire, with its sharp political elbows and partisan name-calling. These verses may also take a bit of a sideswipe at Burns, who could grind personal axes with the best of them, but such satire should not be confused with "poetry." Tannahill's idea of poetry, though constructed in terms of negative opposition, is taking a discernible shape. As we see in the first and second stanzas, a poet must be learned and capable of reproducing and manipulating classical genres and verse forms. Developing this skill requires "scholastic" and assiduous study, not a task for the intellectual lightweight. In the third stanza, the poet eschews the "canker'd, pers'nal satire," the petty subject matter of individual grievance that characterizes much of eighteenth-century poetry.

A further solecism against poetry is committed in the fourth stanza: "Now, see another vent'rer rise / Deep fraught with fulsome eulogies / To win his patron's favor,— / One of those adulating things / That, dangling in the train of kings, / Give guilt a splendid cover." Disappointment in securing patronage is thematic in much of the poetry we are reading, but here the poet seems to assert that anything written in the service of patronage is necessarily false. This view of the matter would disqualify a considerable amount of canonical poetry from the laurels. Nevertheless, the argument is consistent with the poet's conception of the "true" self as the only legitimate source of poetic inspiration. A poet who prostitutes himself or herself to the whims of patronage is at least as deserving of oblivion as one who writes in an effort to propitiate popular or critical taste or demonstrates no competence in using the poetic materials of the past. While the third stanza anathematizes the alienation of the poet's intellectual and aesthetic integrity, the fourth excoriates poetasters who attempt to utilize genres unconnected with the poet's lived experience. This particularly pungent denunciation of "Yon city scribbler" seeking fame in composing Theocritan pastoral, to which the poet delightfully draws attention by consecutive enjambments in the first quatrain (between "common sew'r" and "On rainy days" and "dirt and slime" and "Pour'd turbid"),

[147]

BESIDE THE BARD

applies to any number of Tannahill's predecessors and contemporaries, but just how do we distinguish between "imitation," which the poet appears to accord an appropriate place in his aesthetic, and, for lack of a better term, literary plagiarisms (the "tailor art")? If the "choice epithets in store he gets / From Virgil, Shenstone, Pope" deserve condemnation, what about the ones Virgil, Shenstone, and Pope themselves borrow from their masters? And if poetry must remain free of direct influence, on one hand, and represent the poet's authentic experience, on the other, on what foundation does the poet build? The apparent resolution lies in "Nature":

> But see, rich clad in native worth,
> Yon Bard of Nature ventures forth,
> > In simple modest tale;
> Applauding millions catch the song,
> The raptur'd rocks the notes prolong,
> > And hand them to the gale.
> Pegasus kneels—he takes his seat—
> > Now, see! aloft he towers
> To place him, 'bove the reach of fate,
> > In Fame's ambrosial bowers:
> > > To be enroll'd with bards of old
> > > In ever honour'd station,—
> > The gods, well pleas'd, see mortals rais'd
> > > Worthy of their creation!

This Burnsian apotheosis suggests that only the poet who closes the circuit between the "tale," the "Applauding millions," and Nature itself can "be enroll'd with bards of old." The arbiters of taste—the pedantic literati, fashionable society, partisan or patronage interests, in fact the whole basis of Augustan British culture—have destroyed poetry, leaving its revival to a humble farmer from Ayrshire. This triumphalist version of Burns's aesthetic importance, however, sits uncomfortably beside Burns's co-optation by the very cultural authorities Tannahill rejects. Indeed, Burns's popularity with the "people" might never have occurred without their sanction and the publicity they offered to the penurious poet. In "The Parnassiad," the poet is faced with a Hobson's choice: publicity is necessary to access the literary market, but at the same time producing suitable material for the market requires the poet to satisfy the tastemakers, thus alienating the poet from his "nat'ral" self and falsifying poetry.

The poet's only exit from the paradox is to give up the game:

> Now, mark what crowds of hackney scribblers,
> Imitators, rhyming dabblers,
> > Follow in the rear!

> Pegasus spurns us one by one,
> Yet, still fame-struck, we follow on,
>   And tempt our fate severe:
> In many a dogg'rel Epitaph,
>   And short-lined, mournful Ditty,
> Our "Ahs!—Alases!" raise the laugh,
>   Revert the tide of pity,
>   Yet still we write in Nature's spite,
>   Our last piece aye the best;
>   Arraigning still, complaining still,
>   The world for want of taste!

The speaker strikes a Voltairean pose, urging aspiring poets to tend to their own gardens lest they lose their humanity. But is this renunciation merely a conceit, itself a hackneyed imitation of the trope of the misunderstood artist? To put the question another way, is Tannahill rehearsing the very process the poem appears to abhor, and if so, what does this mean for the idea of poetry? If we read "The Parnassiad" as a challenge to prevailing aesthetic principles and official standards of taste, the poem takes on heavy political freight. It is not simply the conventional diatribe of a disappointed poetaster against critical "vengeance" but a Wordsworthian manifesto for freeing poetry from the hidebound conservatism of the cultural hegemon that regulates poetic production. Moreover, the poem does not advocate this freedom solely as a means of releasing the *poet* from the stranglehold of criticism but of liberating the "public voice" from the disciplinary constraints of official culture. This begs the question of what constitutes a "public," but the poem suggests an answer in terms of the "Applauding millions" whose sanction, "passed" on to Nature, elevates the poet to Parnassus's heights. In Shelley's terms, in this apotheosis the poet realizes his true function as a legislator for the people, whose voice the established order has so long silenced. The real problem with the "crowds of hackney scribblers, / Imitators, rhyming dabblers" is not their ambition but their lack of commitment to the radicalization of poetry itself. While the romantic tropes of the "People" and "Nature" make convenient placeholders for the purpose of opposing the contentless and artificial art demanded by the ruling classes, they speak more directly to the reconception of the poet as a "man speaking to men."

This perspective brings the ostensibly loyal weaver Tannahill into closer political alignment with the radical weaver Wilson. Wilson may have employed republican and reformist codes in the early 1790s, when the possibility of a "constitutional revolution" may still have been imaginable, but we should not judge Tannahill's apparent political quiescence a decade later in those terms. The right turn to "Nature" performed by early nineteenth-century Romantic poets appalled

BESIDE THE BARD

by Napoleon's megalomania, such as Wordsworth, Coleridge, and Southey, finds something of its Scottish parallel in the "Anonymous . . . cries" of an obscure weaver from Paisley:

> But ne'er provoke the critic's stang
>> By premature intrusion.
>>> Lock up your piece, let fondness cease,
>>>> Till mem'ry fail to bear it,
>>> With critic lore then read it o'er,
>>>> Yourself may judge its merit.

Just as Protestantism revolutionized Christianity by giving the "people" direct access to scripture, thus reconceiving personal literacy as both a religious duty and an economic necessity, poets must lead a Reformation of their own medium to meet the demands of a "nat'ral" life, thus reconceiving poetry as a language suitable to the modern conditions of commercial capitalism. This reconception may be achieved only by "locking up" the phony imitations or formulaic doggerel "Till mem'ry fail to bear it." While preserving the universal structure and language of poetry, exemplified by the classical models that the poet must study and internalize, the poet must avoid "premature intrusion" by rushing products to market before either they—or the market itself—are ready. "To lighten life, a wee bit sang / Is sure a sweet Illusion" seems perhaps too modest and homiletic a statement of purpose, at least in the context of defenses of poesy familiar to readers of English Romanticism. But in its understatement lies its power. It is well to recall once more that most English Romantic poets spoke from positions of high cultural authority rather than from the industrial underside of late eighteenth-century Britain. Absent those considerable advantages, laboring-class poets used similar materials for similar purposes; for them, a "wee bit sang" may be a "sweet Illusion," but the important fact remains, in the poet's words, that art *is* an illusion. As such, art cannot be invested with human hopes, fears, ambitions, and aspirations but only with facsimiles thereof rendered by the artist in relation to the natural world, whether that world is a placid hilltop in England or a noisy, grimy industrial town in Scotland.

"Writing in Burns's shadow invited inevitable comparisons, particularly when one wrote in Scots and/or came from a labouring-class background," Corey Andrews observes. "The need to justify one's works was felt personally by such poets, who . . . frequently addressed the matter in poems to or about Burns."[36] In this sense, it might be said that *all* Scottish poetry composed after the Kilmarnock poems fell within Burns's penumbra. Tannahill's advice to poets—"Yourself may judge its merit"—may be a defensive reaction to this fact, but it might at the

[150]

"IN THE SHADOW OF BURNS"

same time offer a reason to keep Burns's flame alight. To be a "Scottish" poet at the end of the eighteenth century, in Tannahill's words, is to be "just" a poet. To claim poets for "Scotland" means no less than to acknowledge that Scotland, regardless of its political status, has always had a large part to play in European, British, Anglophone, and transnational culture. Tannahill, in a Humean mood ("Let mankind live, ae social core, / An drap a selfish quar'ling"), sees it this way:

> This warl's a Tap-room owre an owre,
>   Whar ilk ane tak's his caper,
> Some taste the sweet, some drink the sour,
>   As waiter Fate sees proper;
> Let mankind live, ae social core,
>   An drap a selfish quar'ling,
> An whan the Landlord ca's his score,
>   May ilk ane's clink be sterling.[37]

Burns could not have said it better.

[151]

6

BURNS AND THE JACOBINS

James Kennedy and Alexander Geddes

ROBERT BURNS FAMOUSLY DID NOT EMIGRATE to Jamaica to take up occupation on a sugar plantation.[1] In the wake of heightened scrutiny of Scotland's complicity in the Atlantic slave economy, Burns scholars have taken a fresh look at the poet's attitudes toward the peculiar institution and his real intentions about becoming "a Negro driver."[2] The present discussion does not enter this debate but rather takes Burns's ambivalence toward the divisive political issue of slavery, his serious consideration of emigration in the face of economic distress, and his subsequent attempts to balance his republican ideals with his employment by the British state as indicative of the complexities facing late eighteenth-century Scottish writers with powerful political commitments. To what extent was Burns's pathway through this political and ethical minefield directed by his celebrity and command of a considerable measure of cultural patronage in Scotland and beyond? Addressing this question presents a variation of Corey Andrews's examination of the cultural construction of Burns's "genius" in Enlightenment Edinburgh, in which Burns's validation by elite literary tastemakers both created the tantalizing prospect of publishing success by plebeian poets and restricted their entry into the literary marketplace. In the context of the early 1790s, however, market conditions shifted, at first encouraging the expression of reformist or radical viewpoints elicited by events in France and then savagely repressing them as conservative reaction set in.[3] As we have seen, Burns walked a fine line between extremes, turning primarily to songwriting and collecting but keeping a hand in politics, particularly his poetic interventions in the Dumfries burgh elections in 1790 and 1795.[4]

But other poets did not follow Burns's line and paid a price for it. This chapter examines the work of two such poets working in Burns's penumbra, James Kennedy and Alexander Geddes, whose Jacobinism resembled Burns's radicalism

[153]

BESIDE THE BARD

in some respects but whose uncompromising political views effectively exiled them from Scottish society. During the turbulent 1790s, Kennedy and Geddes achieved considerable notoriety in Lowland Scotland and have reemerged in both historical and literary scholarship as significant figures of the period and in Scottish political and intellectual history more generally. Still, it is difficult to assess either the contemporary or subsequent cultural imprint of radical poets such as Kennedy and Geddes, partly because they spoke from the margins of Lowland society and partly because their political commitments forced them to abandon Scotland altogether. As one historian points out in his history of Thomas Muir and the British government's response to radical politics of this period, anyone voicing antiestablishment opinions, from artisans "blacklisted" by "loyalist employers" to "troublemakers of the officer class" shipped out to "distant empire service" to distinguished Whig lawyers who fell out of favor with the Lord Advocate and his judges, could seldom withstand the combined coercion of officialdom and conservative opinion.[5] Indeed, further research into the scope and depth of consistent antiestablishment sentiment in face of government repression and its links to emergent trade-union and later home-rule movements in the nineteenth century and beyond may reveal the full extent of the influence of exiled and other silenced radical poets. This study takes a first step in reading the poetry of a pair of Scottish exiles whose uncompromising political positions cost them dearly.

As we will see, Kennedy's activism (and possible subsequent flight to Canada to avoid the fate meted out to the "Scottish martyrs") produced an evocative strain of Jacobin verse that, among other things, adapts tropes of exile to the revolutionary context. Geddes's Jacobinism, on the other hand, takes apparently divergent forms, drawing on both the traditions of vernacular Jacobite lyric and medieval Scots-Latinate verse. Like Burns, both poets make rich and allusive use of the linguistic and cultural materials of a diverse Scottish nation contained within an increasingly homogenized British state.

JAMES KENNEDY AND THE POETICS OF EXILE

A friend of Alexander Wilson (who borrowed money from him), James Kennedy made a tenuous living by weaving gauze and muslin in Edinburgh.[6] In the wake of the notorious sedition trials of Muir and Thomas Fysche Palmer, he published a broadside against the government entitled *Treason!!! Or, Not Treason!!! Alias the Weaver's Budget* (1795).[7] Published under his own name, with the added epithet describing himself as a "Scotch Exile," Kennedy announces his offensive against a corrupt, warmongering government dedicated to the slaughter of its young men

[154]

abroad and the starvation of laborers, women, and children at home. For him, poetry is a blunt instrument to be used for the purpose of bludgeoning the conscience of the ruling elites. But it is also the instrument of the political exile; indeed, Kennedy places himself in the rather elevated company of the stateless who refused to go quietly into the Cimmerian darkness: Socrates, Cicero, Boethius, Dante, Bunyan, Milton:

> GEORGE GUELPH the Third, to you I call!
>> Slight not Advice in season:
> Remember CHARLIE STUART's Fall—
>> Kings *can* commit High Treason!

As can poets, but Kennedy does not seem deterred. He was involved in the Robert Watt and David Downie conspiracy in Edinburgh, was arrested, and spent ten weeks in jail.[8] Upon his return to London, he published yet another seditious text, *The Pitiful Plaint of a Hen-Pecked Prodigal: Dedicated to the Daughter of the Duke Bobadil*, a satire on the prince regent.[9] We then lose sight of him; John Barrell thinks he may have fled to Canada to avoid prosecution (and the very great possibility of transportation) for explicitly "imagining," if not threatening to cause, "the king's death."[10] In any event, the personal stakes of publishing poetry of this kind were extremely high, indeed.

What does it mean for Kennedy to represent himself as a "Scotch exile" as opposed simply to a friend of liberty? *Treason!!! Or, Not Treason!!!* opens with an address to "The Reader":

> Chas'd from my calling to this hackney'd trade,
> By persecution a poor Poet made—
> Yet favour court not, scribble not for fame;
> To blast Oppressors is my only aim.
> With pain I started from a private life;
> In sorrow left my Children and my Wife!
> But though fair Freedom's foes have turned me out,
> At every resting-place I'll wheel about,
> And charge the Villains!—

There is no aspiration to scale the heights of Parnassus here: poetry is the last resort of a persecuted man, his only remaining weapon against his "Oppressors" and "fair Freedom's foes." Unlike his friend Wilson, who shared similar political commitments, Kennedy articulates no aesthetic raison d'être for poetry distinct from its function as revolutionary discourse. Poetry, he argues, is the form of language best suited to the condition of exile; "made by Persecution," the poet lives not in an

[155]

BESIDE THE BARD

ecstatic state of mystical converse with Nature but in "pain" and "sorrow," bereft of intimate relationships and the pleasures of a sociable life. The ultimate causes of human suffering are not personal and emotional, not the vicissitudes of fortune, but deliberately political and remediable by direct political action. Kennedy's Paineite view stems from the very Enlightenment thinking that has made common cause with the British state that "chas'd" him "from his calling," destroying his ability to support a family in an honest trade simply by virtue of his republicanism. Politics makes exiles, and exiles respond by making poetry.[11]

But what change can poetry effect, sourced as it is in the most politically impotent, the dispossessed and the stateless? The first poem in Kennedy's pamphlet, "The Exile's Reveries, Dedicated to the Scourge of Scotland, Harry Dundas," announces an explicitly Jacobin and insurrectionary call to arms:

> Do we toil while others reap?
>> Do we starve while others feast?
> Are we sold and shorn like sheep?
>> By the Despot and the Priest?
>
> Are we born for them alone?
>> If by Right Divine they rule,
> Yonder *idiot* on a Throne,
>> Reigns by Right Divine a *fool*.
>
> Masters of the *puppet show*,
>> Long they've made us dance at will;
> Should we down the curtain throw,
>> Farewell to their magic skill.

While this may be standard fare for radical verse of the period, Kennedy prefaces his rising revolutionary zeal and anger with a reflection on the exile's eternal condition as a "marked man": "Here no rotten-hearted Spy, / Spider like, the snare extends, / Though on grassy couch I lie, / I am guarded by my friends." Then, as now, the state's spies were notoriously effective at identifying political agitators and promoters of sedition. The actual physical banishment of the subject was only the most extreme form of exile; for thousands of reformists at home, the unceasing surveillance of the "dangerous" subject isolated them just as effectively as transportation to Botany Bay. In the poem, the exile feels the temptation to succumb to the peace and solitude that Nature offers him, imagining himself secure from discovery by Dundas's agents. What prevents Nature from exercising its narcotic effect is the "child of woe," the consciousness of exile from which the poet can never find relief, even in the relative safety of Nature.

[156]

BURNS AND THE JACOBINS

In contrast, Wordsworth's marvelous freedom to wander and "become" a poet of Nature in the first book of *The Prelude* owes everything to his privileged political position, which produces the benefits of economic and social security. His rejected Jacobinism is a broken fragment of himself, the cause and consequence of an emotional breakdown vaguely attributed to his shock and dismay at the Reign of Terror and the imperial pretensions of Napoleon. Wordsworth figures his passage from revolutionism to quiescence as healing, a wholesome return to his "right mind."[12] His exile was a temporary insanity, not a self-identity, as it is for Kennedy, who enjoys none of Wordsworth's advantages. Wordsworth's "Nature" approaches the Divine, the Objective Universal existing over and above the machinations of human societies, whereas for Kennedy it is simply a production of "culture," controlled and regulated by the ruling elites for the purpose of depriving the great majority of human subjects of a fair share of the fruits of their toil. Thus, even when the exile is beguiled by the natural beauty and repose of his "grassy couch," he recognizes that accepting the illusion as real gives "the Despot and the Priest" the final victory. Any art, any aesthetic principle, produced under their hegemony is necessarily false and oppressive, and it must be resisted: "Should the *Sans-Cullottes* come here, / We may gain, but cannot lose; / Freedom's friends we do not fear, / Tyrants only are our foes." These are fighting words, indeed, inviting the Jacobins to duplicate their slaughter of priests and aristocrats in England's green and pleasant land. The poet laments the fates of Palmer and Muir ("injur'd Scotia's shining gem"), Maurice Margarot and William Skirving, and other transported patriots, victims of judicial murder: "Britons, blush! the tale is true; / Britons, from your stupor, rise! / Are not fetters forg'd for you, / By the shameful sacrifice?" Turning from the martyred Friends of the People to his own domestic sacrifice, the poet once more laments his forced separation from wife and children:

> Fond, I hop'd, my efforts joined
>   To thy Mother's virtuous care,
> Would have stor'd thy rising mind
>   With ideas as free as air,
>
> Mitres, crowns, and titled things
>   Early taught thee to despise;
> Noblest fame true merit brings,
>   The *good* are *great*, the *just* are *wise*.

Revolution is thus figured as a family pietá, a domestic tragedy. What is sacrificed is not so much the poet's injured political sensibilities, as compelling as they are, but his "efforts joined / To thy Mother's virtuous care." The enjambment powerfully

[157]

marks the magnitude of the loss; it severs the line through the word "joined" just as the repressive state decapitates the domestic unit "joined" in marriage and parenthood. Moreover, the revolutionary poet must choose between submission to that state, requiring him to surrender "ideas as free as air," and the maintenance of those ideas at the debilitating expense of the very domesticity that state ideology idealizes. This verse additionally lays bare the illusory nature of the Lockean state as a consensual body that its citizens "join" in order to foster the liberties of "free-born" Britons. It thus makes a mockery of the theoretical right of citizens to withdraw their consent when confronted by tyranny. So just as the poet must sacrifice the domestic security and affection of the family in order to assert his privileges as a "citizen" (ironically the name of his son), he must go into exile in order fully to realize his identity as a citizen of the state that has placed a price on his head.

The Popean format of the poem, recalling *The Essay on Man*, demonstrates just how deeply even plebeian citizens have internalized the British state's language of liberty. But Kennedy does not stop with simply using this language against his oppressors. In the final quatrains of the poem, he proposes a new basis for reconstituting the liberty of the subject from the broken fetters forged by Locke and the Revolution Settlement:

> Must I no more remain your prop?
>   No more your kind embraces meet?
> Hark! SCOTIA calls, "These ravings drop!"
>   "Gain Freedom, or a winding sheet!"

> "My Sons, beneath Corruption's yoke,
>   "Enfeebled and degraded, groan:
> "ROUSE! Fav'rites ROUSE! The SPELL IS BROKE!
>   "THE PROUD OPPRESSOR'S POW'R IS GONE!"

This ecstatic vision imagines Scotia's intervention to restore liberty to the cowed and tyrannized Britons of the previous quatrains. When Scotland rouses the poet from his own "stupour" and sentimental attachment to his family, it is not to reclaim its ancient independence but to redeem the meaning and value of Britishness itself. The poet's move is somewhat ironic, given Scotia's history of repressive and autocratic feudal and Kirk government. Rather, his selective revision of this history emphasizes Scotland's collective experience of repression by its more powerful and imperious neighbor. Here the poet defines "Scottishness" in terms of "Freedom," "Britain" in terms of oppression, emptying out any ethnic or "national" content from these terms and recasting them as markers of a purely political identity. As any republican the world over can become "French" by virtue of his or her adherence to the revolution, anyone can be Scottish, and hence British, if imbued with the same revolutionary ethos of citizenship. In this sense, the poet's son, whom he addresses as "Citizen," embodies the central ideological argument of the poem: what we call things matters. The signs we use to indicate national allegiance, while not entirely arbitrary because of, if nothing else, their historical usage, are nevertheless plastic and malleable. Kennedy's propagandistic sensibility in the poem predicts one of the Foucauldian premises of "modernity"—that political power depends on the command of definitions as much as on a monopoly of violence.

Much of Kennedy's other poetry in this volume deploys a satiric mode, sometimes descending to near scurrility. His critique of Edmund Burke, "the most sublime apostate from the cause of liberty," strikes a common pose in the radical poetry of the period. In a song titled "Swinish Gruntings," the poet calls on the porcine multitude to rise up against their "drivers":

> What! shall a base, deceitful crew,
> Supported by our labours,
> Gainsay our wills—wage wicked war,
> With our good Apeish neighbours?
> Forbid it, Heaven! forbid it, Earth!
> Ye Grunters brave, forbid it!
> Nor let your haughty rulers tell,
> With your consent they did it.

While formulaic and unremarkable with regard to its critique of political and economic repression at home and unpopular war abroad, the poem reveals a palpable tension between reformation and retribution. Here we see the "constitutional" phase of British reformism of the 1780s, of which Burke was a part and which stood for varying degrees of democratization and the elimination of "Old Corruption," giving way to the more radical, Jacobin rhetoric of the people as vengeful Nemesis:

> To view our dear-bought rights o'erstep'd,
> By crazy Capernonians,
> Our Patriots banish'd, dragg'd in chains,
> Alarms us Grumbletonians.
> But rank unjust oppressive deeds,
> And fiery persecution,
> Shall only hasten the day
> Of downright retribution.

BESIDE THE BARD

> *Come Rouse, ye slumb'ring Grunters, Rouse!*
> *Shake off inglorious slav'ry!*
> *Like Swine! assert your native rights,*
> *Make Drivers dread your brav'ry.*

Kennedy's rhyme of the now-forgotten terms "Capernonians" and "Grumbletonians" jars the aesthetic sensibilities, but to contemporary readers it signifies the prevailing reactionary stance of the Scottish judiciary toward the Friends of the People, particularly, its punitive and unjudicial treatment of the radicalized working class in the Scotland's central industrial belt.[13] Once again, we see Kennedy dealing with British politics in a Scottish context. Scotland has become the site of contestation between "native rights" and "fiery persecution," the political space that fully reveals the ruling elites' naked exploitation of the "slumb'ring Grunters." The poem's characterization of the people as "slaves" contradicts James Thomson's proud assertion that "Britons never will be slaves" and compares the condition of the workers to the coerced African laborers toiling on West Indian plantations, a common figure for radical poetry of the period.[14] But whereas the previous poem locates hopes for the renewal of British liberty in Scotland, this one specifically identifies the oppressors as Scottish, rather than referring to the monarch and his Scottish henchmen, such as Henry Dundas.

For Kennedy tyranny is a native British product, as is resistance to it. The English "other" has no particular negative valence, identifying Kennedy, like Alexander Wilson, as a self-consciously laboring-class poet. This Marxian quality of Kennedy's class analysis of the nation, while characteristic of the radical literature in support of the Friends of the People movement generally, nevertheless reverses the unidirectional energy of much late eighteenth-century poetry that asserts Scottish national difference from England and uses iconic historical features such as the Wars of Independence and Jacobite risings to reclaim a peculiar collective identity. As indicated in Kennedy's poetry, this type of special pleading played into the hands of Dundas and his minions in the Scottish judiciary because it elided the exploitation of labor as the cause of state-sponsored oppression. As long as Scotland's grievances, however they are defined, can be "nationalized" in this fashion, the existing class structure might be discomfited, but it can hardly be fundamentally threatened. The bigwigs are still big, whether they wear the tartan or not, and ennobling a wage laborer with the honor of "Scottishness" merely reinforces his or her historical subjection to exploitation.

When the narrative turns personal, however, Kennedy's verses transcend the standard political line. Consider these verses from a poem entitled "Dedicated to the Majesty of the People":

[160]

Thank Heaven! delusion's pow'r's decline;
    King-Priest-craft, Superstition,
In melancholy mania pine,
     Fast sinking to perdition:
     Their vot'ries now with dire dismay,
     Set all their legions in array—
     Go, Friends of Man! at Freedom's call
     With *Reason arm'd*, attack them all!

· ·

Must I no more remain your prop?
    No more your kind embrace meet?
Hark SCOTIA calls, "These ravings drop!
    Gain Freedom, or a winding sheet!"

Kind Reader, let me wisper by the way—
    To do too much at one time is imprudent;
(This trick of Lawyers charms the novice student)
'Tis fools make speed when gaining by delay.
    Let's imitate sly Justice EYRE;
    For mutual benefit, retire:
The Muse, refresh'd from twistings and distortions,
May, like the *Court*, produce some great ABORTIONS!

Andrew Noble calls this the "finest poem in the collection *Treason!!! Or, Not Treason!!!* . . . The poem, too, seethes not with only Burns's contempt for the imposed German royalty but for the equally degenerate aristocracy of the Hanoverian state and its tribe of placemen and informers."[15] But noting John Barrell's "praise of the poem's ambiguity," Noble queries the apparent irony of the poem's final octave, in which the speaker abruptly turns from his clarion call—"Hark SCOTIA calls, "These ravings drop! / Gain Freedom, or a winding sheet!"—to "wisper" in the reader's ear.[16] He suggests somewhat cryptically that Kennedy might have believed that his own radical republican vision for Scotland was a pipe dream, an imaginary already negated by the reality of British state power.[17] I would suggest, rather, that "Scotia's" call for Kennedy to his "ravings drop" registers the fundamental incompatibility of working-class revolution with national reformation. In the revolutionary state that Kennedy projects, the mythical nation would melt into thin air, revealing Scotia, Albion, Britannia, Gallica, or any other national personification as the "King-Priest-craft, Superstition" they are. In fact, the true call in the poem is "Go, Friends of Man! at Freedom's call / With *Reason arm'd*, attack them all!" Once "Reason" enters the fray, the myth of the "nation" must go the same way as the oppressive mystifications of king and church. When Scotia calls, however, it urges the poet to take up arms against the edifice of national

[161]

BESIDE THE BARD

ideology, a futile gesture that can only result in a "winding sheet" because "Freedom" itself is a product of that same ideology. Scotia thus lures the laboring-class poet away from the only revolution that can liberate him: the class revolution that dissolves national difference. In this sense, maybe Noble is right: "Harry Dundas, thinly disguised by various coats of ideological paint, has remained in constant charge—perhaps never more so than at the present moment."[18]

Historians have still to settle definitively the question of whether the Scots, like the Irish, might have organized a rebellion in the 1790s.[19] Scottish historiography tends to view this question in relation to the considerable residual strength of the ruling classes, but it is worth examining it from the perspective of Kennedy and other radical poets. Advocates of a more aggressive interpretation of the revolutionary potential of Scottish dissent point to a relatively large volume of (mainly) ephemera espousing the people's cause, the evident apprehension of the authorities of any hint of working-class aggregation, the overbearing loyalist reaction (of which the sedition trials are only one facet), and periodic rioting throughout the decade as evidence of widespread disaffection that, given the right combination of circumstances, could have been organized into an armed uprising. Those who believe the Scots were essentially quiescent have a strong case as well. They cite the overwhelming preponderance of loyalist literature at the state and local levels, the small and poorly organized radical cells that were so easily infiltrated and broken up, the absence of a single purpose or organizing principle for the rioting and scattered violence that did occur, and the general enthusiasm for which Scots appeared to identify with the British state, especially under the Napoleonic threat. Both views appear plausible, and it also seems reasonable to construct a synthesis of these positions that acknowledges the coexistence of radical and reactionary Scotlands that, at least for brief moments in time during the period, might have hung in the balance.

When analyzed in this fashion, a weaver poet such as Kennedy may be read in very different ways. Kennedy and his compatriots represent the political and social views held by a considerable proportion of the laboring poor and circulated in the cheap broadsheet and chapbook print that circulated freely in the Lowlands, as well as in the popular culture of the tavern, taproom, artisanal societies, parochial meetings, and other sites of plebeian "sociability." The poems of Kennedy and others were likewise "set to Jacobite tunes" or "popular songs dealing with" themes of exile and return.[20] They thus spread widely in Scotland (and among affiliated groups in England and Ireland as well) and indicated a relatively formidable, if only loosely organized, mass political movement.[21] For those who are persuaded by the "uninflammability" thesis, however, Kennedy represents a relatively small fringe of activism that was so weakened by state repression as to become

[162]

BURNS AND THE JACOBINS

moribund by the turn of the nineteenth century. Nevertheless, as Gordon Pentland has argued, the laboring-class dissent in the revolutionary period should be linked both to the so-called Radical War of 1820 (which made martyrs of the hanged weavers Andrew Hardie and John Baird) and the rise of Chartism in the 1840s.[22] Viewed in this context, networks established by radicals like Kennedy, who also provided the popular rhetoric necessary to fuel their spread, survived long after the poet disappeared, possibly, into the wilds of Canada.

By any reckoning, James Kennedy as an individual did not pose a clear and present danger to the British crown, government, armed forces, or constitution, but when he refused to keep his opinions to himself, the full weight of those powers descended upon him and his radical colleagues:

> By them traduc'd, by them belied
> > Unjustly charg'd with Treason,
> Had I not fled, I might have died,
> > Or languish'd, starv'd in prison.
> > By lawless violence opress'd,
> > Where shall the injur'd be redress'd—
> > When Pow'rs base minions, fir'd with fury,
> > Are stern Accusers, Judge and Jury?
>
> What can be done in such a case?
> > Mean inter'st says, "Knock under;
> "Kneel—kiss the breech of knaves in place
> > "Their crimes praise loud as thunder,"
> > No—crouch I won't; I can't endure
> > To see oppressors ride secure:
> > Tho' quite unequal to the task,
> > I'll strive to tear the villain's mask.

Citing these verses, Noble compares Kennedy to the American poet Joel Barlow "in his confrontational style and his desire for violent political solutions."[23] But I am not so sure. Though Kennedy's overheated rhetoric in the poem purports to represent the poet's personal experience, the poet nevertheless distances himself from the violence he suggests. While he proclaims that he will "strive to tear the villain's mask," the poem as a whole decries the "lawless violence" that forced the poet to flee. His legitimacy rests, as we have seen, on the argument that he faces persecution simply by virtue of enjoying the constitutional liberty of a freeborn Briton—Britons never will be slaves. To advocate actual physical violence, as opposed to the rhetorical violence of metaphorical figures ("hurl the sanguine Tyrant down"; "tear the villain's mask"), would cost the poet everything. The choice

[163]

BESIDE THE BARD

of poetry matters; for the same reason that Burns sometimes telegraphed his republican views in verse, Kennedy uses poetry to refuse the violence to which he has been subjected. One wonders what Burns, who likewise shrunk from "violent political solutions," might have written if he had been arrested, imprisoned, and exiled for composing the explicitly Paineite "A Man's a Man." As for Kennedy, I surmise that the poet would have prevailed over the *sansculotte*.

ALEXANDER GEDDES, BRITISH LIBERTY, AND EUROPEAN IDENTITY

Cairns Craig poses the question, "Where are we in history? Ask first whose history, what are its limits. Take your eyes away from the stage: listen for the voices from the dark, listen to the mingling of the voices in and out of history."[24] But which voices do we hear and which do we not? One suspects that many readers of the periodical, pamphlet, and poetry wars of the 1790s agreed with the assessment of the radical newspaper the *Edinburgh Gazetteer*, in the first issue of which the editors denounced opposing political factions:

> Two political parties are understood to exist in the British Government; that of the Ministry, and that of the Opposition. Wise men have long distrusted both of them, and the kingdom at large seems at last disposed to regard them with jealousy, as in a great measure, consisting of men who are little interested in the national welfare, and who contend only about the possession and disposal of the spoils of the people. They have repeatedly exhibited the indecent picture of the leaders of a great empire, courting popularity as the means of obtaining power, but depending on a flagitious corruption of its security.[25]

This is a critique to which Burns and all of the poets studied here would accede. To the extent that a crisis existed in late eighteenth-century Scotland and Britain that threatened the stability of the state, these poets perceived it as civil and political in nature. While they might invoke the Jacobin bogeyman, either as a potential liberator (for Kennedy) or a usurper (for Burns), poets and observers seem more interested in Jacobinism as a trope for emphasizing the apparent breakdown of constitutional government in Britain itself. Events in France became one act in a British political drama that played out in the domestic, Habermasian public sphere, centered largely in the cities and larger towns where much of the unrest and intermittent violence actually occurred. What distinguishes the late eighteenth-century drama is the eruption of laboring-class poets such as Wilson and Kennedy into

[164]

that sphere as representatives of a new "public." Once the working man or woman can compose in the same aesthetic form and language as Alexander Pope, Thomas Gray, or William Shenstone (much less Virgil or Horace), it is clear that poetry and politics can never be the same again. That Romantic poets were already in the process of breaking down these older aesthetic models in the age of revolution might owe something to the plebeian poets in Scotland (as well as in Ireland and England) who contributed, usually under exigent circumstances, to poetry's democratization.

The Catholic priest, Enlightenment intellectual, and Jacobin Alexander Geddes seems an odd player in this game. He was born 1737 in Rathven, Aberdeenshire. His father farmed land belonging to the Gordon estates, allowing the young Geddes to receive instruction from, among others, Catholic priests who served the Gordon family and later at seminary in Glenlivet. At the age of twenty-one, Geddes matriculated at the Scots College in Paris, where he studied rhetoric, Greek, and Latin. He later studied Hebrew at the Sorbonne. Refusing a teaching appointment in Paris, Geddes took up the ministry, first in Dundee and then as chaplain to the Catholic family of John Stewart, 6th Earl of Traquair, and brother of the committed Jacobite Charles Stewart, whom he succeeded. In 1769, Geddes became parish priest in Auchinhalrig. In 1779, he published a financially successful English translation of selected Horatian satires (lauded by Samuel Johnson) and was befriended by James Beattie. Geddes's decision to accept an invitation to attend an Episcopalian service resulted in his forced resignation from his parish in 1781.[26]

Geddes moved to London, where, under the patronage of Lord Petre, he pamphleteered on behalf of Catholic emancipation and published his *Idea of a New English Catholic Edition of the Holy Bible for the Use of the Roman Catholics of Great Britain* (1782) and *Prospectus of a New Translation of the Holy Bible* (1786). Though Geddes abandoned his plan for a new Catholic Bible, he undertook a historical examination of the Old Testament with the support of Robert Lowth, the Anglican bishop of London. Geddes's interest in German biblical criticism landed him in hot water with Catholic authorities but earned him the admiration of radicals such as Joseph Priestley.[27] Geddes may also have helped persuade his publisher, Joseph Johnson, to publish *Rights of Man*, while contributing to the growing body of periodical literature and political satire championing the French Revolution.[28] He composed a lengthy Latin poem (with a corresponding English translation), "Carmen sæculare pro Gallica gente tyrannidi aristocraticæ erepta" (1790), to help reassure French revolutionists of British support for their cause, and two years later added to his growing palette of political activism the satirical prose narrative *An Apology for Slavery* (1792). Also in that year, his publication of a heterodox exegesis entitled *The Holy Bible; or, The Books Accounted Sacred by Jews and Christians;*

[165]

Otherwise Called the Books of the Old and New Covenants resulted in his suspension from holy orders. Indeed, Geddes linked the history of the ancient Hebrews to the republican present; according to Mark Goldie, he "turned the Hebrew commonwealth into a republic and Moses into a Jacobin."[29] At the same time, Geddes became acquainted with leading radical voices in Scotland and joined the Society for Constitutional Reform. His contributions to the pamphlet and newspaper wars of the 1790s include essays on British policy toward France and a significant amount of anonymously published radical poetry. His connection with fellow Catholic David Downie (with whom Kennedy likewise associated), a member of the Scottish Friends of the People who was convicted of high treason along with Robert Watt in Edinburgh in 1794, raised questions about the loyalty of Geddes and other Catholics to Britain, prompting Geddes to write to Henry Dundas attesting his allegiance to the sovereign.[30] Geddes nevertheless continued to publish prorevolution poetry and associate with noted radicals such as Samuel Johnson, as well as the English poets William Blake and Samuel Taylor Coleridge.[31] Geddes died in London on February 26, 1802.

As Gerard Carruthers notes, Geddes composed a significant amount of politically radical poetry, much of which appeared anonymously in the *Morning Chronicle*, edited by Geddes's friend and "fellow Aberdeenshire man" James Perry.[32] Carruthers claims that several poems attributed to Burns by Patrick Scott Hogg actually belong to Geddes, including "Exhortatory Ode to the Prince of Wales on Entering His 34th Year" (1795), "The Ewe Bughts" (1794), "The Cob Web—A Song" (1795), "Address to Justice," "Ode Inscribed to Certain Jurymen" (1794), and "Ode for the Birthday of C. J. Fox."[33] On the basis of the quality Geddes's poetry and his broad influence on British biblical scholarship, Carruthers argues that "Geddes is the second most significant Scottish poet of the 1790s," an "unjustly little-known figure . . . important in Scottish, British, and, indeed, European history and letters."[34]

Geddes's contributions to the Scottish Enlightenment debate over the status of Scots as a "national" language has also received increasing critical attention. As Colin Kidd has shown, Geddes vigorously endorsed the Scots vernacular revival as an expression of true British indigeneity. Scottish writers and scholars of medieval Scottish literature, in Geddes's words, demonstrated that "English and Scots were originally but one language." According to Kidd, "Geddes detected a richness, energy and harmony in Scots, which modern English—absorbed by so many 'French usages'—had lost. Geddes promoted the idea of a Scots dictionary— in his words 'a Scoto-Saxon lexicon'—as 'a desideratum in English literature.'"[35] Geddes composed the article quoted by Kidd for the first volume of the *Transactions of the Society of Antiquaries of Scotland* (1792). Lord Buchan, a radical Whig, had founded the society in 1780 to promote the enlightened political and religious

[166]

BURNS AND THE JACOBINS

values of Scottish moderates in the increasingly fractious Kirk contest with the evangelicals, which broke into open violence over the introduction of the Scottish (Catholic) Relief Bill in 1779.[36] As Mark Goldie puts it, Geddes "celebrated modern Britain's debt to Caledonian culture, Napier in mathematics, Pitcairne in medicine, Arbuthnot in wit, Thomson in poetry, Blair in preaching, Smollett in the novel, Hume in history, Kames in criticism, and Home in tragedy, regretting only that they had not undertaken a linguistic renaissance, for would not Adam Smith's works have had as much 'pith' in Scots?"[37] Curiously, though the article laments "the neglect of the Scots tongue since Allan Ramsay's day," it does not acknowledge Fergusson's or Burns's poetry as exemplifying the very "renaissance" that Geddes otherwise calls for and later, in his own vernacular poetry, helped to enact.[38] In view of the scholarly cast of the society's membership and work, however, Geddes seems to have written here for an audience of moderate clergy, professors, intellectuals, and professionals. The humbler origins of Fergusson or Burns apparently did not fit the bill.

How, then, are we to understand Geddes's immensely erudite poem "Carmen sæculare, pro Gallica gente tyrannidi aristocraticæ erepta" (1790) as "radical" in the same sense as poetry by Burns, Wilson, or Kennedy? For Robert Crawford, Geddes's choice of Latin draws attention to the poem's "Scottishness." The poem "sounds the last trump for Scottish Latinity," a venerable tradition in Scottish letters commencing with the first Christian mission and, for all practical purposes, terminating at the end of the eighteenth century.[39] Crawford regrets Latin's "considerable government-backed repression in the Scottish state-school system" as a potentially irretrievable loss to the study and appreciation of Scottish history, literature, and culture.[40] By invoking this rich cultural tradition, Geddes may identify Scotland with broadly humanist values over against the darker anti-intellectualism of orthodox Presbyterianism, particularly of the anti-Catholic stripe responsible for the Scottish Relief Bill riots. "Carmen sæculare" remarkably "was read to the assembly of deputies in Paris at a time of particular nervousness among the revolutionaries so as to reassure its members that international intellectual support held firm" (indicating that at least some of the elected representatives of Gaul could still conduct business in the lingua franca of medieval Europe); publisher Joseph Johnson provided an English translation for the poem's British audience.[41] The poem thus addresses multiple communities of readers: French revolutionaries, British democrats and friends of reform, and, presumably, members of a classically educated English elite that can recognize a hendecasyllabic verse when they see one. When in London, Geddes frequented Joseph Johnson's home in St. Paul's Churchyard, where he mingled with all manner of reformist and revolutionary intellectuals, including Richard Price, Joseph Priestley, William Godwin, Joel Barlow,

[167]

BESIDE THE BARD

Tom Paine, Horne Tooke, Gilbert Wakefield, Anna Barbauld, and Mary Woll-stonecraft.[42] But just as the poem revives an ancient language associated with Roman *libertas*, its translation from Horatian Sapphic into stately iambic pentameter resurrects the eighteenth-century neoclassical poetry celebrating the "modern" form of British liberty that emerged from the Union, successful wars against absolutist France, and the Hanoverian succession. Geddes's linguistic choices thus inscribe both cosmopolitan and specifically imperial codes in a poem that urges the leveling of aristocratic power and privilege.

Geddes's poem likewise flies directly in the face of both the triumph of national languages over monologic Latin and the assumption that the modern state, as it appeared in the late eighteenth century, would inevitably capture and replace popular allegiance to other forms of self- and collective identification.[43] Rather than reading the poem as "the last trump" of ancient Scottish Latinity—a belated and perhaps nostalgic gesture toward pre-Union Scottish intellectual traditions—we might read it as a rejection of national language, together with its construction of the imaginary nation and its "history," in favor of the universal language of a "single cultural system" in which national languages exist for use in everyday life but do not canonize the nation as the bearer of a unique and "better" culture.[44] This reading too might indulge in nostalgia, but Geddes's face in the poem seems firmly set toward a future defined by *libertas*, as opposed to one culturally dominated by English "liberty" or French *liberté*. To achieve this future, wars and revolutions seem inevitable, aided no doubt by the command and control of the national languages that enable them. For Geddes, however, if these conflicts result only in the creation of "nations" divided by their respective languages, they have signally failed to liberate anyone.

As previously discussed, "Carmen sæculare" announces itself as a Horatian ode, prefaced by Cicero's famous dictum, "Jucundiorem faciet Libertatem Servitutis Recordatio."[45] The poem carries a dedication to the National Constituent Assembly of France, assembled in Paris (called by the full Latin name Lutetiæ Parisiorum). The poem begins with a bardic invocation, bidding the "Sapphic Muse" to inspire his song in praise of "Freedom by Gallia's struggling sons obtain'd": "Canto Saturni repetita regna / Lenis et justi, populique patris: / Et Themin terries cano restitutam, et Aurea sæcla" (I sing Saturnian times return'd: I sing / Once more to Themis earthly temples rear'd, / Under a gentle, just, parental King, / Not dreaded by his people, but rever'd).[46] While in keeping with Latin lyric conventions, the bard's invocation of the "Sapphic Muse" nevertheless marks a point of departure from contemporary lament or panegyric by Burns and others, which invokes "national" muses such as Scotia, Coila, or Britannia. Moreover, while the

[168]

BURNS AND THE JACOBINS

bard deploys the feminine trope of the nation—Gallia—he appeals not to her but to Plato's "Tenth Muse," a progenitor of lyric poetry itself. The poem's address to "Freedom" mimics a lover's address to a beloved; "afflatus subito moveri / Sentio pectus" bespeaks the lover's passionate longing, the pleasurable pain of the heart's desire. The "long-neglected" ancient lyre of the Roman poet likewise contrasts with the bardic harp of James MacPherson's Ossian or James Beattie's minstrel, as well as the traditional musical settings of songs by Burns, Nairne, or Tannahill. Whereas nativist Scottish or British national poetry readily identifies "Freedom" with the Wars of Scottish Independence, distinct Scottish cultural and egalitarian values, or (in loyalist poetics) the British constitutional tradition, here "Freedom" compels the bard to take up an antique art to "resound" not only the victorious "Gallia's struggling sons" but the aesthetic form in which "Freedom" must be expressed: "Galliam, laetus, cano liberatum."

To sing of *libertas* requires, in this sense, an ahistorical language disassociated from national histories and the narratives that produce them. Geddes's poem exemplifies the operation of polyglossia, in that it seeks to set up a unified discursive system through which the interaction of national languages may be synthesized to produce "free" thought, that is, thought free of the "rigid fetters" forged by national languages themselves. For Bakhtin, the modern novel performs this synthesis, dissolving linear—or "historical"—time in the process. Consequently, narratives that use national languages to tell "folk" or national histories, whether those of Scotia, Gallia, or Britannia, attempt to invoke a sense of synchronicity, of the "timelessness" embodied in the concept of the folk or nation, in an idiom that remains obstinately historical and incipient. The phoenix-like nation, always rising from its own ashes, as it were, resists universalization even as it celebrates universal values. Revolutions, from which the modern nation-state emerges, do not move history forward but simply back upon itself. Rather than singing the revolution as a reinscription of Gallic national history in this fashion, however, the bard explicitly invokes the Golden Age under the reign of Themis, upholder of the ancient patriarchal order. This appeal jars a bit, especially when contrasted with Burnsian egalitarianism, Wilsonian dignity of labor, or Kennedy's pan-republicanism. Waiving knowledge of Geddes's political commitments, one might reasonably read the poem as an implicit loyalist paean to benign Hanoverian rule. Yet such a reading overlooks the premised "Saturnian times," which require no external symbols or trappings of power to remind subjects of their subjection; indeed, subjectivity ceases as either signifier or signified. Each lives an objective life in which desire and realization perfectly and spontaneously coincide in each act, and act and thoughts are one. In this sense, then, each "man" is "King," and as "the people" inhere fully in each

[169]

BESIDE THE BARD

"man," there is nothing left to rule. Universal "man" remains as the only object of reverence because he embodies God.

Geddes thus proposes a poetics of universalism with the potential to transcend the operation of polyglossia within a "single cultural system." The next three quatrains revert to *denunciatio*, with the now-familiar warning for tyrants to beware: "Audiant omnes timeantque reges; / Totius terræ timeant tyranny; / Palleat quicunque imitatur illos, / Nomine quovis!" (Let Sov'reigns hear, and tremble!—May the sound / Reach ev'ry tyrant's ear, from pole to pole: / Kings, emp'rors, princes, prelates, popes confound; / And fill with terror each despotic soul!). The bard appears to have taken us unawares into radical territory; Saturnian "gentleness" has become Jovian—or perhaps Jehovah—retribution. Indeed, it seems unclear to which "Father" the bard now refers, as paternal images multiply and contradict each other. Is it the jealous Hebrew God of Genesis, who in his righteous wrath pitches demonic aristocracy into hell, or the Christian counterpart, whose grace and love redeem those who raise the "grateful voice of thanks"? If we read the bard to invoke the Hebrew God, who liberates his chosen people from the thrall of tyrants, must we likewise accept that God's "national" exclusivity? Or can we assume the transcendence of a God available to both Jew and Gentile on equal terms? I would suggest that the poem offers antithetical "gods/fathers" (Saturn/Jove; Jehovah/God; kings/popes) in the same way that it does antithetical theories of "history." As in the first three quatrains, where the bard problematizes "revolution" by placing national, or Gallic, history in opposition to an ahistorical age of gold, here the bard designifies "sovereignty" by collapsing religiomythological, secular, and national variations of the "Father" into a single category: tyrants.

The bard's reduction of "sovereignty" (exercised by "Pow'r Aristocratic") as an equivalent term for tyranny appears reversed in the following quatrains, in which the poet lauds the newly legitimized "felix Ludovice, / Tu tenes tandem innocuam coronam: / Tu tenes tandem maculata nullo / Crimine sceptra!" (Hail, happy Louis! / who can boast, you wear / A crown innocuous, lawfully obtain'd: / Hail, happy Louis, who can boast, you bear / A regal scepter with no crime distain'd!) and compares him to Saint Louis XII (1462–1515) and Henry IV (1553–1610). But at the same time, the terms in which the bard frames his praise of *Le Père du Peuple* and the *le bon roi Henri* reinforce the bard's characterization of aristocratic power as tyrannical by its very nature. Louis, whose "regal scepter with no crime distain'd," wears a "crown innocuous, lawfully obtain'd," exempting him from the "dire, atrocious cruelty" ordinarily associated with dynastic rule. One suspects that this exemption, however, has more to do with Louis's resistance to abso-

[170]

lute monarchy and unwillingness to concentrate power in his hands than it does his saintly character. A king who leaves his subjects alone might well seem innocuous, indeed. Henry, whom the bard cannot bring himself to praise as either "innocuous" or entirely "distain'd," merits mention simply as sire of the House of Bourbon, whose historical purpose, according to the bard, is to put kings out of business altogether. When the bard attributes to these figures "holy rapture" to "find on France bestow'd / Another monarch, like themselves," the "likeness" inheres in the current incumbent's historical importance as the last in a trinity of French kings instrumental in the downfall of the "Pow'r Aristocratic." Thus the bard's ostensible gesture toward an acceptable form of benign (constitutional?) monarchy melts away, leaving us on solid—if radical—republican ground. Indeed, one may ask whether the poet's preservation of the "happy Louis" as a puppet king masks the true extent of the poem's radicalism, particularly in view of Geddes's brush with the government over the firmness of his (and other Catholics') loyalty. The following stanzas suggest that nobility can be reconciled with liberty if sanctified by a holy purpose: "Gaudeant ipsi, generosa pubes / Nata praeclaris atavis, et exhinc / Creditent solam meritis parari / Nobilitatem" (Rejoice, ev'n Ye, who boast a noble birth; / Vain, idle, foolish boast in Wisdom's eye / And henceforth learn to know, that nought on earth, / But worth and virtue, makes Nobility).

When compared to the explicit revolutionism of the *denunciatio*, this aspiration appears conventionally anodyne. The bard anchors himself to safe allegorical ground in the comparison of French bondage to that of the ancient Hebrews. His appeal to ministers of religion to forsake the comforts of their ecclesiastical establishments and to embrace vows of poverty would not overly trouble the conscience of a voluptuary, whether Catholic or Protestant. And "ev'n Ye, who boast of noble birth," may seek redemption from their inherited taint by devotion to "worth and virtue," as if they could re-create themselves as medieval crusaders or figures of chivalric romance. This stuff hardly breathes fire, but the conservative turn evident in these quatrains in the poem gives way to white heat in the following ones, which exhort, "fortis juvenis, lubensque / Velle, testetur patrias ad aras, / Se prius quam servitium subrire, / Perdere vitam" (Whilst your more vig'rous sons, in youthful age, / Exulting, at the patriot altar swear / Eternal war with tyranny to wage; / And sooner *death*, than *servitude*, to bear). The bard no longer seems anxious to propitiate moderate or conservative opinion but to declare the Rights of Man. Returning to the theme with which the song commences, this revolutionary appeal invokes "heav'n's great God" as the author of Liberty, suppressing national muses and recasting the "patriot altar" as domestic and universal. In this sense, the bard implies that servitude entails the same kind of obedience to "unreal"

BESIDE THE BARD

loyalties that Lady Nairne deplores in her laments. National identities, while apparently celebrated in the previous three quatrains ("Frenchmen, rejoice!"), are now denounced as false illusions that can be manipulated to benefit the aristocratic oppressors: the prelacy and nobility (often the same caste). The bard here proclaims a different form of patriarchy than either feudal or absolutist varieties, a patriarchy founded on filial duty and the sacrament of marriage. This markedly gendered "natural" Liberty figures the community as a kind of Rousseauean polity in which patriarchal rule is tempered by piety and domestic affection, rendering "national" government as unnecessary as it is repressive.

The celebration of domesticity continues in the following three quatrains, which also invite the rest of Europe to join the republican band. The bard appropriates the Burkean appeal to chivalry for republican uses, identifying women as primary beneficiaries of a "race of freemen, citizens, compeers / The faithful guardians of their sires and you." His suggestion of the matrilineal origin of this "race" emphasizes its difference from the ancien régime's reliance on church and crown to oppress its subjects. The aristocratic tradition of arranged marriage (and perhaps the popular myth of *droit du seigneur*) figures in this critique as both sexually exploitative and destructive of the marriage institution itself. In the absence of "free choice" in marriage, women become prostitutes, sex becomes rape, and marriage becomes unholy, prefiguring Blake's overtly radical lines:

> But most thro' midnight streets I hear
> How the youthful Harlots curse
> Blasts the new-born Infants tear
> And blights with plagues the Marriage hearse[47]

Just as the poem reverses Burke's paean to aristocratic traditions as "beautiful," it thus identifies radical republicanism with Christian virtue, refuting Burke's denunciation of the revolutionaries as placing their faith in deistic (or even atheistic) and materialist discourses of "moral" philosophy. Though the poem purports to address the French Assembly, it speaks directly to English fears that, if not put down by the concerted effort of European aristocracies, the revolution will continue to spread. But whereas Burke and the apologists raise the specter of a godless rabble bursting into the bedrooms of people of property and burning their family Bibles (or their copies of Magna Carta), the bard figures the revolution as the restoration of Christ's law: faith, hope, and charity. Aristocratic rule has co-opted the Christian religion and placed it in the service of an illegitimate and criminal syndicate. It is no wonder, then, that the bard calls on other subjected European peoples to overthrow their own nobles and prelates, no doubt stoking loyalist paranoia of Jacobinical wolves at the door.

[172]

BURNS AND THE JACOBINS

Indeed, as the bard turns his gaze from France and Europe to the Isles, he issues a challenge and an implied warning:

Albion! sed te potiore plausu
Liberos Fallos decet æmulari;
Æmlans Gallos, tibi gratularis
　　　　Terra Britanna!

Inclyti Heroes Runimedis agri,
Qualis, O, vobis stupor atque sensus?
En! magis clarum Runimedis agro
　　　　Cernitis agrum!

Mira! nunc Lutetia puriore
Gaudet unda, quam Trinobantium urbs; et
Thamesis quam, liberiore crusu
　　　　Sequana sertur.

But, Britons! ye should raise the loudest note,
　　　　For Freedom granted to a sister state:
While ye, with France, this day to joy devote,
　　　　Britons! yourselves ye do but gratulate.

Immortal heroes of that famous field,
　　　　Where was achiev'd the great, the glorious Deed!
What was your wonder, when ye, late, beheld
　　　　A *Field* more famous, ev'n than *Runimede*?

'Tis strange, 'tis passing strange! and, yet, 'tis plain,
　　　　Parisians quaff a purer draught than *We!*
And once sluggish, slow and soilly *Seine*,
　　　　Than *Thames* itself, flows freer to the sea!

British liberty, embodied in the Great Charter and immemorial Blackstonian custom, comes down to little more than a vestige of long-forgotten feudal conflicts, a pathetic historical footnote. While one might read these lines naïvely, the bard's palpable sense of shame and humiliation (the Parisians, of all people, have perfected human freedom) undercuts the Hanoverian constitutionalist narrative. In this rendition of "Whig" history, the torch has already passed to republican France, leaving the moldering carcass of British exceptionalism to poison the lifeline to its maritime empire. The bard's association of the failed Charter with the Thames likewise suggests Blake's dystopian "London":

[173]

BESIDE THE BARD

> I wander thro' each charter'd street,
> Near where the charter'd Thames does flow.
> And mark in every face I meet
> Marks of weakness, marks of woe.

For Blake, the synecdochic "charter" overdetermines English history as a continuous narrative of the aristocracy's enslavement and exploitation of the people ("every face") for its own interests, both at the imperial center ("each charter'd street") and the periphery ("where the charter'd Thames does flow"). Geddes's bard, however, appears to memorialize the "charter" in terms of the "Immortal heroes of that famous field," the barons who forced King John to restore their feudal privileges and now look on in "wonder" as the French discard the last vestiges of them. But the bard's comparison of Magna Carta to the *Declaration of the Rights of Man and of the Citizen* (1789), for which all Britons "should raise the loudest note, For Freedom granted to a sister state," indirectly emphasizes the dystopian condition of contemporary Britain that Blake explicitly invokes. Instead of rejoicing in the spread of liberty to a "sister state," the aristocratic "Britons" (and their Burkean fellow travelers), who by virtue of their own revolutions subjected the monarch to Parliamentary sovereignty, now plan a counterrevolution to return the absolutist Bourbons to power. The bard thus ironizes the British claim to have invented the liberty of the subject, when in fact the "Immortal heroes" of Runnymede were concerned merely with securing their own power vis-à-vis the monarch. This historical obfuscation has muddied the semiotic waters; only a Paineite revolution can purify the British nation and free it from its "charter'd" past.

Geddes's bard thus preserves the categories of "Britain" in order to expose the hypocrisy of claims to constitutional and political legitimacy based on a contract to which the vast majority of "Britons" are not and never have been parties. Republicanism, on the other hand, derives legitimacy from the inclusiveness of the political process that produces it. Thus Britain, to the extent it refers to a constitutionally constructed entity, does not exist and cannot command the loyalty or patriotism of most of its subjects. Does the bard nevertheless recognize that "Britons" may exist without the fiction of "Britain"? The answer may lie in the poem's Latinity itself, which posits "Britannia" as part of a unitary Roman culture that contains and reconciles national difference. Viewed in this context, the bard's invitation to "all nations round"—encompassing Iberi, Belgi, Batavi, Allemanni, and Helvetiique—can be read as proposing the "re-Romanization" of Europe in the republican mode. According to Geddes's bard in "Carmen sæculare," the French Revolution marks a return to the true history of Europe as a

[174]

single culture, an awakening from a dark millennium of schism, confessional violence, and nativist aberration.[48]

Though as a matter of history most of Scotia remained beyond the limits the Roman rule, Geddes's Latinity speaks for a Scottish ecclesiastical, juridical, and court tradition that participated in a pan-European discursive and cultural community largely defined by its Roman antecedents. In learned men such as Duns Scotus, George Buchanan, and Hector Boece, this Scotland can justifiably claim an immense contribution to the collective intellectual project of "Europe" as part of a Britannic identity that privileges its Roman origins over, for example, the fictional indigeneity of Tudor mythology or later Stuart Celticism. When Geddes's bard appeals to "Britons," he means the people whom Rome constituted. When Burns apostrophizes Scotia, rather, he means the people whom the Romans called *Scoti*, the Gaels who descended from union of the Irish Gathelas and the Graeco-Egyptian Scota, pharaoh's daughter. As Murray Pittock puts it, "the Scottish crown's descent from Irish kings, though less emphasized as the Middle Ages progressed, was an important indicator of difference from England and Wales, and indeed betokened a continuing consciousness of cultural alliance with Ireland: the Scottish kingdom was born of Irish immigration."[49] Burns's and other Scottish poets' invocation of Scotia thus revives this emphasis on a Hiberno-Scottish origin, as opposed to the Anglo-Welsh Arthurian mythology.[50]

Geddes's Scottish poetry offers an alternative discourse for identifying radical alterity within the imperial British state to that of "Carmen sæculare." As previously noted, the vernacular poem "The Ewe Bughts" and the Anglicized "The Cob Web" had been attributed to Burns until a little more than a decade ago, when Gerard Carruthers adduced evidence of Geddes's authorship.[51] If Carruthers is correct that the two lost poems are indeed Geddes's, then, taken together with "Carmen sæculare," they reveal the full range of available idiolects that embody the project of Scottish poetry in the Age of Burns. "The Ewe Bughts" was published in the *Morning Chronicle*, on July 10, 1794.[52] The poem announces itself as pastoral:

> 'Will you go to the Ewe-bughts, Marian,
>   'And wear in the sheep wi' me?
> 'The mavis sings sweetly, my Marian,
>   'But not sae sweetly as thee.'
> These aft were the words of my Sandy,
>   As we met in the how of the glen,
> But nae mair shall I meet wi' my Sandy,
>   For Sandy to Flanders is gane.

BESIDE THE BARD

This somewhat-irregular variant of common meter, which includes lines of iambic pentameter as well as anapestic trimeter, heptameter, and octameter, resists easy scansion, drawing attention to the lover's broken and forlorn plaint. In the first octave, the rhymed lines repeat the same term, the names of the lovers, as if they were carved indelibly in stone. This poem reinforces the union of the lovers by putting Sandy's words into Marian's mouth, so that the voices of the lovers blend into a single "sweet" song, shared and amplified by that of the ubiquitous song thrush. The repetitive use of the possessive pronoun "my" produces the effect of a low cry, sounding the lover's loss. The near rhyme of "Sandy"/"Flanders" in the last line of the octave may forebode Sandy's death in battle, his lonely burial in the foreign dust. The separation of the lovers materializes in the imperfect rhyme "glen"/"gane," signifying the violence with which Sandy has been wrenched from the land and his lover's embrace.

In the second octave, the lover projects her sorrow outward, directly addressing unspecified observers: "But, oh, tis the fault o' them a', Sirs, / In search of gowd and of fame, / The lads daily wander awa', Sirs, / And leave their poor lasses at hame." Here the lover rehearses the immemorial masculine allurements of war: excitement and change, plunder and celebrity. She makes no mention of patriotic fervor or duty, indicating the fictionality of abstract appeals of this sort, possibly even those offered by the gentlemanly "Sirs" whom she addresses. The lover's question—"Oh, could na' the Ewe-bughts and Marian / Please mair than the horrors of war?"—appears unanswerable. In relation to pastoral, it is unanswerable, but not so in epic, which celebrates young men who leave home "In search of gowd and of fame." The lover thus touches on the relationship between gender and genre; whereas "soft" pastoral poetry traditionally features rustic lovers ("Ewe-bughts and Marian") engaged in a stylized discourse about love, epic concentrates on "the trumpets loud clarion" and the "horrors of war." But both discourses remain ineluctably masculine, in that love and war become interchangeably masculine fields of conquest. That shepherd "lads wander awa' / And leave their poor lasses at hame" only makes sense in this unitary masculine economy, which the lover recognizes when she blames "them a'" for her abandonment.

The functional equivalence of masculine poetic discourses has real and catastrophic material effects. The pastoral lyric of the first octave and the epic lines of the second give way to the lover's clear-eyed social critique in the third: "Ilka Laird in the Highlands is rueing, / That he drove his poor tenants away, / For naething is seen here but ruin, / As the haughs are a' lying in lay." We see a sharpening of the lover's vernacular, as if cutting through the more formal genres rehearsed before. She tasks the observers to view the economic "ruin" they have caused and alludes to the clearances (that, ironically, have freed up

[176]

pasturage for the sheep Sandy tends), connecting war and "improvement" as twin aspects of the same masculine desire for self-aggrandizement. Here the lover seems to speak in her own voice, maintaining aesthetic form but filling the container with the materiality of lived domestic struggle. In this real world, ruin means starvation and death for the women and children left to shift for themselves. No pastoral or epic poetry can recuperate this condition—nothing comes from "naething."

The increasing bitterness of the lover's animus for masculine desire and the aesthetic forms that cloak it in glory bursts forth in the final octave:

> There's gowd in the garters of Sandy,
>   And silk in his blue-bonnet lug,
> And I'm not a kaerd nor a randy,
>   Nor a lass without blanket or rug;
> Then why should he fight sae for riches,
>   Or seeks for a sodger's degree,
> Or fling by his kilt for the breeches,
>   And leave the dear Ewe-Bughts to me?

Finally, the lover directs her anger at Sandy himself and, through him, at the masculine economy. The mournful love song of the first stanza, with its gesture toward the conventional sentimentality of love and loss, transforms into self-assertion and a different vision for sustaining the community. For the first time in the poem, the lover refers to herself, defining herself against "low" types, a "kaerd" (wool carder) or a "randy" (one who is coarse or rude, frequently associated with beggars).[53] Marian implies that by rejecting her and seeking a "sodger's degree," Sandy proves little more than a fool, seduced by aesthetically beautiful but barren discourses of male desire.[54] Marian's rejection of her lover suggests the possibility of an alternative world in which women "wear in the sheep" without a male auxiliary too stupid to know when he has it so good. From this perspective, the poem does not oppose war except insofar as war reflects the same masculine predilection for violent competition, whether in love or in war. This is not to say that the poem does not articulate more contemporary war-weariness but that the poem views war and masculine aggression from the perspective of those who have to pay the heaviest price for it. Here Geddes creates a "new radical text" that diagnoses British warmongering as in part a product of the aesthetic forms in which men celebrate (and perhaps prove to one another) their own masculinity.

Another of the lost poems, "The Cob Web—A Song," appeared in the *Morning Chronicle* on August 22, 1795.[55] The poem begins in the same vein as "Carmen

[177]

BESIDE THE BARD

sæculare" ends. The speaker, who identifies himself as "A. Briton,"[56] apostrophizes Britons for their traditional love of liberty:

> The sweets of a blessing
> Are had by possessing,
> Hail! Britons! the cause is your own;
>   You are wonderful great,
>   You have Princes and State,
> And the wisest and best on a Throne![57]

The first stanza features three strong rhymes: "blessing"/"possessing"; "great"/"State"; and "own"/"Throne". These rhymes suggest the intimate connection in loyalist polemics between God-granted British exceptionalism (blessing), property (own and possess), and the institutional church-state, unified in the person of the monarch. As the poem continues, the speaker contrasts France, but not in the absolutist and popish terms we might expect to see in loyalist texts. Instead, the speaker emphasizes Britain's "flourishing Trade, / Plenty, beer, meat, and bread," shifting the poem's focus from the ancient constitutional establishment of liberty (on display in "Carmen sæculare") to a specifically eighteenth-century discourse of "improvement" and commercial affluence.[58] This allusion reflects Enlightenment apologetics that link Britain's apparent economic success to its politico-legal institutions, complete with the Lockean equation between liberty, property, and "happiness." But the use of the term "happy" is almost certainly ironized in terms of the judicious Richard Hooker's definition of "happiness" as a life of virtue.[59] The problem for the unlucky, starving, and "unfree" French seems to inhere in their lack of security of property, though in their starvation "to be free" they seem to reject Locke's happiness for Hooker's.

In the third stanza, the speaker abandons the ironized discourse of exceptionalism of the first two, lamenting in chastened tones a lost past of real British freedom: "It was once so for us, / Indeed it was thus." This couplet, so beautiful in its simplicity, reverses the speaker's perspective, casting the French struggles in universalist terms. As it was with us, so it shall be with you—national signifiers dissolve in the essential unity of God and man. We are all the same in him, seeking "The blessing that God, / Sent to cheer man's abode, / And preserve free from blemish or stain." Having reestablished the common basis of human desire in humble domestic virtue, the speaker returns to the historical moment in the following stanzas. As in "Carmen sæculare," the speaker questions why Britons cannot see themselves in their French compatriots. The repetition of "free," "freemen," and "freedom" in the fourth stanza reveals the speaker's disinterest in

[178]

national signifiers. Instead, he refers to both "they" and "we" as "freemen," a common "People." In the following stanza, however, national prejudice wedges itself back into the poem. In Britain the "freedom for which the French rue" signifies "a good, full of evil, / Devis'd by the Devil." This appalling hypocrisy seems to shock the speaker, and he completes the metonymic association of the Devil, the British government, and the gravest of sins, fraud ("We offer'd Court blessings to treat them"). When the French naturally reject this Faustian offer, the British use that rejection as a pretext for a "just" and "holy" war ("And force us, unwilling, to beat them").

The bitterness of the speaker's denunciation of *la perfide Albion* continues in the following stanzas, in which the speaker refers to William Pitt's unsuccessful strategy to invest British and royalist hopes in the Dauphin and the First Coalition's military reverses. When these measures fail, Pitt's tactics turn to subversion and economic blockade, alluding to the great naval battle of June 1, 1794, when the Royal Navy failed to stop a convoy of ships bringing grain to France. The speaker ironically observes that rather than starving French women and children, the government has managed only to starve its own people—especially Scots, who in the 1790s experienced several years of food shortages, high grain prices, and rampant price inflation.[60] The speaker in "The Cob Web" registers this distress, reinforcing the pervasive impression that Britain is caught in downward social spiral:

> But courage my Friends
> We may yet gain our ends,
> Perhaps in a circle they'll meet:
> When, nine out of ten
> They've kill'd of our men,
> And the rest are left something to eat.

Geddes's beautiful Jacobite lyric "Lewie Gordon" equals similar compositions of Burns and Nairne and demonstrates Geddes's comprehensive poetic range:[61]

> O send Lewie Gordon hame,
> And the lad I daurna name!
> Though his back be at the wa',
> Here's to him that's far awa'.
> > Ohone! my Highlandman;
> > Oh! my bonnie Highlandman!
> > Weel wad I my true love ken
> > Amang ten thousand Highlandmen.

[179]

BESIDE THE BARD

> Oh! to see his tartan trews,
> Bonnet blue, and laigh-heeled shoes,
> Philabeg abune his knee!—
> That's the lad that I'll gang wi'.
> > Ohone! my Highlandman.

> Princely youth of whom I sing,
> Thou wert born to be a king!
> On thy breast a regal star
> Shines on loyal hearts afar.
> > Ohone! my Highlandman.

> Oh! to see the wished-for one
> Seated on a kingly throne!
> All our griefs would disappear,
> We should hail a joyful year,
> > Ohone! my Highlandman.

Geddes's lyric reflects all of the features of the Jacobite song with which we are familiar: the speaker's mingled sexual and emotional desire for the conflated figure of her beloved and Prince Charlie; the sartorial typology of the Highlandman; the lover's consciousness of the permanence of the Highlandman's exile; the millenarian association of Charlie's coming with the onset of a new age. Geddes's version of the song, however, operates on two discursive levels: the first two stanzas use the Scots vernacular to voice the lover's lament for her Highland laddie, while the last two address the "wished-for one" in limpid English (though the refrain returns to the vernacular). This discursive shift produces profoundly different effects, as the sexualized love lyric celebrating "the lad I daurna name" pulls apart from the transcendent desire for spiritual unity, embodied by the "wished-for one / Seated on a kingly throne." Geddes's use of Jacobite lyric seems quite distinct from that of Burns, who, as William Donaldson argues, deploys the Jacobite lyric in pursuit of "the preservation and renewal of the *Kulturstaat*," the Scottish "nation, defined as a sense of collective identity based on a common cultural tradition."[62] As we have seen in Geddes's Latin, English, and vernacular poetry, his interest lies not in the recovery of the imaginative artifacts of an endangered Scottish *Volk* but in the disassociation of Scottishness from any and all forms of historical, religious, or cultural exceptionalism (or, one might say, parochialism). His vision spurns "Britain" as well, whose assimilationist narrative, so insistently promoted by the learned literati (which might be said to include Geddes himself),[63] remains far too constricted for Geddes's expansive conception of Scottish identity as both ahistorical and deracinated in nature. In Geddes's Jacobite lyric, the eponymous

[180]

figure of Lewie Gordon, the "Highlandman," refers not just to a feudal remnant of the Scottish past but to an eternal and republican Scotland with which any humane soul may self-identify. To this extent, Geddes's Jacobitism retains political purchase, even while it cuts "Scottishness" loose from both its ancestral and Ossianic tethers. For Geddes, to identify as Scottish simply means that one embraces a forgiving Christian God and rejects tyranny in any form. Though this category remains explicitly European and Latin, as we have seen, it is nevertheless theocentric and refuses national inflections.

CONCLUSION

THIS STUDY HAS SOUGHT TO TRACE the emergence of a literarily and historically significant body of Scottish Lowland poetry produced during and in the immediate aftermath of the life of Robert Burns. It has also sought to establish the "national" characteristics of this poetry in the terms of the critical and popular success of the "Scotch Bard," whose immense talent as a poet and adept self-fashioning opened up the possibility of literary fame for poets from the laboring and middle ranks of Scottish society but at the same time limited their access to a market defined by the critical response to Burns's genius. Most of these poets failed to "succeed" in the Burns fashion and generally survive today as characters in Burns biographies and monographs (not to mention as entries in *The Burns Encyclopedia*). Some, however, such as Lady Nairne and Robert Tannahill, enjoyed significant nineteenth-century reputations as songwriters suitable for polite performances in Victorian parlors and have seen renewed interest in their work in our own time. Another, Alexander Wilson, became a leading Enlightenment figure in the United States after his radical political views and legal problems drove him from Scotland. In a rare bit of poetic justice, his fame as an "American" has sparked long overdue interest in his Scottish poetry (and politics) in current scholarship.

But as I hope to have shown, while these poets may have labored in vain to reproduce Burns's winning formula, they each responded to the pressures and hardships of historical, economic, and social change in late eighteenth-century Scotland in their own ways and according to their own lights. If we allow Burns's poetry alone to determine the full scope and content of "Scottish literature" of the period, we come away with a distorted perspective not only on what makes a particular text "Scottish" but on what may constitute a "national" literature, if we can say that such a category exists. Surely, in order to be "national," a literature ought to speak from within the broadest possible range of linguistic and formal choices available to its poets. It ought to represent in the broadest possible terms the gender, class, and social positions of its poets. And it ought to engage with the greatest possible depth the political, social, and intellectual commitments of its poets. In these terms, there can be no question that late eighteenth-century Scot-

[183]

BESIDE THE BARD

land produced a "national" literature, or at least a literature that registers the ambiguities and ambivalences of a nation trying to find an independent footing in a hegemonic "British" world.

All inquiries of this nature raise as many new questions as they answer and suggest possible directions for future research. In attempting to assess the effect of the "canonization" of Burns on his contemporary Lowland poets, I have been struck by the extent to which, in Scotland, the canonical succession of Ramsay, Fergusson, and Burns has determined analysis of the precise nature of the relationship between the individual poet, the figure of the "bard," and the characteristics of national art. While other poets, such Macpherson, Beattie, Scott, and Hogg (the autodidactic or self-taught poet model does not fit all cases) enter into the question as well, those who do not conform to this partly retrospective standard of "Scottishness" find themselves in a critical dead zone of inferiority and exclusion. Additionally, because the figure of the Scottish bard and its importance to the national canon is so decidedly masculine, women poets need not even apply. In my readings, Janet Little, Isobel Pagan, and Lady Nairne speak to the condition of Scotland in complex ways from a wide range of social positions, but each of them does so from outside the magic circle inscribed by, in Nairne's words, the "Lords of Creation." They thus share a common position from which to produce an "alternative tradition" to the masculine canon. I hope that this study demonstrates how we might evaluate the contribution of these poets to Scottish national literature and identify the specific ways these poets complicate the Burnsian figure of the "Scotch Bard." Much work remains to be done, however, to establish the influence of women poets on national literature, not only in the Scottish case but more generally. In what ways do women poets (or any marginalized poets, for that matter) participate in a literary culture they had no part in creating? How do national literatures come into being, how permanent are they, and why and under what circumstances do they change? These questions remain open to further investigation and rethinking.

One of the difficulties of working in this period is the lack of scholarly editions of Burns's contemporaries. As Gerard Carruthers has rightly lamented, for example, "we remain far short of having all the necessary materials for a longer and much-needed cultural study of [Alexander] Wilson."[1] The same could be said for, I would argue, Alexander Geddes, Lady Nairne, and Robert Tannahill, particularly if we take into account Geddes's significant contributions to biblical criticism, political satire, and historical analysis. Further, the "imitators" of Burns, among them four of the poets studied here, John Lapraik, David Sillar, Janet Little, and Isobel Pagan, might be aggregated into a scholarly revision of James Paterson's *The Contemporaries of Burns*, which is still a valuable resource for the Ayrshire

[184]

CONCLUSION

"bardies." Finally, a definitive scholarly study of late eighteenth-century radical Scottish poetry and the British state's reactionary response to poets in particular remains to be done. Such a study would include poets such as Wilson, his friend James Kennedy, and the group of poets attracted to Thomas Muir but would also encompass the significant amount of anonymous poetry published in politically progressive media and other more ephemeral forms. It would also assess with more precision the circulation of this poetry in the laboring and artisanal classes from which the poetry came. The subsequent history of the Scottish working class and the eventual rise of home-rule parties in Scottish national politics surely owes something to this eighteenth-century radical tradition, brief though it was in the face of savage repression.

Another set of questions that merit further research involves the influence of late eighteenth-century Scottish poets on British and Anglophone literature and culture in more general terms. What did innovations in Scottish poetry contribute to archipelagic literary production in the nineteenth century? How did Scottish poetry interact with national literatures in England, Ireland, and Wales? Beyond the Isles, what effects and influences did Scottish diasporic poets have in the transatlantic and imperial domains in the nineteenth century and beyond? What continuities and disjunctions exist between domestic Scottish national literature and Scottish literature produced *outre mer*? What came back home to Scotland from abroad, and what did not? To what extent does international "Scottishness" interact with and influence the rise of Scottish nationalism since the second half of the nineteenth century? How did the eighteenth-century tradition of plebeian Lowland Scottish poetry inform Scotland's unique political development vis-à-vis England? While much has been done in recent years to address these questions, much scope for research remains.

This study does not address the integration of Highland poetry in Gaelic, Scots, or English into late eighteenth-century Scottish national literature. While in recent years scholars have paid increasing attention to Scottish poets writing in Gaelic, the terms of analysis for placing Lowland and Highland poetry in the same national framework await full articulation.[2] For example, how might the historical experience of civil war, economic deprivation, and imperial subjection inflect Lowland and Highland poetry? Does the use of Gaelic in Highland poetry express historical experience so distinctly that it constitutes a discrete category of poetry with its own interpretive standards? Does Scotland have one "national" literature or more than one? And when the Highland clearances started in earnest after the Napoleonic wars, what was lost to Scottish literature, and, conversely, what did Anglophone literature gain from migrants from the homeland? Some of these answers can no doubt be found, for example, in studies of the national literatures

[185]

BESIDE THE BARD

of the United States and the white settler dominions. In this regard, the lovely volume *Alexander Wilson: Enlightened Naturalist* brings Wilson's Scottish and American careers into the same focus, and its wonderful essays suggest approaches to transnational literary analysis that could fruitfully be developed for other diasporic poets, Scottish and otherwise.[3]

Finally, I marvel that in the late eighteenth century a small and relatively poor country on the northwest fringe of Europe, attached to a powerful and acquisitive neighbor striving to dominate it economically and culturally, produced such a rich culture of men and women of "independent mind," tongue, and pen. I am not here under the spell of claims of Scottish exceptionalism of the "how Scotland invented the modern world" type but am referring to a lived reality in which tenant farmers, ploughmen, packmen, weavers, schoolteachers, howff proprietors, dairy maids, aristocratic women under cover, political undesirables, and defrocked Catholic priests consolidated a national literary tradition that in many ways anticipated the ways and means of national culture formation in nineteenth-century Europe and beyond. That they accomplished this feat while facing economic precarity; sudden downward turns in fortune; gender, class, and religious prejudice; legal and political persecution; depression; disappointment; suicide; and for some the very real threat of imprisonment and exile only emphasizes the magnitude of their achievement. As we have seen, their quest left few sacred cows undisturbed: the political and social order, the existing hierarchies of gender and class, the triumphalist claims of nationalism and imperialism, and, not least, the critical standards by which intellectual elites determine literary merit. This study is dedicated to the men and women who made Scottish Lowland literature in the Age of Burns.

[186]

ACKNOWLEDGMENTS

I am deeply grateful my colleagues at the University of Texas at Austin for their support, encouragement, and advice on the preparation of this book, especially Brian Levack, Sam Baker, James Vaughn, Roger Louis, and Judith Coffin. My thanks, too, to the wonderful staff at the Harry Ransom Research Center and Perry-Castañeda Library at the University of Texas, National Library of Scotland, Edinburgh University Library, and Paisley Central Library. Finally, nothing ever would have been done but for the love, friendship, patience, and humor of Betsy, Leah, Kathryn, and George Christian and Sarah Christian Brothers.

I also wish to thank Taylor & Francis Ltd. for permission to reprint in chapter 4 parts of my essay "Gendering the Scottish Nation: Rereading the Songs of Lady Nairne," *European Romantic Review* 29, no. 6 (2019): 681–709.

NOTES

INTRODUCTION

1. Robert Crawford, "Scottish Literature and English Studies," in *The Scottish Invention of British Literature*, ed. Robert Crawford (Cambridge: Cambridge University Press, 1998), 240.

2. Gerard Carruthers, ed., *The Edinburgh Companion to Robert Burns* (Edinburgh: Edinburgh University Press, 2009); Nigel Leask, *Robert Burns and Pastoral: Poetry and Improvement in Late Eighteenth-Century Scotland* (Oxford: Oxford University Press, 2010); Corey Andrews, *The Genius of Scotland: The Cultural Production of Robert Burns, 1785–1834* (Leiden: Brill Rodopi, 2015); Alex Broadhead, *The Language of Robert Burns: Style, Ideology, and Identity* (Lewisburg, PA: Bucknell University Press, 2014).

3. Corey E. Andrews, "'Far Fam'd RAB': Scottish Labouring-Class Poets Writing in the Shadow of Robert Burns, 1785–1792," *Studies in Hogg and His World*, January 1, 2013, 41–42. Nigel Leask has problematized Burns's characterization as a "laboring class" poet. Leask points out that as a tenant farmer, Burns "occupied the middle rung on the social hierarchy of the rural Lowlands," whose "social peers" included "lawyers, land agents, . . . carters, carriers, and innkeepers: booksellers, printers, schoolteachers, entertainers, and clerks: drapers, grocers, druggists, stationers, ironmongers, shopkeepers of every sort" (*Robert Burns and Pastoral*, 17–18).

4. David Daiches adds William Hamilton of Gilbertfield to this list. See Daiches, "Eighteenth-Century Vernacular Poetry," in *Scottish Poetry: A Critical Survey*, ed. James Kinsley (Norwood, PA: Norwood Editions, 1976), 154. Maurice Lindsay discusses a somewhat more eclectic selection of poets in his chapter on the eighteenth century, including Alexander Pennecuik, Hamilton, Alexander Ross, David Malloch, Tannahill, Elizabeth Hamilton, Baillie, and Nairne. See Lindsay, *History of Scottish Literature* (London: R. Hale, 1977), chap. 4.

5. Robert Crawford, *Scotland's Books: A History of Scottish Literature* (Oxford: Oxford University Press, 2009), 329–383.

6. Andrews, "Far Fam'd RAB," 59.

7. Robert Burns to Mrs. Dunlop, March 4, 1789, in *Letters of Robert Burns*, 2nd ed., 2 vols., ed. J. Delancey Ferguson and G. Ross Roy (Oxford, UK: Clarendon, 1985), 1:382.

8. As Andrews notes regarding Burns's "Epistle to Davie," "Burns had addressed 'Davie' Sillar as a 'brother poet'; he would soon discover that other poets viewed him in the same light, reaching out to him as a 'brother poet' in unsolicited verse. Such gestures were expressly calculated to help the authors gain recognition in the literary field, particularly those epistles penned by fellow labouring-class poets. Establishing kinship with Burns began to be perceived by such poets as the necessary first step to entering the literary marketplace as a 'legtimised' author" (*Genius of Scotland*, 94–95). But even as other poets sought his imprimatur, Burns "eventually spurned such admirers as he began to experience the vagaries of fame and his own litany of personal and professional disappointments" (ibid., 96).

9. Michel Foucault, *The Order of Things: An Archaeology of the Human Sciences* (New York: Vintage, 1994), 119.

[189]

NOTES TO PAGES 3-10

10. Broadhead, *Language of Robert Burns*, 31, 34.
11. Bob Harris, "Cultural Change in Provincial Scottish Towns, c. 1700–1820," *Historical Journal* 54, no. 1 (2011): 138–139.
12. Ibid., 140.
13. See Carol McGuirk, *Reading Robert Burns: Texts, Contexts, Transformations* (London: Pickering and Chatto, 2014), xii–xiii.
14. Ibid., 119.
15. Bob Harris, "The Enlightenment, Towns and Urban Society in Scotland, c. 1760–1820," *English Historical Review* 126, no. 522 (2011): 1115–1116. See also Paul Kaufman, "The Rise of Community Libraries in Scotland," *Papers of the Bibliographical Society of America* 59, no. 3 (1965): 233–294. Kaufman laments the spotty nature of source data for determining the scope of library catalogues in the late eighteenth century and the complete absence of evidence of rental shelves by Scottish booksellers.
16. Vivienne Dunstan, "Chapmen in Eighteenth-Century Scotland," *Scottish Literary Review* 9, no. 2 (2017): 45–50.
17. Murray Pittock, "The W. Ormiston Roy Memorial Lecture: Who Wrote the Scots Musical Museum? Challenging Editorial Practice in the Presence of Authorial Absence," *Studies in Scottish Literature* 42, no. 1 (2016): 13.
18. Harris, "Enlightenment," 1122.
19. Ibid., 1129–1130. Dunstan likewise points out that the nature of the archival material skews studies of print distribution in favor of the more affluent classes. Vivienne Dunstan, "Book Ownership in Late Eighteenth-Century Scotland: a Local Case Study of Dumfriesshire Inventories," *Scottish Historical Review* 91, no. 232, pt. 2 (2012): 276.
20. Harris, "Enlightenment," 1132. On the growth and influence of newspapers in Scotland during the 1790s, see Bob Harris, *The Scottish People and the French Revolution* (London: Pickering and Chatto, 2008), chap. 2.
21. Harris, "Enlightenment," 1134. Harris also points out that smaller manufacturing towns or villages with large concentrations of workers engaged in a single occupation "may well have provided more congenial environments for its development partially hidden from often fiercely conservative-minded elites" (ibid., 1130).
22. McGuirk, *Reading Robert Burns*, 30.
23. See Dunstan, "Book Ownership," 276; and Dunstan, "Chapmen," 46. On the parochial library movement initiated in the 1790s, see Jonathan Rose, "Reading," in *The Edinburgh History of the Book in Scotland: Ambition and Industry, 1800–1880*, vol. 3, ed. Bill Bell (Edinburgh: Edinburgh University Press, 2007), 179.
24. See Elizabeth Ewan, Sue Innes, Siân Reynolds, and Rose Pipes, eds., *The Biographical Dictionary of Scottish Women* (Edinburgh: Edinburgh University Press, 2006), 207–208, 286, 289.
25. Gerard Carruthers, *Scottish Literature* (Edinburgh: Edinburgh University Press, 2009), 198.
26. Christopher Harvie, *Scotland and Nationalism: Scottish Society and Politics 1707 to the Present*, 4th ed. (London: Routledge, 2004), 7–8.
27. Quoted in Ibid., 8.
28. Carla Sassi and Silke Stroh, "Nation and Home," in *The International Companion to Scottish Poetry*, ed. Carla Sassi (Glasgow: Scottish Literature International, 2015), 144–145.
29. Robert Crawford, *Devolving English Literature*, 2nd ed. (Edinburgh: Edinburgh University Press, 2000), 313–314.
30. I am borrowing the term "grammar" from Janet Sorenson's brilliant study *The Grammar of Empire in Eighteenth-Century British Writing* (Cambridge: Cambridge University Press, 2000).

[190]

NOTES TO PAGES 10–12

31. Mary Jane Scott, "James Thomson and the Anglo-Scots," in *The History of Scottish Literature*, vol. 2, *1660–1800*, ed. Andrew Hook (Aberdeen: Aberdeen University Press, 1987), 81.

32. Crawford, *Scotland's Books*, 3.

33. H. R. Trevor-Roper, *The Invention of Scotland: Myth and History* (New Haven, CT: Yale University Press, 2008).

34. For purposes of this study, I adopt Liam McIlvanney's definition of "radical" and "radicalism" as denoting "both the practical agitation for political reform that emerged in the wake of the American Revolution, and the intellectual resources of the reform movement—for instance, the contractarian and Real Whig ideas primarily associated with Dissenting and Presbyterian denominations." McIlvanney, *Burns the Radical: Poetry and Politics in Late Eighteenth-Century Scotland* (East Linton, UK: Tuckwell, 2000), 9. In McIlvanney's usage, "radicalism" refers not to specific political affiliations but to a "general nonconformity and contentiousness, the comprehensive dissidence of a man [Burns] who could boast: 'I set as little by kings, lords, clergy, critics, &c. as all these respectable Gentry do by my Bardship'" (ibid., 10). See also Colin Kidd, "Burns and Politics," in Carruthers, *Edinburgh Companion to Robert Burns*, 61–73. Kidd points out that in late eighteenth-century Britain, "all political positions, whatever their superficial differences, were grounded in a common Whiggery. The very hegemony of an unchallenged set of core Whig shibboleths—the mixed constitution, the Hanoverian succession, the Union—created a tolerant political space in which sentimental Jacobitism, for instance, was indulged as a harmless diversion and in which the sacred revolution principles of 1688 took on a different colouring, perhaps even a different meaning, for different kinds of Whigs, conservative or radical" (ibid., 72–73).

35. Carol McGuirk, "Writing Scotland: Robert Burns," in *The Edinburgh History of Scottish Literature*, vol. 2, ed. Ian Brown (Edinburgh: Edinburgh University Press), 176.

36. Here I refer primarily to Bergson's *Matter and Memory* (1896), trans. Arthur Mitchell (New York: Henry Holt, 1911); and *Creative Evolution* (1907), trans. Arthur Mitchell (New York: Henry Holt, 1911).

37. Evan Gottlieb's work on the Scottish Enlightenment doctrine of sympathy and its importance to developing conceptions of Britishness argues that the Scottish literati's ruminations on what we now call cognitive science is of special interest here. See Gottlieb, *Feeling British: Sympathy and National Identity in Scottish and English Writing, 1707–1832* (Lewisburg, PA: Bucknell University Press, 2007). My use of the term "feeling Scottish" refers to self and collective identity formation through specific forms of "remembrance" available to poets and writers of all classes, educational backgrounds, and social and economic conditions. I am also cognizant of Neil Davidson's carefully drawn distinction between "national consciousness" and "nationalism." For Davidson, national consciousness precedes nationalism but does not necessitate it. National consciousness is "a more or less passive expression of collective identification among a social group," whereas nationalism requires "a more or less active participation in the political mobilisation of a social group for the construction *or* defence of a state." Davidson, *The Origins of Scottish Nationhood* (London: Pluto, 2000), 14–15. As we will see in its full amplitude, drawing lines of this sort when reading specific writers and poets in context is enormously difficult.

38. For example, David McCrone has defined Scotland as a "stateless nation," a definition that seems only to emphasize the problem. McCrone, *Understanding Scotland: The Sociology of a Nation*, 2nd ed. (London: Routledge, 2001), 2. Citing this definition, Leith Davis extends McCrone's analysis, suggesting that "if Scotland is a 'stateless nation,' it is possible to think of the wider unit of Britain as a nationless state, as it has always been fraught with contradictions that refuse to settle into any coherent national identity." Davis, *Acts of Union: Scotland the Literary Negotiation of the British Nation* (Stanford, CA: Stanford University Press,

[191]

NOTES TO PAGES 12-13

1998), 11. Even the redoubtable Christopher Smout seems unsure of how to approach terminology in his recent contribution to *The Edinburgh History of Scottish Literature*, referring to Scottishness and Britishness occupying the same cultural spaces in relative intensities. Smout, "Scotland as North Britain: The Historical Background, 1707–1918," in Brown, *Edinburgh History of Scottish Literature*, vol. 2, 1–11.

39. T. C. Smout, "Scotland as North Britain: The Historical Background, 1707–1918" in *The Edinburgh History of Scottish Literature*, vol. 2, ed. Ian Brown (Edinburgh: Edinburgh University Press, 2007), 1–11. Colin Kidd, "North Britishness and the Nature of Eighteenth-Century British Patriotisms," *History Journal* 39 (1996): 363, 364.

40. This view is succinctly stated in T. M. Devine, "In Bed with an Elephant: Almost Three Hundred Years of the Anglo-Scottish Union," *Scottish Affairs* 57 (2006): 1–18. In this article Devine views the independence debate very much in pragmatic terms as a question of shifting economic and social interests that weigh more or less in favor of Unionism under specific historical conditions. In this regard, Michael Fry usefully defines post-Union Scottish "nationalism" as a set of "modes of thought and action," exemplified most notably in the operation of indigenous Scottish institutions such as the nobility, law, schools and universities, and the Kirk. These institutions, Fry argues, continued to function relatively unimpeded by the Treaty of Union well into the nineteenth century, greatly diminishing the "need for Scots to adopt a defensive nationalism against loss of statehood." Whether the longevity of Scotland's feudal and juridical organization entitles what existed in Scotland prior to 1707 to designation as a "state," especially in light of its vexed and often subservient relations with England, might be argued both ways, and even Fry sometimes slides between the terms "Scottishness" and "nationalism" in much the same way as other scholars do. But Fry's gesture toward a form of Scottishness in some way dependent on institutions manned by cultured elites seems overly exclusive. Scottishness must be accessible both vertically and horizontally to constitute a truly "national" consciousness. The poets featured in this study exist within, respond to, and often resist these institutional structures, but they also locate their Scottishness in uniquely personal, idiosyncratic, and affective "modes of thought and action." Fry, *The Dundas Despotism* (Edinburgh: Edinburgh University Press, 1992), 15.

41. As Leith Davis, Ian Duncan, and Janet Sorenson have pointed out, "The French Revolution provoked a crisis of ideological legitimation in this Scottish republic of letters. The Anti-Jacobin crackdown, strengthened by the monopolistic control of institutions under William Pitt's 'Scotch manager,' Secretary of State Henry Dundas, issued in a general repression: the transportation of 'Friends of the People,' official warnings to philo-revolutionary professors like Dugald Stewart and John Millar, and a Tory stranglehold on appointments and promotions. Accordingly, the projects of Enlightenment shifted their institutional base, from the university curriculum to an industrializing literary marketplace." Davis, Duncan, and Sorenson, introduction to *Scotland and the Borders of Romanticism*, ed. Davis, Duncan, and Sorenson (Cambridge: Cambridge University Press, 2004), 11–12.

42. Gerard Carruthers is particularly strong on this point, arguing that for the literati trying to make sense of Burns's "genius," figures such as Henry Mackenzie might position Burns as "the epitome of literary democracy and novelty," but in doing so "the traces of the poet's literary antecedents are kicked over." Carruthers, *Scottish Literature*, 57. Most of Burns's poetry, Carruthers notes, reflects his schooling "in the modes of the eighteenth-century poetry revival (to say nothing of his very wide and catholic reading of all the mainstream poets of eighteenth-century Britain)," as well as his Scottish Enlightenment "mentality" (ibid.).

43. But as Christopher Harvie points out, even at Burns's most subversive in "Scots, wha hae," his attitude toward Scottish nationalism was ambiguous. "His poem is at no point anti-

[192]

NOTES TO PAGE 13

English, was first carried in a London radical paper, the *Morning Chronicle*, in 1794, and its radical Whig argument scarcely differed from that of 'Rule Britannia' by Burns' hero, James Thomson of Ednam, written in 1740" (*Scotland and Nationalism*, 14). Still, as Carruthers notes, Burns had to "watch his step" in the superheated political climate of the 1790s. Carruthers, "Burns and Publishing," in Carruthers, *Edinburgh Companion to Robert Burns*, 19. Carol McGuirk likewise captures the ambiguity of Burns's position, postulating a "two-sided" critical perspective of the poet: Burns the "working-class hero and also the national hero—a super-Scot"; and "Burns as a victim" who died a broken man without "the recognition and support he deserved." McGuirk, "Scottish Hero, Scottish Victim: Myth of Robert Burns," in Hook, *History of Scottish Literature*, 219–238. McGuirk argues that Burns fit neither description and that both devalue the real Burns poet, who "disintegrates" English into the Scots vernacular "in an effort to evoke the 'Scottish' subject matter as truly universal, not local" (ibid., 234). Burns's transformative use of English is itself a form of Scottish rebellion against assimilative culture and a marker of "Scotland's continuing cultural difference" (ibid.). See also McGuirk's discussion of Burns and the literary canon, in which she assesses the critical debate over whether Burns can be read as both a "Scottish" and "English" poet (*Reading Robert Burns*, 8–12).

44. On this subject the introduction to Robert Crawford's wonderful biography is particularly instructive. Crawford, *The Bard: Robert Burns, a Biography* (Princeton, NJ: Princeton University Press), 3–14. See also Richard J. Finlay, "The Burns Cult and Scottish Identity in the Nineteenth and Twentieth Centuries," in *Love and Liberty: Robert Burns, a Bicentenary Celebration*, ed. Kenneth Simpson (East Linton, UK: Tuckwell, 1997), 69–78. Perhaps the definitive study to date of Burns's "production" as a literary icon is Andrews, *Genius of Scotland*. Andrew Noble's introduction to his and Patrick Scott Hogg's controversial Canongate edition of Burns's poetry actively seeks to disinter the "real" Burns from a tomb safeguarded by the cultural and political conservatives who prevailed in the political struggles of the late eighteenth century. "Consequent on such a new explication of Burns's political values and poetry, will be an exploration into the calculated and deeply successful manner in which, from the moment of his death, his achievement as a radically dissenting democratic poet was denied and suppressed," Noble asserts. "Indeed, what is revealed is the degree to which a whole segment of late-enlightenment liberal, Scottish culture of which Burns was an integral part was, as far as possible, obliterated from the national memory by reactionary forces which were quick to build on their total victory in the 1790s." Noble, introduction to *The Canongate Burns: The Complete Songs and Poems of Robert Burns*, ed. Noble and Hogg (Edinburgh: Canongate, 2001), x.

45. As Leith Davis and Maureen McLane have observed, "For poets, antiquarians and collectors, the complex situation of orality turned out to be in some ways a boon, particularly in post-Culloden Scotland, when the volatility of political Jacobitism gave way to a milder cultural nationalism: an illustrious Scottish national past—an oral past—could be celebrated without necessarily challenging British hegemony." Davis and McLane, "Orality and Public Poetry," in Brown, *Edinburgh History of Scottish Literature*, vol. 2, 126. The authors align Ramsay, Burns, and Hogg, however, with the more radical and subversive possibilities of "representations of orality" (ibid.).

46. Trevor-Roper, *Invention of Scotland*.

47. Susan Manning, "Post-Union Scotland and the Scottish Idiom of Britishness," in Brown, *Edinburgh History of Scottish Literature*, vol. 2, 48–49. David Daiches similarly argues that antiquarianism became an acceptable form of nationalism, while overt protests against the Union were politically "incorrect" expressions of national sentiment. Daiches, *The Paradox of Scottish Culture: The Eighteenth-Century Experience* (London: Oxford University Press, 1964), 28. As Daiches indicates, as long as "Scottish nationalism" had no reference to an

[193]

NOTES TO PAGES 13–14

entity that might be oppositionally (to England) identified as Scotland, one could enjoy his or her Scottish nationalism in relative peace and security.

48. Manning, "Post-Union Scotland," 49–50.

49. Sorenson, *Grammar of Empire*, 25–27. Sorenson advocates a "transnational explanation of the multiple, layered senses of what it means to be English, Scottish, Celtic, and British," a process by which imperial Britain imposed Standard English on its geographic periphery as a common "dominant language" that constructed, differentiated, and hierarchized internal stratifications of class and gender. She thus refigures Michael Hechter's provocative characterization of Scotland as an "internal colony" of England as a dialectical relation in which the English and Scottish Lowland cultural elites participated in the creation, epitomized in Dr. Johnson's *Dictionary*, of an "imperial grammar" or "national language" that no British subject actually spoke (ibid., 16–21).

50. Virginia Woolf, *Three Guineas* (London: Harcourt Brace, 1938), 78.

51. Leith Davis, "From Fingal's Harp to Flora's Song: Scotland, Music and Romanticism," *Wordsworth Circle* 31, no. 2 (2000): 94.

52. J.G.A. Pocock, *The Discovery of Islands: Essays in British History* (Cambridge: Cambridge University Press, 2005), 145.

53. On this point, see Caroline McCracken-Flesher, "Scotland as Theory: Otherness and Instantiation from Mackenzie to the Last Minstrel," *International Journal of Scottish Literature* 3, no. 3 (2007): 1–17. Reading Hume, Mackenzie, and Scott, McCracken-Flesher views Scottish literature as theoretical in nature: "I too am reluctant to make any claim for *How the Scots Invented the Modern World*. But it does seem from the nature of genre-bending practiced by these three authors that, because of their situations in a Scotland colonial and yet post-, they develop a literature that theorises resistance to the assumption of situatedness—and it is situatedness, the relation between texts in traditions, on which the notion of a literary canon depends. No wonder Scottish literature fits neither the traditions of text nor those of theory" (ibid., 13).

54. In this vein, Leith Davis details the vexed history of Scottish literature's relation to English studies in "Scottish Literature and 'Engl. Lit.,'" *Studies in Scottish Literature* 38, no. 1 (2012): 20–27. She concludes that Scottish literature studies should develop its identity as a "national literature" as part of an interconnected field with English studies and as part of a transnational, diasporic literature.

55. On the existence of a general Whig consensus in late eighteenth-century Britain, see Kidd, "Burns and Politics."

56. I do not have the space to discuss the wealth of social and economic history written about Scotland in the past forty years. This history reveals both the expansion of the Scottish agricultural and commercial economy in the run-up to and aftermath of the Union and the parallel marginal subsistence, lack of investment capital, and insufficient economic and social opportunity. See, for example, T. M. Devine, *The Scottish Nation: A History, 1700–2000* (New York: Viking, 1999); T. M. Devine, C. H. Lee, and G. C. Peden, eds., *The Transformation of Scotland: The Economy since 1700* (Edinburgh: Edinburgh University Press, 2005); Bruce Lenman, *Integration, Enlightenment and Industrialisation: Scotland, 1746–1832* (Toronto: Hodder Arnold, 1981); Lenman, *Enlightenment and Change: Scotland, 1746–1832*, 2nd ed. (Edinburgh: Edinburgh University Press, 2009); Christopher Whatley, *Scottish Society, 1707–1830: Beyond Jacobitism, towards Industrialization* (Manchester: Manchester University Press, 2000); Michael Lynch, *The Oxford Companion to Scottish History* (Oxford: Oxford University Press, 2001); and Louis M. Cullen and T. Christopher Smout, *Comparative Aspects of Scottish and Irish Economic and Social History, 1600–1900* (Edinburgh: J. Donald, 1976). This increasing body of economic history can seem curiously detached from

[194]

NOTES TO PAGE 15

questions of Scottish identity, as if the individual experiences of ordinary life had little to do with more abstract questions of national feeling. This study seeks to redress this imbalance to some extent.

57. The extent of Scottish "flammability" during the revolutionary period is undergoing scholarly revision. For variations on the traditional view of a more or less quiescent, or "inflammable," Scotland, see William Law Mathieson, *The Awakening of Scotland: A History from 1747 to 1797* (Glasgow: J. Maclehose, 1910), esp. chap. 2; T. C. Smout, *A History of the Scottish People, 1560–1830* (New York: Fontana, 1977), 412–416; T. M. Devine, "The Failure of Radical Reform in Scotland in the Late Eighteenth Century: The Social and Economic Context," in *Conflict and Stability in Scottish Society, 1700–1850*, ed. Devine (Edinburgh: J. Donald, 1990); Devine, *Scottish Nation*, 215–219; Lenman, *Enlightenment and Change*; Bruce Lenman, *An Economic History of Modern Scotland, 1660–1976* (London: B. T. Batsford, 1977), esp. chap. 5; Linda Colley, *Britons: Forging the Nation, 1707–1837*, 2nd ed. (New Haven, CT: Yale University Press, 2012); and Kidd, "North Britishness." For a discussion of both orthodox views and new lines of inquiry, see Bob Harris, "Introduction: Scotland in the 1790s," in *Scotland in the Age of the French Revolution*, ed. Harris (Edinburgh: J. Donald, 2005), 1–22. In classic arguments for a more politically volatile Scotland, Henry Meikle emphasizes Thomas Paine's influence on a general expansion of Scots' political consciousness during the revolutionary period, while Thomas Johnston's iconic Marxian analysis recounts the development of working-class consciousness rooted in feudal authoritarianism and eighteenth- and nineteenth-century economic transformation. See especially Meikle, *Scotland and the French Revolution* (Glasgow: J. Maclehose, 1912), 67–111; and Johnston, *A History of the Working Classes in Scotland*, 3rd ed. (Glasgow: Forward, 1929), esp. chaps. 6–11. Other notable contributions to this literature include John Brims, "From Reformers to 'Jacobins': The Scottish Association of the Friends of the People," in Devine, *Conflict and Stability in Scottish Society*, 31–50; Brims, "'The Scottish Jacobins,' Scottish Nationalism and the British Union," in *Scotland and England, 1286–1815*, ed. Roger Mason (Edinburgh: J. Donald, 1987), 247–265; D. J. Brown, "The Government Response to Scottish Radicalism: 1792–1802," in Harris, *Scotland in the Age of the French Revolution*, 99–124; T. Clarke and T. Dickson, "Class and Class Consciousness in Early Industrial Capitalism: Paisley, 1770–1850" and "The Making of a Class Society: Commercialisation and Working Class Resistance, 1780–1830," both in *Capital and Class in Scotland*, ed. T. Dickson (Edinburgh: J. Donald, 1982), 8–60, 137–180; W. Hamish Fraser, *Conflict and Class Scottish Workers, 1700–1838* (Edinburgh: J. Donald, 1988); Val Honeyman, "'A Very Dangerous Place'? Radicalism in Perth in the 1790s," *Scottish Historical Review* 87, no. 2 (2008): 278–305; Kenneth Logue, *Popular Disturbances in Scotland, 1780–1815* (Edinburgh: J. Donald, 1979); Elaine McFarland, *Ireland and Scotland in the Age of Revolution: Planting the Green Bough* (Edinburgh: Edinburgh University Press, 1994); McFarland, "Scottish Radicalism in the Later Eighteenth Century: 'The Social Thistle and Shamrock,'" in *Eighteenth Century Scotland: New Perspectives*, ed. T. M. Devine and J. R. Young (East Linton, UK: Tuckwell, 1999), 275–297; and Christopher Whatley, especially in "An Uninflammable People?," in *The Manufacture of Scottish History*, ed. Ian Donnachie and Christopher Whatley (Edinburgh: Polygon, 1992), 51–71; and "Roots of 1790s Radicalism: Reviewing the Economic and Social Background," in Harris, *Scotland in the Age of the French Revolution*, 23–48.

58. Colin Kidd, "British Literature: The Career of a Concept," *Scottish Literary Review* 8, no. 1 (2016): 14.

[195]

NOTES TO PAGES 19–23

1. BURNS'S AYRSHIRE "BARDIES"

1. Burns exchanged poetry with other friends and colleagues in the Tarbolton Bachelors' Club as well, including William Simpson, James Smith, and John Rankine. See Nigel Leask, *Robert Burns and Pastoral: Poetry and Improvement in Late Eighteenth-Century Scotland* (Oxford: Oxford University Press, 2010), 86.
2. Ibid., 10.
3. Ibid., 10–11.
4. Andrew Noble, introduction to *The Canongate Burns: The Complete Poems and Songs of Robert Burns*, ed. Andrew Noble and Patrick Scott Hogg (Edinburgh: Canongate, 2001), x.
5. See also John Strawhorn, "Everyday Life in Burns's Ayrshire," in *Burns Now*, ed. Kenneth Simpson (Edinburgh: Canongate Academic, 1994), 13–30.
6. As Bruce Lenman points out, although "Ayrshire was often regarded as rather backward, and it is true that the upland parishes of its southern areas were quite unenclosed as late as 1793," rapid commercialization was achieved in the period after 1760. This was largely the result of two major developments: heavy liming of artificial grasslands and the introduction into Ayrshire of a "new type of lease . . . whereby the tenant might not plough more than a third to a quarter of his land in any one year, and no land was to be cultivated for more than three years in succession." Lenman notes that this modern lease arrangement, brought to Ayrshire by a certain Mr. Fairlie, manager of the Eglington estates after 1770, after he observed its beneficial effects in Lothian, promoted crop rotation, encouraged enclosure, and ended the ancient "infield-outfield" system of cultivation. Lenman, *An Economic History of Modern Scotland, 1660–1976* (London: B. T. Batsford, 1977), 138.
7. John Barrell, *The Idea of Landscape and the Sense of Place: An Approach to the Poetry of John Clare* (Cambridge: Cambridge University Press, 1972), 1 (quoted in Leask, *Robert Burns and Pastoral*, 18).
8. Leask, *Robert Burns and Pastoral*, 18.
9. For an earlier but similar view of Burns's class position, see Annette Wheeler Cafarelli, "The Romantic 'Peasant' Poets and their Patrons," *Wordsworth Circle* 26, no. 2 (1995): 77–87. Cafarelli notes that "his status as son of a tenant-farmer placed him high in the agrarian hierarchy, and he was for most of his life a man who had farm servants" (ibid., 82). She characterizes Burns in terms of a working-class intellectual model that included poets such as Samuel Bamford, Robert Bloomfield, Janet Little, and Ebenezer Elliott.
10. Leask, *Robert Burns and Pastoral*, 18–19. Murray Pittock also characterizes Burns as a "member of the fringes of middle class Scotland," favorably comparing his salary as an exciseman with a contemporary clergyman's living in southwestern Scotland. See Pittock, "The W. Ormiston Roy Memorial Lecture: Who Wrote the Scots Musical Museum? Challenging Editorial Practice in the Presence of Authorial Absence," *Studies in Scottish Literature* 42, no. 1 (2016): 15–16.
11. Carol McGuirk, *Reading Robert Burns: Texts, Contexts, and Transformations* (London: Pickering and Chatto, 2014), 63.
12. Gerard Carruthers, "Robert Burns's Scots Poetry Contemporaries," in *Burns and Other Poets*, ed. David Sergeant and Fiona Stafford (Edinburgh: Edinburgh University Press, 2012), 39, 41. Carruthers cites a number of such imitators who published volumes with the same title as the Kilmarnock edition, including David Morison (1790), David Crawford (1798), the Reverend James Nichol (1805), Thomas Donaldson (1809), Peter Forbes (1812), David Anderson (1826), and the list goes on (ibid., 41).
13. Ibid.
14. Leask, *Robert Burns and Pastoral*, 86–87.
15. Ibid., 86.

[196]

NOTES TO PAGES 23-26

16. Fiona Stafford, "Scottish Poetry and Regional Literary Expression," in *The Cambridge History of English Literature, 1660–1780*, ed. John Richetti (Cambridge: Cambridge University Press, 2008), 362.

17. Burns, *Canongate Burns*, 151.

18. On the bank's establishment and failure, see Lenman, *Economic History of Modern Scotland*, 93. See also James Paterson, *The Contemporaries of Burns and the More Recent Poets of Ayrshire, with Selections from Their Writings* (Edinburgh: H. Paton, 1840), 21–23.

19. See Leask, *Robert Burns and Pastoral*, 89.

20. Paterson, *Contemporaries of Burns*, 17–34; see also T. W. Bayne, "Lapraik, John (1727–1807)," revised by Gerard Carruthers, in *Oxford Dictionary of National Biography* (Oxford: Oxford University Press, 2004).

21. The song, "When I upon Thy Bosom Lean," is the subject of some controversy. According to J. L. Hempstead, it may have been plagiarized from an earlier version of the song, published in the *Weekly Magazine* on October 14, 1773. Hempstead, *Burns Chronicle*, February 1994, 94–101. See also Burns, *Canongate Burns*, 137; and John Strawhorn, "Burns and the Bardie Clan," *Scottish Literary Journal*, December 1, 1981, 17. In any event, Burns revised the song for James Johnson's *The Scots Musical Museum* (Edinburgh, 1787–1803).

22. Robert Burns, *The Poems and Songs of Robert Burns*, 3 vols., ed. James Kinsley (Oxford, UK: Clarendon, 1968), 1:85; Burns, *Canongate Burns*, 133. Kinsley relates Burns's "improvement" of Lapraik's song "When I upon thy bosom lean" for Johnson's *Scots Musical Museum* (*Poems and Songs*, 3:1058).

23. Burns, *Canongate Burns*, 137.

24. Robert Crawford, *The Bard: Robert Burns, a Biography* (Princeton, NJ: Princeton University Press, 2009), 188–189.

25. Leask, *Robert Burns and Pastoral*, 89n28.

26. Maurice Lindsay, *The Burns Encyclopedia*, 4th ed., ed. David Purdie, Kirsteen McCue, and Gerard Carruthers (London: Robert Hale, 2013), 185.

27. See, for example, T. M. Devine, "The Transformation of Agriculture: Cultivation and Clearance," in *The Transformation of Scotland: The Economy since 1700*, ed. T. M. Devine, C. H. Lee, and G. C. Peden (Edinburgh: Edinburgh University Press, 2005), 71–99. Lapraik probably would have agreed much more with Tony Dickson's analysis of the costs of "client capitalism" and agricultural improvement. Dickson, chapter 6 in *Scottish Capitalism: Class, State and Nation from before the Union to the Present*, ed. Dickson (London: Lawrence and Wishart, 1980), 128–130.

28. John Lapraik, *Poems on Several Occasions* (Kilmarnock, UK: John Wilson, 1788), 118–122.

29. See Leask, *Robert Burns and Pastoral*, 7–8. Leask notes that the Habbie stanza was associated with comedy and satire in earlier periods of the Scottish vernacular revival, but Burns adapts it for use in "a more sentimental and sententious manner" (ibid., 8). See also Robert Crawford, "Robert Fergusson's Robert Burns," in *Robert Burns and Cultural Authority*, ed. Crawford (Edinburgh: Edinburgh University Press, 1997), 3.

30. In this study I use the term "moral economy" in E. P. Thompson's sense of a "popular consensus . . . grounded upon a consistent traditional view of social norms and obligations, of the proper economic functions of several parties within the community, which, taken together, can be said to constitute the moral economy of the poor. An outrage to these moral assumptions, quite as much as actual deprivation, was the usual occasion for direct action." Thompson, "The Moral Economy of the English Crowd in the Eighteenth Century," *Past & Present* 50 (1971): 79.

31. Louisa Gairn, "Nature, Landscape and Rural Life," in *The International Companion to Scottish Poetry*, ed. Carla Sassi (Glasgow: Scottish Literature International, 2015), 136. For further discussion of Burns's debt to Smith's theory of sympathy, see also Sarah Dunnigan,

[197]

NOTES TO PAGES 26-30

"Burns and Women," in *The Edinburgh Companion to Robert Burns*, ed. Gerard Carruthers (Edinburgh: Edinburgh University Press, 2009), 31. For a general discussion of Smith's theory, see Ian Duncan, "The Pathos of Abstraction: Adam Smith, Ossian and Samuel Johnson," in *Scotland and the Borders of Romanticism*, ed. Leith Davis, Ian Duncan, and Janet Sorenson (Cambridge: Cambridge University Press, 2004), 44–45.

32. See, for example, Leask's treatment of these poems in *Robert Burns and Pastoral*, 118–125.

33. It should be noted that Burns too can deploy high Anglicized diction "with fashionable echoes of Shenstone, and the 'graveyard poets' Blair and Young" in estates poetry as well, for example, in "A Man Was Made to Mourn." See ibid., 122–123.

34. Drawing on Raymond Williams, John Barrell, Annabel Patterson, and Michael McKeon, Leask makes a distinction between "hard" and "soft" pastoral. "Hard" pastoral "tends to a more political engagement with other genres such as georgic in its 'realist' representation of rural labour, whereas 'soft' pastoral celebrates the privileged *otium* of Tityrus, ornamental, eroticized, and 'apolitical,' as the poet 'sports with Amaryllis in the shade'" (ibid., 51).

35. Lapraik, *Poems*, 101–106.

36. On the rise of New Light moderatism in the mid-eighteenth century and its influence, see Liam McIlvanney, *Burns the Radical: Poetry and Politics in Late Eighteenth-Century Scotland* (East Linton, UK: Tuckwell, 2000), 127–135. For an interesting discussion of the interaction between Kirk moderates and leading Scottish Catholics Bishop George Hay (1729–1811), Bishop John Geddes (1735–1799), and John's cousin Alexander Geddes (1737–1802), a priest, intellectual, and poet, see Mark Goldie, "The Scottish Catholic Enlightenment," *Journal of British Studies* 30, no. 1 (1991): 20–62.

37. Lapraik's anti-Catholicism was widely shared by Scots, regardless of their particular stamp of Protestantism. Indeed, serious anti-Catholic riots broke out in Edinburgh and Glasgow in 1779 when Henry Dundas proposed easing the penal laws. See Richard Finlay, "Keeping the Covenant: Scottish National Identity," in *Eighteenth-Century Scotland: New Perspectives*, ed. T. M. Devine and J. R. Young (East Linton, UK: Tuckwell, 1999), 128. See also Christopher Whatley, *Scottish Society, 1707–1830: Beyond Jacobitism, towards Industrialization* (Manchester: Manchester University Press, 2000), 164–170.

38. This reference may also allude to Martin Luther's essay "On the Jews and Their Lies" (1543), which dismisses the book of Esther as too "Jewish" and formed the basis of later antisemitic claims that Haman deserved praise for plotting to murder the Jews. See Emil Fackenheim, "The Jewish Bible after the Holocaust: A Re-reading," in *The Jewish Philosophy Reader*, ed. Daniel H. Frank, Oliver Leaman, and Charles Manekin (London: Routledge, 2000), 540–542.

39. See Paterson, *Contemporaries of Burns*, 21–23.

40. Andrew Kerr, *The History of Banking in Scotland*, 4th ed. (London: A. & C. Black, 1926), 109.

41. Lapraik, *Poems*, 47–50.

42. *Oxford English Dictionary*, 2nd ed. (Oxford: Oxford University Press, 1989), s.v. "hornings."

43. Sc. Acts Rob. III (1844) I 574/1; *Oxford English Dictionary*, s.v. "hornings."

44. Proverb 30 reads in full,

> Two things I ask of thee; take not favour from me before I die.
> 1. Remove far from me vanity and falsehood: and give me not wealth *or* poverty; but appoint me what is needful and sufficient:
> 2. Lest I be filled and become false, and say, Who see me? or be poor and steal, and swear *vainly* by the name of God.
> 3. Deliver not a servant into the hands of his master, lest he curse thee, and thou be utterly destroyed.
> 4. A wicked generation curse their father, and do not bless their mother.

[198]

NOTES TO PAGES 31–35

> 5. A wicked generation judge themselves to be just, but do not cleanse their way.
>
> 6. A wicked generation have lofty eyes, and exalt themselves with their eyelids.
>
> 7. A wicked generation have swords *for* teeth and jaw-teeth *as* knives, so as to destroy and devour the lowly from the earth, and the poor of them from among men.

Sir Lancelot Charles Lee Brenton, *English Translation of the Septuagint* (London: S. Bagster, 1844).

45. Alex Broadhead, *The Language of Robert Burns: Style, Ideology, and Identity* (Lewisburg, PA: Bucknell University Press, 2014), 12–19.

46. Christopher Harvie, *Scotland and Nationalism: Scottish Society and Politics 1707 to the Present*, 4th ed. (London: Routledge, 2004), 87–88.

47. Christopher Harvie, *Scotland and Nationalism: Scottish Society and Politics 1707 to the Present*, 4th ed. (London: Routledge, 2004), 7–8.

48. Broadhead, *Language of Robert Burns*, 52.

49. Ibid.

50. For a brief discussion of Maxwell's poem, see Leask, *Robert Burns and Pastoral*, 194–195. Leask notes that "Maxwell castigated Burns's liberal theology from a conservative (though not, it seems, an orthodox) position, especially 'Address to the Deil.' But Maxwell also had a lot to say about 'The Holy Fair,' discovering blasphemy in the poem's very title. . . . Conceding that the festal sacrament was indeed 'grossly abused' by many celebrants, Maxwell identified Burns with the 'rakes and harlots' described in his poem, calling down the wrath of an avenging God to punish him" (ibid.).

51. James Maxwell, "On L——'s Poems. Another A——sh——e Bard," in *Animadversions on Some Poets and Poetasters of the Present Age, Especially R——t B——s, and J——n L——k, with a Contrast of Some of the Former Age* (Paisley, UK: J. Neilson, 1788).

52. Leask, *Robert Burns and Pastoral*, 199. Leask goes on to say of Maxwell, "The 'auld lichts' didn't *always* have the best tunes" (ibid.).

53. Corey E. Andrews, "'Far Fam'd RAB': Scottish Labouring-Class Poets Writing in the Shadow of Robert Burns, 1785–1792," *Studies in Hogg and His World*, January 1, 2013, 48.

54. An excerpt of the article can be found on the website dedicated to Lapraik and his poetry, http://www.lapraik.com/history/memorial.htm (accessed July 26, 2018).

55. Crawford, *Bard*, 85. See also Robert Chambers, ed., *The Life and Works of Robert Burns*, 4 vols. (Edinburgh: W. & R. Chambers, 1896); and Andrews, "Far Fam'd RAB," 48–49.

56. Charles Rogers and J. C. Craig, *The Book of Robert Burns: Genealogical and Historical Memoirs of the Poet, His Associates and Those Celebrated in His Writings*, vol. 3 (Edinburgh: Edinburgh Grampian Club, 1889–1891), 28.

57. Ibid.

58. Burns, *Poems and Songs*, 1:65; Burns, *Canongate Burns*, 97.

59. Richard Henry Stoddard, *Under the Evening Lamp*, vol. 1 (New York: Scribner, 1892), 8–12.

60. Andrews, "Far Fam'd RAB," 50.

61. See, for example, Maurice Lindsay, *The Burns Encyclopedia*, 3rd ed. (New York: St. Martin's Press, 1980), 332; Hans Hecht, *Robert Burns: The Man and His Work*, trans. Jane Lymburn (Alloway, UK: Ayr, 1991), 78; Crawford, *Bard*, 85–90. For a contrary opinion, see Carruthers, "Robert Burns's Scots Poetry Contemporaries," 39.

62. This may account for Nigel Leask's judgment that Sillar has more poetic talent than Lapraik (*Robert Burns and Pastoral*, 89, n28).

63. All poems are quoted from David Sillar, *Poems* (Kilmarnock, UK: John Wilson, 1789).

64. "Here the author admits his ignorance of classical learning, and is apparently quite unambitious of the honours of scholarship" (Paterson, *Contemporaries of Burns*, 39).

65. Robert Crawford likewise notes Sillar's occasional jealousy of Burns's success but emphasizes the poets' close friendship and Burns's debt to Sillar's musicality. Sillar too composed

[199]

NOTES TO PAGES 35–39

songs and inspired Burns to take up the fiddle (unsuccessfully, as things turned out). Crawford, *Bard*, 85–90. Kinsley adds that though "a poor poet," Sillar "was something of a fiddler, and the author of the air" for "The Rosebud" (1788) (Burns, *Poems and Songs*, 3:1039).

66. Sillar, *Poems*, 53–56.

67. That is, the Coila of Ramsay and Fergusson.

68. Lapraik, *Poems*, 35–40.

69. In Corey Andrews's reading, "defensive and self-deprecatory, angry yet resigned" verses such as these "speak to Lapraik's age and experience and suggest his sense of the chasm separating his literary efforts from Burns's" ("Far Fam'd Rab," 48).

70. Sillar, *Poems*, 87–90.

71. See Thomas Crawford, ed., *Love, Labour and Liberty: The Eighteenth-Century Scottish Lyric* (Cheadle, UK: Carcanet, 1976).

72. Sillar, *Poems*, 17–30.

73. Broadhead, *Language of Robert Burns*, 147. Broadhead draws on the work of the sociolinguists Li Wei and Peter Auer for this concept, complicating earlier interpretations that read Burns's multilingualism in terms of the rhetorical theory of *copia verborum* (Jeremy Smith and Nigel Leask), Bakhtinian heteroglossia (David Morris and Thomas Preston), or postcolonial hybridity (Corey Andrews) (ibid., 10–11).

74. See Colin Kidd, "British Literature: The Career of a Concept," *Scottish Literary Review* 8, no. 1 (2016): 3–12. Kidd cautions against late twentieth- and early twenty-first-century tendencies to view the past in terms of binaries like England/Scotland or core/periphery, "which we inherit directly from the discipline of Scottish cultural studies, and at one remove from its own origins in the inter-war Scottish literary renaissance [associated with MacDiarmid, etc.]" (ibid., 3). He further discusses the medieval view that Scots and English were cognate languages that reflected the common ethnic origins of each, noting that the vernacular revival in eighteenth-century Scottish letters (Ramsay, Fergusson, and Burns) runs parallel with "a wider antiquarian project to recover a medieval literary inheritance; a British inheritance no less. Eighteenth-century literary antiquarianism was not a straightforwardly nationalist enterprise" (ibid.).

75. See Benedict Anderson, *Imagined Communities: Reflections on the Origin and Spread Nationalism* (London: Verso, 1983).

76. In another context, Ian Duncan has suggested that this aesthetic or cultural nationalism is a product of both Maria Edgeworth's and Walter Scott's invention of the "Scottish" novel and the periodical wars between the Whig-controlled *Edinburgh Review* and *Blackwood's Magazine*'s "Tory Romanticism." See Duncan, *Scott's Shadow: The Novel in Romantic Edinburgh* (Princeton, NJ: Princeton University Press, 2007).

77. The term "Caledonian antisyzygy" refers to the proposition, advanced in 1919 by G. Gregory Smith, professor of English at Queen's College, Belfast, that Scottish literature evinces a fundamental bipolarity of realism and fantasy. Smith identifies this tradition as medieval and based on a unique instability of Scottish culture. The concept continues to influence Scottish literary criticism and inform notions of Scottish exceptionalism. See Gerard Carruthers, *Scottish Literature* (Edinburgh: Edinburgh University Press, 2009), 11–14.

78. Sillar, *Poems*, 57–60.

79. Liam McIlvanney, "Presbyterian Radicalism and the Politics of Robert Burns," in *Love and Liberty: Robert Burns, a Bicentenary Celebration*, ed. Kenneth Simpson (East Linton, UK: Tuckwell, 1997), 179.

80. On Burns's use of this tradition, see Kenneth Simpson, "Burns and the Legacy of Flyting," in *Critical Essays on Robert Burns*, ed. Carol McGuirk (New York: G. K. Hall, 1998), 151–162.

81. *Oxford English Dictionary*, 2nd ed., s.v. "flyting."

[200]

NOTES TO PAGES 40–48

82. Corey E. Andrews, *The Genius of Scotland: The Cultural Production of Robert Burns, 1785–1834* (Leiden: Brill Rodopi, 2015), 65.
83. Ibid., 94–95.
84. Andrews, "Far Fam'd RAB," 53.
85. Ibid.
86. Ibid.

2. BURNS AND THE WOMEN "PEASANT" POETS

1. In Valentina Bold, "Janet Little 'The Scotch Milkmaid' and 'Peasant Poetry,'" *Scottish Literary Journal* 20, no. 2 (1993): 21–30.
2. On Burns's rejection of Little, see Corey E. Andrews, *The Genius of Scotland: The Cultural Production of Robert Burns, 1785–1834* (Leiden: Brill Rodopi, 2015), 101–102.
3. See Corey E. Andrews, "'Far Fam'd RAB': Scottish Labouring-Class Poets Writing in the Shadow of Robert Burns, 1785–1792," *Studies in Hogg and His World*, January 1, 2013, 59. See also Annette Wheeler Cafarelli, "The Romantic 'Peasant' Poets and their Patrons," *Wordsworth Circle* 26, no. 2 (1995): 81.
4. Andrews, "Far Fam'd RAB," 60.
5. See James Paterson, *The Contemporaries of Burns and the More Recent Poets of Ayrshire, with Selections from Their Writings* (Edinburgh: H. Paton, 1840), 116.
6. Ibid., 122.
7. James Taylor, "Muirkirk: About 100 Years Ago," *Muirkirk Advertiser*, accessed July 13, 2018, http://www.ayrshirehistory.com/ref_muirkirk_100_years_ago.html. All spelling in the original.
8. Bob Harris, "The Enlightenment, Towns and Urban Society in Scotland, c. 1760–1820," *English Historical Review* 126, no. 522 (2011): 1101.
9. Ibid., 1098.
10. Ibid., 1129–1130.
11. Paterson, *Contemporaries of Burns*, 79.
12. See Paterson's biography, ibid., 78–91.
13. Janet Little, *The Poetical Works of Janet Little, the Scotch Milkmaid* (Ayr, UK: John and Peter Wilson, 1792).
14. Paterson, *Contemporaries of Burns*, 83, 44 (on Sillar), 29–30 (on Lapraik).
15. See Bold, "Janet Little," 21–22.
16. Moira Ferguson's chapter on Little in her *Eighteenth-Century Women Poets: Nation, Class, and Gender* (Albany: State University of New York Press, 1995), for example, helped to revive critical interest in Little's poetry.
17. Here I differ somewhat from Moira Ferguson, who argues that Little writes from "a recognizably Scottish patriotic position" in addition to her gender and class opposition to the literati (ibid., 4–5).
18. Andrews, *Genius of Scotland*, 98.
19. Andrews, "Far Fam'd RAB," 55.
20. Ibid., 57.
21. Little, *Poetical Works*, 160–161.
22. Moira Ferguson likewise reads this poem as valorizing the Scots vernacular, although I would add that Little does this in order to emphasize Burns's "Britishness." See Ferguson, *Eighteenth-Century Women Poets*, 96–98.
23. Little, *Poetical Works*, 153–154.
24. Moira Ferguson's reading of the panegyric to Rowe emphasizes Little's preference for Rowe's "piety" over Lady Mary's aristocratic social milieu, though the poem acknowledges the

[201]

NOTES TO PAGES 48–51

importance of Montagu's importance as a woman poet. In this respect, Ferguson argues, Little "prioritizes a precarious gendered subjectivity over a nationalist politic" (*Eighteenth-Century Women Poets*, 101). I agree with this aspect of her reading, though I also interpret the poem as Little sharply differentiating herself from the Augustan tradition that Rowe exemplifies.

25. Little, *Poetical Works*, 112–116.

26. For a perceptive analysis of this poem, see Margery McCulloch, "The Lasses Reply to Mr Burns: Women Poets and Songwriters in the Lowlands," in *Crossing the Highland Line: Cross-Currents in Eighteenth-Century Scottish Writing*, ed. C.J.M. MacLachlan, Association for Scottish Literary Studies Occasional Papers 14 (Glasgow: Association of Scottish Literary Studies, 2009), 137–152. McCulloch similarly argues that Little "makes an assault on all three hierarchies in relation to literary recognition—nation, class and gender" (ibid., 143).

27. As Andrews notes, "To the extent that Burns could (or wanted to) utilise his fame to promote the work of 'brother' and 'sister' poets like Lapraik and Little, his 'power of consecration' relied on the 'credit' he had gained in the literary marketplace. This 'credit' was in turn bestowed upon Burns by his critics, who had 'consecrated' him as an exceptional 'poetic genius'" (*Genius of Scotland*, 99).

28. See Leith Davis, "Gender and the Nation in the Work of Robert Burns and Janet Little," *Studies in English Literature, 1500–1900* 38, no. 4 (1998): 621–645. In a reading inspired by Benedict Anderson's thought, Davis connects Burns's privileged gender position with political agency to produce a powerful Scottish national poetics capable of undermining dominant English cultural discourse. As a woman poet of low social standing, Little has neither, viewing "the alignment of masculinity, literary power, and national identity at the same time as she demonstrates the construction of women within the nation." See also Susanne Kord's discussion of this poem in *Women Peasant Poets in Eighteenth-Century England, Scotland, and Germany: Milkmaids on Parnassus* (Rochester, NY: Camden House, 2003), 220–223. Kord places Little in context with primarily English and German women lower-class poets, such as Mary Collier, Molly Leapor, Ann Yearsley, Jane West, and Anna Louisa Karsch, though she briefly discusses Jeanie Glover, Christian Milne, Jean Murray, and Isobel Pagan.

29. Little, *Poetical Works*, 111–112.

30. McCulloch reads the poem as a "balance between the mock heroic portrait of the national icon and a genuine non-ironic acknowledgement of his achievement" ("Lasses Reply to Mr Burns," 142). I interpret the poem as more ironic and self-reflexive in this respect.

31. Little, *Poetical Works*, 171–172.

32. Ferguson argues that Little's "second poem to Burns suggests an attraction for Burns that collides with her opposition to his sexual conduct. Put more bluntly, Little's understated challenge to Burns is freighted with unstated feelings for the poet whose attentions to women she deplores" (*Eighteenth-Century Women Poets*, 107). Ferguson's larger point is that Little's engagement with Burns assisted her development as a poet: "Through personal negotiations with Burns, she begins to see the construction of her gendered and class identity, and, by extension, how she might oppose that construction through braiding social with confrontational verse" (ibid., 108).

33. Kord argues that for lower-class women who aspired to write poetry in the late eighteenth century, including Little, "gender becomes the crucial aspect sanctioning the poetic activity of the male peasant and banning that of the female. What is withheld from the writing of lower-class women in the creation of this gender divide is a contextualization of their work that could lead to an interpretation of that work, read collectively, within a *tradition* of lower-class writing. Without such a tradition, aspirations to posthumous fame are futile; preempted by the critical response, there is literally no context in which the work of peasant

[202]

NOTES TO PAGES 51-57

women can be read" (*Women Peasant Poets*, 230). Kord briefly notes Little's satire of Burns in "On Seeing Mr.——Baking Cakes" at 218.

34. Little, *Poetical Works*, 164–166.

35. Andrews, *Genius of Scotland*, 99.

36. Robert Burns, *The Poems and Songs of Robert Burns*, 3 vols., ed. James Kinsley (Oxford, UK: Clarendon, 1968), 1:57, ll. 55–58.

37. As Corey Andrews has pointed out, Burns's attitude toward his critics assumed a similar form. For the most part an accomplished, generous, and constructive critic himself, "Burns never received the kind of honest, understanding critical response that he proved capable of giving. His later criticism shows an increasing distance between his own criticisms and those he received; as [Kenneth] Simpson has remarked, 'Burns recognised the widening gap between the creative impulse . . . and the legislative nature of Scottish criticism.'" Andrews, "Burns the Critic," in *The Edinburgh Companion to Robert Burns*, ed. Gerard Carruthers (Edinburgh: Edinburgh University Press, 2009), 121.

38. Little, *Poetical Works*, 125–128.

39. Alfred Lutz, "Representing Scotland in *Roderick Random* and *Humphry Clinker*: Smollett's Development as a Novelist," *Studies in the Novel* 33, no. 1 (2001): 6–7.

40. For a superb discussion of the poem's antecedents and Burns's negotiation of class in the poem, see Nigel Leask, *Robert Burns and Pastoral: Poetry and Improvement in Late Eighteenth-Century Scotland* (Oxford: Oxford University Press, 2010), 118–123.

41. Little, *Poetical Works*, 129–131. For an interesting reading of the poem as a savvy performance of Little's position as a laboring-class worker and poet, see Anne Milne, "Dogs and the 'Talking Animal Syndrome' in Janet Little's 'From Snipe, a Favourite Dog, to His Master' (1791)," *Scottish Studies Review*, March 1, 2003, 69–81.

42. Little, *Poetical Works*, 206–207.

43. Quoted in Paterson, *Contemporaries of Burns*, 113. Paterson appends the following comment: "This is a sweet little lyric; and its great superiority to the other known effusions of Isobel, is well calculated to raise a doubt whether it be really hers or not." Paterson concludes that the song is Pagan's. Robert Archibald Smith published a truncated version of the song, omitting stanzas 2, 4, and 5, in *The Scottish Minstrel: A Selection from the Vocal Melodies of Scotland, Ancient and Modern, Arranged for the Piano Forte* by R. A. Smith, 6 vols. (Edinburgh: Robt. Purdie, 1821), 4: 82.

44. Elizabeth Amelia Sharp, ed., *Women's Voices: An Anthology of the Most Characteristic Poems by English, Scotch, and Irish Women* (London: Walter Scott, 1887), 22–23. This volume also includes poems and songs of Anne Grant, Jean Glover, Elizabeth Hamilton, Joanna Baillie, and Lady Nairne.

45. Ibid., ix. For an argument that Sharp's anthology pushed back against Victorian critical standards and sought justice for neglected women poets, see Deborah Bennett Tyler, "'Women's voices speak for them-selves': Gender, Subversion and the *Women's Voices* Anthology of 1887," *Women's History Review* 4, no. 2 (1995): 165–174, https://doi.org/10.1080/09612029500200079. In this regard see also Margaret Kelleher, "Writing Irish Women's Literary History," *Irish Studies Review* 9, no. 1 (2010): 5–14, https://doi.org/10.1080/09670880020032654.

46. See Sir Arthur Thomas Quiller-Couch, ed., *The Oxford Book of English Verse, 1250–1900* (Oxford, UK: Clarendon, 1919), 473, 506.

47. See T. W. Bayne, "Pagan, Isobel," revised by Jane Potter, in *Oxford Dictionary of National Biography* (Oxford: Oxford University Press, 2004). Burns's versions can be found in Robert Burns, *Poems and Songs*, 2:738–739; and Burns, *The Canongate Burns: The Complete Poems and Songs of Robert Burns*, ed. Andrew Hogg and Patrick Scott Noble (Edinburgh: Canongate, 2003), 338, 823–824. According to Pagan's entry in the most recent edition of

[203]

NOTES TO PAGES 57-61

Maurice Lindsay's *The Burns Encyclopedia*, in a letter to George Thomson Burns recalled hearing "Ca' the Yowes" sung by the Reverend John Clunie (1759–1819), a schoolmaster at Markinch in Fife and later minister at Borthwick, Midlothian. Clunie's local reputation as a songwriter led Kinsley to believe that he composed the song, though the *Encyclopedia* editors attribute it to Pagan. See Maurice Lindsay, *The Burns Encyclopedia*, 4th ed., ed. David Purdie, Kirsteen McCue, and Gerard Carruthers (London: Robert Hale, 2013), 247.

48. Quoted in Paterson, *Contemporaries of Burns*, 114. See also Allan Cunningham, *The Songs of Scotland, Ancient and Modern, with an Introduction and Notes, Historical and Critical, and Characters of the Lyric Poets* (London: J. Taylor, 1825), 276. The poem is also included in George Eyre-Todd, *Scottish Poetry of the Eighteenth Century*, vol. 2 (Glasgow: W. Hodge, 1896), 36–37; and in the *Anthology of Scottish Women Poets*, ed. Catherine Kerrigan (Edinburgh: Edinburgh University Press, 1991), 164.

49. Paterson, *Contemporaries of Burns*, 114.

50. Margery McCulloch, "Women, Poetry and Song in Eighteenth-Century Lowland Scotland," in "Scottish Women's Writing," special issue, *Women's Writing* 10, no. 3 (2003): 453–468, accessed at Scottish Corpus of Texts & Speech, https://www.scottishcorpus.ac.uk/document/?documentid=1437.

51. Kirsteen McCue, "Women and Song, 1750–1850," in *A History of Scottish Women's Writing*, ed. Douglas Gifford and Dorothy McMillan (Edinburgh: Edinburgh University Press, 1997), 60.

52. Leask, *Robert Burns and Pastoral*, 255.

53. Isobel Pagan, *A Collection of Songs and Poems on Several Occasions* (Glasgow: Niven, Napier and Khull, 1803).

54. Bayne, "Pagan, Isobel."

55. Paterson, *Contemporaries of Burns*, 116.

56. Ibid., 122. For an additional short biography of Pagan, see Kord, *Women Peasant Poets*, 268–269. See also Valentina Bold's entry for Pagan in *The Biographical Dictionary of Scottish Women*, ed. Elizabeth Ewan, Sue Innes, Siân Reynolds, and Rose Pipes (Edinburgh: Edinburgh University Press, 2006), 289.

57. Bayne, "Pagan, Isobel."

58. Paterson, *Contemporaries of Burns*, 117.

59. Valentina Bold, *James Hogg: A Bard of Nature's Making* (Oxford, UK: Peter Lang, 2007), 245.

60. Ibid., 297–298.

61. Pagan, *Songs and Poems*, 5.

62. "The Crook and Plaid" is quoted in full in Paterson, *Contemporaries of Burns*, 119–120. It is also found in the *Anthology of Scottish Women Poets*, ed. Catherine Kerrigan (Edinburgh: Edinburgh University Press, 1991), 165.

63. Nigel Leask's distinction between "hard" and "soft" pastoral is instructive here. According to Leask, "'Hard' pastoral "tends to a more political engagement with other genres such as georgic in its 'realist' representation of rural labour, whereas 'soft' pastoral celebrates the privileged *otium* of Tityrus, ornamental, eroticized, and 'apolitical,' as the poet 'sports with Amaryllis in the shade'" (*Robert Burns and Pastoral*, 51). Pagan's vernacular treatment of "soft" pastoral emphasizes its erotic energy over its patrician origins.

64. On the Jacobite song's erotic fascination with the "laddie wi' the tartan plaidie," see William Donaldson, *The Jacobite Song: Political Myth and National Identity* (Aberdeen: Aberdeen University Press, 1988), 54–58.

65. Pagan, *Songs and Poems*, 19.

[204]

NOTES TO PAGES 61–68

66. The text of the poem uses the Scots word "pout," which means both a game bird and a young girl or sweetheart. See *Dictionary of the Scots Language*, s.v. "pout," accessed January 9, 2019, http://www.dsl.ac.uk/entry/snd/pout.
67. Paterson, *Contemporaries of Burns*, 115.
68. Pagan, *Songs and Poems*, 24–26.
69. Ibid., 26–27.
70. Ibid., 49–51.
71. See Christopher Whatley, *Scottish Society, 1707–1830: Beyond Jacobitism, towards Industrialization* (Manchester: Manchester University Press, 2000), 170–174.
72. William Blake, *The Complete Poetry and Prose of William Blake*, ed. David V. Erdman (New York: Random House, 1965, 1982, 1988), 13.
73. Burns, *Poems and Songs*, 1:208, ll. 254–257.
74. Pagan, *Songs and Poems*, 75–76.
75. Indeed, Jean Victor Marie Moreau (1763–1813), a republican military hero for his victories over the Austrians, became disenchanted with Napoleon's imperial pretensions. His flirtation with royalists seeking to restore the Bourbons resulted in his exile to the United States. But he was no Scot, and it is conceivable that Pagan confuses Moreau with Étienne-Jacques-Joseph-Alexandre MacDonald (1765–1840), another French revolutionary war hero whose Jacobite father, Neil MacDonald, hailed from South Uist and took up exile in France following the 1745 uprising. MacDonald became one of Napoleon's most successful generals but fell under suspicion for supporting Moreau's alleged royalist plot in 1805. He subsequently rejoined Napoleon, serving in Spain and Russia, but, following the emperor's abdication, threw his support to the Bourbons. See "Victor Moreau," *Encyclopædia Britannica*, accessed January 9, 2019, http://www.britannica.com/EBchecked/topic/392063/Victor-Moreau.
76. On Scottish Jacobitism generally, see Murray G. H. Pittock, *Poetry and Jacobite Politics in Eighteenth-Century Britain and Ireland* (Cambridge: Cambridge University Press, 1994), esp. 50–58.
77. Whatley, *Scottish Society*, 251. On the Highlanders' mixed motives for enlisting in the British military during this period, see Andrew Mackillop, "For King, Country and Regiment? Motive and Identity within Highland Soldiering, 1746–1815," in *Fighting for Identity: Scottish Military Experience, c. 1550–1900*, ed. Steve Murdock and Andrew Mackillop (Leiden: Brill, 2002), 185–211.
78. Pagan, *Songs and Poems*, 16–18.
79. J. W. Fortescue, *The British Army, 1783–1802* (London: Macmillan, 1905), 20.
80. On the history of the Duke of Gordon's fencibles, see C. G. Gardyne, *The Life of a Regiment: The History of the Gordon Highlanders* (Edinburgh: D. Douglas, 1901).
81. Pagan, *Songs and Poems*, 47–49.
82. Thomas Johnston details the long struggle of colliers for emancipation from the legal serfdom in this way: "The poor unfortunates condemned to this servitude in the mines and salt works became as a race apart; they were buried in unconsecrated ground; some of them wore metal collars round their necks; they were bought and sold and gifted like cattle; unless in certain extraordinary instances, like the lead miners at the Leadhills in Lanarkshire, they were wholly unlettered; they developed a jargon of their own, and were regarded with superstitious fear and terror by the majority of their fellow-countrymen; they lived in colonies; and in every old mining district in Scotland local tradition still tells of how the 'brown yins' or the 'black folk' allowed no stranger near their habitations. Their alleged 'privileges' consisted in exemption from taxation and from military service and in the legal obligation which rested with the owner to provide for them in sickness and in old age, and to supply a coffin for their burial. Lord Cockburn, the Whig jurist, who wrote shortly after the serfs

[205]

NOTES TO PAGES 68-71

were freed, declared that while the collier and salter slaves could not legally be 'killed or directly tortured by their masters,' in every other respect they were held to be 'cattle,' possessing no human rights." Johnston, *A History of the Working Classes in Scotland*, 3rd ed. (Glasgow: Forward, 1929), 79–80.

83. As the economic historian Bruce Lenman describes, "The Scottish coal industry had a rather curious history in the decades after 1780. Coal prices rose steeply, to the extreme distress of consumers who sought about for culprits to blame for the problem. . . . On the other hand, wages in mines did undoubtedly rise sharply until about 1810. Between 1715 and 1785 rates of pay for hewers roughly doubled and then between 1785 and 1808 they more than doubled again. Much of this increase was due to shortage of labour in a very labour-intensive industry. The servile status of colliers undoubtedly made it difficult to increase the labour supply, thus placing the very unservile serfs in Scottish coalmines in a very strong bargaining position. Emancipation was embarked upon late and falteringly. By 1800 effective legislation to this end was a fact but it had comparatively little impact on wages for a couple of decades, when a flow of cheap Highland and above all Irish labour helped to solve the recruitment crisis and simultaneously strengthen the hand of the employer in wage negotiation. However, it would be wrong to blame all the increase in coal prices between 1780 and 1810 on labour costs. All prices rose within the British economy in the period 1792–1813. One price index shows an increase of over 100 percent in domestic prices between 1792 and 1812–13." Lenman, *An Economic History of Modern Scotland, 1660–1976* (London: B. T. Batsford, 1977), 132. See also Johnston, *History of the Working Classes*, 82. Johnston's argument that Parliament abolished tied labor in Scottish mines only after it became unprofitable for the coal masters anticipates Eric Williams's brilliant and unorthodox thesis regarding slavery and the slave trade by two decades. See Williams, *Capitalism and Slavery* (Chapel Hill: University of North Carolina Press, 1944).

84. Johnston, *History of the Working Classes*, 83.

85. This does not mean, as Chris Whatley has pointed out, that colliers were at the complete mercy of the masters. Noting the long history of colliers' strikes in Scotland since the seventeenth century, Whatley argues that "Scottish collier serfs . . . could and did withdraw their labour. . . . While it would be mistaken to claim that there existed in the Scottish mining districts 'formal continuous associations' of the 1800s, there is a great deal of evidence to suggest that . . . within the Scottish collier communities there were deeply embedded traditions of collective activity, which surfaced whenever opportunities for material advances were perceived, or when the need for mutual defence arose." Whatley, "'The Fettering Bonds of Brotherhood': Combination and Labour Relations in the Scottish Coal-Mining Industry, c. 1690–1775," *Social History* 12, no. 2 (1987): 142–143.

86. Johnston, *History of the Working Classes*, 154: "It was they who were to be freed, first, from a mass of estate custom and legal decisions which made labour recruitment difficult and its retention insecure, and second from the restraining force of organized labour. For the colliers it was hoped by their masters that emancipation would lead to lower wages and a loosening of their employees' grip over the pace and organization of underground operations. The colliers' legal servitude was to be replaced by the far more effective subjugation of a combination-free labour market."

87. Pagan, *Songs and Poems*, 20–22.

3. ALEXANDER WILSON AND THE PRICE OF RADICALISM

1. Alexander Wilson to David Brodie, April 28, 1788, in *The Life and Letters of Alexander Wilson*, ed. Clark Hunter (Philadelphia: American Philosophical Society, 1983), 119–121, 121–122n1.

[206]

NOTES TO PAGES 71-75

2. Indeed, David Hill Radcliffe calls Wilson, "who was able to continue his education to the advanced age of thirteen, . . . both a more competent poet than Turnbull and a more successful social rebel." Radcliffe, "Imitation, Popular Literacy, and 'The Cottar's Saturday Night,'" in *Critical Essays on Robert Burns*, ed. Carol McGuirk (New York: G. K. Hall, 1998), 265.

3. Michael Ziser, "Introduction to Alexander Wilson, Poems, Prose, and Journalism," Early Americas Digital Archive, accessed July 18, 2018, http://eada.lib.umd.edu/text-entries /introduction-to-alexander-wilson-poems-literary-prose-and-journalism/.

4. Kenneth Simpson, *The Protean Scot: The Crisis of Identity in Eighteenth-Century Scottish Literature* (Aberdeen: Aberdeen University Press, 1989).

5. Richard Price, "Robert Burns and the Scottish Renaissance," in *Love and Liberty, Robert Burns: A Bicentenary Celebration*, ed. Kenneth Simpson (East Linton, UK: Tuckwell, 1997), 128.

6. See Ziser, "Introduction to Alexander Wilson."

7. Andrew Noble, "Displaced Persons: Burns and the Renfrew Radicals," in *Scotland in the Age of the French Revolution*, ed. Bob Harris (Edinburgh: J. Donald, 2005), 201.

8. See Frank Egerton, "Wilson, Alexander, 1766–1813," in *Oxford Dictionary of National Biography* (Oxford: Oxford University Press, 2004). Wilson's American career also inspired the establishment of the Wilson Ornithological Society in 1888. See Wilson Ornithological Society, http://www.wilsonsociety.org/about-wos/about/ (accessed August 8, 2019).

9. For a recent discussion of Burns's influence on Wilson, see Gerard Carruthers, "Alexander Wilson: Scots Poet," in *Alexander Wilson: Enlightened Naturalist*, ed. Edward H. Burtt Jr. (Lewisburg, PA: Bucknell University Press, 2016), 1–15.

10. See Clark Hunter, "The Life of Alexander Wilson," in Hunter, *Life and Letters of Alexander Wilson*, 33–36.

11. In *Radical Renfrew: Poetry from the French Revolution to the First World War*, ed. Tom Leonard (Edinburgh: Polygon, 1990), 13–16.

12. The poem begins with an epigraph from the contemplative poem *The Grave* (1743), by the Presbyterian clergyman and poet Robert Blair (1699–1746): "—Unheard of tortures / Must be reserv'd for such: these herd together; / The common damn'd shun their society, / And look upon themselves as fiends less foul."

13. See T. M. Devine, "Industrialisation," in *The Transformation of Scotland: The Economy since 1700*, ed. T. M. Devine, C. H. Lee, and G. C. Peden (Edinburgh: Edinburgh University Press, 2005). By the turn of the nineteenth century in Glasgow, Devine notes, "it was reckoned that around half the [cotton] mill workforce in the city was either Irish-born or of Irish descent. By that time, national population growth in Scotland was starting to accelerate and in the cities the swelling number of migrants was relieving any scarcities that had previously existed in the labor market" (ibid., 51). Wilson would certainly have experienced this migrant workforce firsthand.

14. William Henry, "Answers for Alex Wilson," July 15, 1790, in Hunter, *Life and Letters of Alexander Wilson*, 421. For the full text see ibid., 420–424.

15. Pagan's libels, presumably because they were composed by a destitute woman of ill fame who could not be expected to pay damages and whose imprisonment would probably draw down even greater fulminations on the head of the injured party, were not worth the cost of the lawsuit.

16. Richard Sher gives us a good idea of Wilson's audience in the following passage: "Paisley was one of the central sites of Scottish industrialization in the late eighteenth century. It featured pious handloom weavers and other tradesmen laboring in cottages and small workshops, along with workers in rural and semirural factories driven by waterpower. We can see many of their names in a subscription list appended to the eight-volume duodecimo

[207]

NOTES TO PAGES 75–81

edition of *The Whole Works of Reverend Robert Millar, A.M.*, which appeared in Paisley in 1789; more than a thousand names appear, most of them identified by their occupations as artisans and tradesmen, including more than 350 weavers from Glasgow, Renfrewshire, and Ayrshire." Sher, *The Enlightenment and the Book: Scottish Authors and Their Publishers in Eighteenth-Century Britain, Ireland, and America* (Chicago: University of Chicago Press, 2006), 276–277.

17. Millar, the son of a Church of Scotland clergyman and educated at the University of Glasgow, authored one of the great works of early eighteenth-century Scottish literature, *The History of the Propagation of Christianity, and Overthrow of Paganism.* His sons John and Henry held parishes in Old Kilpatrick in Dunbartonshire and Neilston (near Paisley), and his daughter, Elizabeth, married James Hamilton, who succeeded Millar as minister of the Abbey Kirk, Paisley. A third son, Andrew Millar (1705–1768), was, according to Sher, "the greatest bookseller and publisher of the mid-eighteenth century" and at the center of the intellectual renaissance of the Scottish Enlightenment. Sher, *Enlightenment and the Book*, 275–277.

18. Hunter, "Life of Alexander Wilson," 41.

19. Alexander Wilson, *The Poems and Literary Prose of Alexander Wilson*, ed. Rev. Alexander B. Grosart (Paisley: A. Gardner, 1876), 17–23.

20. As Ziser notes, "Having gained a measure of notoriety in the capital, Wilson arranged to have the unsold copies of his 1790 collection reissued with a few changes in a new edition, which were soon sold out" ("Introduction to Alexander Wilson").

21. Carruthers reads this poem to demonstrate that the "shift in the association of Scots language, away from a literary culture toward common speech and the culture of the hoi polloi, represents a historic phenomenon that has largely endured down to the twenty-first century. It represents, paradoxically, an anti-intellectualism that both helps feed the Romantic movement and inserts into Scottish culture an amnesia about its own Scots literary heritage (before Burns)" ("Alexander Wilson: Scots Poet," 15).

22. Alexander Wilson, *The Poems and Literary Prose of Alexander Wilson*, ed. Rev. Alexander B. Grosart (Paisley: A. Gardner, 1876), 24–26. Also in Leonard, *Radical Renfrew*, 20.

23. Hunter, "Life of Alexander Wilson," 46.

24. Wilson, *Poems and Literary Prose*, 57–62.

25. Hunter, "Life of Alexander Wilson," 52.

26. Ibid., 56.

27. Wilson went to prison on January 4, 1794, but he was soon released for lack of evidence. See Edward Burtt Jr., "Biographical Sketch," in Burtt, *Alexander Wilson*, xxix.

28. Colin Kidd, "Burns and Politics," in *The Edinburgh Companion to Robert Burns*, ed. Gerard Carruthers (Edinburgh: Edinburgh University Press, 2009), 72.

29. See, for example, Carol McGuirk's discussion of Burns's political troubles in *Reading Robert Burns: Texts, Contexts, and Transformations* (London: Pickering and Chatto, 2014), 22–26.

30. Carruthers, "Alexander Wilson: Scots Poet," 19.

31. See Ziser, "Introduction to Alexander Wilson."

32. Hunter, "Life of Alexander Wilson," 48. See also Noble, who describes these satires as "bitter, brilliant, seminal poems of the weaving industry on the brink of industrial exploitation" ("Displaced Persons," 202).

33. In this vein, see Leith Davis, "At 'sang about': Scottish Song and the Challenge to British Culture," in *Scotland and the Borders of Romanticism*, ed. Leith Davis, Ian Duncan, and Janet Sorenson (Cambridge: Cambridge University Press, 2004), 188–203. Davis suggests that "Burns wanted to establish the collecting of Scottish music as an alternative to the marketing of poetry. Burns's work . . . establishes a different relationship between author and reader than that involved in poetic composition. Burns as author in fact disappears,

[208]

NOTES TO PAGES 81–88

since he does not discriminate between songs which he writes and those he revises or merely transmits from available sources" (ibid., 198). She also points out that Burns accepted no money for his work.

34. Quoted in Hunter, "Life of Alexander Wilson," 42–43.

35. With respect to Little and the tailor-poet Thomas Walker, Valentina Bold observes that "Burns was less than wholly encouraging to those who tried to jump on his bandwagon." We can add Wilson to that list. Bold, "Inmate of the Hamlet: Burns as Peasant Poet," in *Love and Liberty: Robert Burns, a Bicentenary Celebration*, ed. Kenneth Simpson (East Linton, UK: Tuckwell, 1997), 49–50.

36. Wilson, *Poems and Literary Prose*, 3–10.

37. See Ziser, "Introduction to Alexander Wilson." See also G. Ross Roy, "Robert Burns and the Brash and Reid Chapbooks of Glasgow," in *Literatur in Kontext: Festschrift für Horst W. Drescher*, ed. Joachim Schwend, Susanne Hagemann, and Hermann Völkel (Frankfurt am Main: Peter Lang, 1992), 53–69. Roy surveys the publication of cheap eight-page, one-penny chapbooks by the Glaswegian firm Brash and Reid during the period between 1795 and 1817. While he focuses on the reprinting of Burns's poems in this format, he notes that Wilson's "Watty and Meg" appears in the fifth number of the first volume (ibid., 55).

38. On the poem's misattribution, see Burtt, *Alexander Wilson: The Scot Who Founded American Ornithology*, 21. See also G. Ross Roy, "Poems and Songs Spuriously Attributed to Robert Burns," in *Critical Essays on Robert Burns*, ed. Carol McGuirk (New York: G. K. Hall, 1998), 229.

39. See Anna Clark, *Struggle for the Breeches: Gender and the Making of the British Working Class* (Berkeley: University of California Press, 1995).

40. Gerard Carruthers likewise reads the poem as "soaked in the carousing phraseology" of "Tam o' Shanter" (1790) but reads it as "straightforwardly didactic, which is to say simply sexist." Carruthers, "Alexander Wilson: The Rise and Fall and Rise of a Laboring Class Writer," in *A History of the British Working Class*, ed. John Goodridge and Bridget Keegan (Cambridge: Cambridge University Press, 2017), 75.

41. Tytler wrote, "Had you never written another syllable, [this poem] would have been sufficient to have transmitted your name down to posterity with high reputation. In the introductory part, where you paint the character of your hero, and exhibit him at the alehouse ingle, with his tippling cronies, you have delineated nature with an honour and naivete, that would do honour to Matthew Prior; but when you describe the unfortunate orgies of the witches' sabbath, and the hellish scenery in which they are exhibited, you display a power of imagination, that Shakespeare himself could not have exceeded." Quoted in Robert Burns, *The Canongate Burns: The Complete Poems and Songs of Robert Burns*, ed. Andrew Noble and Patrick Scott Hogg (Edinburgh: Canongate, 2003), 270. Burns composed the poem for Francis Grose's *Antiquities of Scotland* because Grose wanted a tale of superstition and witchcraft to pair with a romantic drawing of Alloway Kirk. The resulting product certainly fits the purpose.

42. Robert Burns, *The Poems and Songs of Robert Burns*, ed. James Kinsley, 3 vols. (Oxford, UK: Clarendon, 1968), 2:558; Burns, *Canongate Burns*, 263.

43. Wilson, *Poems and Literary Prose*, 13–17.

44. Ibid., 50–53.

45. Ibid., 91–94.

46. William Wordsworth, "Tintern Abbey," in *The Pedlar, Tintern Abbey, The Two-Part Prelude*, ed. Jonathan Wordsworth (Cambridge: Cambridge University Press, 1985), 33–40.

47. I would argue that Wilson is ahead of his time here. As Wilson McLeod and Alan Riach have pointed out, "Much political poetry expressed regret for what had happened in tones of nostalgia, lament and exile, but in the later nineteenth century a new tone was heard,

[209]

NOTES TO PAGES 89–98

demanding change. Industrialising Scotland altered the nation's character. The rate of urbanisation in Scotland, the rising number of emigrants leaving the country in the early nineteenth century, and the increasing concentration of the population in the cities, particularly in Glasgow, had a deep legacy." McLeod and Riach specifically cite the poetry of Thomas Campbell (1777–1844), Elizabeth Hamilton (1758–1816), William Thom (1799–1848), and Marion Bernstein (1846–1906). McLeod and Riach, "Protest and Politics," in *The International Companion to Scottish Poetry*, ed. Carla Sassi (Glasgow: Scottish Literature International, 2015), 156–168 (quote on 161).

48. Wilson, *Poems and Literary Prose*, 71–75.

49. Virginia Woolf, *Three Guineas* (London: Harcourt Brace, 1938), 78.

50. Wilson, *Poems and Literary Prose*, 212–216.

51. The quoted phrase belongs to P. J. Cain and A. G. Hopkins in *British Imperialism, 1688–2000*, 2nd ed. (New York: Routledge, 2002). Based on the concept of "gentlemanly capitalism," Cain and Hopkins posit the emergence of a powerful service sector centered within the confines of the City of London, which both preexisted the manufacturing classes created by the Industrial Revolution and outlived the decline of British manufacturing after 1914. The service sector, which encompassed financial, insurance, professional, transportation, and communications-related industries, was closely connected to the ruling elite, shared the public-school values of generations of British landed aristocrats, and formed an enduring symbiosis with Whitehall and its "official mind." This alliance of the political and economic elite ultimately directed British policy toward overseas expansion in order to preserve privilege, prestige, and property at home, while creating a world economic system mediated by British sterling and fueled by British credit and investments.

52. Noble, "Displaced Persons," 206.

53. Robert Tannahill, *The Poems and Songs and Correspondence of Robert Tannahill, with Life and Notes*, ed. David Semple (Paisley, UK: A. Gardner, 1874), 78–80.

54. Indeed, Gerard Carruthers views Wilson's Scottish career as demonstrating "the possibility in late eighteenth-century Scotland for the rise of a laboring class writer and the danger of his downfall if he were to become too political" ("Rise and Fall and Rise," 70).

55. Wilson, *Poems and Literary Prose*, 225–227.

4. LADY NAIRNE

1. Valentina Bold, *James Hogg: A Bard of Nature's Making* (Bern: Peter Lang, 2007), 295.

2. McGuirk, *Reading Robert Burns: Texts, Contexts, and Transformations* (London: Pickering and Chatto, 2014), 127.

3. See Margery McCulloch, "The Lasses Reply to Mr Burns: Women Poets and Songwriters in the Lowlands," in *Crossing the Highland Line: Cross-Currents in Eighteenth-Century Scottish Writing*, ed. C.J.M. MacLachlan, Association for Scottish Literary Studies Occasional Papers 14 (Glasgow: Association of Scottish Literary Studies, 2009), 149. On the attribution controversy, see McGuirk, *Reading Robert Burns*, 143; and G. Ross Roy, "Poems and Songs Spuriously Attributed to Robert Burns," in *Critical Essays on Robert Burns*, ed. Carol McGuirk (New York: G. K. Hall, 1998), 229–230.

4. The most recent reprint of Lady Nairne's poems and songs, together with an updated biography, can be found in Freeland Barbour, *The White Rose of Gask, the Life and Songs of Carolina Oliphant, Lady Nairne* (Edinburgh: Birlinn, 2019).

5. McGuirk, *Reading Robert Burns*, 127. As Kirsteen McCue likewise points out, Nairne "was serious about her alter-ego and dressed as Mrs Bogan of Bogan, a 'country lady of a former generation,' for meetings" with her publisher. She also used a distinct hand for her manuscripts and "tried to conceal from the committee who read them that they were the work

[210]

NOTES TO PAGES 98-99

of a woman." McCue, "Women and Song, 1750–1850," in *A History of Scottish Women's Writing*, ed. Douglas Gifford and Dorothy McMillan (Edinburgh: Edinburgh University Press, 1997), 66. Here she cites Margaret Stewart Simpson's biography of Nairne, *The Scottish Songstress: Caroline Baroness Nairne* (Edinburgh: Oliphant, Anderson and Ferrier 1894).

6. Quoted in McGuirk, *Reading Robert Burns*, 127.

7. William Donaldson, "Oliphant, Carolina, Lady Nairne (1766–1845)," in *Oxford Dictionary of National Biography* (Oxford: Oxford University Press, 2004).

8. Ian Duncan and Sheila Kidd, "The Nineteenth Century," in *The International Companion to Scottish Poetry*, ed. Carla Stassi (Glasgow: Scottish Literature International, 2015), 69.

9. Leith Davis, *Music, Postcolonialism, and Gender: The Construction of Irish National Identity, 1724–1824* (Notre Dame, IN: University of Notre Dame Press, 2006), 9. Drawing on the work of Homi Bhabha, Davis argues further, "The discourse on Irish music reflects a continuous negotiation between the original cultures of the native Irish and the dominant culture, both Anglo-Irish and English. . . . The readings I offer—of eighteenth-century printed collections of Irish tunes of historiographies that promote Irish bardic culture, of translations of Irish songs and of novels that highlight Irish musical culture, to name only a few—are all characterized by the hybridity derived from encounter and translation, despite the creators' frequent claims for the purity of the musical tradition on which they draw" (ibid.).

10. Carol McGuirk, "Jacobite History to National Song: Robert Burns and Carolina Oliphant (Baroness Nairne)," *Eighteenth Century* 47, nos. 2–3 (2006): 254.

11. Maurice Lindsay previews something of the postcolonial potential of Nairne studies when, in a reference to her Jacobite lyric "Will Ye No Come Back Again?," he observes that because of "a disastrous quirk in the native temperament, which enables Scots to profess sentimental devotion to one cause while giving practical support to another, often diametrically opposed, this song has long been used to sublimate regret, not merely for an unrestorable monarchical house, but for that 'auld sang' the ending of which Lord Seafield proclaimed so contemptuously to the last Scottish Parliament in 1707." Lindsay, *History of Scottish Literature* (London: R. Hale, 1977), 228. Lindsay also ascribes this sense of "regret" to songs such as "The Rowan Tree," "The Auld House," and "The Land o' the Leal" (ibid., 228). In a similar vein, Leith Davis contends that poems such as "Bonny Gascon Ha'," "The Auld House," and "The Banks of the Earn" "emphasize a rural, unthreatening Scotland" that suggests "the ultimate defeat of the Scottish cause." Davis, "Gender, Genre and the Imagining of the Scottish Nation" (2002, unpaginated copy of the essay provided to me by the author). McGuirk distinguishes "Scotland's two greatest writers of national song" on the basis of their treatment of Scotland's present. For Burns, the Scottish present suggested "a means to a future for which he had hopes." By contrast, Nairne "is the belated survivor of an Old House, a lost world of loyalty and honour." McGuirk, *Reading Robert Burns*, 150.

12. Catherine Kerrigan, introduction to *Anthology of Scottish Women Poets*, ed. Kerrigan (Edinburgh: Edinburgh University Press, 1991), 5. Kirsteen McCue's discussion of Joanna Baillie, Elizabeth Hamilton, Anne Grant, and Nairne stresses the gendered provenance of balladry in the "folk songs or ballads which were most often performed by other women, such as grandmothers, aunts, mothers and nannies" ("Women and Song," 59). Mary Ellen Brown suggests further that associating balladry with women composers, performers, and readers has deeply influenced the "genres known and performed, the subject matter chosen, the style and venue of performance, and the meaning/significance of the material." Brown, "Old Singing Women and the Canons of Scottish Balladry and Song," in Gifford and McMillan, *History of Scottish Women's Writing*, 51.

[211]

NOTES TO PAGES 99–102

13. Most of Nairne's songs were composed prior to her marriage in 1806. See McGuirk, "Jacobite History to National Song," 255. But as McGuirk points out, most of Nairne's songs date from the 1790s, at the same time Burns submitted material for Johnson's *Scots Musical Museum* (1787–1803) and Thomson's *Select Collection of Original Scottish Airs* (1793–1841) (*Reading Robert Burns*, 128).

14. Colin Kidd, "Burns and Politics," in *The Edinburgh Companion to Robert Burns*, ed. Gerard Carruthers (Edinburgh: Edinburgh University Press, 2009), 72.

15. Ibid.

16. Murray G. H. Pittock, *Poetry and Jacobite Politics in Eighteenth-Century Britain and Ireland* (Cambridge: Cambridge University Press, 1994), 222.

17. See Murray G. H. Pittock, *Material Culture and Sedition, 1688–1760: Treacherous Objects, Secret Places* (Basingstoke, UK: Palgrave Macmillan, 2013), esp. 151–158.

18. Quoted in McCulloch, "Lasses Reply to Mr Burns," 149.

19. Rev. George Henderson, *Lady Nairne and Her Songs*, 3rd ed. (Paisley, UK: A. Gardner, 1905), 51.

20. Colin Kidd, "British Literature: The Career of a Concept," *Scottish Literary Review* 8, no. 1 (2016): 8.

21. McCulloch, "Lasses Reply to Mr Burns," 148.

22. McCulloch, "Lasses Replay to Mr Burns," 148. See also McGuirk's discussion of the martial musical settings of the two songs in Jacobite terms in *Reading Robert Burns*, 141–144. "Nairne takes 'Hey tutie tatey' far from Burns's context of battle songs and raucous drinking stanzas; indeed, the song marks a break from her own early work," McGuirk observes. "After her conversion, her songs continue to use Jacobite images but to employ them, often more dogmatically than in these graceful stanzas, to project evangelically tinged scenes of future bliss" (ibid., 143). For McGuirk's earlier reading of the poem's Jacobite shadows, see McGuirk, "Jacobite History to National Song," 262–263.

23. McCulloch, "Lasses Reply to Mr Burns," 151.

24. Quoted in McCulloch, "Lasses Reply to Mr Burns," 149. In a similar vein, while naming Lady Nairne as "one of Scotland's greatest songwriters" whose "social status did not prevent her from imaginatively identifying with other people in a variety of very different situations, not the least those of suffering women," Robert Crawford classes her with the aristocratic, "sentimental Jacobite" Lady Anne Barnard. Crawford, *Scotland's Books: A History of Scottish Literature* (Oxford: Oxford University Press, 2009), 374–375. Steve Newman's emphasis on the importance of popular song in the Scottish Enlightenment's theorization of sympathy as the crucial social bond in "modern" commercial society includes only Ramsay, Home, and Burns, but his argument extends to Nairne as well. See Newman, *Ballad Collection, Lyric, and the Canon: The Call of the Popular from the Restoration to the New Criticism* (Philadelphia: University of Pennsylvania Press, 2007).

25. Robert Archibald Smith, *The Scottish Minstrel: A Selection from the Vocal Melodies of Scotland, Ancient and Modern, Arranged for the Piano Forte by R. A. Smith*, 6 vols. (Edinburgh: Robt. Purdie, 1821), 3:54–55.

26. For a reading of the poem's Jacobite shadows, see McGuirk, "Jacobite History to National Song," 262–263.

27. Lady Nairne (Carolina Oliphant), *Lays of Strathearn, the Symphonies and Accompaniments by the Late Finlay Dun*, new ed. (Edinburgh: Paterson, 185?), 1–5.

28. McGuirk makes this point in her discussion of Nairne's drawing of the Old House at Gask. The drawing shows a rustic structure next to a public road, with a beggar in the foreground. Victorian renditions of the drawing show the house on a grander scale, the public road replaced by a private drive, and no beggar. McGuirk, *Reading Robert Burns*, 147–149.

[212]

NOTES TO PAGES 102–109

29. My discussion of the rural values of eighteenth-century English poetry remain deeply informed by Raymond Williams, *The Country and the City* (Oxford: Oxford University Press, 1973), chap. 8.

30. See, for example, Samuel Taylor Coleridge, *Reflections on Having Left a Place of Retirement* (1796), lines 4–6: "In the open air / Our Myrtles blossomed; and across the porch / Thick Jasmins twined"; and George Crabbe, "The Parish Register," pt. 3, in *Poems* (1807), 107: "Where Jasmine trails on either side the Door." See Crabbe, *The Poetical Works of The Rev. George Crabbe* (Edinburgh: Gall and Inglis, 18?), 74.

31. Murray Pittock shrewdly refers to this pacification as the "tartan curtain" drawn by Scott's fiction over "the 'old' Scotland of Jacobite-nationalist threat" (*Poetry and Jacobite Politics*, 234).

32. McCue sees this song as "anticipating nineteenth-century Kailyard sentimentality. . . . The migration of families from country to city, or to foreign lands, naturally encouraged this highly charged emotional view of home and nation" ("Women and Song," 64). Leith Davis reads the poem as alluding to Nairne's father, Laurence Oliphant, an aide to Charles Edward Stuart during the '45, and more generally to the lost Jacobite cause ("Gender, Genre and the Imagining of the Scottish Nation"). For a brief history of the Old House at Gask, Nairne's birthplace, as well as a discussion of Nairne's drawing of the house and subsequent Victorian editing, see McGuirk, *Reading Robert Burns*, 130, 148–149.

33. Lady Nairne (Carolina Oliphant), *Life and Songs of the Baroness Nairne: With a Memoir and Poems of Caroline Oliphant the Younger*, ed. Rev. Charles Rogers (London: C. Griffin, 1869), 11–12.

34. Nairne, *Lays of Strathearn*, 19–20.

35. The Earn empties out of Loch Earn near St. Fillans in Pertshire and flows east and south through Strathearn, joining the Tay near Abernethy.

36. Robert Burns, *The Canongate Burns: The Complete Poems and Songs of Robert Burns*, ed. Andrew Noble and Patrick Scott Hogg (Edinburgh: Canongate, 2003), 474.

37. Ibid., 475. See also Liam McIlvanney's discussion of Burns's response to the "crisis" brought on by the sedition trials in *Burns the Radical: Poetry and Politics in Late Eighteenth-Century Scotland* (East Linton, UK: Tuckwell, 2000), 212–215.

38. Linda Colley, *Britons: Forging the Nation, 1707–1837*, 2nd ed. (New Haven, CT: Yale University Press, 2012), 56.

39. While the 1707 Treaty of Union opened the way for free trade and navigation with England and the empire, it also subjected Scots to liability for a portion of the English national debt. Though the treaty temporarily softened the blow by exempting Scotland from temporary duties on stamped paper, windows, coal, and malt and (controversially) granted compensation for losses incurred by investors in the Company of Scotland Trading to Africa and the Indies and for private individuals as a result of the recall of Scots coinage, it eventually burdened Scottish consumers with substantially higher excise taxes on consumables. "What Scots objected to," notes Bruce Lenman, "was the very existence of an institution [the new customs and excise service] to which their previous history offered no parallel." Lenman, *An Economic History of Modern Scotland, 1660–1976* (London: B. T. Batsford, 1977), 61.

40. See John Brewer, *The Sinews of Power: War, Money and the English State, 1688–1783* (London: Routledge, 1989), chaps. 4, 7.

41. Nairne, *Life and Songs*, 41–42.

42. Mikhail M. Bakhtin, *The Dialogic Imagination*, ed. Michael Holquist, trans. Caryl Emerson and Michael Holquist (Austin: University of Texas Press, 1981), 31–32.

43. Ibid., 32.

44. Steven R. McKenna, "Burns and Virgil," in *The Edinburgh Companion to Robert Burns*, ed. Gerard Carruthers (Edinburgh: Edinburgh University Press, 2009), 149.

[213]

NOTES TO PAGES 111–120

45. Bakhtin, *Dialogic Imagination*, 35.
46. On the development of this art in the form of Macpherson's *Ossian*, see Pittock, *Poetry and Jacobite Politics*, 178–186.
47. Nairne, *Lays of Strathearn*, 71–72.
48. Burns, *Canongate Burns*, 360.
49. Ibid., 360–361.
50. *Edinburgh Morning Chronicle*, August 1795.
51. Burns, *Canongate Burns*, 298.
52. Ibid., 298.
53. On links between the Scottish and Irish radicals in the 1790s, see Elaine W. McFarland, "Scottish Radicalism in the Later Eighteenth Century: 'The Social Thistle and Shamrock,'" in *Eighteenth Century Scotland: New Perspectives*, ed. T. M. Devine and J. R. Young (East Linton, UK: Tuckwell, 1999), 275–297. John Stevenson puts Scottish radicalism in the larger context of the Atlantic world in "Scotland and the French Revolution: An Overview," in *Scotland in the Age of the French Revolution*, ed. Bob Harris (Edinburgh: J. Donald, 2005), 247–264.
54. As McCue puts it, Nairne and other women songwriters "were generally uninterested in the nationalist element of Jacobitism, but they were clearly attracted by the idea of the Highland soldier and the Prince himself" ("Women and Song," 64).
55. Smith, *Scottish Minstrel*, 6:86–87.
56. The MacDonalds of Sleat fought on the Hanoverian side and retained their property, though the majority of MacDonalds were out for Charlie. Angus MacDonald and Archibald MacDonald, *The Clan Donald*, vol. 3 (Inverness, UK: Northern Counties, 1900), 84–92.
57. See Louis Althusser, *On the Reproduction of Capitalism: Ideology and Ideological State Apparatuses* (New York: Verso, 2014).
58. Smith, *Scottish Minstrel*, 4:41.
59. As Murray Pittock has argued, the encounter between the "Highland lad" and the "Lowland lassie," which originates in a "fabliau tale of rape, seduction, or lover's defiance," is converted in the Jacobite lyric into "a vision of sexual, personal and national liberation, which reached its expressive peak after 1745. The Lowland woman, a paradigm of the Scotland which has been faithless, is returned to a relationship of true identity after yielding to the Highland patriot" (*Poetry and Jacobite Politics*, 141).
60. Nairne, *Life and Songs*, 84.
61. Robert Burns, *The Poems and Songs of Robert Burns*, 3 vols., ed. James Kinsley (Oxford, UK: Clarendon, 1968), 2:572; Burns, *Canongate Burns*, 367.
62. Burns, *Canongate Burns*, 367. They refer to Alexander Cunningham's commentary on the poem: "When Political combustion ceases to be the object of Princes & Patriots, it then, you know, becomes the lawful prey of Historians & Poets" (ibid.).
63. Nairne, *Life and Songs*, 33–34. The song also appears in Smith, *Scottish Minstrel*, 5:53.
64. Burns, *Poems and Songs*, 2:687; Burns, *Canongate Burns*, 411.
65. Smith, *Scottish Minstrel*, 1:17.
66. See Pittock, *Poetry and Jacobite Politics*, 137. Pittock observes this close link between Jacobite eroticism and a "strong, even ferocious nationalism which sits awkwardly with the Stuart aim of being restored in three kingdoms" (ibid.). He also alludes to the homoerotic nature of some Jacobite poetry when he quotes this song from Hogg's *The Jacobite Relics*:

> Great James, come kiss me now, now,
>> Great James, come kiss me now;
> Too long I've undone myself these years bygone,
>> By basely forsaking you.
>
> See James Hogg, *The Jacobite Relics of Scotland; Being the Songs, Airs, and Legends of the Adherents to the House of Stuart* (Paisley: Alexander Gardner, 1874), 144–146.

[214]

NOTES TO PAGES 121–128

67. Nairne, *Life and Songs*, 138–139.

68. David Herd, *Ancient and Modern Scottish Songs, Heroic Ballads, Etc.*, vol. 2 (Edinburgh: John Wotherspoon, 1776), 179–180; Burns, *Poems and Songs*, 2:532–533; Burns, *Canongate Burns*, 358.

69. In the traditional version published in Herd, the second couplet of the first stanza reads, "O he is forced frae me to gae, / Over the hills and far away." Burns appears to soften the coercive implication of the original.

70. For the full text of Thomson's ode, see David Mallet, *Alfred: A Masque, in The Works of David Mallet*, vol. 3 (London: A. Millar, 1759), 67–69. The ode's allusion to Britannia's "native oak" is in the fourth stanza on page 67.

71. Nairne, *Lays of Strathearn*, 73–74.

72. Gowrie, or *Gobharaidh* in Gaelic, is the ancient appellation of what is now eastern Perthshire. The "Carse o' Gowrie" is the region extending from Perth eastward to Dundee. The kings of Scotland were coronated at Scone.

5. "IN THE SHADOW OF BURNS"

1. David Semple, introduction to *The Poems and Songs and Correspondence of Robert Tannahill, with Life and Notes*, by Robert Tannahill (Paisley, UK: A. Gardner, 1876), lxxxiii–lxxxiv; see also William Donaldson, "Tannahill, Robert (1774–1810)," in *Oxford Dictionary of National Biography* (Oxford: Oxford University Press, 2004).

2. Ian Duncan and Sheila Kidd, "The Nineteenth Century," in *The International Companion to Scottish Poetry*, ed. Carla Sassi (Glasgow: Scottish Literature International, 2015), 67.

3. For a discussion of the original music of Barr and Smith composed for Tannahill's songs, see Steve Sweeney-Turner, "Pagan Airts: Reading Critical Perspectives on the Songs of Burns and Tannahill," in *Critical Essays on Robert Burns*, ed. Carol McGuirk (New York: G. K. Hall, 1998), 194–196.

4. Donaldson, "Tannahill, Robert."

5. Penny Fielding, *Scotland and the Fictions of Geography: North Britain, 1760–1830* (Cambridge: Cambridge University Press, 2008), 65.

6. Whether Burns saw song collecting this way is another question. For example, Nigel Leask ties Burns's "rapturous" reception in Edinburgh by the "anglicizing Scottish literati" in part to the poet's deliberate performance of the "farmer poet" role. "By the mid-1780s," Leask writes, "the civic virtue of agricultural improvement had become an ideological obsession with the British ruling classes, as well as the professional classes and the 'middling sort.'" Leask, *Robert Burns and Pastoral: Poetry and Improvement in Late Eighteenth-Century Scotland* (Oxford: Oxford University Press, 2010), 38.

7. Corey E. Andrews, *The Genius of Scotland: The Cultural Production of Robert Burns, 1785–1834* (Leiden: Brill Rodopi, 2015), 221.

8. James Hogg visited Paisley and met Tannahill just before his death in the spring of 1810. See Semple, introduction to *Poems and Songs*, lxxx.

9. A copy is located in the National Library of Scotland, catalogued under Evans, printer, Long-Lane, London; Shelfmark: L.C.1269 (118).

10. Semple, introduction to *Poems and Songs*, lxxii.

11. See Claire Casey, introduction to *The Weaver Poet: The Songs & Poems of Robert Tannahill* (CreateSpace, 2016), 9–14.

12. These include editions by G. Cowie in London (1817); Broderick and Ritter in New York (1819); A. Fullarton in Glasgow, Dublin, and London (1838 and 1899); and Alexander Gardner in Paisley (1873 and 1876).

[215]

NOTES TO PAGES 129–130

13. Christopher Harvie, "'It Is Said That Burns Was a Radical': Contest, Concession, and the Political Legacy of Robert Burns, ca. 1796–1859," *Journal of British Studies* 50, no. 3 (2011): 639–666.

14. Sweeney-Turner, "Pagan Airts," 199. Sweeney-Turner also points out that Tannahill's uncle John Tannahill attended a meeting in Edinburgh of the Friends of the People in 1793.

15. Ibid., 200. Sweeney-Turner postulates a sharp contrast between a "pre-capitalist" Burns and a "para-capitalist" Tannahill, who offers "an alternative *locus* to the new metropolitan worker—the pastoral not as a mythical past, but as a contemporary alterity" (ibid.).

16. Robert Tannahill, *The Poems and Songs and Correspondence of Robert Tannahill, with Life and Notes*, ed. David Semple (Paisley, UK: A. Gardner, 1874), 109–112.

17. Andrew Noble and Patrick Scott Hogg's commentary on Burns's poem harmonizes his republican support of French revolutionary principles while opposing the postrevolutionary tyranny now threatening a British invasion. Robert Burns, *The Canongate Burns: The Complete Poems and Songs of Robert Burns*, ed. Andrew Noble and Patrick Scott Hogg (Edinburgh: Canongate, 2003), 419.

18. G. Ross Roy notes the resemblance of this section of Tannahill's ode to Burns's poem, in his article "'The Mair They Talk, I'm Kend the Better': Poems about Robert Burns to 1859," in *Love and Liberty, Robert Burns: A Bicentenary Celebration*, ed. Kenneth Simpson (East Linton, UK: Tuckwell, 1997), 58–59.

19. Andrews reads the poem as almost painfully self-conscious, "expressing much self-doubt along with validation of his subject" (*Genius of Scotland*, 222). On poetry written in the twenty-five years after Burns's death, see ibid., chap. 5.

20. For an analysis of the concept of "North Britain" as both a geographic and imaginative construct, see Fielding, *Scotland and the Fictions of Geography*. Fielding argues that Scottish romanticism can be distinguished from its English counterpart in their conceptions of the relation between local, national, and global space. According to Fielding, "To think of Scotland as 'North Britain' is already to shape it geographically. 'North Britain' is a term that at once homogenises and divides, and it does so in various ways. First, it confers a unity upon both the nation-state of Britain and a Scotland whose internal divisions are thereby blurred. 'North' becomes a general signifier for Scotland in the decades preceding its adoption as a common term for the north of England following the industrialization of parts of that region. Although 'North Britain' was a commonplace term for Scotland throughout the eighteenth century, its meanings were not straightforward, and the term 'north' was loaded, divided and sometimes ambiguous" (ibid., 15).

21. Thomas Preston argues, for example, that "Burns's poetry as a whole constitutes both a Britannic and Scottish political agenda—that of proposing a non-anglicizing cultural identity and future for Scotland within a British polity in which England must inevitably retain superiority of size in geography, population, and economic resources, but not uncontested moral and cultural authority." In this regard, "Does Haughty Gaul" calls on "united Britons" to "correct British political ills," enabling both the pro-liberty and anti-Gallic interpretations of the poem. Preston, "Contrary Scriptings: Implied National Narratives in Burns and Smollett," in Simpson, *Love and Liberty*, 204.

22. Robert Burns, *The Poems and Songs of Robert Burns*, 3 vols., ed. James Kinsley (Oxford, UK: Clarendon, 1968), 2:756. As Liam McIlvanney argues, Burns's ideological commitment to "civic humanism" goes hand in hand with his "radical" politics. Burns's opposition to foreign invasion expresses "the Real Whig ethos of British radicalism," which sought constitutional reform at home in an effort to vindicate the "liberty" of free-born Britons. McIlvanney, *Burns the Radical: Poetry and Politics in Late Eighteenth-Century Scotland* (East

[216]

NOTES TO PAGES 130–153

Linton, UK: Tuckwell, 2000), 237–237. Tannahill, however, does not appear attracted to Burns's specific form of "Real Whig" radicalism in his ode.

23. Robert Tannahill, *The Soldier's Return: A Scottish Interlude in Two Acts, with Other Poems and Songs, Chiefly in the Scottish Dialect* (Paisley, UK: Stephen Young, 1807).

24. T. M. Devine, *The Scottish Nation: A History, 1700–2000* (New York: Viking, 1999), 233.

25. Ibid., 234.

26. Tannahill, *Poems and Songs* (1874), 163–165.

27. Tannahill, *Poems and Songs* (1876), 247.

28. Robert Tannahill, *The Works of Robert Tannahill*, ed. Philip A. Ramsey (London: A. Fullarton, 1838), 82.

29. Ibid., 72–74.

30. Ibid., 74.

31. See C. S. Lewis, *The Allegory of Love: A Study in Medieval Tradition* (New York: Oxford University Press, 1958), 13.

32. Tannahill, *Poems and Songs* (1874), 171–173. Victorian critics lauded the first two stanzas of the song while regretting the later addition of the "inferior" third stanza. See Tannahill, *Poems and Songs* (1876), 208; and Tannahill, *Works*, 4–5.

33. Tannahill, *Works*, 4.

34. Tannahill, *Poems and Songs* (1876), 75–80.

35. Marilyn Butler and others have answered this question in the negative. Although most agree that Burns privately sympathized with the reform cause in private, he generally devoted his energies in the 1790s to "Scottish song, with its potentially much wider, more open popular market." Butler, "Burns and Politics," in Simpson, *Love and Liberty*, 88–89.

36. Andrews, *Genius of Scotland*, 193.

37. Tannahill, *Poems and Songs* (1876), 171 ("The Tap-Room").

6. BURNS AND THE JACOBINS

1. See particularly T. M. Devine, ed., *Recovering Scotland's Slavery Past: the Caribbean Connection* (Edinburgh: Edinburgh University Press, 2015); and Michael Morris, *Scotland and the Caribbean, c. 1740–1833: Atlantic Archipelagos* (New York: Routledge, 2015).

2. For example, see Nigel Leask, "Burns and the Poetics of Abolition," in *The Edinburgh Companion to Robert Burns*, ed. Gerard Carruthers (Edinburgh: Edinburgh University Press, 2009), 47–60; Corey E. Andrews, "'Ev'ry Heart can Feel': Scottish Poetic Responses to Slavery in the West Indies, from Blair to Burns," *International Journal of Scottish Literature* 4 (Spring–Summer 2008), http://www.ijsl.stir.ac.uk/issue4/index.htm; Clark McGinn, "The Scotch Bard and 'The Planting Line': New Documents on Burns and Jamaica," *Studies in Scottish Literature* 43, no. 2 (2017): 255–266. As McGinn notes, the generally accepted narrative that Burns accepted a job from Patrick Douglas on his brother's plantation near Port Antonio in a desperate bid to escape prosecution for debt and begin anew with his lover Mary Campbell, only to be "saved" by the financial and critical success of his poems, is now in question. Relying on newly discovered correspondence between the Douglas brothers, McGinn finds that Burn's own accounts of the episode "are clearly at odds with the Douglas correspondence. The job offered to the poet was more vile than we had imagined and was to be undertaken for paltry sums. He certainly represented it as a better outcome than that to his friends" ("Scotch Bard," 265). Indeed, McGinn pulls no punches, concluding that the poet "sought to prosper from chattel slavery and only dropped the opportunity because a better offer came along, not because of any moral scruples over human suffering" ("Scotch Bard," 265). Nigel Leask's argues less

[217]

NOTES TO PAGES 153–156

bluntly, based on his reading in an abolitionist context of Burns's poem "Is There for Honest Poverty" (1795), that "Burns's difficult attitude to slavery" does not necessarily "qualify his radical credentials in 1795, however much it may qualify our admiration for this ethical outlook in general" ("Burns and the Poetics of Abolition," 58).

3. As Leith Davis, Ian Duncan, and Janet Sorenson observe, "The French Revolution provoked a crisis of ideological legitimation in this Scottish republic of letters. The Anti-Jacobin crackdown, strengthened by the monopolistic control of institutions under William Pitt's "Scotch manager," Secretary of State Henry Dundas, issued in a general repression: the transportation of 'Friends of the People,' official warnings to philo-revolutionary professors like Dugald Stewart and John Millar, and a Tory stranglehold on appointments and promotions. Accordingly, the projects of Enlightenment shifted their institutional base, from the university curriculum to an industrializing literary marketplace." Davis, Duncan, and Sorenson, introduction to *Scotland and the Borders of Romanticism*, ed. Davis, Duncan, and Sorenson (Cambridge: Cambridge University Press, 2004), 11–12.

4. On Burns's involvement, see Colin Kidd, "Burns and Politics," in Carruthers, *Edinburgh Companion to Robert Burns*, 68–73. Kidd concludes that Burns's politics during this period "must remain a matter of puzzlement" (ibid., 72).

5. Hector MacMillan, *Handful of Rogues: Thomas Muir's Enemies of the People* (Argyll, UK: Argyll, 2005), 150. Listing a number of leading Enlightenment intellectuals in Scottish universities, including the philosophers Dugald Stewart (Edinburgh) and George Jardine (Glasgow), the legal scholar John Millar (Glasgow), and James Brown (St. Andrews), as well as distinguished nobleman, attorneys, and teachers, MacMillan argues that support for the French was probably broader based in Scottish society at large than conservative historians would like to admit. He calls for further research into "family papers that were perhaps thought best kept out of view during an extended and intense period of North British prejudice" (ibid., 220).

6. Andrew Noble, "Displaced Persons: Burns and the Renfrew Radicals," in *Scotland in the Age of the French Revolution*, ed. Bob Harris (Edinburgh: J. Donald, 2005), 212.

7. James Kennedy, *Treason!!! Or, Not Treason!!! Alias the Weaver's Budget* (London, 1795).

8. Noble, "Burns and the Renfrew Radicals," 214. See also Gordon Pentland, "Radical Returns in an Age of Revolutions," *Études écossaises* 13 (2010): 91–92. Robert Watt and David Downie were defendants in a celebrated state trial in Edinburgh that commenced August of 1794. Charged with high treason for allegedly conspiring with rebels in Ireland and England to mount an armed insurrection against the government, Watt and Downie were convicted and sentenced to death. Although the trial adduced little evidence that the plot had advanced beyond seditious speech and the collection of about four dozen weapons, the government sought conviction on the capital charge of treason as part of a crackdown on allegedly treasonous activities by the London Corresponding Society and sister organizations in Scotland and Ireland. Watt was executed; Downie, however, received a pardon after the jury recommended clemency. See Thomas Erskine May, *The Constitutional History of England Since the Accession of George III, 1760–1860*, vol. 2 (New York: A.C. Armstrong and Son, 1880), 154–155.

9. James Kennedy. *The Pitiful Plaint of a Hen-Pecked Prodigal: Dedicated to the Daughter of the Duke Bobadil Manifesto* (London: the author, 1797).

10. See John Barrell, *Imagining the King's Death: Figurative Treason, Fantasies of Regicide, 1793–1796* (Oxford: Oxford University Press, 2000), 116–117.

11. Gordon Pentland argues that this poem indicates "the centrality of ideas of 'exile' to the language and symbolism of population politics" ("Radical Returns," 91). He further notes that Kennedy and other radicals deployed the trope of exile to dramatize "the conflict

[218]

NOTES TO PAGES 157–163

between the state and radical reformers" and to bring attention to "the tyranny of Scottish law" (ibid., 92).

12. For a perceptive reading of Wordsworth's mediation of his experiences of the French Revolution in *The Prelude*, see Eugene L. Stelzig, "'The Shield of Human Nature': Wordsworth's Reflections on the Revolution in France," *Nineteenth-Century Literature* 45, no. 4 (1991): 415–431.

13. The trial of Thomas Muir exemplifies this perception. Muir's trial took place on August 30, 1793, before Scotland's criminal court, the high court of justiciary. Lord Advocate Robert Dundas, Henry Dundas's nephew, appeared for the prosecution. Five judges heard the case, presided over by Robert Macqueen, Lord Braxfield. Braxfield's conduct of the trial has passed into some Whig histories of eighteenth-century Scotland as a scandalous travesty of justice, though these accounts can be exaggerated. According to Henry W. Meikle, the great early twentieth-century historian of the period, "most of the injustice was due to the panic pervading all classes, including the bench." Meikle bases much of his famous narrative of Muir's trial on Henry Cockburn's *An Examination of the Trials for Sedition in Scotland* (New York: A. M. Kelley, 1970). See Meikle, *Scotland and the French Revolution* (Glasgow: J. Maclehose, 1912), 131–136. For a political biography of Muir and his compatriots, see MacMillan, *Handful of Rogues*.

14. As Nigel Leask points out, the eighteenth-century usage of the term "slave" possessed multiple connotations. It could be used to refer to the subjects of French and Spanish Catholic absolutism, as well as, in Burns for example, the laboring poor subjected to feudal dependence. Leask, "Burns and the Poetics of Abolition," 47–48. For the full text of Thomson's ode, see David Mallet, *Alfred; A Masque,* in *The Works of David Mallet,* vol. 3 (London: A. Millar, 1759), 67-69. The ode's allusion to Britannia's "native oak" is in the fourth stanza on page 67.

15. Noble, "Burns and the Renfrew Radicals," 220, 222.

16. Ibid., 223.

17. Ibid., 224.

18. Ibid.

19. J. E. Cookson, for example, argues that "there was an enormous gap between the threat of revolution as imagined by the government and ruling groups and the innocuousness of physical force protest in the actual event. Violent disorder, for the most part, remained localized, limited in its aims, and easily subdued." Cookson, *The British Armed Nation, 1793–1815* (Oxford, UK: Clarendon, 1997), 182. On the other hand, Roger Wells concludes from essentially the same evidence that the threat of revolution "must be taken very seriously indeed." Wells, *Insurrection: The British Experience, 1795–1803* (Gloucester, UK: A. Sutton, 1983), xiv. J. W. Fortescue notes in his history of the British army during the period that "the home army . . . was not designed primarily for defence against foreign enemies, but simply and solely for the purpose of domestic police," indicating a relatively high level of anxiety that, even if exaggerated, was nevertheless real. Fortescue, *The British Army, 1783–1802* (London: Macmillan, 1905), 20. See also the more extensive list of scholarship in note 57 to the introduction to this work.

20. Pentland, "Radical Returns," 91.

21. Pentland's study of the few transported Jacobins who returned to Britain, including Maurice Margarot, who showed up in Scotland and northern England 1812 to continue his radical activities, much to the consternation of the magistrates, provides evidence of "the tenacity of these radical networks" and suggests that they endured well beyond the usual dating of their demise in the latter half of the 1790s (ibid., 96).

22. Ibid., 96–99.

[219]

NOTES TO PAGES 163–168

23. Noble, "Burns and the Renfrew Radicals," 217.
24. Cairns Craig, *Out of History: Narrative Paradigms in English and Scottish Culture* (Edinburgh: Polygon, 1996), 255.
25. *Edinburgh Gazetteer*, November 16, 1792.
26. Gerard Carruthers, "Geddes, Alexander (1737–1802)," in *Oxford Dictionary of National Biography* (Oxford: Oxford University Press, 2004).
27. According to Jerome McGann, "Geddes was the chief conduit in England for the ideas which were being pursued and elaborated by the new German scholars of the Bible." McGann, "The Idea of an Indeterminate Text: Blake's Bible of Hell and Dr. Alexander Geddes," *Studies in Romanticism* 25 (1986): 309. Geddes's biblical criticism argues that the "received biblical texts were corrupt because they all derived from unreliable base texts" and could only be purified by a new, unadulterated translation of the original Hebrew texts, i.e., the Samaritan Pentateuch" (ibid., 310–311).
28. Gerard Carruthers, "Alexander Geddes and the Burns 'Lost Poems' Controversy," *Studies in Scottish Literature* 31 (1999): 83.
29. Mark Goldie, "Alexander Geddes at the Limits of the Catholic Enlightenment," *Historical Journal* 53, no. 1 (2010): 80.
30. Carruthers, "Geddes, Alexander." See also Mark Goldie, "The Scottish Catholic Enlightenment," *Journal of British Studies* 30, no. 1 (1991): 20–62.
31. McGann contends that "Blake's *Urizen* follows Geddes' idea, which he shared with the leading contemporary German scholars, that Genesis represents an edited collection of mythological narratives which have their basis in the cultural history of the ancient Hebrews. . . . His discussion of the 'Mosaic divinity'—the figure Blake will name, recollecting Geddes, Urizen—is particularly apposite in relation to Blake's various accounts of this being" ("Idea of an Indeterminate Text," 318). In McGann's reading, Geddes and his treatment of scriptural texts as "mythologues" constitute a major influence on the development of English Romanticism and nineteenth-century poetry and fiction (ibid., 324).
32. Carruthers, "Alexander Geddes," 84.
33. Ibid., 81–82.
34. Ibid., 82.
35. Colin Kidd, "British Literature: The Career of a Concept," *Scottish Literary Review* 8, no. 1 (2016): 4.
36. For a discussion of the anti-Catholic and antimoderate backlash to the Scottish Relief Bill, as well as the involvement of Geddes's brother, Bishop John Geddes, in the society, see Goldie, "Scottish Catholic Enlightenment."
37. Ibid., 50.
38. Ibid.
39. Robert Crawford, *Scotland's Books: A History of Scottish Literature* (Oxford: Oxford University Press, 2009), 367.
40. Ibid., 369.
41. Carruthers, "Alexander Geddes," 83.
42. Goldie, "Alexander Geddes at the Limits," 84.
43. For an analysis of how "national" languages overwhelmed Latin as a linguistic medium for elite control of European state, church, and society, while at the same time limited the potentially infinite diversity of local idiolects to a relatively small number of languages that began to look "national" in character, see Benedict Anderson, *Imagined Communities: Reflections on the Origin and Spread of Nationalism* (London: Verso, 1983), chap. 3.
44. Mikhail M. Bakhtin, *The Dialogic Imagination*, ed. Michael Holquist, trans. Caryl Emerson and Michael Holquist (Austin: University of Texas Press, 1981), 431. Michael Holquist has synthesized the sense in which Bakhtin employs the term *polyglossia*, defining it as the

[220]

NOTES TO PAGES 168–177

"simultaneous presence of two or more national languages interacting within a single cultural system (Bakhtin's two historical models are ancient Rome and the Renaissance)" (ibid., 431). According to Bakhtin, *heteroglossia* refers to "the problem of internal differentiation, the stratification characteristic of any national language" (ibid., 67). A "national language," according to Holquist, means the "traditional linguistic unities (English, Russian, French, etc.) with their coherent grammatical and semantic systems" (ibid., 430).

45. Alexander Geddes, *Carmen sæculare, pro Gallica gente tyrannidi aristocraticæ erepta* (London: J. Johnson, 1790). The preface may be translated, "Liberty is made even more precious by the recollection of servitude." Geddes's contemporary biographer John Mason Good takes a dim view of the poem: "animated with the sacred fury of the moment, which seems to have borne down every breast before it, [Geddes] flies to his muse, to give vent to the rapturous feelings that agitated him. The muse, however, in direct contradiction to what might have been expected, does not appear to have been propitious. There is a tameness and insipidity pervading the entire ode—an occasional inattention to prosody and grammar which renders it equally unworthy of its subject and the poet: no prominent event is seized possession of; no sentiment auspiciously conveyed." Good, *Memoirs of the Life and Writings of the Reverend Alexander Geddes, LL.D.* (London: R. Wilks, 1803), 265. Good (1764–1827) is an interesting figure in his own right. Son of a Congregationalist minister, he studied medicine and practiced surgery in Suffolk and London; authored a history of medicine; acquired a number of foreign languages, including Hebrew, Latin, Greek, Spanish, Portuguese, Arabic, Persian, Russian, Sanskrit, and Chinese; and wrote and translated Latin poetry. Good met Geddes in 1792 and undertook his biography upon Geddes's death. See G. T. Bettany, "Good, John Mason (1764–1827)," revised by Patrick Wallis, in *Oxford Dictionary of National Biography* (Oxford: Oxford University Press, 2004).

46. The English translation appears at the foot of each page of the original text.

47. William Blake, *Songs of Innocence and of Experience*, Copy B, Object 36, "London" (1789, 1794), accessed March 27, 2014, http://blakearchive.org.

48. As Mark Goldie points out, Geddes "adopted an historicist progressivism. He was impatient with the 'barbarism' of primitive ages. . . . Geddes rejoiced that he lived 'in a more enlightened and less superstitious age' and that 'a considerable revolution' in the minds of Catholics had occurred in modern times" ("Alexander Geddes at the Limits," 78).

49. Murray G. H. Pittock, *Celtic Identity and the British Image* (Manchester: Manchester University Press, 1999), 15.

50. Ibid., 14–16.

51. See Carruthers, "Alexander Geddes." Noble and Hogg, while attributing the poem to Burns, note that "the song is based on an old song named 'Will Ye Go to the Ewe Bughts, Marion' and its tune of the same name, which melody Burns had already set to 'Will Ye Go to the Indies, My Mary.' This new version is significantly adapted from Allan Ramsay's earlier 'Ewe Bughts, Marion.'" Robert Burns, *The Canongate Burns: The Complete Poems and Songs of Robert Burns*, ed. Andrew Noble and Patrick Scott Hogg (Edinburgh: Canongate, 2003), 492.

52. Alexander Geddes(?), "The Ewe Bughts," in Burns, *Canongate Burns*, 491–493. Carruthers bases his claim for Geddes's authorship of "The Ewe Bughts" on a number of circumstantial factors: Geddes's frequent contributions to the *Morning Chronicle*, his consistent critique of Pitt's war policy, his long association with the Gordons of Aberdeenshire, and his composition and revision of other Scots songs, such as "Lewie Gordon." As Carruthers adds, "If I were to push my case, I might even point to the song's lament for 'Sandy,' the soldier abroad on duty in Flanders, and suggest a playful piece of self-reference" ("Alexander Geddes," 84).

53. Noble and Hogg translate "kaerd" as "gypsy" (Burns, *Canongate Burns*, 492).

54. Noble and Hogg observe in their discussion of the poem as one of Burns's lost poems, "Like Burns's treatment of *Logan Braes*, the new lyric has been transformed into a war-broken

[221]

NOTES TO PAGES 177-184

love song. The simple language and style is enhanced by the evocative use of the feminine voice: a characteristic trait of Burns's lyrics. Ramsay's version is written in the male voice. No poet of the eighteenth-century possessed Burns's skill in employing the female voice in song" (ibid.). While I would argue that Lady Nairne is at least one other eighteenth-century poet who could match Burns in this respect, Noble and Hogg's discussion does not account for the reversal of the poem's "feminine voice" from the "war-broken love song" of the first half to the assertive, self-aware critic of the follies of men in the second half. This reversal would seem to undercut their argument that the poem represents a "new radical text" in opposition to war.

55. Ibid., 528. In attributing the poem to Burns, Noble and Hogg argue that nowhere does Geddes "display the Burnsian skill of ironic assent to what he is actually attacking so evident here" (ibid.). Geddes's familiarity with Horatian satire, his marvelous nine-canto mock-epic "The Battle of Bangor, or the Church's Triumph," and his pungent *An Apology for Slavery; or, Six Cogent Arguments against the Immediate Abolition of the Slave-Trade* (1792) might argue the case against Burns's clear superiority with respect to ironic assent.

56. With respect to the pseudonym "A. Briton," Carruthers notes that Geddes used similar pseudonyms elsewhere, including "A Patriot" and "A True Briton" in the months leading up to publication of the poem ("Alexander Geddes," 85). Noble and Hogg dismiss this claim, arguing that "A. Briton" points to Burns because he had recently used it to identify an essay addressed to the editor of the *Morning Chronicle* (Burns, *Canongate Burns*, 526).

57. Geddes, "The Cob Web: A Song," in Burns, *Canongate Burns*, 524–526.

58. Noble and Hogg point out the irony of the speaker's allusion to "plenty," given the widespread food shortages in Scotland during the mid-1790s (ibid., 527).

59. Richard Hooker, *Of the Laws of Ecclesiastical Polity* (Cambridge: Cambridge University Press, 1989), book 1, chap. 10.

60. As one concerned magistrate observed, "The Farmers in this Country are very much more disposed to sell their Grain by the lump for shipping, than in small quantities for the consumpt of certain classes of People at home; because though the price may be the same, they thereby avoid the trouble attending the sale of small quantities in the public market, when, on the other hand, they sell and deliver in large quantities, and receive their payment in one sum." David Staig, Dumfries, to Robert Dundas, December 27, 1795, National Records of Scotland, Melville Castle Papers, GD 51/5/226/1, quoted in Bob Harris, "Introduction: Scotland in the 1790s," in Harris, *Scotland in the Age of the French Revolution*, 9.

61. Robert Chambers, *The Scottish Songs: Collected and Illustrated by Robert Chambers*, vol. 1 (Edinburgh: W. Tait, 1829), 186–187.

62. Donaldson borrows this term from Johann Gottfried von Herder. William Donaldson, *The Jacobite Song: Political Myth and National Identity* (Aberdeen: Aberdeen University Press, 1988), 87–88. For an excellent overview of Herder's philosophy of history, see George G. Iggers, *The German Conception of History: The National Tradition of Historical Thought from Herder to the Present*, rev. ed. (Middletown: Wesleyan University Press, 1968, 1983), chap. 1.

63. Carruthers suggests just this: "A short sketch of his life and the recent powerful re-awakening of interest in Geddes gives a sense of the fact that, in spite of his subsequent relative anonymity, Geddes is one of the major intellects to emerge from eighteenth-century Scotland, and this is to place him among no small rank in the milieu of the Scottish Enlightenment" ("Alexander Geddes," 82).

CONCLUSION

1. Gerard Carruthers, "Alexander Wilson: The Rise and Fall and Rise of a Laboring Class Writer," in *A History of British Working Class Poetry*, ed. John Goodridge and Bridget Keegan (Cambridge: Cambridge University Press, 2017), 70.

[222]

NOTES TO PAGES 185–186

2. See, for example, Robert Dunbar, "Vernacular Gaelic Tradition"; Anja Gunderloch, "The Heroic Ballads of Gaelic Scotland"; Jason Marc Harris, "Nineteenth-Century Highland and Island Folklore"; and Michael Newton, "Tradition and Innovation in Twentieth-Century Scottish Gaelic Literature," all in *The Edinburgh Companion to Scottish Traditional Literatures*, ed. Sarah Dunnigan and Suzanne Gilbert (Edinburgh: Edinburgh University Press, 2013).
3. Edward H. Burtt Jr., ed., *Alexander Wilson: Enlightened Naturalist* (Lewisburg, PA: Bucknell University Press, 2016).

BIBLIOGRAPHY

Althusser, Louis. *On the Reproduction of Capitalism: Ideology and Ideological State Apparatuses.* New York: Verso, 2014.

Anderson, Benedict. *Imagined Communities: Reflections on the Origin and Spread of Nationalism.* London: Verso, 1983.

Andrews, Corey E. "'Almost the Same, but Not Quite': English Poetry by Eighteenth-Century Scots." *Eighteenth Century* 47, no. 1 (2006): 59–79.

———. "Burns the Critic." In *The Edinburgh Companion to Robert Burns,* edited by Gerard Carruthers, 110–124. Edinburgh: Edinburgh University Press, 2009.

———. "'Ev'ry Heart can Feel': Scottish Poetic Responses to Slavery in the West Indies, from Blair to Burns." *International Journal of Scottish Literature* 4 (Spring–Summer 2008). http://www.ijsl.stir.ac.uk/issue4/index.htm.

———. "'Far Fam'd RAB': Scottish Labouring-Class Poets Writing in the Shadow of Robert Burns, 1785–1792." *Studies in Hogg and His World,* January 1, 2013, 41–67.

———. "The Genius of Scotland: Robert Burns and His Critics, 1796–1828." *International Journal of Scottish Literature* 6 (2010): 1–16.

———. *The Genius of Scotland: The Cultural Production of Robert Burns, 1785–1834.* Leiden: Brill Rodopi, 2015.

Atchison, Peter, and Andrew Cassell. *The Lowland Clearances: Scotland's Silent Revolution, 1760–1830.* East Linton, UK: Tuckwell, 2003.

Bainbridge, Simon, *British Poetry and the Revolutionary and Napoleonic Wars: Visions of Conflict.* Oxford: Oxford University Press, 2003.

Bakhtin, Mikhail M. *The Dialogic Imagination.* Edited by Michael Holquist. Translated by Caryl Emerson and Michael Holquist. Austin: University of Texas Press, 1981.

Barbour, Freeland. *The White Rose of Gask, the Life and Songs of Carolina Oliphant, Lady Nairne.* Edinburgh: Birlinn, 2019.

Barrell, John. *The Idea of Landscape and the Sense of Place: An Approach to the Poetry of John Clare.* Cambridge: Cambridge University Press, 1972.

———. *Imagining the King's Death: Figurative Treason, Fantasies of Regicide, 1793–1796.* Oxford: Oxford University Press, 2000.

Bayne, T. W. "Lapraik, John (1727–1807)." Revised by Gerard Carruthers. In *Oxford Dictionary of National Biography.* Oxford: Oxford University Press 2004.

———. "Pagan, Isobel." Revised by Jane Potter. In *Oxford Dictionary of National Biography.* Oxford: Oxford University Press, 2004.

Behrendt, Stephen C., ed. *Romanticism, Radicalism, and the Press.* Detroit: Wayne State University Press, 1997.

Bell, Eleanor, and Gavin Miller, eds. *Scotland in Theory: Reflections on Culture and Literature.* Amsterdam: Brill, 2004.

Bergson, Henri. *Creative Evolution.* 1907. Translated by Arthur Mitchell. New York: Henry Holt, 1911.

[225]

BIBLIOGRAPHY

———. *Matter and Memory*. 1896. Translated by Arthur Mitchell. New York: Henry Holt, 1911.

Bettany, G. T. "Good, John Mason (1764–1827)." Revised by Patrick Wallis. *Oxford Dictionary of National Biography*. Oxford: Oxford University Press, 2004.

Black, Ronald, and Gerard Carruthers. "The Eighteenth Century." In *The International Companion to Scottish Poetry*, edited by Carla Sassi, 54–63. Glasgow: Scottish Literature International, 2015.

Blake, William. *The Complete Poetry and Prose of William Blake*, ed. David V. Erdman. New York: Random House, 1965, 1982, 1988).

Bold, Valentina. "Inmate of the Hamlet: Burns as Peasant Poet." In *Love and Liberty, Robert Burns: A Bicentenary Celebration*, edited by Kenneth Simpson, 43–52. East Linton, UK: Tuckwell, 1997.

———. *James Hogg: A Bard of Nature's Making*. Oxford, UK: Peter Lang, 2007.

———. "Janet Little 'The Scotch Milkmaid' and 'Peasant Poetry.'" *Scottish Literary Journal* 20, no. 2 (1993): 21–30.

Brenton, Sir Lancelot Charles Lee. *English Translation of the Septuagint*. London: S. Bagster, 1844.

Brewer, John. *The Sinews of Power: War, Money and the English State, 1688–1783*. London: Routledge, 1989.

Brims, John D. "The Covenanting Tradition and Scottish Radicalism in the 1790s." In *Covenant, Charter, and Party: Traditions of Revolt and Protest in Modern Scottish History*, edited Terry Brotherstone, 50–62. Aberdeen: Aberdeen University Press, 1989.

——— "From Reformers to 'Jacobins': The Scottish Association of the Friends of the People." In *Conflict and Stability in Scottish Society, 1700–1850*, edited by T. M. Devine, 31–50. Edinburgh: J. Donald, 1990.

———. "The Scottish 'Jacobins,' Scottish Nationalism and the British Union." In *Scotland and England, 1286–1815*, edited by Roger Mason, 247–265. Edinburgh: J. Donald, 1987.

Broadhead, Alex. *The Language of Robert Burns: Style, Ideology, and Identity*. Lewisburg, PA: Bucknell University Press, 2014.

Brotherstone, Terry, ed. *Covenant, Charter, and Party: Traditions of Revolt and Protest in Modern Scottish History*. Aberdeen: Aberdeen University Press, 1989.

Brotherstone, Terry, Anna Clark, and Kevin Whelan, eds. *These Fissured Isles: Ireland, Scotland and the Making of Modern Britain, 1798–1848*. Edinburgh: J. Donald, 2005.

Brown, Callum G. *Religion and Society in Scotland since 1707*. Edinburgh: Edinburgh University Press, 1997.

Brown, D. J. "The Government Response to Scottish Radicalism: 1792–1802." In *Scotland in the Age of the French Revolution*, edited by Bob Harris, 99–124. Edinburgh: J. Donald, 2005.

Brown, Ian, ed. *The Edinburgh History of Scottish Literature*. Vol. 2. Edinburgh: Edinburgh University Press, 2007.

Brown, Mary Ellen. *Burns and Tradition*. Urbana: University of Illinois Press, 1984.

———. "Old Singing Women and the Canons of Scottish Balladry and Song." In *A History of Scottish Women's Writing*, edited by Douglas Gifford and Dorothy McMillan, 44–57. Edinburgh: Edinburgh University Press, 1997.

Brown, Robert. *Paisley Poets, with Brief Memoirs of Them and Selections from Their Poetry*. 2 vols. Glasgow: J. & J. Cook, 1889–1890.

Buchan, David. *The Ballad and the Folk*. London: Routledge and Kegan Paul, 1971.

Buchan, James. *Capital of the Mind: How Edinburgh Changed the World*. London: John Murray, 2003.

Burns, Frank L. "Alexander Wilson. VIII. His Early Life and Writings." *Wilson Bulletin* 22, no. 2 (1910): 79–96.

[226]

BIBLIOGRAPHY

Burns, Robert. *The Canongate Burns: The Complete Poems and Songs of Robert Burns*. Edited by Andrew Noble and Patrick Scott Hogg. Edinburgh: Canongate, 2003.
———. *Letters of Robert Burns*. 2nd ed., 2 vols. Edited by J. De Lancey Ferguson and G. Ross Roy. Oxford, UK: Clarendon, 1985.
———. *The Poems and Songs of Robert Burns*. 3 vols. Edited by James Kinsley. Oxford, UK: Clarendon, 1968.
Burtt, Edward H., Jr., ed. *Alexander Wilson: Enlightened Naturalist*. Lewisburg: Bucknell University Press, 2016.
———. "Biographical Sketch." In *Alexander Wilson: Enlightened Naturalist*, edited by Edward H. Burtt Jr., xxvii–xxx. Lewisburg, PA: Bucknell University Press, 2016.
Burtt, Edward H., Jr., and William E. Davis Jr. *Alexander Wilson: The Scot Who Founded American Ornithology*. Cambridge, MA: Harvard University Press, 2013.
Butler, Marilyn. "Burns and Politics." In *Love and Liberty, Robert Burns: A Bicentenary Celebration*, edited by Kenneth Simpson, 86–112. East Linton, UK: Tuckwell, 1997.
Cadogan, Jean K. *Domenico Ghirlandaio: Artist and Artisan*. New Haven, CT: Yale University Press, 2001.
Cafarelli, Annette Wheeler. "The Romantic 'Peasant' Poets and their Patrons." *Wordsworth Circle* 26, no. 2 (1995): 77–87.
Cain, P. J., and A. G. Hopkins. *British Imperialism, 1688–2000*. 2nd ed. New York: Routledge, 2002.
Campbell, R. H. *The Rise and Fall of Scottish Industry, 1707–1939*. Edinburgh: J. Donald, 1980.
———. *Scotland since 1707: The Rise of an Industrial Society*. Edinburgh: J. Donald, 1985.
Carlyle, Thomas. *Past and Present*. London: Chapman and Hall, 1843.
———. "Signs of the Times." *Edinburgh Review* 49 (1829).
Carruthers, Gerard. "Alexander Geddes and the Burns 'Lost Poems' Controversy." *Studies in Scottish Literature* 31 (1999): 81–84.
———. "Alexander Wilson: Scots Poet." In *Alexander Wilson: Enlightened Naturalist*, edited by Edward H. Burtt Jr., 1–21. Lewisburg, PA: Bucknell University Press, 2016.
———. "Alexander Wilson: The Rise and Fall and Rise of a Laboring Class Writer." In *A History of British Working Class Literature*, edited by John Goodridge and Bridget Keegan, 70–84. Cambridge: Cambridge University Press, 2017.
———. "Burns and Publishing." In *The Edinburgh Companion to Robert Burns*, edited by Gerard Carruthers, 6–19. Edinburgh: Edinburgh University Press, 2009.
———, ed. *The Edinburgh Companion to Robert Burns*. Edinburgh: Edinburgh University Press, 2009.
———. "Geddes, Alexander (1737–1802)." In *Oxford Dictionary of National Biography*. Oxford: Oxford University Press, 2004.
———. "Robert Burns's Scots Poetry Contemporaries." In *Burns and Other Poets*, edited by David Sergeant and Fiona Stafford, 38–52. Edinburgh: Edinburgh University Press, 2012.
———. *Scottish Literature*. Edinburgh: Edinburgh University Press, 2009.
Casey, Claire. Introduction to *The Weaver Poet: The Songs & Poems of Robert Tannahill*, 9–14. CreateSpace, 2016.
Chambers, Robert, ed. *The Life and Works of Robert Burns*. 4 vols. Edinburgh: W. & R. Chambers, 1896.
———. *The Scottish Songs: Collected and Illustrated by Robert Chambers*. Vol. 1. Edinburgh: W. Tait, 1829.
Christie, Ian R. *Wars and Revolution: Britain, 1760–1815*. London: E. Arnold, 1982.
Christmas, William. "Introduction: An Eighteenth-Century Laboring-Class Tradition." *Eighteenth Century* 42, no. 3 (2001): 187–194.

[227]

BIBLIOGRAPHY

———. "The Verse Epistle and Laboring Class Literary Sociability from Duck to Burns." In *A History of British Working Class Literature*, edited by John Goodridge and Bridget Keegan, 39–54. Cambridge: Cambridge University Press, 2017.

Clark, Anna. *Struggle for the Breeches: Gender and the Making of the British Working Class*. Berkeley: University of California Press, 1995.

Clark, J.C.D. "A Short History of Scholarship in Jacobitism, 1688–2006." In *Loyalty and Identity: Jacobites at Home and Abroad*, edited P. Monod, M.G.H. Pittock, and Daniel Szechi, 9–56. Basingstoke, UK: Palgrave Macmillan, 2010.

Clark, Peter. *British Clubs and Societies, 1580–1800: The Origins of an Associational World*. Oxford: Oxford University Press, 2000.

Clarke, T., and T. Dickson. "Class and Class Consciousness in Early Industrial Capitalism: Paisley, 1770–1850." In *Capital and Class in Scotland*, edited by T. Dickson, 8–60. Edinburgh: J. Donald, 1982.

———. "The Making of a Class Society: Commercialisation and Working Class Resistance, 1780–1830." In *Capital and Class in Scotland*, edited by T. Dickson, 137–180. Edinburgh: J. Donald 1982.

Cockburn, Henry. *An Examination of the Trials for Sedition in Scotland*. New York: A. M. Kelley, 1970.

———. *Memorials of His Time*. Edited by Karl F. C. Miller. Chicago: University of Chicago Press, 1974.

Colley, Linda, *Britons: Forging the Nation, 1707–1832*. 2nd ed. New Haven, CT: Yale University Press, 2012.

Connolly, S. J., R. A. Houston, and R. J. Morris, eds. *Conflict, Identity and Economic Development: Ireland and Scotland, 1600–1939*. Preston, UK: Carnegie, 1995.

Cooke, A. J., I. Donnachie, A. MacSween, and C. A. Whatley, eds. *Modern Scottish History, 1707 to the Present*. 5 vols. East Linton, UK: Tuckwell, 1998.

Cookson, J. E. *The British Armed Nation, 1793–1815*. Oxford, UK: Clarendon, 1997.

Couper, W. J. *The Edinburgh Periodical Press*. 2 vols. Stirling, UK: E. Mackay, 1908.

Cowan, Edward J. "The Covenanting Tradition in Scottish History." In *Scottish History: The Power of the Past*, edited by Edward J. Cowan and Richard J. Finlay, 121–145. Edinburgh: Edinburgh University Press, 2002.

Cowan, Edward J., and Richard J. Finlay. Introduction to *Scottish History: The Power of the Past*, edited by Edward J. Cowan and Richard J. Finlay, 1–9. Edinburgh: Edinburgh University Press, 2002.

———, eds. *Scottish History: The Power of the Past*. Edinburgh: Edinburgh University Press, 2002.

Crabbe, George. *The Poetical Works of the Rev. George Crabbe*. Edinburgh: Gall and Inglis, 18?.

Craig, Cairns. "Coleridge, Hume and the Chains of the Romantic Imagination." In *Scotland and the Borders of Romanticism*, edited by Leith Davis, Ian Duncan, and Janet Sorensen, 20–37. Cambridge: Cambridge University Press, 2004.

———. *Out of History: Narrative Paradigms in English and Scottish Culture*. Edinburgh: Polygon, 1996.

Craig, David. *Scottish Literature and the Scottish People, 1680–1830*. London: Chatto and Windus, 1961.

Crawford, Robert. *The Bard: Robert Burns, a Biography*. Princeton, NJ: Princeton University Press, 2009.

———. *Devolving English Literature*. 2nd ed. Edinburgh: Edinburgh University Press, 2000.

———, ed. *Robert Burns and Cultural Authority*. Edinburgh: Edinburgh University Press, 1997.

———. "Robert Fergusson's Robert Burns." In *Robert Burns and Cultural Authority*, edited by Robert Crawford, 1–22. Edinburgh: Edinburgh University Press, 1997.

BIBLIOGRAPHY

———. *Scotland's Books: A History of Scottish Literature.* Oxford: Oxford University Press, 2009.

———. "Scottish Literature and English Studies." In *The Scottish Invention of British Literature,* edited by Robert Crawford, 225–246. Cambridge: Cambridge University Press, 1998.

Crawford, Thomas, ed. *Love, Labour and Liberty: The Eighteenth-Century Scottish Lyric.* Cheadle, UK: A Carcanet, 1976.

———. "Lowland Song and Popular Tradition in the Eighteenth Century." In *The History of Scottish Literature,* vol. 2, *1660–1800,* edited by Andrew Hook, 123–138. Aberdeen: Aberdeen University Press, 1987.

———. "Political and Protest Songs in Eighteenth-Century Scotland II: Songs of the Left." *Scottish Studies* 14 (1970): 105–131.

———. *Society and the Lyric: A Study of the Song Culture of Eighteenth-Century Scotland.* Edinburgh: Scottish Academic Press, 1979.

Cullen, Louis M., and T. Christopher Smout. *Comparative Aspects of Scottish and Irish Economic and Social History, 1600–1900.* Edinburgh: J. Donald, 1977.

Cunningham, Allan. *The Songs of Scotland, Ancient and Modern, with an Introduction and Notes, Historical and Critical, and Characters of the Lyric Poets.* London: J. Taylor, 1825.

Daiches, David, "Eighteenth-Century Vernacular Poetry." In *Scottish Poetry: A Critical Survey,* edited by James Kinsley, 150–184. Norwood, PA: Norwood Editions, 1976.

———. *The Paradox of Scottish Culture: The Eighteenth-Century Experience.* London: Oxford University Press, 1964.

Davidson, Neil. *The Origins of Scottish Nationhood.* London: Pluto, 2000.

Davis, Leith. *Acts of Union: Scotland and the Literary Negotiation of the British Nation.* Stanford, CA: Stanford University Press, 1998.

———. "At 'sang about': Scottish Song and the Challenge to British Culture." In *Scotland and the Borders of Romanticism,* edited by Leith Davis, Ian Duncan, and Janet Sorenson, 188–203. Cambridge: Cambridge University Press, 2004.

———. "From Fingal's Harp to Flora's Song: Scotland, Music and Romanticism." *Wordsworth Circle* 31, no. 2 (2000): 93–97.

———. "Gender and the Nation in the Work of Robert Burns and Janet Little." *Studies in English Literature, 1500–1900* 38, no. 4 (1998): 621–645.

———. "Gender, Genre and the Imagining of the Scottish Nation" (2002). An unpaginated copy of this essay was provided to me by the author.

———. *Music, Postcolonialism, and Gender: The Construction of Irish National Identity, 1724–1824.* Notre Dame, IN: University of Notre Dame Press, 2006.

———. "Scottish Literature and 'Engl. Lit.'" *Studies in Scottish Literature* 38, no. 1 (2012): 20–27.

Davis, Leith, Ian Duncan, and Janet Sorenson. Introduction to *Scotland and the Borders of Romanticism,* edited by Leith Davis, Ian Duncan, and Janet Sorenson, 1–19. Cambridge: Cambridge University Press, 2004.

———, eds. *Scotland and the Borders of Romanticism.* Cambridge: Cambridge University Press, 2004.

Davis, Leith, and Maureen N. McLane. "Orality and Public Poetry." In *The Edinburgh History of Scottish Literature,* vol. 2, edited by Ian Brown, 125–142. Edinburgh: Edinburgh University Press, 2007.

Devine, T. M., ed. *Conflict and Stability in Scottish Society, 1700–1850.* Edinburgh: J. Donald, 1990.

———. "The Failure of Radical Reform in Scotland in the Late Eighteenth Century: The Social and Economic Context." In *Conflict and Stability in Scottish Society, 1700–1850,* edited by T. M. Devine, 51–64. Edinburgh: J. Donald, 1990.

———. "In Bed with an Elephant: Almost Three Hundred Years of the Anglo-Scottish Union." *Scottish Affairs* 57 (2006): 1–18.

[229]

BIBLIOGRAPHY

———. "Industrialisation." In *The Transformation of Scotland: The Economy since 1700*, edited by T. M. Devine, C. H. Lee, and G. C. Peden, 34–70. Edinburgh: Edinburgh University Press, 2005.

———, ed. *Recovering Scotland's Slavery Past: the Caribbean Connection*. Edinburgh: Edinburgh University Press, 2015.

———, ed. *Scotland and the Union, 1707–2007*. Edinburgh: Edinburgh University Press, 2008.

———. *Scotland's Empire and the Shaping of the Americas, 1600–1815*. Washington, DC: Smithsonian Books, 2003.

———. *The Scottish Nation: A History, 1700–2000*. New York: Viking, 1999.

———. "Social Responses to Agrarian 'Improvement': The Highland the Lowland Clearances in Scotland." In *Scottish Society 1500–1800*, edited by R. A. Houston and I. D. Whyte, 146–168. Cambridge: Cambridge University Press, 1989.

———. "The Transformation of Agriculture: Cultivation and Clearance." In *The Transformation of Scotland: The Economy since 1700*, edited by T. M. Devine, C. H. Lee, and G. C. Peden, 71–99. Edinburgh: Edinburgh University Press, 2005.

———. *The Transformation of Rural Scotland: Social Change and the Agrarian Economy, 1660–1815*. Edinburgh: Edinburgh University Press, 1994.

Devine, T. M., C. H. Lee, and G. C. Peden, eds. *The Transformation of Scotland: The Economy since 1700*. Edinburgh: Edinburgh University Press, 2005.

Devine, T. M., and J. R. Young, eds. *Eighteenth Century Scotland: New Perspectives*. East Linton, UK: Tuckwell, 1999.

Dewar, Robert. "Burns and the Burns Tradition." In *Scottish Poetry: A Critical Survey*, edited by James Kinsley, 185–211. Norwood, PA: Norwood Editions, 1976.

Dickinson, H. T., ed. *Britain and the French Revolution, 1789–1815*. Basingstoke, UK: Palgrave Macmillan, 1989.

———. *The Politics of the People in Eighteenth-Century Britain*. Basingstoke, UK: Palgrave Macmillan, 1995.

Dickson, Tony. *Capital and Class in Scotland*. Edinburgh: J. Donald, 1982.

———, ed. *Scottish Capitalism: Class, State and Nation from before the Union to the Present*. London: Lawrence and Wishart, 1980.

Dirks, Nicholas G. *Scandal of Empire: India and the Creation of Imperial Britain*. Cambridge, MA: Harvard University Press, 2009.

Donaldson, William. *The Jacobite Song: Political Myth and National Identity*. Aberdeen: Aberdeen University Press, 1988.

———. "Oliphant, Carolina, Lady Nairne (1766–1845)." In *Oxford Dictionary of National Biography*. Oxford: Oxford University Press, 2004.

———. "Tannahill, Robert (1774–1810)." In *Oxford Dictionary of National Biography*. Oxford: Oxford University Press, 2004.

Donnachie, Ian, and Christopher Whatley, eds. *The Manufacture of Scottish History*. Edinburgh: Polygon, 1992.

Duncan, Ian. "The Pathos of Abstraction: Adam Smith, Ossian and Samuel Johnson." In *Scotland and the Borders of Romanticism*, edited by Leith Davis, Ian Duncan, and Janet Sorensen, 38–46. Cambridge: Cambridge University Press, 2004.

———. *Scott's Shadow: The Novel in Romantic Edinburgh*. Princeton, NJ: Princeton University Press, 2008.

Duncan, Ian, and Sheila Kidd. "The Nineteenth Century." In *The International Companion to Scottish Poetry*, edited by Carla Sassi, 64–73. Glasgow: Scottish Literature International, 2015.

Dunnigan, Sarah. "Burns and Women." In *The Edinburgh Companion to Robert Burns*, edited by Gerard Carruthers, 20–33. Edinburgh: Edinburgh University Press, 2009.

[230]

BIBLIOGRAPHY

Dunnigan, Sarah, and Suzanne Gilbert, eds. *The Edinburgh Companion to Scottish Traditional Literatures*. Edinburgh: Edinburgh University Press, 2013.

Dunstan, Vivienne. "Book Ownership in Late Eighteenth-Century Scotland: A Local Case Study of Dumfriesshire Inventories." *Scottish Historical Review* 91, no. 232, pt. 2 (2012): 265–286.

———. "Chapmen in Eighteenth-Century Scotland." *Scottish Literary Review* 9, no. 2 (2017): 41–57.

———. "Professionals, Their Private Libraries, and Wider Reading Habits in Late Eighteenth- and Early Nineteenth-Century Scotland." *Library & Information History* 30, no. 2 (2014): 110–128.

Durey, Michael. *Transatlantic Radicals and the Early American Republic*. Lawrence: University Press of Kansas, 1997.

Egerton, Frank N. "Wilson, Alexander, 1766–1813." In *Oxford Dictionary of National Biography*. Oxford: Oxford University Press, 2004.

Erdman, David V. *Blake, Prophet against Empire: A Poet's Interpretation of the History of His Own Times*. Princeton, NJ: Princeton University Press, 1984.

Ewan, Elizabeth, Sue Innes, Siân Reynolds, and Rose Pipes, eds. *The Biographical Dictionary of Scottish Women*. Edinburgh: Edinburgh University Press, 2006.

Eyre-Todd, George. *Scottish Poetry of the Eighteenth Century*. Vol. 2. Glasgow: W. Hodge, 1896.

Fackenheim, Emil. "The Jewish Bible after the Holocaust: A Re-reading." In *The Jewish Philosophy Reader*, edited by Daniel H. Frank, Oliver Leaman, and Charles Manekin, 538–546. London: Routledge, 2000.

Ferguson, Moira. *Eighteenth-Century Women Poets: Nation, Class, and Gender*. Albany: State University of New York Press, 1995.

———. "Janet Little and Robert Burns: An Alliance with Reservations." *Studies Eighteenth-Century Culture* 24 (1995): 155–174.

———. "Janet Little and Robert Burns: The Politics of the Heart." In *Romantic Women Writers: Voices and Countervoices*, edited by Theresa M. Kelley and Paula R. Feldman, 207–219. Hanover, NH: University Press of New England, 1995.

Ferguson, William. *Scotland: 1689 to the Present*. Edinburgh: Oliver and Boyd, 1968.

Ferris, Ina. "Melancholy, Memory, and the 'Narrative Situation' of History in Post-Enlightenment Scotland." In *Scotland and the Borders of Romanticism*, edited by Leith Davis, Ian Duncan, and Janet Sorenson, 77–93. Cambridge: Cambridge University Press, 2004.

Fielding, Penny. "Burns's Topographies." In *Scotland and the Borders of Romanticism*, edited by Leith Davis, Ian Duncan, and Janet Sorenson, 170–187. Cambridge: Cambridge University Press, 2004.

———. *Scotland and the Fictions of Geography: North Britain, 1760–1830*. Cambridge: Cambridge University Press, 2008.

———. "Writing at the North: Rhetoric and Dialect in Eighteenth-Century Scotland." *Eighteenth Century* 39, no. 1 (1998): 25–43.

Finlay, Richard J. "The Burns Cult and Scottish Identity in the Nineteenth and Twentieth Centuries." In *Love and Liberty: Robert Burns, a Bicentenary Celebration*, edited by Kenneth Simpson, 69–78. East Linton, UK: Tuckwell, 1997.

———. "Keeping the Covenant: Scottish National Identity." In *Eighteenth Century Scotland: New Perspectives*, edited by T. M. Devine and J. R. Young, 121–133. East Linton, UK: Tuckwell, 1999.

Fortescue, J. W. *The British Army, 1783–1802*. London: Macmillan, 1905.

Foucault, Michel. *The Order of Things: An Archaeology of the Human Sciences*. New York: Vintage, 1994.

[231]

BIBLIOGRAPHY

Foyster, E., and C. A. Whatley, eds. *A History of Everyday Life in Scotland, 1600–1800*. Edinburgh: Edinburgh University Press, 2010.

Fraser, G. M. *The Strathspey Mutineers: A History of the First Highland Fencible Regiment, 1793–1799*. Kinloss, UK: Librario, 2003.

Fraser, W. Hamish. *Conflict and Class: Scottish Workers, 1700–1838*. Edinburgh: J. Donald, 1988.

———. *Scottish Popular Politics: From Radicalism to Labor*. Edinburgh: Polygon, 2000.

Fry, Michael. *The Dundas Despotism*. Edinburgh: Edinburgh University Press, 1992.

———. "Macqueen, Robert, Lord Braxfield (1722–1799)." In *Oxford Dictionary of National Biography*. Oxford: Oxford University Press, 2004.

———. "The Whig Interpretation of Scottish History." In *The Manufacture of Scottish History*, edited by Ian Donnachie and Christopher Whatley, 72–89. Edinburgh: Polygon, 1992.

Gairn, Louisa. "Nature, Landscape and Rural Life." In *The International Companion to Scottish Poetry*, edited by Carla Sassi, 132–143. Glasgow: Scottish Literature International, 2015.

Gardyne, C. G. *The Life of a Regiment: The History of the Gordon Highlanders*. Edinburgh: D. Douglas, 1901.

Geddes, Alexander. *An Apology for Slavery: or, Six Cogent Arguments against the Immediate Abolition of the Slave Trade*. London: J. Johnson, 1792.

———. *Carmen sæculare pro Gallica gente tyrannidi aristocraticæ erepta*. London: J. Johnson, 1790.

Gifford, Douglas, and Dorothy McMillan. *A History of Scottish Women's Writing*. Edinburgh: Edinburgh University Press, 1997.

Goldie, Mark. "Alexander Geddes at the Limits of the Catholic Enlightenment." *Historical Journal* 53, no. 1 (2010): 61–86.

———. "The Scottish Catholic Enlightenment." *Journal of British Studies* 30, no. 1 (1991): 20–62.

Good, John Mason. *Memoirs of the Life and Writings of the Reverend Alexander Geddes, LL.D.* London: R. Wilks, 1803.

Goodridge, John, and Bridget Keegan, eds. *A History of British Working Class Literature*. Cambridge: Cambridge University Press, 2017.

Gottlieb, Evan. *Feeling British: Sympathy and National Identity in Scottish and English Writing, 1707–1832*. Lewisburg, PA: Bucknell University Press, 2007.

Gray, William Forbes. *The Poets Laureate of England: Their History and Their Odes*. London: Sir Isaac Pitman, 1915.

Griffin, Dustin H. *Patriotic Poetry in Eighteenth-Century Britain*. Cambridge: Cambridge University Press, 2002.

Hadden, J. C. "Maxwell, James (1720–1800)." Revised by Gerard Carruthers. In *Oxford Dictionary of National Biography*. Oxford: Oxford University Press, 2004.

Hamilton, Henry. *An Economic History of Scotland in the Eighteenth Century*. Oxford, UK: Clarendon, 1963.

Harris, Bob. "Cultural Change in Provincial Scottish Towns, c. 1700–1820." *Historical Journal* 54, no. 1 (2011): 105–141.

———. "The Enlightenment, Towns and Urban Society in Scotland, c. 1760–1820." *English Historical Review* 126, no. 522 (2011): 1097–1136.

———. "Introduction: Scotland in the 1790s." In *Scotland in the Age of the French Revolution*, edited by Bob Harris, 1–22. Edinburgh: J. Donald, 2005.

———. "Political Protests in the Year of Liberty, 1792." In *Scotland in the Age of the French Revolution*, edited by Bob Harris, 49–78. Edinburgh: J. Donald, 2005.

———. "Popular Politics in Angus and Pertshire in the Seventeen-Nineties." *Historical Research* 80 (2007): 518–544.

[232]

BIBLIOGRAPHY

———. "The Press, Newspaper Fiction and Literary Journalism, 1707–1918." In *The Edinburgh History of Scottish Literature*, vol. 2, edited by Ian Brown, 308–316. Edinburgh: Edinburgh University Press, 2007.

———. "Print and Politics." In *Scotland in the Age of the French Revolution*, edited by Bob Harris, 164–195. Edinburgh: J. Donald, 2005.

———, ed. *Scotland in the Age of the French Revolution*. Edinburgh: J. Donald, 2005.

———. "Scottish-English Connections in British Radicalism in the 1790s." In *Anglo-Scottish Relations from 1603 to 1900*, edited by T. C. Smout, 189–212. Oxford: Oxford University Press, 2005.

———. *The Scottish People and the French Revolution*. London: Pickering and Chatto, 2008.

Harvie, Christopher. "'It Is Said That Burns Was a Radical': Contest, Concession, and the Political Legacy of Robert Burns, ca. 1796–1859." *Journal of British Studies* 50, no. 3 (2011): 639–666.

———. *Scotland and Nationalism: Scottish Society and Politics 1707 to the Present*. 4th ed. London: Routledge, 2004.

Hecht, Hans. *Robert Burns: The Man and His Work*. Translated by Jane Lymburn. Alloway, UK: Ayr, 1991.

Hechter, Michael. *Internal Colonialism: The Celtic Fringe in British National Development, 1536–1966*. New Brunswick, NJ: Transaction, 1975.

Hempstead, J. L. *Burns Chronicle*, February 1994, 94–101.

Henderson, Rev. George. *Lady Nairne and Her Songs*. 3rd ed. Paisley, UK: A. Gardner, 1905.

Herd, David. *Ancient and Modern Scottish Songs, Heroic Ballads, Etc.* Vol. 1. Glasgow: Kerr and Richardson, 1869. Vol. 2. Edinburgh: John Wotherspoon, 1776.

Hill, George. *The Present Happiness of Great Britain*. 2nd ed. Edinburgh: John Balfour and James Dickson, 1792.

Hogg, James. *The Jacobite Relics of Scotland; Being the Songs, Airs, and Legends of the Adherents to the House of Stuart*. Paisley: Alexander Gardner, 1874.

Honeyman, Val. "'A Very Dangerous Place'? Radicalism in Perth in the 1790s." *Scottish Historical Review* 87, no. 2 (2008): 278–305.

Hook, Andrew, ed. *The History of Scottish Literature*. Vol. 2, *1660–1800*. Aberdeen: Aberdeen University Press, 1987.

Hooker, Richard. *Of the Laws of Ecclesiastical Polity*. Cambridge: Cambridge University Press, 1989.

Houston, R. A. *Literacy in Early Modern Europe: Culture and Education, 1500–1800*. London: Longman, 1988.

Houston, R. A., and I. D. Whyte, eds. *Scottish Society, 1500–1800*. Cambridge: Cambridge University Press, 1989.

Hume, J. R., and Michael S. Moss. *Workshop of the British Empire*. Rutherford, NJ: Farleigh Dickinson University Press, 1977.

Hunter, Clark, ed. *The Life and Letters of Alexander Wilson*. Philadelphia: American Philosophical Society, 1983.

Iggers, George G. *The German Conception of History: The National Tradition of Historical Thought from Herder to the Present*, rev. ed. Middletown: Wesleyan University Press, 1968, 1983.

Innes, Sue, and Jane Rendall, "Women, Gender and Politics." In *Gender in Scottish History since 1700*, edited by Lynn Abrams, Eleanor Gordon, Deborah Siminton, and Eileen Janes Yeo, 43–83. Edinburgh: Edinburgh University Press, 2006.

Jarrell, Mackie, and William Meredith. *Eighteenth-Century English Minor Poets*. New York: Dell, 1968.

Johnston, Thomas. *A History of the Working Classes in Scotland*. 3rd ed. Glasgow: Forward, 1929.

[233]

BIBLIOGRAPHY

Jones, Charles, and Wilson McLeod. "Standards and Differences: Languages in Scotland, 1707–1918." In *The Edinburgh History of Scottish Literature*, vol. 2, edited by Ian Brown, 21–32. Edinburgh: Edinburgh University Press, 2007.

Kaufman, Paul. "The Rise of Community Libraries in Scotland." *Papers of the Bibliographical Society of America* 59, no. 3 (1965): 233–294.

Kaulbach, Ernest. *Imaginative Prophecy in the B Text of "Piers Plowman."* Cambridge, UK: D. S. Brewer, 1993.

Keegan, Bridget. "Cobbling Verse: Shoemaker Poets of the Long Eighteenth Century." *Eighteenth Century* 42, no. 3 (2001): 195–217.

Kelleher, Margaret. "Writing Irish Women's Literary History." *Irish Studies Review* 9, no. 1 (2010): 5–14. https://doi.org/10.1080/09670880020032654.

Kelly, Gary. *Women, Writing and Revolution, 1790–1827*. Oxford: Oxford University Press, 1993.

Kennedy, James. *The Pitiful Plaint of a Hen-Pecked Prodigal: Dedicated to the Daughter of the Duke Bobadil Manifesto*. London: the author, 1797.

———. *Treason!!! Or, Not Treason!!! Alias the Weaver's Budget*. London, 1795.

Kerr, Andrew William. *The History of Banking in Scotland*. 4th ed. London: A. & C. Black, 1926.

Kerrigan, Catherine, ed. *Anthology of Scottish Women Poets*. Edinburgh: Edinburgh University Press, 1991.

———. Introduction to *Anthology of Scottish Women Poets*, edited by Catherine Kerrigan, 1–11. Edinburgh: Edinburgh University Press, 1991

Kidd, Colin. "British Literature: The Career of a Concept." *Scottish Literary Review* 8, no. 1 (2016): 1–16.

———. "Burns and Politics." In *The Edinburgh Companion to Robert Burns*, edited by Gerard Carruthers, 61–73. Edinburgh: Edinburgh University Press, 2009.

———. "Eighteenth-Century Scotland and the Three Unions." In *Anglo-Scottish Relations from 1603 to 1900*, edited by T. C. Smout, 171–188. Oxford: Oxford University Press, 2005.

———. "North Britishness and the Nature of Eighteenth-Century British Patriotisms." *History Journal* 39 (1996): 361–382.

———. "'The Strange Death of Scottish History' Revisited: Constructions of the Past in Scotland, c. 1790–1914." *Scottish Historical Review* 76, pt. 1: "Writing Scotland's History": Proceedings of the 1996 Edinburgh Conference (1997): 86–102.

———. *Subverting Scotland's Past: Scottish Whig Historians and the Creation of an Anglo-British Identity, 1689–c. 1830*. Cambridge: Cambridge University Press, 1993.

———. *Union and Unionisms: Political Thought in Scotland, 1500–2000*. Cambridge: Cambridge University Press, 2008.

Kinsley, James, ed. *Scottish Poetry: A Critical Survey*. Norwood, PA: Norwood, 1976.

Kord, Susanne. *Women Peasant Poets in Eighteenth-Century England, Scotland, and Germany: Milkmaids on Parnassus*. Rochester, NY: Camden House, 2003.

Landry, Donna. *The Muses of Resistance: Laboring-Class Women's Poetry in Britain, 1739–1796*. Cambridge: Cambridge University Press, 1990.

Langford, Paul. *A Polite and Commercial People: England, 1727–1783*. Oxford: Oxford University Press, 1989.

Langland, William. *The Vision of Piers Plowman, A Complete Edition of the B-Text*, edited by A.V.C. Schmidt. London: J. M. Dent, 1978.

Lapraik, John. *Poems on Several Occasions*. Kilmarnock, UK: John Wilson, 1788.

Leask, Nigel. "Burns and the Poetics of Abolition." In *The Edinburgh Companion to Robert Burns*, edited by Gerard Carruthers, 47–60. Edinburgh: Edinburgh University Press, 2009.

———. *Robert Burns and Pastoral: Poetry and Improvement in Late Eighteenth-Century Scotland*. Oxford: Oxford University Press, 2010.

[234]

BIBLIOGRAPHY

———. "Scotland's Literature of Empire and Emigration." In *The Edinburgh History of Scottish Literature*, vol. 2, edited by Ian Brown, 153–162. Edinburgh: Edinburgh University Press, 2007.

Lee, C. H. "Economic Progress: Wealth and Poverty." In *The Transformation of Scotland: The Economy since 1700*, edited by T. M. Devine, C. H. Lee, and G. C. Peden, 128–156. Edinburgh: Edinburgh University Press, 2005.

———. *Scotland and the United Kingdom: The Economy and the Union in the Twentieth Century*. Manchester: Manchester University Press, 1995.

Lenman, Bruce. *An Economic History of Modern Scotland, 1660–1976*. London: B. T. Batsford, 1977.

———. *Enlightenment and Change: Scotland, 1746–1832*. 2nd ed. Edinburgh: Edinburgh University Press, 2009.

———. *Integration, Enlightenment and Industrialisation: Scotland, 1746–1832*. Toronto: Hodder Arnold, 1981.

Leonard, Tom, ed. *Radical Renfrew: Poetry from the French Revolution to the First World War*. Edinburgh: Polygon, 1990.

Lewis, C. S. *The Allegory of Love: A Study in Medieval Tradition*. New York: Oxford University Press, 1958.

Lindsay, Maurice. *The Burns Encyclopedia*. 3rd ed. New York: St. Martin's, 1980.

———. *The Burns Encyclopedia*. 4th ed. Edited by David Purdie, Kirsteen McCue, and Gerard Carruthers. London: Robert Hale, 2013.

———. *History of Scottish Literature*. London: R. Hale, 1977.

Little, Janet. *The Poetical Works of Janet Little, the Scotch Milkmaid*. Ayr, UK: John and Peter Wilson, 1792.

Logue, Kenneth. *Popular Disturbances in Scotland, 1780–1815*. Edinburgh: J. Donald, 1979.

Low, Donald A., ed. *Robert Burns: The Critical Heritage*. London: Routledge and Kegan Paul, 1974.

Lutz, Alfred. "Representing Scotland in *Roderick Random* and *Humphry Clinker*: Smollett's Development as a Novelist." *Studies in the Novel* 33, no. 1 (2001): 1–17.

Lynch, Michael. *The Oxford Companion to Scottish History*. Oxford: Oxford University Press, 2001.

MacDonald, Angus, and Archibald MacDonald. *The Clan Donald*. Vol. 3. Inverness, UK: Northern Counties, 1900.

Macdonald, Catriona M. M. "'Their Laurels Wither'd, and their Name Forgot': Women and the Scottish Radical Tradition." In *Scottish History: The Power of the Past*, edited by Edward J. Cowan and Richard J. Finlay, 225–252. Edinburgh: Edinburgh University Press, 2002.

MacDonald, J. R. "Paul, Hamilton (1773–1854)." Revised by Douglas Brown. In *Oxford Dictionary of National Biography*. Oxford: Oxford University Press, 2004.

Macinnes, Allan I. "Jacobitism in Scotland: Episodic Cause or National Movement?" *Scottish Historical Review* 86, no. 2 (2007): 225–252.

———. "Scottish Jacobitism: in Search of a Movement." In *Eighteenth Century Scotland: New Perspectives*, edited by T. M. Devine and J. R. Young, 70–89. East Linton, UK: Tuckwell, 1999.

———. *Union and Empire: The Making of the United Kingdom in 1707*. Cambridge: Cambridge University Press, 2007.

Macinnes, Allan I., and T. M. Devine, eds. *Scotland and the British Empire*. Oxford: Oxford University Press, 2011.

Mackillop, Andrew. "For King, Country, and Regiment? Motive and Identity within Highland Soldiering, 1746–1815." In *Fighting for Identity: Scottish Military Experience, c. 1550–1900*, edited by Steve Murdock and Andrew Mackillop, 185–211. Leiden: Brill, 2002.

[235]

BIBLIOGRAPHY

MacLachlan, Christopher, ed. *Before Burns: Eighteenth-Century Scottish Poetry*. Edinburgh: Canongate Classics, 2002.

MacMillan, Hector. *Handful of Rogues: Thomas Muir's Enemies of the People*. Argyll, UK: Argyll, 2005.

Mallet, David. *Alfred; A Masque,* in *The Works of David Mallet*. Vol. 3. London: A. Millar, 1759.

Manning, Susan. *Fragments of Union: Making Connections in Scottish and American Writing*. Basingstoke, UK: Palgrave Macmillan, 2002.

———. "Post-Union Scotland and the Scottish Idiom of Britishness." In *The Edinburgh History of Scottish Literature*, vol. 2, edited by Ian Brown, 45–56. Edinburgh: Edinburgh University Press, 2007.

Marshall, P. J. ed. *The Oxford History of the British Empire*. Vol. 2, *The Eighteenth Century*. Oxford: Oxford University Press,1998.

Mason, Roger, ed. *Scotland and England, 1286–1815*. Edinburgh: J. Donald, 1987.

Mathieson, William Law. *The Awakening of Scotland: A History from 1747 to 1797*. Glasgow: J. Maclehose, 1910.

Maxwell, James. *Animadversions on Some Poets and Poetasters of the Present Age, Especially R—t B—s, and J—n L—k, with a Contrast of Some of the Former Age*. Paisley, UK: J. Neilson, 1788.

———. *On the French Revolution. A Moral Essay on the Rights of Man*. Paisley, UK: J. Neilson, 1792.

———. *A Touch on the Times; or, Observations on Mr. Paine's Letter to Mr Secretary Dundas, Set Forth in the Following Dialogue*. Paisley, UK: J. Neilson, 1793?

———. *War against Heaven Openly Declared by Multitudes in This Degenerate Age; Who Say to the Almighty, Depart from Us; For We Desire Not the Knowledge of Thy Ways. A Seasonable and Serious Exhortation for All Sorts to Consider of Their Ways, before It Is Too Late*. Paisley, UK: J. Neilson, 1796.

May, Thomas Erskine. *The Constitutional History of England Since the Accession of George III, 1760–1860*. Vol. 2. New York: A.C. Armstrong and Son, 1880.

McCracken-Flesher, Caroline. "Scotland as Theory: Otherness and Instantiation from Mackenzie to the Last Minstrel." *International Journal of Scottish Literature* 3, no. 3 (2007): 1–17.

McCrone, David. *Understanding Scotland: The Sociology of a Nation*. 2nd ed. London: Routledge, 2001.

McCue, Kirsteen. "Women and Song, 1750–1850." In *A History of Scottish Women's Writing*, edited by Douglas Gifford and Dorothy McMillan, 58–70. Edinburgh: Edinburgh University Press, 1997.

McCulloch, Margery Palmer. "The Lasses Reply to Mr Burns: Women Poets and Songwriters in the Lowlands." In *Crossing the Highland Line: Cross-Currents in Eighteenth-Century Scottish Writing*, edited by C.J.M. MacLachlan, Association for Scottish Literary Studies Occasional Papers 14, 137–152. Glasgow: Association of Scottish Literary Studies, 2009.

———. "Women, Poetry and Song in Eighteenth-Century Lowland Scotland." In "Scottish Women's Writing," special issue, *Women's Writing* 10, no. 3 (2003): 453–468. Accessed at Scottish Corpus of Texts & Speech, https://www.scottishcorpus.ac.uk/document/?documentid=1437.

McFarland, Elaine W. *Ireland and Scotland in the Age of Revolution: Planting the Green Bough*. Edinburgh: Edinburgh University Press, 1994.

———. "Scottish Radicalism in the Later Eighteenth Century: 'The Social Thistle and Shamrock.'" In *Eighteenth Century Scotland: New Perspectives*, edited by T. M. Devine and J. R. Young, 275–297. East Linton, UK: Tuckwell, 1999.

McGann, Jerome J. "The Idea of an Indeterminate Text: Blake's Bible of Hell and Dr. Alexander Geddes." *Studies in Romanticism* 25 (1986): 303–324.

[236]

BIBLIOGRAPHY

McGinn, Clark. "The Scotch Bard and 'The Planting Line': New Documents on Burns and Jamaica." *Studies in Scottish Literature* 43, no. 2 (2017): 255–266.

McGuirk, Carol. "Burns, Bakhtin, and the Opposition of Poetic and Novelistic Discourse: A Response to David Morris." *Eighteenth Century* 32, no. 1 (1991): 58–72.

———, ed. *Critical Essays on Robert Burns.* New York: G. K. Hall, 1998.

———. "Jacobite History to National Song: Robert Burns and Carolina Oliphant (Baroness Nairne)." *Eighteenth Century* 47, nos. 2–3 (2006): 253–287.

———. *Reading Robert Burns: Texts, Contexts, and Transformations.* London: Pickering and Chatto, 2014.

———. *Robert Burns and the Sentimental Era.* Athens: University of Georgia Press, 1985.

———. "Scottish Hero, Scottish Victim: Myths of Robert Burns." In *The History of Scottish Literature,* vol. 2, *1660–1800,* edited by Andrew Hook, 219–238. Aberdeen: Aberdeen University Press, 1987.

———. "Writing Scotland: Robert Burns." In *The Edinburgh History of Scottish Literature,* vol. 2, edited by Ian Brown, 169–177. Edinburgh: Edinburgh University Press, 2007.

McIlvanney, Liam. *Burns the Radical: Poetry and Politics in Late Eighteenth-Century Scotland.* East Linton, UK: Tuckwell, 2000.

———. "Hugh Blair, Robert Burns, and the Invention of Scottish Literature." *Eighteenth-Century Life* 29, no. 2 (2005): 25–46.

———. "Presbyterian Radicalism and the Politics of Robert Burns." In *Love and Liberty: Robert Burns, a Bicentenary Celebration,* edited by Kenneth Simpson, 168–182. East Linton, UK: Tuckwell, 1997.

McKenna, Steve. "Burns and Virgil." In *The Edinburgh Companion to Robert Burns,* edited by Gerard Carruthers, 137–149. Edinburgh: Edinburgh University Press, 2009.

McLane, Maureen, and Laura Slatkin. "British Romantic Homer: Oral Tradition, 'Primitive Poetry' and the Emergence of Comparative Poetics in Britain, 1760–1830." *ELH* 78, no. 3 (2011): 687–714.

McLeod, Wilson, and Alan Riach. "Protest and Politics." In *The International Companion to Scottish Poetry,* edited by Carla Sassi, 156–168. Glasgow: Scottish Literature International, 2015.

Meikle, Henry W. *Scotland and the French Revolution.* Glasgow: J. Maclehose, 1912.

Miller, Gavin. "'Persuade without convincing . . . represent without reasoning': The Inferiorist Mythology of the Scots Language." In *Scotland in Theory: Reflections on Culture and Literature,* edited by Eleanor Bell and Gavin Miller, 197–209. Amsterdam: Rodopi, 2004.

Milne, Anne. "Dogs and the 'Talking Animal Syndrome' in Janet Little's 'From Snipe, a Favourite Dog, to his Master (1791).'" *Scottish Studies Review,* March 1, 2003, 69–81.

Monod, P. K. *Jacobitism and the English People, 1688–1788.* Cambridge: Cambridge University Press, 1995.

Monod, P. K., M.G.H. Pittock, and D. Szechi, eds. *Loyalty and Identity: Jacobites at Home and Abroad.* Basingstoke, UK: Palgrave, 2010.

Morris, Michael. *Scotland and the Caribbean, c. 1740–1833: Atlantic Archipelagos.* New York: Routledge, 2015.

Murdoch, Alexander J. *British History, 1660–1832: National Identity and Local Culture.* Basingstoke, UK: Palgrave, 1998.

———. "Scotland and the Idea of Britain in the Eighteenth Century." In *Eighteenth Century Scotland: New Perspectives,* edited by T. M. Devine and J. R. Young, 106–120. East Linton, UK: Tuckwell, 1999.

———, ed. *The Scottish Nation: Identity and History: Essays in Honour of William Ferguson.* Edinburgh: J. Donald, 2007.

BIBLIOGRAPHY

Murphy, Peter T. *Poetry as an Occupation and an Art in Britain, 1760–1830*. Cambridge: Cambridge University Press, 1993.

Murray, N. *Scottish Handloom Weavers, 1790–1850*. Edinburgh: J. Donald, 1978.

Nairn, Tom. *The Break-Up of Britain: Crisis and Neo-Nationalism*. London: New Left Books, 1977.

——. "Break-Up: Twenty Five Years On." In *Scotland in Theory: Reflections on Culture and Literature*, edited by Eleanor Bell and Gavin Miller, 17–33. Amsterdam: Rodopi, 2004.

Nairne, Carolina, Baroness (Carolina Oliphant). *Lays of Strathearn, the Symphonies and Accompaniments by the Late Finlay Dun*. New ed. Edinburgh: Paterson, 185?

——. *Life and Songs of the Baroness Nairne: With a Memoir and Poems of Caroline Oliphant the Younger*, edited by Rev. Charles Rogers. London: C. Griffin, 1869.

Nenadic, Stana. "Necessities: Food and Clothing in the Long Eighteenth Century." In *A History of Everyday Life in Scotland, 1600–1800*, edited by E. Foyster and C. A. Whatley, 137–163. Edinburgh: Edinburgh University Press, 2010.

Newman, Steve. *Ballad Collection, Lyric, and the Canon: The Call of the Popular from the Restoration to the New Criticism*. Philadelphia: University of Pennsylvania Press, 2007.

——. "'Hodden-Gray': Pastoral, Enlightenment Re-Mediation, and the Proverbial Allan Ramsay." *Scottish Literary Review* 10, no. 1 (2018): 1–18.

Noble, Andrew. "Displaced Persons: Burns and the Renfrew Radicals." In *Scotland in the Age of the French Revolution*, edited by Bob Harris, 196–225. Edinburgh: J. Donald, 2005.

——. Introduction to *The Canongate Burns: The Complete Songs and Poems of Robert Burns*, edited by Andrew Noble and Patrick Scott Hogg, ix–xcii. Edinburgh: Canongate, 2001.

O'Gorman, F. *The Long Eighteenth Century: British Political and Social History, 1688–1832*. London: Bloomsbury,1997.

Pagan, Isobel. *A Collection of Songs and Poems on Several Occasions*. Glasgow: Niven, Napier and Khull, 1803.

Paine, Thomas. "Letter Addressed to the Addressers on the Late Proclamation." In *The Thomas Paine Reader*, edited by Michael Foot and Isaac Kramnick, 34. New York: Penguin Books, 1987.

Paterson, James. *The Contemporaries of Burns and the More Recent Poets of Ayrshire, with Selections from Their Writings*. Edinburgh: H. Paton, 1840.

Paul, Hamilton. *The Wail of Scotia, in Which the Former and Present States of Scotland Are Contrasted*. Glasgow, 1794.

Paulson, Ronald. *Representations of Revolution (1780–1830)*. New Haven, CT: Yale University Press, 1983.

Pentland, Gordon. "Radical Returns in an Age of Revolutions." *Études écossaises* 13 (2010): 91–102.

——. "'We Speak for the Ready': Images of Scots in Political Prints, 1707–1832." *Scottish Historical Review* 90, no. 229, pt. 1 (2011): 64–95.

Phillipson, Nicholas, and Rosalind Mitchison, eds. *Scotland in the Age of Improvement: Essays in Scottish History in the Eighteenth Century*. Edinburgh: Edinburgh University Press, 1970.

Philp, Mark, ed. *The French Revolution and British Popular Politics*. Cambridge: Cambridge University Press, 1991.

Pittock, Murray G. H. "Allan Ramsay and the Decolonisation of Genre." *Review of English Studies* 58, no. 235 (2007): 316–337.

——. *Celtic Identity and the British Image*. Manchester: Manchester University Press, 1999.

——. *The Invention of Scotland: The Stuart Myth and the Scottish Identity, 1638 to the Present*. London: Routledge, 1991.

——. *Inventing and Resisting Britain: Cultural Identities in Britain and Ireland, 1685–1789*. Basingstoke, UK: Palgrave, 1997.

BIBLIOGRAPHY

―――. *Jacobitism*. Basingstoke, UK: Palgrave, 1998.

―――. *Material Culture and Sedition, 1688–1760: Treacherous Objects, Secret Places*. Basingstoke, UK: Palgrave Macmillan, 2013.

―――. *Poetry and Jacobite Politics in Eighteenth-Century Britain and Ireland*. Cambridge: Cambridge University Press, 1994.

―――. *Scottish Nationality*. Basingstoke, UK: Palgrave, 2001.

―――. "Scottish Song and the Jacobite Cause." In *The Edinburgh History of Scottish Literature*, vol. 2, edited by Ian Brown, 105–109. Edinburgh: Edinburgh University Press, 2007.

―――. "The W. Ormiston Roy Memorial Lecture: Who Wrote the Scots Musical Museum? Challenging Editorial Practice in the Presence of Authorial Absence." *Studies in Scottish Literature* 42, no. 1 (2016): 3–27.

Pocock, J.G.A. *The Discovery of Islands: Essays in British History*. Cambridge: Cambridge University Press, 2005.

Porter, Roy. *The Creation of the Modern World: The Untold Story of the British Enlightenment*. New York: Norton, 2000.

Porter, Roy, and Mikulas Teich, eds. *The Enlightenment in National Context*. Cambridge: Cambridge University Press, 1981.

Prebble, J. *The Highland Clearances*. London: Penguin, 1969.

―――. *Mutiny: Highland Regiments in Revolt, 1743–1804*. London: Secker and Warburg, 1975.

Preston, Thomas. "Contrary Scriptings: Implied National Narratives in Burns and Smollett." In *Love and Liberty, Robert Burns: A Bicentenary Celebration*, edited by Kenneth Simpson, 198–216. East Linton, UK: Tuckwell, 1997.

Price, Richard. "Robert Burns and the Scottish Renaissance." In *Love and Liberty, Robert Burns: A Bicentenary Celebration*, edited by Kenneth Simpson, 128–144. East Linton, UK: Tuckwell, 1997.

Quiller-Couch, Sir Arthur Thomas, ed. *The Oxford Book of English Verse, 1250–1900*. Oxford, UK: Clarendon, 1919.

Radcliffe, David Hill. "Imitation, Popular Literacy, and 'The Cottar's Saturday Night.'" In *Critical Essays on Robert Burns*, edited by Carol McGuirk, 251–279. New York: G. K. Hall, 1998.

Rendall, Jane. "Clio, Mars and Minerva: The Scottish Enlightenment and the Writing of Women's History." In *Eighteenth Century Scotland: New Perspectives*, edited by T. M. Devine and J. R. Young, 134–151. East Linton, UK: Tuckwell, 1999.

―――. *The Origins of the Scottish Enlightenment*. London: Macmillan, 1978.

Renfrew, Alastair. "Brief Encounters, Long Farewells: Bakhtin and Scottish Literature." *International Journal of Scottish Literature* 1 (Autumn 2006): 1–18.

Richards, Eric. *A History of the Highland Clearances*. 2 vols. London: Croom Helm, 1985.

Robb, William. *The Patriotic Wolves: A Fable. By a Scotch Episcopal Clergyman*. 2nd ed. Edinburgh: A. Guthrie, 1793.

Robertson, Ian C. "The Bard and *The Minstrel*." *Scottish Literary Review* 8, no.1 (2016): 133–142.

―――. "Beattie's *The Minstrel*: A Missing Link in Scottish Poetry." *Studies in Scottish Literature* 43, no. 2 (2017): 237–254.

Robertson, John, ed. *The Scottish Enlightenment and the Militia Issue*. Edinburgh, J. Donald, 1985.

―――. *A Union for Empire: Political Thought and the British Union of 1707*. Cambridge: Cambridge University Press, 1995.

Rogers, Charles, and J. C. Craig. *The Book of Robert Burns: Genealogical and Historical Memoirs of the Poet, His Associates and Those Celebrated in His Writings*. Vol. 3. Edinburgh: Edinburgh Grampian Club, 1889–1891.

Rogers, Nicholas. *Crowds, Culture, and Politics in Georgian Britain*. Oxford: Oxford University Press, 1998.

[239]

BIBLIOGRAPHY

Rose, Jonathan. "Reading." In *The Edinburgh History of the Book in Scotland: Ambition and Industry, 1800–1880*, vol. 3, edited by Bill Bell, 173–189. Edinburgh: Edinburgh University Press, 2007.

Roy, G. Ross. "'The Mair They Talk, I'm Kend the Better': Poems about Robert Burns to 1859." In *Love and Liberty, Robert Burns: A Bicentenary Celebration*, edited by Kenneth Simpson, 53–68. East Linton, UK: Tuckwell, 1997.

———. "Poems and Songs Spuriously Attributed to Robert Burns." In *Critical Essays on Robert Burns*, edited by Carol McGuirk, 225–237. New York: G. K. Hall, 1998.

———. "Robert Burns and the Brash and Reid Chapbooks of Glasgow." In *Literatur in Kontext: Festschrift für Horst W. Drescher*, edited by Joachim Schwend, Susanne Hagemann, and Hermann Völkel, 53–69. Frankfurt am Main: Peter Lang, 1992.

Sassi, Carla, ed. *The International Companion to Scottish Poetry*. Glasgow: Scottish Literature International, 2015.

Sassi, Carla, and Silke Stroh. "Nation and Home." In *The International Companion to Scottish Poetry*, edited by Carla Sassi, 144–155. Glasgow: Scottish Literature International, 2015.

Scott, Mary Jane. "James Thomson and the Anglo-Scots." In *The History of Scottish Literature*, vol. 2, *1660–1800*, edited by Andrew Hook, 81–98. Aberdeen: Aberdeen University Press, 1987.

Scrivener, Michael, ed. *Poetry and Reform: Periodical Verse from the English Democratic Press, 1792–1824*. Detroit: Wayne State University Press, 1992.

Semple, David. Introduction to *The Poems and Songs and Correspondence of Robert Tannahill, with Life and Notes*, by Robert Tannahill, xxvi–lxxxviii. Paisley, UK: A. Gardner, 1876.

Sharp, Elizabeth Amelia, ed. *Women's Voices: An Anthology of the Most Characteristic Poems by English, Scotch, and Irish Women*. London: Walter Scott, 1887.

Shaw, John Stuart. *The Political History of Eighteenth-Century Scotland*. Basingstoke, UK: Palgrave, 1999.

Sher, Richard B. *The Enlightenment and the Book: Scottish Authors and Their Publishers in Eighteenth-Century Britain, Ireland, and America*. Chicago: University of Chicago Press, 2006.

Sillar, David. *Poems*. Kilmarnock, UK: John Wilson, 1789.

Simpson, Kenneth. "Burns and the Legacy of Flyting." In *Critical Essays on Robert Burns*, edited by Carol McGuirk, 151–162. New York: G. K. Hall, 1998.

———, ed. *Burns Now*. Edinburgh: Canongate Academic, 1994.

———, ed. *Love and Liberty, Robert Burns: A Bicentenary Celebration*. East Linton, UK: Tuckwell, 1997.

———. *The Protean Scot: The Crisis of Identity in Eighteenth-Century Scottish Literature*. Aberdeen: Aberdeen University Press, 1989.

Simpson, Margaret Stewart. *The Scottish Songstress: Caroline Baroness Nairne*. Edinburgh: Oliphant, Anderson and Ferrier, 1894.

Smith, Angela, "Scottish Literature and the British Empire." In *Scotland and the British Empire*, edited by John M. MacKenzie and T. M. Devine, 255–279. Oxford: Oxford University Press, 2011.

Smith, G. Gregory. *Scottish Literature: Character and Influence*. London: Macmillan, 1919.

Smith, Robert Archibald. *The Scottish Minstrel: A Selection from the Vocal Melodies of Scotland, Ancient and Modern, Arranged for the Piano Forte by R. A. Smith*. 6 vols. Edinburgh: Robt. Purdie, 1821.

Smout, T. C., ed. *Anglo-Scottish Relations from 1603 to 1900*. Oxford: Oxford University Press, 2005.

———. *Comparative Aspects of Scottish and Irish Economic and Social History, 1600–1900*. Edinburgh: J. Donald, 1976.

BIBLIOGRAPHY

————. *A History of the Scottish People, 1560–1830*. New York: Fontana, 1977.

————. "Scotland as North Britain: The Historical Background, 1707–1918." In *The Edinburgh History of Scottish Literature*, vol. 2, edited by Ian Brown, 1–11. Edinburgh: Edinburgh University Press, 2007.

Sorenson, Janet. *The Grammar of Empire in Eighteenth-Century British Writing*. Cambridge: Cambridge University Press, 2000.

————. "Varieties of Public Performance: Folk Songs, Ballads, Popular Drama and Sermons." In *The Edinburgh History of Scottish Literature*, vol. 2, edited by Ian Brown, 133–142. Edinburgh: Edinburgh University Press, 2007.

Stafford, Fiona. "Scottish Poetry and Regional Literary Expression." In *The Cambridge History of English Literature, 1660–1780*, edited by John Richetti, 340–362. Cambridge: Cambridge University Press, 2008.

————. *Starting Lines in Scottish, Irish, and English Poetry: From Burns to Heaney*. Oxford: Oxford University Press, 2000.

————. *The Sublime Savage: A Study of James MacPherson and the Poems of Ossian*. Edinburgh: Edinburgh University Press, 1988.

Stelzig, Eugene L. "'The Shield of Human Nature': Wordsworth's Reflections on the Revolution in France." *Nineteenth-Century Literature* 45, no. 4 (1991): 415–431.

Stevenson, John. "Scotland and the French Revolution: An Overview." In *Scotland in the Age of the French Revolution*, edited by Bob Harris, 247–264. Edinburgh: J. Donald, 2005.

Stoddard, Richard Henry. *Under the Evening Lamp*. Vol. 1. New York: Scribner, 1892.

Strawhorn, John. "Burns and the Bardie Clan." *Scottish Literary Journal* (December 1, 1981): 5–23.

————. "Everyday Life in Burns's Ayrshire." In *Burns Now*, edited by Kenneth Simpson, 13–30. Edinburgh: Canongate Academic, 1994.

Sunter, R. *Patronage and Politics in Scotland, 1707–1832*. Edinburgh: J. Donald, 1986.

Sweeney-Turner, Steve. "Pagan Airts: Reading Critical Perspectives on the Songs of Burns and Tannahill." In *Critical Essays on Robert Burns*, edited by Carol McGuirk, 182–207. New York: G. K. Hall, 1998.

Tait, Alexander. *Poems and Songs*. Paisley, UK, 1790.

Tannahill, Robert. *The Poems and Songs and Correspondence of Robert Tannahill, with Life and Notes*. Edited by David Semple. Paisley, UK: A. Gardner, 1874.

————. *The Poems and Songs and Correspondence of Robert Tannahill, with Life and Notes*. Edited by David Semple. Paisley, UK: A. Gardner, 1876.

————. *The Poetical Works of Robert Tannahill: With Life of the Author, and a Memoir of Robert A. Smith*. London: A. Fullarton 18?

————. *The Soldier's Return: A Scottish Interlude in Two Acts, with Other Poems and Songs, Chiefly in the Scottish Dialect*. Paisley, UK: Stephen Young, 1807.

————. *The Songs and Poems: With Biography, Illustrations, and Music*. Edinburgh: J. & R. Parlane, 1911.

————. *The Works of Robert Tannahill*. Edited by Philip A. Ramsey. London: A. Fullarton, 1838.

Thompson, Alistair. "The Use of Libraries by the Working Class in Scotland in the Early Nineteenth Century." *Scottish Historical Review* 42, no. 133, pt. 1 (1963): 21–29.

Thompson, E. P. "The Moral Economy of the English Crowd in the Eighteenth Century." *Past & Present* 50 (1971): 76–136.

Trevor-Roper, H. R. *The Invention of Scotland: Myth and History*. New Haven, CT: Yale University Press, 2008.

Tyler, Deborah Bennett. "'Women's voices speak for them-selves': Gender, Subversion and the *Women's Voices* Anthology of 1887." *Women's History Review* 4, no. 2 (1995): 165–174. https://doi.org/10.1080/09612029500200079.

Tytler, Sarah, and J. L. Watson. *The Songstresses of Scotland*. 2 vols. London: Strahan, 1871.

[241]

BIBLIOGRAPHY

Vincent, Emma. "The Responses of Scottish Churchmen to the French Revolution." *Scottish Historical Review* 73, no. 2 (1994): 191–215.

Walker, Marshall. *Scottish Literature since 1707*. London: Longman, 1997.

Watson, Roderick. *The Literature of Scotland*. New York: Palgrave, 2007.

Watt, Douglas. *The Price of Scotland: Darien, Union and the Wealth of Nations*. Edinburgh: Luath, 2007.

Wells, Roger. *Insurrection: The British Experience 1795–1803*. Gloucester, UK: A. Sutton, 1983.

Whatley, Christopher. *Bought and Sold for English Gold? Explaining the Union 1707*. 2nd ed. East Linton, UK: Tuckwell, 2001.

———. "The Dark Side of the Enlightenment? Sorting Out Serfdom." In *Eighteenth Century Scotland: New Perspectives*, edited by T. M. Devine and J. R. Young, 259–274. East Linton, UK: Tuckwell, 1999.

———. "'The Fettering Bonds of Brotherhood': Combination and Labour Relations in the Scottish Coal-Mining Industry, c. 1690–1775." *Social History* 12, no. 2 (1987): 139–154.

———. "'It Is Said That Burns Was a Radical': Contest, Concession, and the Political Legacy of Robert Burns, ca. 1796–1859." *Journal of British Studies* 50, no. 3 (2011): 639–666.

———. "Roots of 1790s Radicalism: Reviewing the Economic and Social Background." In *Scotland in the Age of the French Revolution*, edited by Bob Harris, 23–48. Edinburgh: J. Donald, 2005.

———. *Scottish Society, 1707–1830: Beyond Jacobitism, towards Industrialization*. Manchester: Manchester University Press, 2000.

———. "An Uninflammable People?" In *The Manufacture of Scottish History*, edited by Ian Donnachie and Christopher Whatley, 51–71. Edinburgh: Polygon, 1992.

Williams, Eric. *Capitalism and Slavery*. Chapel Hill: University of North Carolina Press, 1944.

Williams, Raymond. *The Country and the City*. Oxford: Oxford University Press, 1973.

Wilson, Alexander. *The Laurel Disputed; or, The Merits of Allan Ramsay and Robert Fergusson Contrasted*. Edinburgh: A. Guthrie, 1791.

———. *The Poems and Literary Prose to Alexander Wilson*. Paisley, UK: A. Gardner, 1876.

Wold, Atle L. "Scottish Attitudes to Military Mobilisation and War in the 1790s." In *Scotland in the Age of the French Revolution*, edited by Bob Harris, 141–163. Edinburgh: J. Donald, 2005.

Wollstonecraft, Mary. *A Vindication of the Rights of Woman*. Boston: Peter Edes, 1792.

Woolf, Virginia. *Three Guineas*. London: Harcourt Brace, 1938.

Wordsworth, William. "Tintern Abbey." In *The Pedlar, Tintern Abbey, The Two-Part Prelude*, edited by Jonathan Wordsworth, 33–40. Cambridge: Cambridge University Press, 1985.

Young, J. D. *The Rousing of the Scottish Working Class*. London: Croom Helm, 1979.

Ziser, Michael. "Introduction to Alexander Wilson, Poems, Literary Prose, and Journalism." Early Americas Digital Archive. Accessed July 18, 2018, http://eada.lib.umd.edu/text-entries /introduction-to-alexander-wilson-poems-literary-prose-and-journalism/.

INDEX

Alexander Wilson: Enlightened Naturalist, 186
Althusser, Louis, 115
American Ornithology, 73, 80
Anderson, Benedict, 37, 202n28
Andrews, Corey, 1, 8, 19, 44; on Burns's effect
  on other laboring-class poets, 40, 41; on
  Burns's "genius," 153, 193n44; on Burns's
  response to his critics, 203n37; on David
  Sillar's "Epistle to R. Burns," 33, 34; on
  Janet Little's relationship with Burns, 46,
  47, 49, 52; on John Lapraik, 32; on the
  "shadow of Burns," 128, 150, 153
Ane Satyre of the Thrie Estatis, 26
Antiquary, The, 140
Armour, Jean, 6
Audubon, John James, 73
Augustan poetry, 47, 48, 91, 104, 105, 110,
  130, 137
autodidactic poets: and Alexander Wilson,
  73; and contemporaries of Burns, 97; and
  Isobel Pagan, 58, 59
Ayr Bank failure, 23, 29, 32, 197n18
Ayrshire, 4, 19, 25, 36; and globalization, 20,
  22; and improvement, 23, 25, 32, 69, 89, 178

Baillie, Joanna, 58–59
Bakhtin, Mikhail, 108, 110; and polyglossia,
  169, 170, 220n44
ballad, 5, 193n45, 211n12
Barbauld, Anna, 167–168
Barlow, Joel, 163, 167–168
Barrell, John, 20, 155, 161
Beattie, James, 2, 24, 165, 169, 184
Bell, Maria, 59
Bergson, Henri, 11
Bernstein, Marion, 59
Bhabha, Homi, 98, 211n9
*Biographical Dictionary of Scottish Women,
  The*, 7
Blackstone, William, 173

Blair, Hugh, 21, 89
Blair, Robert, 40, 73, 75, 207n12
Blake, William, 63, 64, 67, 88, 94, 130, 166,
  172–174
Boece, Hector, 175
Boethius, 155
Bold, Valentina, 7, 8, 43, 58, 97
Boswell, James, 2, 43, 72
Bradford, Samuel, 73
Britannia, 37, 38, 92, 93, 146, 151, 168, 174
Britishness, 10, 21, 37, 91, 93, 102, 134, 158,
  192n38
British Parliament, 68
Broadhead, Alex, 1, 31, 37, 200n73
Brodie, David, 71, 79
Brown, Mary Ellen, 211n12
Buchanan, George, 175
Bunyan, John, 83, 155
Burke, Edmund, 54, 55, 62, 64, 65, 90, 159,
  172, 174
Burns, Robert: Alexander Wilson's criticism
  of, 81; Alexander Wilson's emulation of,
  73; and the Board of Excise, 79; and
  Burns scholarship, 1, 2; and "Ca' the
  Yowes," 60, 204n47; in comparison to
  Alexander Geddes, 166–169; in comparison to John Lapraik, 31, 32; in comparison
  to Robert Tannahill, 129, 150; and
  criticism, 203n37; as farmer poet, 215n6;
  and "genius," 7, 40, 41, 59, 94, 145, 153,
  192n42, 194n44; and his invocation of
  Scotia, 175; and his Jacobite poetry,
  97–100, 111–114, 117–119, 121, 122; and
  improvement in Ayrshire, 19–21; and
  the influence of other Ayrshire poets,
  21–23; and Jamaica, 6, 153, 217n2l;
  and Janet Little, 48–52, 202nn27–28,
  202n32; and laboring class poets, 189n3;
  and linguistic heterogeneity, 3; as a
  national poet, 11–13; and orality, 193n45;

[243]

INDEX

Burns, Robert (cont.)
and Presbyterianism, 39; relationship
with David Sillar, 33, 34; and Robert
Tannahill, "The Parnassiad: A Visionary
View," 144–147; as Robt. Burness, 6, 21;
and "Scotch bard," 2, 76, 140, 183, 184;
and Scottish nationalism, 192n43; and
Scottish song, 208n33, 217n35; and the
sedition trials of Thomas Muir and Rev.
Thomas Fyshe Palmer, 106; and Standard
Habbie, 26; and Whiggery, 216n22; and
William Wallace, 109
Burns, Robert, works of: "Address to the
Deil," 32; "The Cottar's Saturday Night,"
7, 86; "Does Haughty Gaul Invastion
Threat," 130; "Epistle to Davie, a Brother
Poet," 33; "Epistle to J. Lapraik: An Old
Scotch Bard," 24, 52; *The First Common-
place Book*, 6; "Frae the Friends and Land
I Love," 112; "The Jolly Beggars, a Cantata,"
64; *The Kilmarnock Manuscript*, 6; "The
Scotian Muse: An Elegy," 106; "Scots
Wha Hae," 100, 105; "The Sodger's Return,"
119; "Strathallan's Lament," 113; "Tam
O'Shanter," 81, 83, 209n41; "There'll
Never Be Peace till Jamie Comes Home,"
117; "The Twa Dogs: A Tale," 54; "The
Vision," 91, 145, 146; "The White
Cockade," 121
Burns Encyclopedia, The, 183
Butler, Marilyn, 217n35

Cafarelli, Annette Wheeler, 196n9
Cain, Peter, 210n51
Caledonian antisyzygy, 37, 200n73
Cameron Highlanders, 130
Cameronians, 140, 141
Carlyle, Thomas, 9
Carruthers, Gerard, 1, 7, 8, 21, 79, 166, 175,
184, 192n42, 193n43, 196n12, 208n21
Carse o' Gowrie, 123–125
Cervantes, 54
chapbooks, 5
chapmen, 5
Chartism, 163
Cherry and Slae, 22
Christ's Kirk stanza, 74, 78, 85
Cicero, 155
Clan Donald, 114
Clark, Anna, 82

Cockburn, Henry, 219n13
code-switching: in the poetry of Robert
Burns and David Sillar, 37, 38, 200n73
Coleridge, Samuel Taylor, 150, 166
colliers: and emancipation, 206n85; and
serfdom, 66–68, 85, 86, 205n82; and
strikes, 206n86
commercialization of literature, 5, 7, 51
Constable, Archibald, 128
Contemporaries of Burns, The, 184
Cowper, William, 25, 102
Crabbe, George, 25, 102
Craig, Cairns, 164
Crawford, Robert, 1, 2, 10, 11, 24, 167, 193n44
Crawford, Thomas, 36
Crichton of Paisley, Thomas, 73
Cumnock, 66, 67
Cunningham, Allan, 57

Daiches, David, 193n47
Dante, 53, 145
Davidson, Neil, 191n37
Davis, Leith, 13, 46, 49, 98, 191n38, 192n41,
193n45, 194n54, 202n28, 208n33, 211n9,
218n3
*Declaration of the Rights of Man and of the
Citizen*, 174
"The Deserted Village," 91
Devine, Thomas M., 12, 133, 192n40,
207n13
Devolving English Literature, 2
Donaldson, William, 98, 127, 128, 180
Douglas, Heron & Company, 32. *See also*
Ayr Bank failure
Downie, David, 155, 166, 218n8
Duff, William, 40
Duke of Gordon's Fencibles, The, 66
Dumfries, 43
Dumfries Volunteers, 130
Dunbar, William, 39
Duncan, Ian, 98, 127, 192n41, 200n76
Dundas, Henry, 63, 156, 160, 162, 192n41,
218n3
Dunlop, Frances, 2, 15, 43, 45, 49, 81
Dunstan, Vivienne, 5

East India Company, 103
Edinburgh Gazetteer, 6, 106, 164
Edinburgh literati, 2, 36, 37, 48, 49, 76, 153,
192n42, 215n6

[244]

INDEX

elegy, 16, 104
"Eloisa to Abelard," 47
Engels, Friedrich, 29
epic poetry, 109–111, 176, 177
Erskine, David Steuart (Lord Buchan), 166
Essay on Man, The, 158
estates satire, 62, 67, 73, 88

Ferguson, Moira, 46, 57, 100, 101, 202n24, 202n32
Fergusson, Robert, 2, 22, 24, 35, 76, 77, 130, 167, 184
Fielding, Penny, 128, 216n20
"The Flyting betwixt M. and Polwart," 39
"The Flyting of D. and Kennedie," 39
Fortescue, J. W., 66
Foucault, Michel, 3, 9, 159
freemasons, 4
French Revolution, 12, 91, 165, 174, 218n3, 218n5
Fry, Michael, 192n40
Fulton, Robert, 73

Gairn, Louisa, 26
Gardner, Alexander, 80
Geddes, Alexander, 100, 153, 154, 220n27, 220n31; and attribution controversy, 175, 222n5; life and works of, 165, 166; and linguistic choices, 168; and polyglossia, 169, 170; and Scots language, 166; and the Scottish Enlightenment, 167
Geddes, Alexander, works of: "Address to Justice," 166; *An Apology for Slavery*, 165; "Carmen sæculare pro Gallica gente tyrannidi aristocraticæ erepta," 165, 167–174, 177, 178, 221n45; "The Cob Web—A Song," 166, 175, 177; "The Ewe Bughts," 166, 175–177; "Exhortatory Ode to the Prince of Wales on Entering his 34th Year," 166; *The Holy Bible; or, The Books Accounted Sacred by Jews and Christians; Otherwise Called the Books of the Old and New Covenants*, 165; *The Idea of a New Catholic Edition of the Holy Bible for the Use of the Roman Catholics in Great Britain*, 165; "Lewie Gordon," 179; "Ode Inscribed to Certain Jurymen," 166; "Ode to the Birthday of C J Fox," 166; *Prospectus of a New Translation of the Holy Bible*, 165

Geddes, Bishop John, 197n36
gentlemanly capitalism, 92, 210n51
Glasgow, 43, 44, 74, 207n13
Glover, Jean, 59
Godwin, William, 167
Goldie, Mark, 166, 167, 198n36
Goldsmith, Oliver, 22, 72, 91, 102
Gottlieb, Evan, 191n37
Graham of Fintry, Robert, 79
"The Grave," 207n12
Gray, Thomas, 22, 25, 165
Grosart, The Reverend Andrew, 80

Habermas, Jürgen, 164
Hamilton, Janet, 59
Harris, Bob, 4, 5, 22, 45
Harvie, Christopher, 8, 9, 31, 103, 108, 129, 192n43; and red/black Scots, 9, 31, 103, 108
Hay, Bishop George, 197n36
Henderson, George, 100, 101
Henderson, John, 80
Henry, William, 73, 75, 78
Herd, David, 121
Hogg, James, 44, 83, 97, 98, 127, 128, 184, 193n45, 194n53, 214n66
Hogg, Patrick Scott, 11, 24, 113, 117, 166, 193n44
"Holy Thursday," 63
Home, John, 72
Homer, 145
Hooker, Richard, 178
Hopkins, A.G., 210n51
Horace, 165
Hume, David, 151, 194n53
Humphry Clinker, 53
Hunter, Clark, 79, 80
Hutcheson, Thomas Smith, 80

Iliad, The, 109, 135
Irvine, 4, 33

Jacobinism, 16, 48, 153, 156, 157, 164
Jacobite poetry, 9, 16, 38, 60, 65, 73, 85, 98, 99, 100, 107, 140, 180, 214n59, 214n65; and the Charlie trope in Lady Nairne's songs, 113–117; and Robert Tannahill's "Loudon's Bonnie Woods and Braes," 135, 136; and Robert Tannahill's "The Soldier's Return," 131, 132; and women, 119–122

[245]

INDEX

Jefferson, Thomas, 73
Johnson, Joseph, 165, 167
Johnson, Samuel, 47, 48, 49, 51, 165
Johnston, Ellen, 59
Johnston, Thomas, 68, 195n57, 205n82, 206n86
Johnstone, Jeannie, 59

Kennedy, James, 71, 167, 185; compared to Joel Barlow, 163; and his critique of Edmund Burke, 159; and involvement in the Watt and Downie conspiracy, 155; as a laboring-class poet, 160; life, 154
Kennedy, James, works of: "Dedicated to the Majesty of the People," 160; "The Exile's Reveries, Dedicated to the Scourge of Scotland, Harry Dundas," 152; "The Pitiful Plaint of a Hen Pecked Prodigal: Dedicated to the Daughter of the Duke of Bobadil," 155; "Swinish Gruntings" 159; "Treason!!!, or, Not Treason!!! Alias the Weaver's Budget," 154, 155, 161
Kerrigan, Catherine, 99, 211n12
Kidd, Colin, 12, 15, 37, 79, 99, 166, 191n34, 200n74
Kidd, Sheila, 98, 127
Knox, Isabella Craig, 59
Kord, Susanne, 202n33

laboring class poets, 1, 2, 7, 15, 20, 21, 34, 45, 48, 59, 81, 150, 160, 164
laboring class women poets, 15, 45, 48, 59
Lady Nairne. See Oliphant, Carolina
Lady Nairne and Her Songs, 98
Lapraik Burns Club, 32
Lapraik, John, 2, 6, 7, 15, 19, 37, 55, 184; and the Ayr Bank failure, 29; as a "black" Scot, 31; Burns's effect on, 40, 41; in comparison to Robert Burns, 32; and his criticism of the landlord class, 27, 28; friendship with Burns, 24; and improvement, 20, 21; life of, 23, 24; reception of, 23; and representation of the laboring poor, 26
Lapraik, John, works of: "Epistle to R****T B***S," 35; "Honest John's Opinion of Patronage," 27, 29, 30, 40; "Observations on the D—S AND H—N B—K," 29; "On the Distressed Condition of Honest Farmers," 25, 26, 28, 29; *Poems on Several*

Occasions, 24; "When I upon Thy Bosom Lean, 197nn21–22
Lawson, Alexander, 73
Leask, Nigel, 1, 19, 22, 24, 32, 57, 197n29, 198n34, 199n50, 204n63, 215n6, 217n2
Lenman, Bruce, 196n6, 206n83, 213n39
Leonard, Tom, 73
Lewis, C.S., 139
Lindsay, Sir David, 26
"Lines Composed a Few Miles above Tintern Abbey, on Revisiting the Banks of the Wye during a Tour, July 13, 1798," 87
Little, Janet, 2, 6, 7, 15, 19, 21, 43, 184; in comparison to Burns, 47; effect of Burns on, 48–51; and exclusion from literary success, 54, 55; gender and Augustan verse, 48; and her critique of the Edinburgh *literati*, 52, 53; life of, 45, 46; recent scholarship, 46
Little, Janet, works of: "An Epistle to a Lady," 52, 54; "An Epistle to Mr Robert Burns, Dates July 12, 1789," 47; "Given to a Lady Who Asked Me to Write a Poem," 48; "To a Lady Who Sent the Author Some Paper with a Reading of Sillar's Poems," 55; "To My Aunty," 51; "On a Visit to Mr. Burns," 49; "On Reading Lady Mary Montague and Mrs. Rowe's Letters," 47; "On Seeing Mr.—Baking Cakes," 50, 54; *The Poetical Works of Janet Little, the Scotch Milkmaid*, 43; "From Snipe, a Favourite Dog, to His Master," 54
Locke, John, 158, 178
Lowth, Robert, 165
Lutz, Alfred, 53

MacDonald, Étienne-Jacques-Joseph-Alexandre, 205n75
MacDonalds of Sleat, 214n56
Mackenzie, Henry, 52
Macpherson, James, 2, 13, 72, 169, 184
MacQueen, Robert (Lord Braxfield), 219n13
Magna Carta, 173, 174
Manning, Susan, 13
Marx, Karl, 29, 160
Masson, David Mather, 100, 101
Maxwell, James, 31, 32, 199n50
McCracken-Flesher, Caroline, 194n53
McCrone, David, 191n38
McCue, Kirsteen, 57, 214n54

[246]

INDEX

McCulloch, Margery Palmer, 46, 57, 100, 101, 202n26, 202n30, 212n22
McDiarmid, Hugh, 72
McDowell, William, 73
McGuirk, Carol, 1, 6, 11, 21, 98, 99, 193n43, 210n5, 212n22
McIlvanney, Liam, 11, 39, 191n34, 197n36, 216n22
McKenna, Steven, 109
McLane, Maureen, 193n45
Meikle, Henry, 195n57, 219n13
Millar, John, 192n41
Millar, Robert, 75, 208n17
Miller, John, 128
Milton, John, 72, 124, 145, 155
Montague, Lady Mary, 47, 55
Montgomerie, Alexander, 39
moral economy, 26, 30, 67, 69, 74, 80, 107, 197n30
moral philosophy, 89, 90, 92
Moreau, Jean Victor Marie, 205n75
Morning Chronicle, 6, 113, 166, 175, 177, 193n43
Muir, Thomas, 106, 113, 114, 154, 157, 185; trial of, 219n13
Muirkirk, 23, 24, 32, 44, 45, 58, 67
Muirkirk Advertiser, 32
Muirkirk Iron Company, 44

Napoleon, 16, 65, 141, 150, 157
Neilson, John, 73, 80
neoclassical, 13, 168
Nietzsche, Friedrich, 138
Noble, Andrew, 11, 20, 24, 72, 92, 106, 113, 117, 161, 163, 193n44
North British, 12, 14, 126, 132, 216n20

"Ode: Rule, Britannia," 123, 193n43
Oliphant, Carolina (Lady Nairne), 7, 9, 16, 59, 183, 194; and anonymity, 97, 99; and hybridity, 98, 99; life of, 99, 100; and nationalism, 114, 117, 126; and recent scholarship, 98; and reception, 100
Oliphant, Carolina (Lady Nairne), works of: "The Auld House," 102; "The Banks of the Earn," 105, 110, 123, 126; "Bonny Gascon Ha,'" 108, 111–113; "Caller Herrin," 102; "Her Home She Is Leaving," 103, 105; "The Laird o' Cockpen," 138; "The Land o' the Leal," 97, 100, 102, 105, 136; "The

Lass of Livingstane," 118, 120; "The Lass o' Gowrie," 123; "My Bonnie Hieland Laddie," 119, 120; "Songs of My Native Land," 112; "Wha'll Be King but Charlie," 114, 117; "The White Rose o' June," 121; "The Women Are A' Gane Wud," 116, 117; "Ye'll Mount, Gudeman," 117
Oliphant, Laurence, laird of Gask, 99
"On the Death of Mr Thomas Rowe," 47, 48, 55, 201n24
Ossian, 22, 169, 181
Oxford Book of English Verse, The, 1250–1900, 57
"Ozymandias," 108, 109

Pagan, Isobel, 7, 9, 21, 184; and anticapitalism, 69; attribution to Burns of "Ca' the Yowes to the Knowes," 57; and her communitarian ethos, 67; and her social marginalization, 44, 45; life of, 58; reception of, 56, 57
Pagan Isobel, works of: "Account of the Author's Lifetime," 58; "Ca' the Yowes to the Knowes," 43, 56, 60; "The Crook and the Plaid," 60; "The Laird of Glenlee," 61; "A Letter to a Gentleman on the Death of His Pointer," 62; "Muirkirk Light Weights," 69; "A New Song," (I) 61; "A New Song," (II) 64; "A New Song," (III) 67; "A New Song on the Times," 63, 64; "On Burns and Ramsay," 59; "Song," 66
Paine, Thomas, 156, 168, 174, 195n57
Paisley, 4, 71, 72, 75, 129, 134, 207n16
Paisley Burns Club, 127
Paisley Friends of Reform, 79
Palmer, The Reverend Thomas Fyshe, 106, 113, 114, 154, 157
Paradise Lost, 124
pastoral: in "The Ewe Bughts," 176, 177; "hard" and "soft," 204n63; "The Lass o' Gowrie," 124, 125; in Robert Tannahill, 216n15
Paterson, James, 34, 45, 57, 58, 61, 184, 203n43
Pentland, Gordon, 163
Perry, James, 166
Pitt, William (the Younger), 12, 63, 66, 175
Pittock, Murray, 5, 99, 100, 175, 196n10, 214n59, 215n65
Pocock, J.G.A., 14

[247]

INDEX

Poems, Chiefly in the Scottish Dialect, 6, 21, 73
Poetical Works of Janet Little, the Scotch Milkmaid, The, 2
Poets and Poetry of Scotland, The, 98
Pope, Alexander, 24, 47, 54, 72, 148, 165
Prelude, The, 145, 157
Presbyterianism: and Auld Licht, 7, 16, 28, 32, 39; and New Licht, 16, 28, 32, 39, 40, 94, 198n36
Preston, Thomas, 216n21
Price, Richard, 167
Priestly, Joseph, 165, 167
Purdie, Robert, 97
Pyper, Mary, 59

Quiller-Couch, Arthur, 57

Radical War of 1820, 163
Ramsay, Allan, 2, 22, 24, 34, 35, 59, 60, 76, 77, 130, 167, 184
Ramsay, Philip, 138, 141, 142
Raphael, 53, 54
Rawdon-Hastings, Francis (2nd Earl of Moira), 134
Renfrewshire, 73, 75, 78, 80
republicanism, 14, 16, 129, 156, 174
Rights of Man, The, 78, 79, 90, 93, 105
Robert I (Robert the Bruce), 65
romance, 125; in tales of chivalry, 139, 140
romanticism, 149, 150, 165
Ross, John, 127, 130
Rousseau, Jean-Jacques, 172
Rowe, Elizabeth, 47, 48, 55, 201n24
Russell, Jessie, 59

Sassi, Carla, 9
Scotia, 105, 107, 108, 145, 158, 161, 162, 168, 175
Scotland: and agricultural improvement, 19, 25; and Anglicization, 12, 105, 131, 194n49; and anti-Catholic riots, 28; and antiquarianism, 16, 193n47; and the Auld Alliance, 65, 131; and Calvinism, 4, 28, 29, 69, 90; and clearances, 176; and coal mining, 206n83; and Covenanting, 89, 140; and domestic violence, 82; economic history of, 194n56; and the Enlightenment, 4, 78, 89, 92, 94, 166; and famine, 63; and Gaelic poetry, 185; and illegal distillation, 107, 108; and improvement, 4, 7; and industrialization, 16, 88, 89, 92, 107; and

the Jacobite rebellion of 1745, 40; and the Kirk, 7, 28, 29, 39, 89, 140; and the laboring class, 5, 7, 26, 44, 55; and Latinity, 167, 168; and literacy, 20; and modernization, 8, 19; and national identity, 8, 9, 11, 36, 180, 191n38, 193n47, 200n76, 216n21; and nationalism, 9, 37, 120, 191n37, 192n40; and national literature, 8, 111, 184, 185, 194n54; and patriotism, 119, 131, 135, 138; and radicalism, 16, 73, 79, 90, 92, 114, 129, 136, 153, 162, 171, 191n34, 218n53; and the 1707 Treaty of Union, 12, 14, 107, 108, 115, 133, 192n40, 193n45, 194n54, 208n33, 211n9, 218n3; and tenant farmers, 20; and threat of revolution, 195n57; and Wars of Independence, 106, 130, 169
Scotland's Books, 2
Scots Chronicle, 6
Scots Magazine, 128
Scots Minstrel, 98, 99
Scots Musical Museum, The, 56
Scots vernacular: in Alexander Geddes's poetry, 180; Alexander Geddes's support for revival of, 166; in Alexander Wilson's poetry, 73, 76, 77, 208n21; in David Sillar's poetry, 34; and English as a cognate language, 100, 200n74; in Isobel Pagan's poetry, 59, 60; in Janet Little's poetry, 47; in Lady Nairne's poetry, 102, 105; in Robert Burns's poetry, 31, 193n43
Scott, Mary Jane, 10
Scott, Sir Walter, 2, 11, 13, 83, 128, 140, 184, 194n53
Scottish Friends of the People, 76, 78, 90, 107, 114, 129, 157, 160, 166
Scottish lowlands: and book clubs, 6; and bookselling, 5; and industrialization, 209n47; and print culture, 5, 7; and subscription libraries, 5; and urban culture, 4, 5, 20, 22, 26, 45
Scottishness, 10, 21, 37, 158, 160, 167, 180, 181, 184, 192n38, 192n40
Scottish Parliament, 67
Scottish Relief Bill of 1779, 167
Scotus, Duns, 175
Semple, David, 127, 134, 135
sentimentalism, 16, 99
Shakespeare, William, 48, 124
Sharp, Elizabeth Amelia, 56–57

[248]

INDEX

Sharp, William, 72, 75, 78
Shelley, Percy Bysshe, 149
Shenstone, William, 22, 127, 144, 148, 165
Sher, Richard, 207n16, 208n17
Sillar, David, 2, 6, 7, 15, 184, 199n65; association with Burns, 33, 34; Burns's effect on, 40, 41; and improvement, 20, 21; and Janet Little, 55; life of, 33; and nationalism, 35; reception of, 23; and use of Scots vernacular, 34–36
Sillar, David, works of: "The Duel," 36–38, 40; "Epistle to J. W****, Student of Divinity, Edinburgh," 38, 39; "Epistle to R. Burns," 35; "Epistle to the Author, by J. H*******N," 36; *Poems*, 34; "To the Critics, an Epistle," 34
Simpson, Kenneth, 72
Sinclair, Sir John, 44
Skirving, William, 157
Smith, Adam, 11, 26, 69, 92; and sympathy, 191n37, 197n31
Smith, Robert, 80, 101
Smith, Robert Archibald, 127, 128, 142, 208n43
Smollett, Tobias, 53, 54, 72
Smout, T. C., 12, 192n38
Society for Constitutional Reform, 166
Socrates, 155
Songs of Innocence, The, 63
Songs of Scotland, The, 97
Songstresses of Scotland, The, 97
Sorenson, Janet, 13, 192n41, 194n49, 218n3
Southey, Robert, 150
Stafford, Fiona, 23
Standard Habbie, 22, 26, 29, 35, 36, 59, 144, 197n29
Statistical Account of Scotland, 44
Steele, Richard, 24
Stewart, Dugald, 192n41
Stewart, John, 6th Earl of Traquair, 165
Stroh, Silke, 9
Sweeney-Turner, Steve, 129, 216n15
Swift, Jonathan, 157

Taming of the Shrew, The, 81
Tannahill, Robert, 6, 183; life of, 127; and politics, 129, 130; popularity with Victorians, 136, 139, 142, 143; reception of, 128; and the rejection of allegory, 146; and rejection of critical standards, 148

Tannahill, Robert, works of: "Britons, Who for Freedom Bled," 129; "Gloomy Winter's Now Awa," 127; "Jessie, the Flower o' Dunblane," 127, 128, 142; "The Kebbuckston Wedding," 138; "Loudon's Bonnie Woods and Braes," 134–138; "Oh, Are Ye Sleeping, Maggie," 127; "The Old Beggar," 128; "Parnassus, a Vision," 144–149; "The Recruiting Drum," 128; "The Soldier's Funeral," 137; "The Soldier's Return," 128, 130–134; "The Tap-Room," 151; "Thou Bonnie Wood o' Craiglea," 127
Tarbolton, 4, 33
Tarbolton Bachelors' Club, 4, 33, 196n1
Theocritus, 147
Theory of Moral Sentiments, 26
Thomson, James, 10, 123, 127, 130, 160, 193n43
Tooke, Horne, 167–168
Transactions of the Society of Antiquaries of Scotland, 166
Treaty of Amiens (1801), 63
Trevor-Roper, Hugh (Lord Dacre), 11, 13
Turnbull, Gavin, 71
Tytler, A. F. (Lord Woodhouselee), 83

United Scotsmen, 129

Vargas Llosa, Mario, 11
Victorian period, 16, 100, 127, 136, 183, 203n45
Virgil, 145, 148, 165
Voltaire, 149

Wakefield, Gilbert, 168
Wallace, William, 65, 106, 113, 130; and national epic, 108–111
Watt, Robert, 155, 166, 218n8
Whatley, Christopher, 206n85
Whig, 14, 38, 99; and common Whiggery, 191n34, 194n55; and history, 173
Wilson, Alexander, 5, 6, 7, 9, 16, 183, 184; Burns's influence on, 73; in comparison to Burns, 94; and criticism of "Tam o' Shanter," 81; and his legal entanglements, 75, 76; and industrial poetry, 86; and James Kennedy, 154, 155; life of, 71–73; and radical politics, 78, 92; and Robert Tannahill, 149; and use of Augustan aesthetic conventions, 91; and use of Christ's Kirk stanza, 85

[249]

INDEX

Wilson, Alexander, works of: "Address to the Synod of Glasgow and Ayr," 89, 90; "The Disconsolate Wren," 84; "Elegy on an Unfortunate Tailor," 84; "To the Famishing Bard, From a Brother Skeleton," 94; "First Epistle to Mr. William Mitchell," 85; "The Foresters," 80; "The Hollander, or Light Weight," 73, 80, 85; "The Laurel Disputed; or, The Merits of Allan Ramsay and Robert Fergusson Contrasted," 76, 78, 80; "Rab and Ringan," 77, 78, 80; "The Shark, or, Lang Mills Detected," 72, 78, 80; "The Tears of Britain," 90; "Watty and Meg; or, The Wife Reformed," 80–85
Wilson, John and Peter, 5, 46
Witherspoon, John, 94
Wollstonecraft, Mary, 168
Woolf, Virginia, 13, 67, 90
Wordsworth, William, 24, 88, 142, 149, 150, 157

Ziser, Michael, 71–72

[250]

ABOUT THE AUTHOR

George S. Christian teaches British and world literature at the University of Texas at Austin. He holds a law degree and doctorates in English and history from the University of Texas and practices law in Austin. He has published in *Nineteenth-Century Studies*, the *Hardy Review*, *Dickens Studies Annual, LIT: Literature, Interpretation, Theory, European Romantic Review*, and other scholarly journals. He and his wife, Betsy Christian, have also authored two books on Texas history for children and young adults (2013).